DATE DUE

GAYLORD			PRINTED IN U.S.A.

Islamic Thought in the Twentieth Century

Islamic Thought in the Twentieth Century

Edited by
Suha Taji-Farouki and Basheer M. Nafi

I.B. TAURIS
LONDON · NEW YORK

Published in 2004 by I.B.Tauris & Co Ltd
6 Salem Rd, London W2 4BU
175 Fifth Avenue, New York NY 10010
www.ibtauris.com

In the United States of America and in Canada distributed by
St Martin's Press, 175 Fifth Avenue, New York NY 10010

ISBN   1 85043 425 5
EAN   978 1 85043 425 2
ISBN   1 85043 751 3 (pb)
EAN   978 1 85043 751 2

A full CIP record for this book is available from the British Library
A full CIP record for this book is available from the Library of Congress

Library of Congress catalog card: available

Typeset in ITC New Baskerville by Philip Armstrong, Sheffield
Printed and bound in Great Britain by MPG Books Ltd, Bodmin

Nothing that has a history can be defined

Friedrich Nietzsche

Contents

Abbreviations

Q.	Qur'an
BSOAS	*Bulletin of the School of Oriental and African Studies*
EI2	*Encyclopaedia of Islam* (second edition)
IJMES	*International Journal of Middle East Studies*
JAAS	*Journal of Asian and African Studies*
JAIMES	*Journal of Arabic, Islamic and Middle Eastern Studies*
JAOS	*Journal of the American Oriental Society*
JIS	*Journal of Islamic Studies*
MES	*Middle Eastern Studies*
MESA	Middle East Studies Association
MW	*The Muslim World*
WI	*Die Welt des Islams*
WO	*Die Welt des Orients*

Notes on the Contributors

Hibba Abugideiri is Assistant Professor of History, Honors and International Affairs at George Washington University. As an historian of the Middle East who specialises in the fields of gender and women's studies, she has published in such journals as *The Muslim World* and *The American Journal of Islamic Social Sciences*. Her main interest is in women's issues within scriptural Islam, with particular attention to the deconstruction of Islamic discourses.

Ralph M. Coury is Professor of History at Fairfield University in Connecticut. He has published widely on Arab political and cultural history, and Orientalism. His publications include *The Making of an Egyptian Arab Nationalist: The Early Years of Azzam Pasha, 1893–1936* (1998), *The Arab-African and Islamic Worlds: Interdisciplinary Studies* (co-edited, 2000) and 'Who Invented Egyptian Arab Nationalism?', *International Journal of Middle East Studies* (1982).

Abdelwahab El-Affendi is a Senior Research Fellow at the Centre for the Study of Democracy, University of Westminster and Co-ordinator of the Centre's Project on Democracy in the Muslim World. His major publications include *Turabi's Revolution: Islam and Power in Sudan* (1991), *Who Needs an Islamic State?* (1991), *Revolution and Political Reform in Sudan* (1995), *Rethinking Islam and Modernity* (2001), and *For a State of Peace: Conflict and the Future of Democracy in Sudan* (2002).

Hugh Goddard is Reader in Islamic Theology at the University of Nottingham. His recent publications include *Christians and Muslims: From Double Standards to Mutual Understanding* (1995), *Muslim Perceptions of Christianity* (1996), and *A History of Christian-Muslim Relations* (2000).

Basheer M. Nafi teaches History and Islamic Studies at the Muslim College and Birkbeck College, University of London. He has published extensively on Arab nationalism, modern Islam, and the history of *salafiyya*. His publications include *Arabism, Islamism and the Palestine Question: 1908–1941* (1998), *Imperialism, Zionism and Palestinian Nationalism* (in Arabic: 1999), and *The Rise and Decline of the Arab-Islamic Reform Movement* (2000).

William Shepard is Associate Professor of Religious Studies, retired, at the University of Canterbury, Christchurch, New Zealand. He is author of *The Faith of a Modern Muslim Intellectual: the Religious Aspects and Implications of the Writings of Ahmad Amin* (1982), *Sayyid Qutb and Islamic Activism: A Translation and Critical Analysis of 'Social Justice in Islam'* (1996), and articles on aspects of Islam in the modern world.

Elizabeth Sirriyeh is Lecturer in Islamic Studies in the School of Theology and Religious Studies, University of Leeds. Her current interests are Sufism and its critics since the seventeenth century. She is author of *Sufis and Anti-Sufis: the Defence, Rethinking and Rejection of Sufism in the Modern World* (1999), and *Visionary of Ottoman Damscus: 'Abd al-Ghani al-Nabulusi, 1641–1731* (forthcoming).

Suha Taji-Farouki is Lecturer in Modern Islam at the Institute of Arab and Islamic Studies, University of Exeter, and Research Associate at The Institute of Ismaili Studies, London. Her publications include *A Fundamental Quest: Hizb al-Tahrir and the Search for the Islamic Caliphate* (1996), *Muslim Identity and the Balkan State* (co-edited, 1997), *Muslim–Jewish Encounters: Intellectual Traditions and Modern Politics* (co-edited, 1998), and *Modern Muslim Intellectuals and the Qur'an* (edited).

Jacques Waardenburg has carried out research and taught at several universities internationally, including the University of California at Los Angeles, the University of Utrecht, and the University of Lausanne, where he held the Chair of Science of Religions, from which he recently retired. His extensive publications include most recently *Islam et sciences des religions* (1998), *Islam et Occident face à face: Regards de l'histoire des religions* (1998); *Muslim Perceptions of Other Religions: A Historical Survey* (edited, 1999); *Islam: Historical, Social and Political Perspectives* (2002). His interests centre on relationships between Islam and the West, the Arab World and Europe, and Islam and Christianity.

Rodney Wilson is Professor of Economics at the Institute for Middle Eastern and Islamic Studies, University of Durham. He currently chairs the academic committee of the Institute of Islamic Banking and Insurance (London), and his recent work includes business reports on *Islamic Finance* (1997) and *Banking and Finance in the Middle East* (1998) for Financial Times Publications (London). He is co-editor of a series, *The Political Economy of the Middle East* (1996), which includes a volume on Islamic economics.

Introduction

Basheer M. Nafi and Suha Taji-Farouki

Why Study Islamic Thought in the Twentieth Century?

The question that perhaps poses itself at the outset in relation to this volume is why such a study of Islamic thought in the twentieth century should be undertaken. There is, of course, no simple answer to this question. Yet even in the Western context, the twentieth century seems to mark a turning point in human history. Relating the condition of modernity to the movement of modernisation during the twentieth century, Marshall Berman writes:

> The maelstrom of modern life has been fed from many sources: great discoveries in the physical sciences, changing our images of the universe and our place in it; the industrialisation of production, which transforms scientific knowledge into technology, creates new human environments and destroys old ones, speeds up the whole tempo of life, generates new forms of corporate power and class struggle; immense demographic upheavals, severing millions of people from their ancestral habitats, hurling them halfway across the world into new lives; rapid and often cataclysmic urban growths; systems of mass communication, dynamic in their development, enveloping and binding together the most divers people and societies; increasingly powerful national states, bureaucratically structured and operated, constantly striving to expand their powers; mass social movements of people, and peoples, challenging their political and economic rulers, striving to gain some control over their lives;

finally, bearing and driving all these people and institutions along, an ever-expanding, drastically fluctuating capitalist world market.[1]

Berman's view of the social processes unleashed by these changes, which constitute what we know as 'modernisation', is very much influenced by his understanding of the Western (that is, European and North American) experience. Yet the impact of these changes has been felt not only in Western but also in non-Western societies, and especially in Muslim countries, as the twentieth century has become a major arena of disruption and dynamism in intellectual, social and political life. In the Middle East of 1900, for example, less than 10 per cent of the inhabitants were city dwellers; by 1980, 47 per cent were urban. In 1800, Cairo had a population of 250,000, rising to 600,000 by the beginning of the twentieth century. The unprecedented influx of immigrants from rural areas brought the population of Cairo to almost 8 million by 1980.[2] Massive urbanisation altered patterns of living, of housing and architecture, of the human relation with space and land, of marketing, employment and consumption, and the very structure of family and social hierarchy. Programmes of modernisation were launched in several parts of the Muslim world in the second half of the nineteenth century; however, by the end of the Second World War, the accelerated rate of change had reached almost every corner of Islamic life. Modern transformation brought with it pervasive and ever-expanding nation-states; centralised education and legal systems; telegraph and telephone lines, railways and highways; printing and visual media; and finally satellite dishes, mobile phones and digital communication.

But the difference between the Western and the Islamic experiences of the modern is significant. While modern changes were intrinsic to Western historical development, they were largely seen by Muslims as alien and enforced. Intellectual and social resistance to modern changes, which are still visible in Western societies, were sometimes – and remain – pronounced and powerful in the Muslim world. The Muslim perspective on the modern was fundamentally different in another way, for even when modern systems, institutions and instruments were welcomed, it did not escape the Muslim collective consciousness that these were articulated in foreign languages, and were premised on foreign values. Muslim peoples' relation to the modern was moreover complicated by the imperialist project, and the role that the imperialist administrations played in the process of change in Muslim societies.

Yet modernity was never triumphant in the Muslim world; while the new became irreversibly integrated into Muslim realities, it could not totally obliterate the old and the traditional.[3] In many cases, imperatives of survival and adaptation forced both the old and the new to exchange concessions; in others, relations between the two were marked by a state of conflict. This situation became a source of continuous tension in Muslim societies, turning Islamic discourse in the twentieth century into a discourse of crisis. The modern Muslim lives in the middle of countless moments of apparently irreconcilable differences. These include the values taught and promoted in the mosque, and the morality of the secular public sphere; the laws emanating from the sacred book, and the official law of the land; the inherently pervasive and centralised modern state, and the unrepresentativeness of the body politic; the world-view advanced by modern education, and that associated with traditional texts and Islamic schools. Conscious of the philosophical underpinnings of modernity, twentieth-century Islamic thought reflects a continuous intellectual struggle to define the place of the sacred and the place of human reason, to decipher the implications engendered by identifying with Islam in a world characterised by a fractured, multi-dimensional sense of identity, and to chart a meaningful way between an ever-persisting past, and an ever-changing reality. In many respects, therefore, what is 'Islamic' in modern Islamic thought is largely a construct, a construct in which a complex nexus of forces and cognitions are at play in the context of modernity, and which defies easy labels and definitions. As Roxanne L. Euben has concluded, even the ideas of Sayyid Qutb, a 'fundamentalist' par excellence among twentieth-century Muslim ideologues, cannot be described as either pre-modern, anti-modern or post-modern. Rather they should be understood in terms of 'a dialectical relationship to modernity, one that entails not the negation of modernity but an attempt to simultaneously abolish, transcend, preserve and transform it'.[4] This dialectical relationship to the modern creates a level of discontinuity between Islamic thought in the twentieth century and Islamic intellectual traditions, and provides the crucial framework for the study of this thought. It is often obscured by the fact that much modern Muslim thought, in a reaction to the actual or perceived threat of cultural marginalisation or annihilation, has increasingly become *self-consciously* Islamic. As the Western debate concerning Islam has intensified in the course of the century and particularly since the Iranian revolution, it has pushed the 'other' in this debate to self-identify as such. This Islamic self-conscious-ness at the same time reflects a process in which Islam as a faith has become objectified in the Muslim imagination, partly as a result of the penetration of the Muslim world by multiple ideological and philosophical options with which 'Islam' must compete, and with which it must favourably compare.[5]

In contrast with the ferment and dynamism of the modern period, Islamic thought and Islamic societies of middle Islamic history have often been represented as stagnant and static. The period extend-ing from the Mongol invasion in the mid-thirteenth century to the Muslim-European encounter from the late eighteenth century on-wards has been described as a period of decay and lack of creativity in Muslim history. During this period, according to widespread as-sumptions, speculative thinking declined drastically, *fiqhi* and theo-logical pursuits were frozen, and intellectual reasoning dissipated.[6] As more recent scholarship on this long and complex era of Islamic history makes significant advances, there is an emerging realisation that the stagnation hypothesis may not be correct. Islamic life thus did not cease to change and evolve, whether in intellectual or struc-tural spheres. During the Mamluk era, Middle Eastern Islamic cities re-emerged, remarkably, from the long period of confrontations with the Crusaders and the Mongols, and Islamic learning and culture exhibited the complexity and diversity of a new renaissance. Recent academic glimpses into the early Ottoman period, often assumed to be the nadir of Islamic decline, depict a continuous intellectual dy-namism and change. At the same time, both Iran and Mogul India were living through some of the most prosperous and fruitful eras of their histories.[7] While the focus of the present work is on the twenti-eth century, it is neither premised on nor in any way meant to con-done the view that vitality and diversity characterise Islamic thought in the modern period to the exclusion of Islamic thinking and the intellectual life of Muslim societies of pre-modern eras. Rather its intention is to highlight the fact that the volume and magnitude of change experienced by Islamic societies and culture during the late nineteenth, and particularly the twentieth, centuries, are largely unprecedented in the history of these societies and culture. This change has transformed the discursive underpinnings and assumptions of Islamic thought, as well as its subject matter. It has created overlapping and interacting junctures of intellectual rupture and continuity never witnessed before in Islamic intellectual history. This is what informs our conviction that Islamic thought in the twentieth century constitutes a worthy subject for an undertaking such as that presented here, however incomprehensive it might be.[8]

Towards a General Framework

By their very nature, projects such as this volume, which bring together articles by different contributors, tend to be susceptible to a loss of inner unity and coherence. By emphasising their own areas of specialisation, contributors are naturally less concerned with the overall picture and the ultimate purpose of the project. Bearing this in mind, in what follows in this introductory chapter we attempt to sketch a basic framework for approaching Islamic thought in the twentieth century, constructed around three major themes. First is the making of modern and contemporary spokesmen of Islam, the producers of the range of ideas that form the subject of this volume. Second are the salient features of Islamic discourse in the twentieth century, among which its internal diversity specifically is highlighted. Third are the inter-connections and dis-connections, or ruptures, between Islamic thought and the global intellectual arena (particularly, its dominant Western formulations), or their shared concerns and the gulfs and preoccupations that divide and separate them.

Modern Spokesmen for Islam

Throughout its long history, a single social group spoke for Islam. This was the ulama class. Although Islam was embedded within and expressed by the community as a whole, it was the ulama who held the recognised authority to interpret the Qur'an, to derive the rules of fiqh from their cardinal sources, and to define the religious outlook of society. The role played by the ulama in safeguarding the tenets of religion, holding the societal nexus, and extending legitimacy to the state was unparalleled. This role was achieved through the ulama's occupation and control of the posts of qadis, teachers, muftis, guardians of waqfs, market inspectors, and scribes. With the rise of the bureaucratised Islamic empires in the fifteenth and sixteenth centuries, two major developments came to affect the position of the ulama. First was the incorporation of a large segment of the ulama class into structures of the Ottoman, Safavid and Mogul states.[9] Second was the increasing identification of the Sufi *tariqas* with the ulama institutions.[10] While leading to a marked reduction in intellectual diversity within the ulama class as a whole, and limiting the degree of freedom they enjoyed relative to that of ulama of preceding centuries, these developments did not diminish the influence of the ulama. On the contrary: the pervasive diffusion of Sufi *tariqas* in Muslim society and the instrument of the state that had thus become available to 'official' ulama in fact consolidated and added further dimensions to the ulama's status and influence in society. By the late nineteenth and beginning of the twentieth century, sweeping transformations produced by the modernisation programmes and the experience of European imperialism were leaving their impact on the position of the ulama, opening the doors for the eventual emergence of new spokesmen for Islam.

Modern education brought with it new disciplines, depriving the ulama of their centuries-old monopoly of the educational process. At the same time, it produced new types of professionals and intellectuals, for whom the traditional Islamic knowledge of the ulama was becoming increasingly irrelevant. Similarly, modern court systems based on foreign legal procedures and laws, and the appropriation of the legislation process itself by the centralised state, undermined the foundation of the social identification between the ulama and the law. The waqf sector, a major source of the economic power of the ulama and of their economic independence, was largely taken over by the modern state in the nineteenth century, and finally abolished in many Muslim countries during the course of the twentieth century. To use Pierre Bourdieu's defining concept of the social field,[11] the ulama were rapidly losing much of their economic and cultural capital, as modern schoolteachers, lawyers, engineers, journalists, government officials, army officers and politicians, and even actors and actresses, speaking new languages and promoting different ideals, crowded the social arena.

However, as noted earlier, as the triumph of modernity was never comprehensive or complete, modern social forces in Muslim societies were ideologically divided from the moment of their birth. This division was accentuated under the impact of the political, social, ideological and economic maelstrom of the twentieth century, leading to the fragmentation of cultural expression and the Islamic cultural arena. The modern Muslim intelligentsia might thus espouse an ideal of one of the Marxist variants, or an 'Islamic' political vision, or subscribe to a Sufi *tariqa*, or promote a liberal or a nationalist vision, or be utterly non-committed. For that matter, the ulama have themselves also become widely divided, not only on traditional *madhhabi* and theological lines, but also as reformist/traditional, Sufi/salafi, and political/non-political ulama. One of the salient outcomes of the historical shift encapsulated in the decline of the ulama class was the rising role of the Islamically committed intelligentsia in speaking on behalf of Islam. This intelligentsia occupied much of the space vacated by the ulama, either because of the evident weakening of the ulama as a social force or because of their failure to respond to the modern discursive challenge. The vast majority of illustrative Islamist political leaders and influential Muslim intellectuals in the twentieth century are of non-ulamatic background, including Hasan al-Banna, Abu al-A'la Mawdudi, Sayyid Qutb, Hasan al-Turabi, Neçmettin Erbakan, Rashid al-Ghannushi, Khurshid Ahmad, Tariq al-Bishri, Muhammad Salim al-'Awa, Munir Shafiq and 'Abbasi Madani. The modern Islamist intellectuals and political activists, graduates of the universities of Cairo, Istanbul, Aligarh and Algiers, as well as of London and Paris, speak for Islam using novel idioms and discourses, expressing new concerns and preoccupations, and crystallising the contradictions of modernity while they reflect the ruptures it has brought with Islamic intellectual traditions.[12]

While emphasis must be placed upon such shifts engendered by modernisation, one must not fall into the trap of underestimating the tenacity of the traditional forces, and the ability of these forces, and their associated religious modes and spokesmen, to survive the challenges of the twentieth century. In this volume, chapters by Basheer M. Nafi ('The Rise of Islamic Reformist Thought and its Challenge to Traditional Islam') and Elizabeth Siriyyeh ('Sufi Thought and its Reconstruction') demonstrate that both the ulama class and the Sufi *tariqas* have succeeded in riding the storm of modernisation, albeit with significant concessions and heavy losses. They have survived either by implementing structural changes and embracing reformist thought, or by regrouping. Two of the most influential Sunni ulama of the twentieth-century Arab world, Muhammad Rashid Rida (1865–1935) and Yusuf al-Qaradawi (b. 1926), thus subscribe to a salafi-reformist outlook, while a long process of reform and restructuring has been a major factor behind the enduring influence of al-Azhar university. On the other hand, consolidation and regrouping have been mainly responsible for the survival of the Sufi-oriented Barelwi trend and the Deobandi, orthodox Hanafi school of ulama in the Indo-Pakistani subcontinent. The triumph of the Islamic revolution in 1979, led by Ayatullah Khumayni, is the most startling testimony to the survival and persisting influence of the ulama class and its traditional centres of learning in Shi'i Iran. This persistence must be qualified on at least two significant fronts, however. First, it is necessary to take into account the important contribution of Iranian Islamist intellectuals and professionals to the evolution of the political and cultural environment in which the Islamic revolution was reared, and to the rallying of the masses behind the Khumayni leadership. Second, it must be acknowledged that Khumayni's concept of *wilayat al-faqih*, which played a vital role in imploding the traditional Shi'i ulama institution from within, and in offering a discursive justification for the political responsibility of the ulama to establish an Islamic state in the absence of the Shi'i Imam, singled him out as an *'alim* with a powerful reformist outlook.

The Diversity of Twentieth-Century Islamic Thought

Diversity, to the point of complete fragmentation, is the outstanding feature of Islamic thought in the twentieth century. Unlike traditional Islamic thought, in which ideational differences referred to a common origin and in which an evolving consensus set the boundaries of orthodoxy, modern Islamic thought reflects diverse frames of references and is inspired by an assortment of intellectual, as well as structural, influences. It lacks any level of consensus. In addition to invoking Islam as a source of legitimacy, at the same time it projects Islam, as suggested above, as the object of the intellectual process. This diversity, important aspects of which are illustrated in William Shepard's chapter ('The Diversity of Islamic Thought: Towards a Typology'), is the function of several forces.

First, rather than being a development within cultural traditions that is internally generated, twentieth-century Islamic thought is constitutively responsive; it is substantially a reaction to extrinsic challenges. Thus, Muslim reformist thought was largely an eclectic response to post-Enlightenment European ideas; modern Sufi and neo-Ash'arite tracts are motivated by the combined onslaught of Muslim reformist and Western rationalist thought; liberal Islamists seek to establish a niche for democracy and the multi-party system in modern Islamic political thought, while other forces of political Islam re-imagine the traditional Islamic polity in terms of the modern nation-state. Meanwhile conservative Islamic thinkers reject Islam's westernisation and politicisation, brought about by the rise of reformist thought and political Islam. Second, in its complex relation to modernity, modern Islamic thought has become a reflection of the very nature of modernity itself, from the confidence evinced in Kantian morality and the rise of capitalism, to the loss of certainty engendered by twentieth-century global wars, consumerism, and relativist philosophies. Modernity resulted in undermining centuries-old social institutions, in challenging normative values, in raising doubts about the invincibility of Islamdom, and in offering different and contradictory answers to the very questions it generated. The nineteenth-century Islamic reformists seemed to think that embracing reason and free will would engender a new Islamic revival. In the twentieth century, Muslim thought embraced and subsequently lost faith in the pan-Islamic ideal, nationalism, the effectiveness of the modern state, and socialism. It remains deeply divided on the merits of liberalism and globalisation. In essence, the invocation of Islam in modern Islamic thought was not only an affirmation of continuing commitment to the Islamic faith and heritage. It was also meant to extend a sense of certainty, morality and stability to ever-changing perceptions of the past and present.

Yet, this in itself has become a source of further divergence, for debating Islam has largely turned into a debate about man and the world, at a time when both man and the world are in a state of continuous change and flux.

Diversity in modern Islamic thought was also precipitated by, and has been a major factor behind, the loss of Islamic intellectual authority. Lamenting the intrusion of non-ulamatic elements into the modern cultural arena of Islam, Khaled Abou El Fadl, a Muslim academic, writes:

> … there is a state of virtual anarchy in modern Islam: it is not clear who speaks with authority on religious issues. This state of virtual anarchy is perhaps not problematic in secular societies where religion is essentially reduced to a private matter. But where religion remains central to the dynamics of public legitimacy and cultural meaning, the question of who represents the voice of God is of central significance.[13]

In the pre-modern mode, the authority of the ulama sprang from age-long traditions of learning, a teacher-student system of intimate companionship, established customs of *ijaza*-granting, piety and societal recognition. Major Islamic centres of learning, such as al-Azhar and al-Zaytuna, and numerous madrasas throughout the Muslim world, played a vital role in maintaining these traditions and their associated attributes of Islamic intellectual authority. New spokesmen for Islam, lawyers, teachers, journalists or modern professionals, lacked the formal training of the ulama class along with its established criteria of learning and piety.[14] Above all, they lacked the world-view of this class. What contributed yet further to the rupturing of traditional Islamic authority was the powerful case made by the Muslim reformists for reasserting the primacy of the foundational Islamic texts, the Qur'an and Sunna. As the salafi idea of returning directly to the founding texts gradually displaced the assumption of the ulamatic traditions of learning as the necessary credentials for speaking on behalf of Islam, the Islamic cultural arena became wide open to an assortment of voices, reflecting new notions of authority. Alternative modes of authority were derived from the dominant and pervasive influence of modern education and professions, from political activism, and from the power and influence of modern information technology and modes of communication.[15] In many cases, the intensifying conflict between the ruling classes and political Islamic forces forced even the modern nation-state to appropriate for itself the authority to speak on behalf of Islam. As claims to Islamic intellectual authority continue to multiply and diversify, and the potential choices available to the individual expand, it is increasingly a matter of accident which 'authoritative' voices, texts and discourses are encountered and embraced.

One of the most significant features of twentieth-century Islamic thought, which both contributes to and reflects the trends sketched above, is the blurring of contours between expressions of Islamic intellectualism and the academic study of Islam. The study of Islam, in the modern sense, began with the emergence of Orientalism in the late eighteenth century in modern European educational centres.[16] However, Orientalism did not begin to exercise any tangible influence on Islamic thought until the late nineteenth and early twentieth centuries, and this influence was largely in a negative sense. Increasing numbers of Muslim scholars were encountering the works of Western scholars of Islam, whether in European languages or through translations, and many felt compelled to respond to what they regarded as the Orientalists' distortions of Islam and Islamic realities. Behind the polemics, however, Muslim admiration for the meticulous methods of inquiry adopted by the Orientalists could be discerned.[17] In the course of the twentieth century, as scholars of Area Studies, Humanities and Social Sciences gradually replaced Orientalists, Islamic culture began to develop an affinity of sorts with works produced by new generations of Western scholars of Islam, among whom many were in fact themselves Muslims. Parallel with this development was the institution of the modern university as the bastion of higher education in the Muslim world. Here, the study of Islam would be largely introduced just like any of the other modern areas of specialisation. Gradually, as the chapters in this volume by Hibba Abugideiri ('On Gender and the Family') and Rodney Wilson ('The Development of Islamic Economics: Theory and Practice') testify, the Islamic cultural arena has become a melting-pot of ideas from diverse sources, among which are Muslim thinkers or academics who may or may not have a declared commitment to an Islamic ideal. Alternatively, they might emanate from works produced in

various departments of Western universities. Some of the most il-
lustrious Muslim intellectuals of the twentieth century, from Hasan
al-Turabi, Mohammed 'Abed al-Jabiri to Khurshid Ahmad, have
themselves been trained in the best traditions of modern Humanities and Social Sciences. At the same time, works of Western scholars, such as Joseph Schacht, Henri Laoust, H. A. R. Gibb, Albert
Hourani, and Bernard Lewis have exercised a marked influence on
modern Islamic debates.[18] The impact of modern Humanities and
Social Sciences on modern Islamic thought might in fact prove im-
measurable. Thus while modern Muslim societies and currents of
Islamic thought remain objects of inquiry for students of Islam, the
publications generated by such inquiry are widely read by Muslims,
the very objects of inquiry, thereby producing and reproducing a
novel and unprecedented circle of knowledge, in which external
projections and self-perceptions continuously interact.

Inter-connections and Dis-connections

Coupled with the structural transformation of Muslim societies, the
conscious adoption and unconscious internalisation of Western ideas
and concepts by modern Muslims have led to fundamental changes both in the imagining of the Islamic past, and in the definition
of what constitutes the 'Islamic'. The example of nationalism is a
case in point. From the early twentieth century, Muslim intellectuals demonstrated a clear predisposition to embrace the idea of nationalism, in spite of its Western origins (and despite the persistent
influence of the pan-Islamic project). Typically, this alien idea was
set within an Islamic rubric. Thus Islamist intellectuals in the Arab
world sought in an Islamically-orientated nationalist vision a route
for revitalising Arab society and reawakening the Arab spirit; while
Pakistan's nationalist project was framed not in terms of language
and ethnicity, but in terms of Islam. Similarly, Islam was the defining source of differentiation that informed the struggle of Bosnian
Muslim intellectuals to assert Bosnian independence. The concept
of constitutionalism provides a further example. In the late 1970s,
it laid the foundation for the establishment of the Islamic Republic
of Iran, mirroring the role it had previously played in the Iranian
and Ottoman reformist revolutions of the early twentieth century.

Furthermore, with some minor differences, the philosophical under-pinnings of the Islamic state in Iran, and likewise the assumptions of a wide range of the programmes of political Islamist forces, are heavily indebted to the modern Western concept of the state. Simi-larly, the 'Islamic' debate about civil society, democracy and human rights, which has intensified during the late twentieth century,[19] is only faintly related to Islamic traditions, and is rather a reflection of a global debate that swept the world in the aftermath of the col-lapse of the Soviet bloc.

These few examples illustrate the inter-connections that exist between twentieth-century constructions of the 'Islamic' and the intellectual products of the modern West. Yet, the traumatic experi-ence of Western imperialism and post-colonial Western hegemony, which has unfolded steadily and undeniably during the twentieth century, has also had its share in shaping the Islamic imagining, both of the self-world and of the world at large. Equally, this expe-rience has shaped the manner in which modern Muslims invoke traditional Islamic values and cultural systems, and, crucially, the ends to which such invocation is put. Hence, as much as the West is admired and internalised, it is vilified and consciously rejected. Rashid Rida's revised assessment of the West, motivated by images of carnage during the First World War, would develop as the century progressed into an outright and sweeping condemnation of Western decadence and immorality, as articulated in the writings of Hasan al-Banna, Abu al-A'la Mawdudi and Sayyid Qutb, for example.[20] As illustrated by the chapter in this volume by Abdelwahab El-Affendi ('On the State, Democracy and Pluralism'), more than a century and a half after the beginnings of the Muslim encounter with the modern West, Islamic thought continues in its struggle to reconcile its embrace of modern political ideas and institutions with the West-ern cultural and philosophical roots of those ideas and institutions. However, the Islamic view of the West and its values is most severely put to the test in relation to a cluster of concrete issues of Western policy, and its perceived injustice towards Muslims and matters that are of concern to them. These include the intractable conflict over Palestine, where Western powers play a major role in defending the state of Israel and its policies. They encompass flash-points where Muslim minorities are suffering the heavy-handedness of oppressive non-Islamic states, and where the Western-dominated international system is seen as failing Muslim aspirations. The perception of the West as a threat to Muslim peoples and their sacred heritage is accentuated by the American military presence in the Middle East. A Muslim sense of vulnerability and outrage is further exacerbated by the seemingly unstoppable encroachment of American popular culture and modes of consumerism, and the transparent hypocrisy of the American rhetoric of universal rights and liberty.[21] It is also stoked by Western ambivalence towards economic disparities in the world.

Perceptions of a threatening West have been translated into self-defensive cultural withdrawal on the part of some Islamic circles, which can take the form of passive, introspective Sufi positions on the one hand, or highly aggressive anti-Western postures on the other. The discursive Islamic formulations in which the latter are rooted illustrate the consciously constructed dis-connections between certain modes of Islamic thought and the West, or the modern world at large with which it is equated. Examples of such self-defensive constructs can be found in the assertion of Islamic concepts such as *al-wala' wa'l-bara'* (allegiance to the Islamic side and dissociation from the non-Islamic one), and the division of the world into Islam and *jahiliyya, dar al-Islam* and *dar al-harb*, or Islam and *kufr*. Such bi-polar models and their associated categories are then used to justify the use of violence, whether against 'Western' targets in the international arena or, closer to home, against political enemies within Muslim societies, who are themselves often seen as Western agents. A discourse of dis-connection can thus have drastic implications in shaping the postures adopted from within towards Muslim societies and states. While the state and its various apparatuses are anathematised, specific categories within society can at times pay an especially high price. This has been demonstrated in recent years by the experience of the Copts at the hands of the militant al-Jama'a al-Islami-yya in Egypt, and by that of women under the rule of the Taliban in Afghanistan. Informed by an explicit rejection of a threatening West and an impulse to retrieve a perceived pure Islamic culture as the basis for constructing a pure Islamic society and polity, Islamic discourses of dis-connection are at times nonetheless developed through the assumption of concepts and realities that are connected to, or have been shaped by, the very West that is denied.[22] This underscores the centrality of the Islam-West relation to contemporary Islamic thinking, and points to its complexity.

Muslim views of the West are naturally shaped by contradictory contingencies, aspects of which are discussed in the chapter in this volume by Jacques Waardenburg ('Reflections on the West'). Beyond these, however, it is evident that it is through the *Western* prism specifically (and not through the prism of Chinese, Japanese, Indian, or any other cultural influences)[23] that modern Muslim intellectuals see the world, and define their relations to its diverse cultural actors and currents. Furthermore, even when resisting the hegemonic forces of modernity and struggling to address problems that have been entirely or largely of the West's making, defending what they deem to be the immutable values of their religious traditions, Muslims tend to seek allies in Western forces specifically, be they religious or otherwise. This tendency has been evident on many occasions and in different arenas including, for example, the joint Islamic-Catholic position adopted during the UN International Conference on Population and Development (Cairo, 5–13 September, 1994) and The Fourth World Conference on Women (Beijing, 4–15 September 1995), and the shared activities among Islamic representatives and others at UN World Conferences on the Environment. It is also apparent in various intellectual fora bringing together Muslim and Western intellectuals and academics, an example of which is The Circle of Tradition and Progress, which argues that the modernist project has actually come to pose a threat to life itself.[24] Although the vast majority of Islamic intellectual output with an international perspective remains confined to issues related to the pivotal Islamic-Western relation, Muslim intellectuals are nevertheless becoming increasingly visible in the global debates generated by the twentieth-century experience. They have endeavoured to make a contribution from within the Islamic cultural heritage to efforts addressing issues related to accelerated rates of modernisation and change, and to redress some of their more pernicious effects. Worthy of mention in this regard are arguments rooted in the pivotal Qur'anic concepts of *tawhid* and *khilafa* for a human-oriented and morally-inspired vision of economics and development based on equity and justice and balancing the demands of growth with those of the environment.[25] In addition, resources derived from the universalist ethics of Islam have inspired calls by Muslim intellectuals for a reinstatement of moral dimensions in global politics, through prioritisation of ethical and human issues.[26] Finally, some have drawn attention to the potential dangers posed by unrestrained rates of secularisation,[27] by unbridled scientific and technological advance,[28] and by uncontrolled processes of globalisation.[29]

An appreciation of the three broad themes sketched in the basic framework here informs the overall approach to Islamic thought in the twentieth century adopted in the present volume. These themes are discernible to a greater or lesser extent in the individual chapters, as well as in the volume as a whole.

This Volume

The questions and challenges that have exercised Islamic thought in the twentieth century first came to the fore during the closing decades of the preceding century, when the major responses, faultlines and debates were also adumbrated. The structure of the present volume reflects this. In the context of modernisation projects launched in the face of the growing encroachment of a dominant Europe, the late nineteenth century witnessed the beginnings of a rupture with traditional Islamic modes of thought. As the first three chapters here demonstrate, the Islamic intellectual arena during the twentieth century in many ways reflects this rupture, and the problematic of how to relate to the modern West that had effectively engendered it. Basheer M. Nafi traces the social origins, ideological underpinnings and ultimate fate of the late nineteenth – early twentieth-century salafi reformist project, seeing this as a response to the crisis engendered by the challenge of Europe and the demands of modernisation, and an expression of the inner Islamic impulse of reform and renewal. While acknowledging its shortcomings and the ultimate disintegration of the Islamic-Western (or modern-traditional) synthesis it had endeavoured to forge, Nafi underlines the reformist project's profound, long-term imprint, largely overlooked in assessments of it, on the political and cultural order of modern Muslim societies, and on the evolution of twentieth-century Islamic intellectual currents. For example, the reformists helped prepare the ground for the emerging sense of modern nationhood that would eventually influence all aspects of the modern Muslim experience. By breaking the dominance of traditional modes of Islam and challenging the monopoly of the traditional institutions, they prepared the way for those with no ulamatic training to speak on behalf of Islam. Through their willingness to engage with modernity while retaining their Islamic commitment, they helped pave the way for its assimilation with the least possible losses for Islam. Finally, the reformist vision, in some respects, provided the canonical logic for the ideologisation of Islam manifest in the twentieth-century movements of political Islam.

William Shepard's survey of the ideological dimension of Islamic thinking in the twentieth century bears ample witness to the fact that the problematic of Islam and Western modernity has loomed large throughout. It also illustrates the outcomes of the unravelling of the reformist synthesis. Shepard's typological analysis is framed in terms of responses to two inter-related issues: Islam as a holistic doctrine, and the limits of adoption from the West. Three pure types are identified, which appear in concrete expression in positions of innumerable admixtures and shades, demonstrating the diversity and fragmentation of intellectual life in Muslim contexts. These are secularism, Islamism and traditionalism/neo-traditionalism, the latter being separated from the first two in terms of attitude towards modernity. In 1900, the author notes, all but a limited urban elite in the Muslim world would have been described as 'traditionalists'. In contrast, in the course of the twentieth century, secularism and Islamism (in its modernist and radical expressions) have each flourished in opposition to each other, having reached something of an impasse in their relations at present. Significantly, Shepard points to the decline of the West's moral hegemony as a major factor behind the growth in Islamic self-affirmation during the final quarter of the century. He also underlines the ongoing upward social mobility, acquired through mass education, of Muslims who are responsive to Islamist or neo-traditionalist options, thanks to their traditional backgrounds. Both Shepard and Nafi stress that, while dealt a significant blow by the impacts of modernity and the challenge of alternative formulations of Islam, Islamic traditionalism has not only survived but occasionally gained in force in the twentieth century, having been constrained in many cases to engage in self-reform. As a mode of traditional Islam, *tasawwuf* was the object of a pointed attack among many late nineteenth and early twentieth-century reformists, and remained thus across the twentieth century for many Islamists and other cultural forces. Elizabeth Sirriyeh charts its fortunes. Underscoring once more the grand rupture of the twentieth century, she points out that, in 1900, the Sufi understanding of Islam was mediated to the vast majority of Muslims by Sufi shaykhs or traditional ulama who accepted *tasawwuf* as the inner core of Islam. While it never regained the strength and influence of previous centuries, Sirriyeh's discussion demonstrates that the story of *tasawwuf* by the close of the twentieth century was one of measured success, thanks largely to its flexibility and adaptability. This has been in spite of mid-century predictions of its demise, and the rival campaigns of Islamist movements, whose very successes and excesses may indeed have contributed to *tasawwuf*'s recovered popularity.

Continuities and ruptures in modes of Islam and Islamic intellectual traditions, which are both mediated and magnified by the impacts of modernisation, point to the importance of historical and contextual dimensions in the study of modern Islamic thought. Questions relating to theory and methodology and the assumptions (at times prejudices) that guide these are brought to the fore in chapters by Ralph Coury and Abdelwahab El-Affendi. Focusing on the contentious issue of nationalism in the Muslim world (and the case of Arab nationalism in particular), Coury offers a critique of the widespread assumptions and prominent contemporary theories that shape a significant trend in scholarship. Marshalling an array of evidence, he upholds the view that nationalism has been confirmed as the dominant view of the world among Muslims, and that it has been as 'modular' in the Islamic world as it has been elsewhere. He attributes the widespread opposing assumption (that the Islamic world is virtually immune to nationalism, or is able to produce only nationalisms that parody what exists in the West) to the persistence of Orientalist perspectives. These continue to shape understandings of the history of nationalism in the Islamic world, and its relation to culture. Coury thus points to the reformulation of standard Orientalist motifs in the discourses of post-modernism and neo-modernisation theory, which have risen to prominence in the post-Cold War period. He argues that these have reinforced emphasis on the notion of a uniquely Islamic essence, defined either in terms of Islam as a religion, or in terms of fragmentation. Insisting that Islamic societies are not constituted by an Islamic essence that has been 'everywhere the same and decisive', Coury rejects the totalisation of these societies and their histories as Islamic. As a corollary, he underlines the fallaciousness of interpretations of Islamism as a 'return of the repressed', in societies that are ultimately resistant to nationalism and all other foreign imports. Coury's rejection of the notion of an Islamic essence and his critique of a spectrum of discussions of Arab nationalism have several important implications for the study and understanding both of Arab nationalism specifically, and of Muslim societies and culture more generally. Three of these implications can be mentioned here by way of illustration. First, it makes possible a re-imagining of Arab nationalism from standard tendencies to demonise it in various ways, or to pronounce it dead. Second, it enables more illuminating interpretations of political Islamist movements and their agendas, and of their 'Islamic' identity as manufactured, rather than recovered. Finally, it elucidates the inter-connectedness of the Muslim experience with that of other societies and cultures, and the virtually universal character of what is often attributed to some Islamic 'uniqueness'.

Essentialist assumptions have at times informed the argument that Islamism (and indeed Islam itself) is by nature illiberal, and that anti-democracy tendencies are inherent within it. Pointing up the general ambivalence that characterises Islamist attitudes towards democracy, rooted in the challenge of reconciling its philosophical underpinnings and world-view with fundamental Islamic principles, El-Affendi's discussion demonstrates that the outcomes of this challenge in Islamic discourse have been far from monolithic. Indeed, he notes that, while many Islamists set about 'proving' the compatibility of Islam and democracy, or pragmatically isolate and embrace its procedural aspects and even field candidates in the electoral process, current regimes in Muslim countries and their Western backers reject not only Islamism, but, equally, the democratic option. El-Affendi underlines the importance for understanding the modern Islamic debate on democracy of contextualisation, something that is frequently neglected in discussions of this debate. In charting its course, due consideration must thus be given to the impact of the abolition of the caliphate, the implantation of modern states which have failed substantially to achieve legitimacy in Muslim perceptions, the assertion of democracy as a global norm, and the secularisation debate. As in the case of democracy, El-Affendi's discussion of Islamic responses to the debate concerning human rights and pluralism illustrate Muslim efforts simultaneously to adopt and mimic Western constructs and norms, to defend the distinctiveness of the Islamic experience, and to accommodate and deny existing realities.

Similar concerns and impulses can be discerned in the development of Islamic thinking concerning economics. As Rodney Wilson demonstrates, the mid-century establishment of the science of Islamic economics, conceived as an ideal system rooted in the sources of revelation, has been intimately connected with the elaboration of Islamic critiques of contemporary economic theories, and of responses to the secularist-capitalist structures under which Muslims live. Most recently, the discipline has launched a challenge to development economics, based on alternative concepts of development that emphasise human values, socio-moral regeneration, and justice. Wilson highlights the preoccupation of many Islamic economists, who have often been trained in Western universities, with the problematic of how to narrow the gap between Islamic ideals and the contemporary realities of Muslim countries. Outside of the sphere of finance, where there has been much practical implementation, he notes the lack of commitment in existing Muslim states to addressing this issue.

In comparison with Islamic economics, which has been relatively marginal in modern Islamic thought, debates concerning gender and the family have been prominent and widespread throughout the century. Contrasting this with late nineteenth-century Muslim debates on how the liberation of woman from the role of mother could be achieved, Hibba Abugideiri deconstructs a pervasive, 'taken-for-granted' way of thinking in the twentieth century that has re-inscribed traditional notions of family, and hence of women's roles, in Islamic thought. While turn of the century reformists had conceptualised woman's role as a social, and not exclusively domestic, agent, the discourse analysed by Abugideiri gives primacy to motherhood and woman's role within the family, and views her agency within society as secondary to this role. This perspective, which Abugideiri argues has been constructed at the expense of other legitimate Islamic roles and rights of women, is drawn from an essentialist understanding of woman as relational. She is thus conceived as the unique cementing agent of the family, society and culture, who while binding these together, at the same time confers on them Islamic legitimacy. As the interpreted nature of woman as relational is also central to Islamic cultural authenticity, Abugideiri concludes that modernity, post-coloniality, globalisation and Western cultural hegemony have all served as pretexts for its construction and perpetuation. Noteworthy in recent years is the rise of a counter-discourse that underlines the nature of the interpretive process as a human endeavour and, accordingly, that of gender roles as cultural constructs.

As chapters by Abugideiri and Coury demonstrate, essentialist understandings are by no means the monopoly of certain trends of Western scholarship on Islam, and indeed arise in Islamic constructs of the Muslim other, whether defined in terms of gender, or ideological persuasion. It has been contended that the uniquely Islamic 'essence' constructed by some Western scholarship on Islam has been cast in the role of the other to the distinctiveness, indeed uniqueness, of Western modernity. Some might argue that such a contention can be legitimately inverted, and applied to Muslim constructs of the West and, more broadly, of the non-Muslim other however defined. Acknowledging this debate, the purpose of chapters by Jacques Waardenburg, Hugh Goddard and Suha Taji-Farouki is to investigate perceptions, views and constructs of the non-Muslim other in twentieth-century Islamic thought. An important aspect of these contributions is to map the impact of the transformations engendered by this century on traditional views and perceptions, where appropriate, and to ascertain the extent to which twentieth-century Muslim imaginings have become the subject of consensus, or display fragmentation. The chapters in question consider Islamic thinking concerning three significant non-Muslim others, which are frequently clustered together, or at least associated with each other, in contemporary Islamic discourses. Waardenburg's overview of Muslim reflections on the most significant, and perhaps the defining, non-Muslim other highlights the widely-divergent perceptions and constructions of the West embedded in twentieth-century Muslim discourses. It maps the impact on these of shifting configurations exemplified by the colonial experience, de-colonisation, the Cold War, and the 'New World Order' since 1991. As Waardenburg demonstrates, imaginings of the West are linked to the diverse experiences of particular Muslim intellectuals, social groups, societies and nations. While they are neither monolithic nor static, they bring home the tremendous impact of the West, both as a reality and an idea, on Muslims in the twentieth century. Among these disparate imaginings, the West as a political construct in which the aspect of power predominates has been particularly prominent, reflecting the historical facts and ongoing concerns of various Muslim experiences. Discourses that focus on the religious aspect of the West were preoccupied during the first half of the twentieth century with the activities of Christian missions in Muslim countries, motivating refutations of Christianity. Since then, a major concern has been with the rise of secularism as a subversive influence from the West. As Goddard demonstrates, apart from standard polemical works that are largely faithful to the traditional mould, and with a few important exceptions, intellectual engagement with Christianity *per se* has been less prominent in Muslim writings from the second half of the century. This might be attributed to the fact that, as Waardenburg suggests, Christianity is seen less as an aggressive enemy; at the same time, preoccupation with the West as a political and cultural threat has taken centre stage. Goddard highlights two important areas that speak to the diversity and creativity of Muslim thinking on the Christian other, and the impact of twentieth-century political realities in nurturing Muslim re-imaginings of traditional Islamic concepts and modes. First is the Islamic debate concerning the status of Christians in Islamic societies and states, in which the contemporary validity of the traditional institution of the *dhimma* is questioned, and increasingly denied. Second is the expanding arena of Muslim-Christian dialogue. Such developments can be partly attributed to Muslim perceptions that Christianity no longer constitutes a hostile force (it is in fact often seen as an ally in the struggle against the common enemy of radical secularism), and to the growing and constructive personal contacts between Muslims and

Christians world-wide. With certain qualifications, a useful contrast can be drawn here with Muslim perceptions of the Jewish other, and the realities of Muslim-Jewish relations, in the twentieth century. As Taji-Farouki demonstrates, the profound impact of Zionism and the creation of the Jewish state in Palestine on Muslim perceptions of the Jews and the Muslim-Jewish relationship has issued in significant shifts in traditional Islamic formulations, producing new constructs and traditions. Its broader context has been the ruptures occasioned by modernity and the colonial experience, through which the West, in Muslim perceptions, effectively brought the Jews into the heart of Arab-Muslim existence, as part of its new order for the region. The sense of crisis and mood of self-defence generated by the Muslim experience of modernity, with its perceived imposition of alien concepts and forms, is perhaps nowhere more acute in twentieth-century Islamic discourses than in relation to the issue of the Jews and their state. Taji-Farouki emphasises that to understand contemporary Islamic discourses concerning this issue, as for so many others, it is imperative to return to the Muslim experience of the modern and, in particular, the imperialist project that was seen to be inextricably linked to it.

To conclude this introductory chapter, we would underline the complex, contradictory and overlapping nature of the forces of the twentieth-century experience, which are mirrored in the manifestations and expressions of modern Islamic culture. These forces, which shape the broad context of modern Islamic thought, point to the risks involved in upholding reductionist, one-dimensional approaches to its ideational structures, and its makers and producers. While undercurrents of internal conflict, polarisation, and a strong sense of crisis form significant aspects of modern Islamic thought, these aspects must not be allowed to conceal its essential vitality and dynamism. Nor should they be seen as the end of its journey. In many respects, modern Islamic thought is characterised by a strong sense of the self-learning and experimentation that constitute key features in modern man's struggle to grasp the meaning of his world, and to come to terms with it. It is hoped that the essays collected here might in some way contribute to this struggle.

Notes

1. Marshall Berman, *All That is Solid Melts into Air: The Experience of Modernity* (New York, 1982), p. 16.

2. Dale F. Eickelman, *The Middle East: An Anthropological Approach* (Englewood Cliffs, NJ, 1989), pp. 96–97.

3. Albert Hourani, 'How Should We Write the History of the Middle East?', *IJMES*, 23 (1991), pp. 125–136.

4. Roxanne L. Euben, 'Premodern, Antimodern or Postmodern? Islamic and Western Critiques of Modernity', *Review of Politics*, 59, 3 (1997), pp. 429–460.

5. Recognition of the self-consciously Islamic character of the thinking surveyed in this volume is deliberately reflected in the volume title. On the 'objectification' of Islam in Muslim consciousness see Dale F. Eickelman and James Piscatori, *Muslim Politics* (Princeton, NJ, 1996), pp. 37–45. On the 'ideologisation' of Islam see Bassam Tibi, 'Islam and Modern European Ideologies', *IJMES*, 18 (1986), pp. 15–29.

6. For some aspects of the debate about Islamic decline, see Charles Issawi, 'Europe, the Middle East and the Shift in Power: Some Reflections on a Theme by Marshall Hodgson', in C. Issawi, *The Arab World's Legacy* (Princeton, NJ, 1981), pp. 111–131; Martin Sicker, *The Islamic World in Decline* (New York, 2000).

7. See, for example, Marshall Hodgson, *Rethinking World History*, edited, with an introduction and conclusion, by Edmund Burke III (Cambridge, 1993), pp. 171–206; John O. Voll, 'Hadith Scholars and *Tariqas*: An ulama Group in the 18th Century Haramayn and Their Impact in the Islamic World', *JAAS*, 15, 3–4 (1980), pp. 264–273; John O. Voll, 'Muhammad Hayya al-Sindi and Muhammad ibn Abd al-Wahhab: An Analysis of an Intellectual Group in Eighteenth Century Madina', *BSOAS*, 38, 1 (1974), pp. 32–39. Also, the collection of articles included in N. Levtzion and J. Voll, ed., *Eighteenth-Century Renewal and Reform in Islam* (New York, 1987); Ahmad Dallal, 'The Origins and Objectives of Islamic Revivalist Thought, 1750–1850', *JAOS*, 113, 3 (1993), pp. 341–359; Basheer M. Nafi, 'Tasawwuf and Reform in pre-Modern Islamic Culture: In Search of Ibrahim al-Kurani', *WO*, 42, 3 (2002), pp. 1–49.

8. To complement the present work, a follow-up volume exploring the impact of the twentieth century on the evolution of the Islamic disciplines specifically is planned.

9. Stanford Shaw, *History of the Ottoman Empire and Modern Turkey* (Cambridge, 1976), vol. 1, pp. 134–139; Ira Lapidus, *A History of Islamic Societies* (Cambridge, 1988), p. 324; Marshall Hodgson, *The Venture of Islam* (Chicago,

1974), vol. 3, pp. 105–106.

10. Halil Inalcik, *The Ottoman Empire: The Classical Age, 1300–1600* (London, 1973), pp. 168–202; J. Spencer Trimingham, *The Sufi Orders in Islam* (Oxford, 1971), pp. 99–102; Ishtiaq Husain Qureshi, *The Muslim Community of the Indo-Pakistani Subcontinent, 610–1947* (The Hague, 1962), pp. 125–148.

11. Pierre Bourdieu, *Practical Reason: On the Theory of Action* (Stanford, 1998), pp. 1–18.

12. See, for example, John L. Esposito and John O. Voll, *Makers of Contemporary Islam* (Oxford, 2001); Ali Rahnema, ed., *Pioneers of Islamic Revival* (London and New Jersey, 1994).

13. Khaled Abou El Fadl, 'The Place of Tolerance in Islam', *The Boston Review* (December 2001/January 2002).

14. Timothy Mitchell, *Colonising Egypt* (Cambridge, 1988), p. 84. See also, Dale F. Eickelman, 'The Art of Memory: Islamic Education and Its Social Reproduction', in Juan I. Cole, ed., *Comparing Muslim Societies: Knowledge and the State in a World Civilization* (Ann Arbor, MI, 1992), pp. 97–132; Seyyed Hossein Nasr, 'Oral Transmission and the Book in Islamic Education: The Spoken and the Written Word', *JIS*, 3, 1 (1992), pp. 1–14; Michael Chamberlain, *Knowledge and Social Practice in Medieval Damascus, 1190–1350* (Cambridge, 1994), pp. 69–90.

15. On shifting modes of authority see Dale F. Eickelman, 'Islamic Religious Commentary and Lesson Circles: Is There a Copernican Revolution?' in G. W. Most, ed., *Commentaries – Kommentare* (Göttingen, 1999), pp. 121–146; Dale F. Eickelman, 'Inside the Islamic Reformation', *Wilson Quarterly* (Winter 1998), pp. 80–89; Francis Robinson, 'Technology and Religious Change: Islam and the Impact of Print', *Modern Asian Studies* 27, 1 (1993), pp. 229–251; Dale F. Eickelman and Jon W. Anderson, ed., *New Media in the Muslim World: The Emerging Public Sphere* (Bloomington, IN, 2000).

16. Albert Hourani, *Islam in European Thought* (Cambridge, 1991), pp. 7–60.

17. For examples of some later evaluations and responses by Muslim scholars see Asaf Hussain, Robert Olson and Jamil Qureshi, ed., *Orientalism, Islam and Islamists* (Brattleboro, VT, 1984).

18. See, for example, the impact of Joseph Schacht's theory on the origin of Islamic jurisprudence on the debate among Muslim scholars about early Islamic fiqh and hadith in G. H. A. Juynboll, *The Authenticity of the Tradition Literature: Discussion in Modern Egypt* (Leiden, 1969); Harald Motzki, *The Origins of Islamic Jurisprudence: Meccan Fiqh before the Classical Schools*, tr., Marion Katz (Leiden, 2002), pp. 35–45.

19. For examples of this debate see the website of the Center for the Study of Islam and Democracy (http://www.islam-democracy.org) and its

quarterly newsletter *Muslim Democrat.*

20. Basheer M. Nafi, *The Rise and Decline of the Arab-Islamic Reform Movement* (London, 2000), pp. 55–68.

21. For an incisive recent critique of what the authors term 'American fundamentalism', see Rodney Blackhirst and Kenneth Oldmeadow, 'Shadows and Strife: Reflections on the Confrontation of Islam and the West', *Sacred Web*, 8 (2001), pp. 121–36, esp. pp. 125–128.

22. See, for example, Sami Zubaida, *Islam, the People and the State: Political Ideas and Movements in the Middle East* (London, 1993), pp. 1–63; Suha Taji-Farouki, 'Islamic State Theories and Contemporary Realities', in Anoushiravan Ehteshami and Abdel Salam SidAhmad, ed., *Islamic Fundamentalism* (Boulder, CO, 1996), pp. 35–50.

23. Apart from studies related to the genre of comparative religions, Islamic investigations into non-Western world cultures are virtually non-existent. A rare serious study of the Japanese modern experience in comparison with the Arab modern experience, written in Arabic by an Arab academic, is Mas'ud Dahir, *al-Nahda al-'Arabiyya wa'l-nahda al-Yabaniyya: Tashabuh al-muqaddamat wa ikhtilaf al-nata'ij* (Kuwait, 1999).

24. See 'The Circle of Tradition and Progress', *MESA Newsletter*, 19, 3 (1997), p. 11. For examples of the convergence of opinion among Muslims and Christians on areas of common concern, see Suha Taji-Farouki, 'Muslim-Christian Cooperation in the 21st Century: Some Global Challenges and Strategic Responses', *Islam and Christian-Muslim Relations*, 11, 2 (July 2000), pp. 167–193.

25. For examples of the growing literature on Islamic perspectives on the environmental and ecological challenges see A. R. Agwan, ed., *Islam and The Environment* (New Delhi, 1997); Harfiyah Abdel Haleem, ed., *Islam and The Environment* (London, 1999); Mustafa Abu-Sway, 'Towards an Islamic Jurisprudence of the Environment (*Fiqh al-bi'a fi'l-Islam*)' at http://www.islam-online.net/english/Contemporary/2002/08/Article02.shtml. Established in the mid–1980s, The Islamic Foundation for Ecology and Environmental Sciences describes itself as 'a comprehensive socio-ecological project to respond to the destruction of the environment through application of the Qur'an and Sunna'. As an internationally recognised body, it articulates the Islamic position through educational and awareness-raising activities, while attempting at the same time to give practical expression to this position. See http://www.ifees.org.

26. For explorations of the potential of Islamic resources in this regard see, for example, Sohail Hashmi, 'Is there an Islamic Ethic of Humanitarian Intervention?' *Ethics and International Affairs*, 7 (1993), pp. 55–73; Mohammed A. Muqtedar Khan, 'Islam as an Ethical Tradition of International

Relations', *Islam and Christian-Muslim Relations*, 8, 2 (1997), pp. 177–192.

27. See, for example, the works of 'Abd al-Wahhab al-Massiri in Aziz Al-Azmeh and 'Abd al-Wahhab al-Massiri, *al-'Ilmaniyya taht al-majhar* (Damascus, 2001), and 'Abd al-Wahhab al-Massiri, *al-'Ilmaniyya al-juz'iyya wa'l-shamila: namudhaj tafsiri jadid* (Cairo, 2002), 2 vols.; Munir Shafiq, *al-Dimuqratiyya wa'l-'ilmaniyya fi'l-tajriba al-gharbiyya* (Beirut, 2001).

28. Seyyed Hossein Nasr has been one of the most outspoken Muslim critics of modern secular science. See, for example, *The Encounter of Man and Nature: The Spiritual Crisis of Modern Man* (London, 1968); *Religion and the Order of Nature* (Oxford, 1996). For different perspectives, see Ziauddin Sardar, ed., *Touch of Midas: Scientific Values and the Environment in Islam and the West* (Manchester, 1984).

29. Jalal Amin, *al-'Awlama* (Cairo, 1998); Munir Shafiq, *Fi'l-hadatha wa'l-khitab al-hadathi* (Casablanca, 1999).

The Rise of Islamic Reformist Thought and its Challenge to Traditional Islam

Basheer M. Nafi

The nineteenth century, and especially the later part of it, witnessed some fundamental changes in Islamic thought. These changes touched almost all aspects of the Islamic intellectual debate, altering the nature and focus of many of its issues while bringing to the fore issues that were altogether new. In more than one respect, the Islamic intellectual arena during the twentieth century was a reflection of the late nineteenth-century intellectual rupture. Issues of identity, women, the state, tradition and renewal, text and reason, and Islam and the West, which dominated the Islamic intellectual scene in the twentieth century, had their roots in the discussion of reform and revival that erupted as never before in late nineteenth-century Cairo, Damascus, Istanbul, Tehran, Delhi and elsewhere. Even the Khumaynist revolutionary concept of an Islamic government based on *wilayat al-faqi* cannot be separated from Muhammad Husayn Na'ini's earlier explorations into the nature of relations between the ulama and the temporal authority.[1]

It is perhaps possible to group the evolving intellectual changes in Islamic thought of the nineteenth century into three categories: the first related to the Muslims' views of the primary Islamic texts, the Qur'an and hadith, their role in addressing the challenges facing the world of Islam, and their relation to subsequent Islamic traditions; the second related to understanding and evaluating the prevalent Islamic intellectual modes and their connections to the living conditions of the Muslims; the third related to defining the external, that is the Western challenge, the nature of this challenge and the search for possible intellectual avenues for an Islamic-Western composite. In addition to attempting to delineate the intricate intellectual arena shaped by these issues, this chapter will discuss the origins of the late nineteenth-century Islamic intellectual ferment. It will try to identify the main forces that were associated with major Islamic intellectual developments, as well as the motivations of those who were involved with these developments. One of the principal aims of this chapter is to assess not only the impact of the late nineteenth-century intellectual impulses on the evolution of twentieth-century Islamic intellectual currents, but also trends of rupture and continuity in the modern versus traditional Islamic modes of thinking.

Three important clarifications must, however, be made. First, the term 'traditional' is used specifically here in the general, social-scientific sense to denote *taqlidi*, i.e. dominant, conventional and established. Second, although the subject matter of this chapter relates to the realm of culture, ideas here are to be largely treated in connection with their socio-political conditions, an approach that is believed to be conducive to constructing a more meaningful view of history.[2] Third, the very nature of this chapter as a survey study restricts intricate discussion of the minute details of the intellectual development of any of the main figures mentioned here; hence, the Islamic reformist school is projected as a collective body of ideas and beliefs rather than as individual thinkers. While this approach is bound to blur the significant differences between specific individuals, experiences and situations, it is believed that it will facilitate understanding of the Islamic reformist movement as a whole, and clarify its impact on modern Islamic thought.

Albert Hourani, among others, in his now classic work, *Arabic Thought in the Liberal Age: 1798–1938*,[3] projected nineteenth-century reformist thought in relation to the overwhelming sense of crisis that swept Muslim state and elite circles in the face of the spectacular Western rise and military advances. Seen from this standpoint, Muslim reformists, such as Muhammad 'Abduh, Muhammad Rashid Rida

and Sayyid Ahmad Khan, chose the middle road between those who
rejected any level of interaction with modern Western ideas and those
who advocated a wholesale embrace of Western systems of thought
and social and political institutions. The problem with this characterisation of the Muslim reformist school, or modern *salafiyya* as it is
also known, is the underlying assumption upon which it rests, that is,
defining the reformist trends in Islamic thought merely in terms of
the Western challenge to the world of Islam. A consideration of the
intrinsic origins of Muslim reformism will perhaps provide a more
balanced assessment of the reformist project, its main themes and
its long-lasting impact on Islamic cultural modes.

Inner Impulses

The last attempt at a comprehensive intellectual reform during
the Middle Islamic period was undertaken by Ahmad b. Taymiyya
(1263–1328),[4] the controversial theologian, *faqih* and scholar of hadith. Seen by modern Muslim scholars as the effective founder of
the salafi school of thought,[5] Ibn Taymiyya represented a formidable
challenge to *tasawwuf*, Ash'ari theology and the fanatic adherence
to the *fiqhi* (juristic) schools, or *madhhabs*. Central to Ibn Taymiyya's
reformist project was his emphasis on the primacy of the original
Islamic texts, the Qur'an and hadith; beyond which he saw only the
consensus of the Prophet's Companions and the Companions' Followers as binding. In other words, driven by a search for unity and
the desire to confront foreign influences on Islamic culture (such
as Greek logic and philosophy), Ibn Taymiyya endeavoured to re-
establish the ultimate authority of the earlier, unadulterated views
of Islam. This does not mean that he opted for a simplified reconstruction of religion, for neither was the cultural environment in
which he lived and functioned simple, nor were the opponents he
had to confront easy prey.

Ibn Taymiyya held that the Ash'ari theology, then dominating
Sunni circles, and the Mu'tazali doctrines, embraced by Shi'i scholars, were threatening the viability and balance of Islamic beliefs.
For him, the Ash'aris, especially the late Ash'ari theologians, by trying to allegorically re-interpret the reality of the attributes of God,
were moulding Islamic beliefs in a Greek philosophical cast, and by

denying causation were diminishing the rational bases of religion and the responsibility of man. The Mu'tazili theology, in contrast, undermined the essence of *tawhid*, the bedrock of Islam, by negating any sense of God's attributes, and making reason the sole and supreme reference for man's action. Ibn Taymiyya, therefore, sought to affirm the attributes of God as these are stated in the Qur'anic text while asserting their uniqueness, and to chart a middle way between the irrational Ash'ari principle of *kasb* (acquisition) and the Mu'tazali exclusive emphasis on reason by reconciling the all-embracing power of God and His ultimate will with man's responsibility and rational capacities. For him, it thus follows that the rational and the *shar'i* (pertinent to the Qur'an and Sunna) evidence are essentially uncontradictory; anything that contradicts an accepted part of the texts contradicts reason. Equally essential to Ibn Taymiyya's project was his fierce opposition to popular *tasawwuf,* its excesses and deviation from the strict norms of Islam, and to the theosophism of *wahdat al-wujud* as advanced by Ibn 'Arabi and his disciples, which he regarded as undermining the transcendence of God and His oneness. This position did not entail a complete rupture with *tasawwuf* but rather an attempt to construct a regime of Islamic spirituality and aesthetics on the basis of the Qur'an and Sunna.

As comprehensive and over-reaching as Ibn Taymiyya's project was, however, opposition to him, ranging from the leading ulama of the established Sunni *madhhab*s to the influential figures of *tasawwuf* throughout the Mamluk realm, was even more powerful. Ibn Taymiyya's students and disciples, such as Ibn Qayim al-Jawziyya (691/1292–751/1350) and Ibn Kathir (700/1300–774/1373) held to their position, sometimes in a tempered form, but the rise of the Sufi *tariqa*s and the pervasive but firm identification of the ulama institution with Sufism quelled the reformist voice of the salafi school. From the late fourteenth century onward, the Islamic cultural landscape was dominated by the alliance of traditional *madhhabi* Islam, Ash'ari theology and *tasawwuf.* Equipped by the popular cult of *wilaya* (sainthood), the doctrine of *wahdat al-wujud* and the effective social organisation of the *tariqa,* the grip of Sufism and traditional Islam seemed unbreakable. Not surprisingly, the last of the major responses to Ibn Taymiyya's ideas in the middle Islamic period, came from the influential sixteenth-century scholar Ahmad

b. Hajar al-Haytami (1504–67),[6] a prominent Shafiʻi *faqih*, Ashʻari theologian and defender of Ibn ʻArabi. Instrumental in the monolithic dominance of the Sufi-traditional ulama association was the support lent to it by the state, i.e. the Ottoman, the Mogul and other Islamic states, which found in the conservatism of the traditional ulama class, the other-worldly emphasis of Sufism and the acquiescence of Ashʻari theology, a convenient partner.

It was not until the seventeenth century that tangibly-felt reactions to the dominant cultural modes of traditional Islam began to develop. These reactions were shaped by ulama with diverse intellectual concerns and experiences: Sufis, theologians and scholars of hadith, arose in different parts of the Muslim world and reflected various social and political contexts. What united them, however, was their total unrelatedness to the modern Western intellectual currents, being in essence expressions of the Islamic principal of *islah*,[7] which continued to motivate conscientious ulama throughout the centuries.

Mulla ʻAli al-Qari al-Harawi (d. 1606),[8] an eminent Hanafi *faqih* and hadith scholar of Central Asian origin and resident of the holy city of Mecca, launched a sharp attack on the popular Sufi *tariqas* and their ritual practices of dance and music, and wrote a powerful refutation of the doctrine of *wahdat al-wujud*. In Mogul India, Ahmad Sirhindi (1564–1624),[9] influenced by the orthodox impulses of the Naqshbandi *tariqa* and reacting to Sufi ulama's compliance with emperor Akbar's attempt to formulate a syncretic religion of Islam and other Indian faiths, embarked upon a reformist drive that aimed at both the political authority, the ideological underpinnings of Sufism and traditional ulama. Defending strict Sunnism as the backbone of social morality, he renounced the Sufi customs of dance and *samaʻ*, and sought to reinterpret the Sufi experience in terms of *wahdat al-shuhud* (unity of witness), rather than Ibn ʻArabi's *wahdat al-wujud* that he held to be pantheistic in essence. The influence of Sirhindi, eulogised by his followers as the renewer of the second Islamic millennium, resonated in various parts of the Muslim world, and grew to shape the outlook of many other Sufi ulama, within and without Naqshbandi circles.

Towards the end of the seventeenth century, Ibrahim b. Hasan al-Kurani (1616–1689),[10] a Shafiʻi-Sufi *ʻalim* of Kurdish origin and resident of Medina, inspired by Ibn Taymiyya's ideas, attempted to reconcile Ash'arism with salafi theology, dealing not only with the commonly-debated question of the attributes of God but also with the concept of *kasb*, the most problematic Ash'ari interpretation for human action and natural phenomena. Al-Kurani, as well as many of his followers, would place higher emphasis on Abu al-Hasan al-Ash'ari's (260/875–324/939) last work, *al-Ibana fi usul al-diyana*,[11] in which he declared his adherence to the Hanbali-salafi theological views, than on his earlier works which provided the embryonic ideas for the development of the Ash'ari school of theology. Essentially a Sufi, al-Kurani affirmed his commitment to the doctrine of *wahdat al-wujud* while trying to explain it from within the contours of orthodox Islam. A prolific writer and highly-regarded teacher, al-Kurani left a profound impact on a wide range of students and disciples from Southeast Asia to North Africa. In Medina itself, the eighteenth-century circles of hadith scholarship and Islamic theology, in which many of al-Kurani's ideas were embedded, provided the ferment that contributed to the making of two of the most important Muslim reformists in the pre-modern period.

The first was Shah Wali-Allah Dihlawi (1703–1762)[12] who, faced with the collapse of the Mogul empire and the disintegration of Muslim political unity in India, struggled throughout his intellectual career to strike a balance between the necessities of religious reform and the pre-requisites for reinstituting the communal unity of Indian Muslim society. By recovering the high traditions of orthodox Islam, therefore, he consistently viewed the ends of social organisation in moral terms, without the observance of which society would fail in its purpose. On a cultural level, Dihlawi was the outcome of complex currents of reformist Naqshbandi impulses, Medinan hadith circles and Ibn Taymiyya's ideas, which enabled him to formulate intricate answers to a highly charged and complex situation. He did not refrain from confronting the *madhhabi* divisions by asserting the essential unity of religion and attributing the differences between the grand founders of Islamic schools to the different methodological rationales they followed. Equally daring was his writing of a commentary on the Qur'an in Persian, the cultural language of Mogul India, which, along with his project to revive hadith scholarship in Indian Muslim circles, signified an attempt to restructure Islamic knowledge by transcending the middle traditions and asserting the role of the primary texts of Islam.

The second major eighteenth-century reformist was Muhammad b. 'Abd al-Wahhab (1703–92).[13] Also influenced by the resurgent hadith circles of Medina, and a strict interpreter of Ibn Taymiyya's legacy, Ibn 'Abd al-Wahhab's Najdi environment was less urbane and more insulated than that of his contemporary, Shah Wali-Allah. Despite his potent intellectual impact, his ideas lacked the versatility and subtlety that characterised Dihlawi's, and were certainly more controversial. Like other Islamic reformists, Ibn 'Abd al-Wahhab was motivated by a critical approach to the dominant modes of knowledge and social norms; his teachings, however, were based on a strict judgement of society in pure theological terms, where the denied reality is sharply projected against a direct interpretation of the scripture. He argued that *tawhid* is not only about belief in the oneness of God as the Creator and Lord of the universe (*tawhid al-rububiyya*), but also about holding Him as the master and the ultimate sovereign of life (*tawhid uluhiya*). It thus follows that the association of any other power or entity with God is *shirk*, or a breach of *tawhid*. From there, Ibn 'Abd al-Wahhab launched his fierce theological denunciation of *tasawwuf* and popular religion, providing the legitimating discourse to the Saudi-Wahhabi movement and its long wars against the people of the Arabian peninsula and its vicinity, other local amirs and the Ottoman authorities. Yet, Ibn 'Abd al-Wahhab's acute recovery of the creed of *tawhid*, with its liberating force, from the heavy burden of the dense Islamic traditions propelled the appeal of the Wahhabi enterprise well beyond the traditional and Sufi counter-response and Ottoman political and military reactions.

During the last few decades of the eighteenth century and the first half of the nineteenth century, calls for reform and renewal resonated throughout the Muslim world. Muhammad Murtada al-Zabidi (d. 1791) in Cairo,[14] 'Abd al-'Aziz Dihlawi (1746–1824) in India,[15] Muhammad b. 'Ali al-Sanusi (1787–1859)[16] in the Libyan interior, Abu al-Thana' al-Alusi (1802–54)[17] in Baghdad, Muhammad b. 'Ali al-Shawkani (1760–1834)[18] in Yemen and 'Uthman b. Fodio (1754–1817)[19] in West Africa, all contributed to the infusion of new ideas to the Islamic intellectual landscape and new vitality to

Islamic societies that were on the eve of confronting a totally different challenge in the form of European imperialism. Yet variations
in their educational backgrounds and local environments defined
the thematic variations between their projects.

Al-Zabidi was concerned with reforming *tasawwuf* through a conscious study of hadith as a founding text not only as a sound chain of
authority. 'Abd al-'Aziz Dihlawi, on the other hand, took the teachings of his father to their logical ends by sanctifying the Indian
Muslims' militant response to the Hindu-Sikh encroachments. Both
al-Sanusi and Bin Fodio, though not necessarily in identical manners,
were engaged in constructing an Islamic framework compatible with
the Qur'an and Sunna for emerging societies in non-urban environments and with strong local traditional vestiges. Al-Shawkani, a Zaydi
qadi of Yemen, and al-Alusi, an Ottoman official mufti of Baghdad,
worked to accommodate their salafi and Taymiyyan convictions to
the adverse intellectual and political milieu in which they lived and
functioned. Since the ground had already been prepared by the
grand figures of the eighteenth century, almost all agreed on the
primacy of the Islamic original texts, the urgent need for renewing
the moral fabric of society and a new era of *ijtihad*.

Within Shi'i circles, a different kind of intellectual dynamism
was evolving, though in no way less crucial in its contribution to the
shaping of modern Shi'i Islamic thought, signified in the triumph
of Usulism. In its origin, the divide within the Shi'i body of ulama
between Akhbaris and Usulis went back to the Safavid period and
the rise of Shi'ism and the Shi'i ulama institution in Iran. As the decline of the Safavids in the eighteenth century occasioned a period
of socio-political instability and conflict, conservative currents, represented by the Akhbari school, dominated the Shi'i seminaries and
ulama circles. Akhbaris believe that the field of scholarly investiga-
tion is confined to the Qur'an and the entire body of *akhbar*, or the
traditions and reports of the Prophet and the Shi'i Imams, thereby
restricting, if not entirely rejecting, the process of *ijtihad*. During
the late eighteenth century, Akhbarism was confronted by a revived
Usuli school, led by Aqa Muhammad Baqir Bihbahani (1706–1790),[20]
a renowned *faqih* of Isfahani origins and resident of the 'Atabat
in Iraq. Bihbahani revitalised the Usuli critical approach to traditions and consolidated *ijtihad*, both on the level of jurisprudential

theory and practice. During the first half of the nineteenth century, Usulism in Iran continued its ascendance by overcoming the challenges of mystic Shi'ism (such as the Ni'matullahis) and Shaykhism (an off-shoot of Akhbarism with mystic tendencies and a precursor of Babism and Baha'ism). The triumph of the Usuli school would have dramatic implications for the future course of Shi'i Islam, especially in Iran, for it facilitated the 'intervention of the religious authority in the affairs of the world, and hence provided a new outlook through which the ulama justified their increasingly noticeable presence in society'.[21]

External Challenges

Apart from a vague awareness on the part of 'Abd al-'Aziz Dihlawi of the expanding British penetration of India, the European-imperialist challenge did not figure very prominently in the systems of thought of the eighteenth/early-nineteenth-century Muslim reformers. Their ideas, therefore, reflected a dialogue between a denied reality and the self-past, in which the Western other had yet no instrumental role to play. In contrast, a few decades later, Western superiority would become a major concern for the late-nineteenth-century reformers, be they ulama, statesmen, travellers, or keen observers of the colonial administrations. This late Muslim response to challenges imposed by the Western powers reflected the fact that it was primarily in the battlefields, rather than in fields of law, education and architecture, that Muslims first experienced the rising power of modern Europe. Not surprisingly, first attempts at reform were initiated by Muslim statesmen, the likes of Salim III, Muhammad 'Ali and the Qajar shahs, and were largely limited to military restructuring.[22] Soon, however, it became apparent that Western challenges were more fundamental and that even the attaining of modern military capabilities required wide-ranging social, economic and even political reorganisations. Between the mid-nineteenth century and the end of the First World War, almost all parts of the Muslim world were touched by this process, which amounted to a remoulding of Islamic societies in a modern European cast.

Although the goals and the consequences of the nineteenth and early twentieth-century modernisation programmes in the Muslim world were largely similar, the instruments, machineries and dynamics differed from one region to another. In Egypt, Tunisia, Morocco, Iran and the Ottoman Empire, modernisation was undertaken by the state itself, while in Algeria, Indonesia and India, being early victims to European imperialism, and later in Egypt and North and West Africa, the process of change was the responsibility of the colonial administrations. The most outreaching was the Ottoman modernisation project, which continued without any significant interruption from 1840 to the end of the First World War and the demise of the empire, whereas in other regions of the Muslim world, fierce local resistance, lack of determination, absence of clear vision or a weak state and administrative apparatus, made the process of change largely incohesive and characteristically slow.

One of the major aims of modernisation in the Muslim world, best exemplified by the Ottoman, Egyptian and Qajar experiences, was to assert state control over land and society. This entailed the monopolisation of violence by the state, in the form of modern armies, police force and security systems, as well as a hierarchically accountable, impersonal administration, and the imposition of central rule over locally run and semi-autonomous regions.[23] In order to maintain the hold of the state on its peoples, new roads and railway lines were constructed, telegraphic communication networks were extended,[24] and land reforms, which altered centuries-old modes of land relations, were initiated.[25] The introduction of modern schooling, with uniform curricula, was intended to produce not only the required type of state functionary but also to create a homogeneous nation with a unified outlook.[26] The same logic was applied in the sphere of law where a modern court system replaced the old qadi-court, and after short-lived attempts to codify Islamic sharia, European civil and public laws were imported wholesale.[27] Whether in areas under Muslim rule or in areas under colonial administrations, waqfs were expropriated on a large scale, either because they were seen as a source of power for the anti-modernisation forces or in order to boost the state revenue.[28] Coupled with the increasing European economic penetration and the peripheralisation of the Islamic economies, the period of modernisation left a profound and largely irreversible impact on the fabric of society, state-society relations and social and cultural value systems.

As the new age produced its own men and language, the ulama class, which had held the societal nexus for centuries, dwindled into a marginal position and the traditional moral order began to crumble. Society, to use Edmund Burke's words, 'is joined in perpetuity by a moral bond among the dead, the living, and those yet to be born'.[29] In many parts of the Muslim world, the second half of the nineteenth and the beginning of the twentieth century witnessed the breaking of this bond. Limited attempts at introducing the principles of political representation and constitutionalism in the Ottoman Empire, Egypt or Qajar Iran, with the aim of creating a spirit of citizenship, went hand in hand with the assertion of state power. By undermining what Stanford Shaw called 'the local autonomy' allowed in the traditional mode of social organisation,[30] by enforcing standardised legal and educational systems, by re-appropriating the power of legislation, the modern state reigned supreme, irreversibly tipping the historical balance between the ruler and the ruled in its own favour.

Implicit in the free, relative and diversified discourse of traditional society was the profound belief in the limitations of man and the uncertain nature of his pursuits. The wide variation in the opinions of *fuqaha'*, judges and muftis was a testimony to their deep understanding of the position of man in the world. The discourse of modernity, in contrast, is imbibed with a flagrant sense of certainty. After describing the precision, order and certainty by which British military preparations for the invasion of Egypt in 1882 were carried out, Timothy Mitchell wrote that 'the steadily increasing range, speed and certainty of means of communication coupled with the increasing range, speed and certainty of means of destruction would correspond, and contribute, to the increasing range, speed and certainty, so to speak, of the truth and authority of modern political power'.[31] Man's increasing belief in his righteousness and ability unleashed forces of violence on a scale unprecedented in history, witnessed in the violence of the imperialist project and the violence of the modern state.

The distance that now separated the ruler from the ruled, the heavy sense of alienation that burdened the people's relation with the new laws, the new school and the new culture, elicited strong and pronounced resistance within society. Popular uprisings in Mosul,

Jeddah, Aleppo, Karak and Nablus, during the second half of the nineteenth century and the sectarian events that engulfed the city of Damascus in 1860, all testified to the depth of pain and anger at the loss of livelihood and social stability.[32] Even in Egypt, though sporadic, manifestations of resistance to Muhammad 'Ali's forceful programme of modernisation and reordering were not lacking.[33] In countries that had fallen under foreign rule, such as Algeria and India, Muslim reactions were more militant and more sustained.

The complexity and bewilderment that characterised the period of modernisation and Western challenge made a considerable contribution to the making of Islamic reformist thought in the late-nineteenth and early-twentieth centuries. While some Muslim elements were calling for a rapid and wholesale embrace of Western ideas and institutional models, and others were holding to the past, rejecting any form of change, reformist ulama, intellectuals and statesmen sought to chart a way between accommodating the new condition and preserving the Islamic identity of society. Muhammad 'Abduh (1849–1905) and Muhammad Rashid Rida (1865–1935) in Cairo, Mahmud Shukri al-Alusi (1857–1924) in Baghdad, Tahir al-Jaza'iri (1852–1920) and Jamal al-Din al-Qasimi (1866–1914) in Damascus, Bashir Sfar (d. 1937), 'Abd al-'Aziz al-Tha'alibi (1875–1944) and Muhammad al-Tahir b. 'Ashur (1879–1973) in Tunisia, 'Abd al-Hamid b. Badis (1889–1940), Tayyib al-'Uqbi (1888–1962) and Muhammad al-Bashir al-Ibrahimi (1889–1965) of Jam'iyyat al-Ulama in Algeria, the Young Ottomans and their associates in Istanbul, Jam'iyya Muhammadiyya in Indonesia, Muhammad Husayn Na'ini (1860–1936) in Iran, Sayyid Ahmad Khan (1817–98), Siddiq Hasan Khan (d. 1888) and Ahl al-Hadith, and Shibli Nu'mani (1857–1914) of Nadwatul Ulama in India, all were concerned, in various degrees, as much with safeguarding Islamic tenets and identity in the face of the destabilising and unstoppable currents of modernisation as with purifying religion from the shackles of traditions, whether they were of local, Sufi or unorthodox influences.

The Reformist Ideology

In the wake of Egyptian and Ottoman modernisation, the defeat of the Indian mutiny and the heavy-handed policies of the Dutch and

French imperialist administrations, the main preoccupation of the
reformists was to revive the meaningfulness of religious beliefs and
to maintain the relevance of Islamic faith to the radically changing
times. The unprecedented historical situation in which they found
themselves created its own rules. In order to achieve its goals, the
reformist movement assumed a twofold mission: containing the
Western challenge by creating a synthesis between modern values
and systems and what they perceived as eternal Islamic values and
systems; and questioning the credibility, even the Islamicity, of the
dominant traditional modes of religion by questioning their timelessness and their reality at the same time.

What shaped the development of the reformist critical approach
were not only the antecedents of the eighteenth-century revivalist
attempts but also the social background of the nineteenth-century
reformists. The great majority of the reformist ulama, including
'Abduh, Rida, al-Qasimi and al-Jaza'iri,[34] belonged to rural or small
urban families, not to the entrenched ulama aristocracy of the urban notables. In this sense, the reformists had no particular interest
in maintaining the status quo with its heavy social implications for
the ulama establishment. Yet, the reformist project was primarily
an Islamic project, and to be seen as such it had to employ Islamic
tools and idioms and to express itself in Islamic discourse. Hence,[35]
reformist thought was based on four principles: *tawhid*; return to
the Qur'an and Sunna, the ultimate source of legitimacy in Islam;
assertion of the role of reason; and the call for renewed *ijtihad*.
Largely, however, the reformists viewed and interpreted the principal Islamic texts, understood reason and sought *ijtihad*, through
the prism of modernity; for modernity, however it was perceived,
was the internalised, powerful influence against which the project
of Islamic reconstruction and revival was envisioned.

Tawhid, the essence of Islamic belief, was the cutting edge of
reformist thought, by which they aspired to dislodge the Ash'ari
theological dominance of traditional Islam, and to confront the Sufi
polytheistic manifestations as well as the materialist denial of divine
existence. For the reformists, God's attributes are unique and must
not be confused with natural elements, physical objects or men,
however saintly the latter may be. God's knowledge, power and will
are all-embracing, supreme and incomparable to man's perception

of knowledge, power and will.[36] Although not much different from the Wahhabi conception of *tawhid*, reformist thought had to concern itself also with dissenting modernist Muslim voices that were undermining the role of religion in society by positing a path of regeneration and progress based on modern Western philosophical analyses of man, nature and society. It thus became pertinent to re-establish the unity of God against materialist and positivist doctrines by amassing a body of evidence derived from Qur'anic reasoning, philosophy and logic, as well as modern scientific discoveries.[37] The reformists argued that it was only within the fold of *tawhid* that civilisation and renewal could be achieved, laying thereby the foundations for their apologetic discourse on Islam and modernity. It was, of course, 'Abduh, more than any of his contemporaries, who conceived a comparatively coherent synthesis of this grand idea of the reformist system of thought. For 'Abduh, *tawhid* was seen as liberation from superstition, irrationality and myth, and the source for endowing man with the powers of free will and independence of mind.[38] Having accepted the view that modern Europe was the child of the Reformation, 'Abduh asserted that Western progress was propelled by the embrace of the two principles of free will and independence of mind.

Central to reformist thought was the notion of man's responsibility for his choices and deeds, where the reformists staged the most powerful challenge to the Ash'ari-Sufi theological traditions since Ibn Taymiyya. Affirming their commitment to the salafi school of thought and rejecting both the esoteric and Greek philosophical evidence, the reformists posited an interpretation of the creed of *tawhid* based on direct understanding of the *nass* (the Qur'an and hadith). For the reformists, where God's power is universal and His will is eternally ordained, man is not deprived of free will, nor is he captive to predestination.[39] The essence of man's responsibility is reason, which separates the human race from God's other creation. This does not mean that the reformists went as far as establishing reason as an agent independent from *shar'*; in reality the reason they perceived is not in contradiction with revelation.[40] Only improper reasoning or incorrect understanding of the revealed truth can appear inconsistent. Inherent in this formulation was an inner contradiction that was never resolved since it was proposed by Ibn

Taymiyya and that had now to withstand not only the traditionalist counter-argument but also the very challenge of rationalist modernity that it was conceived of to accommodate in the first place.

Yet, the reformists' embrace of reason and their invocation of the classical Islamic theological debate on its role varied to a large degree. While Siddiq Hasan Khan and Ahl al-Hadith[41] of India and Mahmud Shukri al-Alusi[42] of Iraq expressed definitive salafi views, 'Abduh vacillated between a Mu'tazili and a typical salafi/Taymiyyan position.[43] Rida, on the other hand, showed more Mu'tazali inclinations in the earlier stages of his career than after the end of the First World War when he became associated with Saudi-Wahhabi circles and his salafi convictions became more pronounced. What unified the various reformist currents and groupings, however, was a shared opposition to Ash'ari/Sufi theology and a strong desire to challenge its dominance on the level of the learned classes and on the societal level as well.[44] Only Muhammad Iqbal (1877–1938) among the early twentieth-century reformists would draw heavily on Sufi philosophical traditions and try to construct a view of modernity through their prism.[45]

Beyond the emphasis on the primacy of the Qur'an and Sunna and the forceful challenge to Ash'ari theology was another major goal on the reformists' agenda: the transcending of the middle Islamic traditions, not only in theology and *kalam* but particularly in fiqh and law. With their contempt of their fellow Muslim traditionalists' detachment from the changing reality, and their espousal of the idea of progress, the reformists set out to draw a dividing line between the *nass* and the accumulated output of fiqh. While the first is unchangeable and unalterable, the second, being a product of man's limited and constrained intellect, is subject to change, adjustment and modification. Contending that blind adherence to juristic opinions developed hundreds of years ago was contradictory to the spirit and letter of the faith, the reformists called for *ijtihad*, on every possible level of the sharia, as the only path for restoration and renewal.[46] Yet, carefully argued, the call for *ijtihad* was not advanced as an innovation but fundamentally as a basic principle of Islamic methodology, the raison d'etre of the earlier Islamic florescence, and the way of the great scholars from al-Shafi'i, Abu Hanif and Malik, to Wali-Allah Dihlawi. From the reformists' perspective, if the

Sharia is the prescribed organiser of life, no limits were prescribed for labouring within its framework. It thus follows that *ijtihad* was not only desired or recommended but also required and imperative for Muslims in every age and place, through which the position of the umma in the world is continuously redefined.

At the heart of the reformists' call for *ijtihad* is their belief in the notion of *ta'lil*, or the intelligibility of God's injunction. For long a matter of heated debate between scholars of Islamic legal theory (*usul al-fiqh*), the reformists, like their salafi ancestors, believed that the wisdom behind the divine *nass/hukm* (text/injunction) is amenable to human reason, and is thus open to interpretations. This, of course, entailed a rejection of the Ash'ari principle of *kasb* (acquisition) in favour of belief in the rational comprehension of natural phenomenon, for if the divine injunctions are fathomable, then natural phenomena, which are also manifestations of God's word, are based on a system of causation. Equally informed by the 'ultimate purposes of the sharia theory, formulated by the Andalusian scholar Abu Ishaq al-Shatibi (d. 790/1388),[47] the reformist call for *ijtihad* became a modern-Islamic celebration of reason and rationality. Yet, the reformists were also conscious of the objectivity of the law in Islam, being of divine origin, and the risk involved in the process of unguarded subordination of the *nass* to the contingent.[48] Here again the reformist project was aided by the idea of public welfare (*al-masalih al-mursala*), another of the Maliki *usuli* principles, which informed Rida's call for the reconsideration of the Islamic laws of *mu'amalat* (or transactions),[49] as well as the approach adopted by framers of the *majalla* in their endeavour to develop a codified Ottoman civil law, despite their Hanafi background.

Yet, reformist thought was not a mere reflection of theological and juristic preoccupations; it was not an idealist intellectual exercise, but rather an undertaking embedded in a specific socio-political context. Never since the Umayyad and early Abbasid periods was Islamic thought so interconnected with, and so expressive of, the socio-political questions of the time as reformist thought was; almost every single major idea of the reformists had socio-political implications. The reformist rejection of predestination ('*aqidat al-qadar*, as 'Abduh put it) was not only an attack on the Ash'ari-Sufi ethos but essentially a denunciation of political despotism and its perceived inevitability. In the beginning, the target of reformist theo-political opposition was the Muslim autocratic ruler, Abd al-Hamid II, the khedive, the Sultan of Morocco, but soon it included also the imperialist authority as students of the early generation of reformists emerged to lead the nationalist movements in the Moroccan Rif, Palestine, Indonesia and India. Similarly, the denial of reason was linked, in the reformists' scheme of things, to stagnation and the desire of the dominant political and religious forces to perpetuate the status quo. Reassertion of the primacy of the Qur'an and Sunna was not only meant to circumvent the middle traditions and eclipse their influences, but also to confront the entrenched *madhhabi* and sectarian divisions as well as the social nexus of interest and power associated with them. Above all, however, the Muslim reformists of the late-nineteenth and early-twentieth centuries were concerned with the socio-political consequences of modernisation and the overwhelming Western challenge to Islamdom. And here reformist thought would exhibit some of the gravest of its inner contradictions.

Reformist thought is by definition the product of a crisis situation, a crisis that was made all the more acute by the deepening sense of self-decline and inability to repel Western military, economic and cultural challenges. However, it would be simplistic to interpret the reformists' calling on Islam as a mere stratagem to justify the embrace of modernity: firstly, because Islam represented the only frame of reference that the reformists, whether ulama or statesmen, could imagine; secondly, because the reformists' opposition to the increasing Western penetration of Islamic societies was genuine and reflected a real concern for the position of Islam in the modern world; and thirdly, because the positive projection of the West in reformist thought was equally employed as a weapon in the ongoing conflict with the traditionalist circles as it was an expression of appropriationist and assimilationist attitudes. The reformists were, therefore, uncompromising in their attack on missionary and foreign education, which they saw as incapable of rescuing the Muslim mind and society.[50] Their alternative vision, however, was not based on the return to traditional educational methods and contents but rather a new system of education that combined a dynamic understanding of Islam together with modern methods of learning, the best example of which would be the Free Schools in Morocco, the

Jam'iyyat al-Ulama schools in Algeria, the Jam'iyya Muhammadiyya schools in Indonesia and the Indian Muslim Aligarh College and Darul 'Ulum of Nadwatul Ulama.[51]

On the level of legal reforms, where European legal codes began to have the upper hand, reformists spared no effort to question the legitimacy and utility of the imported European laws, citing their incomprehensibility to the people and inability to command respect or obedience.[52] Yet Islamic legal renewal in the reformist vision was still captive to the Western model of a centralised legal system and uniform laws, a conception that lay behind 'Abduh's proposal for the establishment of the Judicial School (Madrasat al-Qada') independent from al-Azhar.[53] The other approach adopted by the reformists concerned the substance of law, where established Islamic legal concepts were interpreted in light of modern Western sociopolitical discourse.[54] In both an apologetic tone and an expression of fascination, the reformists sought to emphasise the relatedness between the great values of Islam and the modern West, in the sphere of law as well as in the wider realm of social morality.[55] Since the reformists' preoccupations revolved around questions of self-decline and revival, and the answers which they attempted to track down lay in the West's vitality, what they strived for was to grasp elements of Western strength and re-introduce them to their own people. In the end, since the Self/other contrast constituted the point of departure for the reformists' vocation, their perceived knowledge of the West was unreservedly employed to undermine the position of their traditionalist adversaries and their detachment from the ongoing cultural engagement.

Impelled by humiliating feelings of military decline, Muslims were captivated by Western science and industry and modern techniques. Not surprisingly, early Muslim modernist rulers, including Muhammad 'Ali, Sultan Mahmud II and the men of the Tanzimat, all saw in the acquisition of modern science and in industrialisation vital routes for bridging the gap between their countries and the Western powers. But while the Muslim statesmen perceived Western sciences and techniques merely as tools of power in the narrow sense of the word, the late nineteenth-century Arab-Islamic reformists were beginning to discern the philosophical attachments that related science and industry to the larger world-view.[56] In fact, a crucial dimension of the reformist discourse on the compatibility of *shar'* and reason was meant to legitimise the appropriation of Western sciences. Increasingly, the reformists would see Western scientific achievements not only as a major source of power, but also as an important means for arriving at a better understanding of religion and for generating the process of social and moral reconstruction that would free Muslims from the shackles of traditions.[57] Akin to this current of thought was the movement of translation of scientific texts and other technical manuals from European languages, which was encouraged by leading reformists and flourished within their circles.[58]

It is important, however, to recognise that the reformists' approach to the West was largely selective and non-historical, mainly because of the limitations arising from their Islamic-religious background, the recentness of the encounter with the West and the overwhelming force of the Western experience in the nineteenth century, which precluded, even in European intellectual circles, the emergence of a serious critique of the Enlightenment and its modern consequences. While critical of despotism, for example, the Muslim reformists could not foresee the maximisation of power implied in centralisation, uniformity and codification that became the essence of the process of modernisation. And although they played a fundamental role in disseminating the culture of constitutionalism, the reformist's heart was much less with full representative polity than with the idea of a just ruler, accounting to *ahl al-hall wa'l-'aqd*, not to the people as a whole.[59] One suspects that the reformist ulama, with their fascination with the notion of the Protestant origins of modern Europe, saw themselves as the core of *ahl al-hall wa'l-'aqd* and sought in their oppositional political discourse to revive their own declining role in society.

Yet, one of the most problematic aspects of the reformists' characterisation of the modern European experience was their failure to discern the imperialist dimensions of the Western enterprise, and their silence over the early imperialist atrocities in Algeria, India and elsewhere. Equally, the reformists were unable to establish the interconnectedness between imperialism, capitalism and Western achievements in the nineteenth century; their projection of the West was thus devoid of the inhumane misery that industrialisation and rationalisation inflicted on the European societies themselves. This partial, non-historical imagination of the West exposed the reformist side to the severe accusation of Europeanisation and undermining Islam and the foundations of the Islamic society. While the reformists' theological discourse stood on solid ground, their socio-political vision seemed shaky and incoherent. It was not until the outbreak of the First World War, and the images of the carnage of the trenches associated with it, that the Muslim reformists began to develop a more profound, critical view of the West and modernity.[60] By then, of course, European imperialism was becoming a global phenomenon, touching the life of almost all Muslims.

Islamic Reformism and Nationalism

If the Muslim reformists meant to take a determined position concerning a wide range of Islamic and socio-political issues, as well as in relation to the Islamic encounter with the modern West, the role they played in the emergence of nationalism in the Muslim world was largely the result of sheer objective circumstances. The development of the reformist project in the late nineteenth/early twentieth-century coincided with some fundamental changes in terms of communications, urbanisation and education, which were highly conducive to the evolution of the sense of nation-ness outside of Western Europe where nationalism was first born.[61] Being an integral part of this process of change, Islamic reformist circles provided a ferment for the novel sense of national identity that would grow to influence all other aspects of the modern Islamic experience.[62]

In Islamic societies, programmes of modernisation, coupled with the destabilising impact of Western economic penetration, were the main forces altering old patterns of associations: the tribal, the artisan and trade guilds and the local modes of identification. This trend was enhanced by the reformists' attack on Sufi and *madhhabi* divisions, and their promotion of the modern institutions of education, judiciary, representation, political parties and civil societies, which were bound to weaken socio-cultural barriers in society and contribute to the development of what Renan described as 'the shared amnesia',[63] or the collective forgetfulness of traditional modes of association and identification. By weakening segmental vehicles of identity, especially in swelling urban centres, Muslim reformists

and modernists prepared the ground for the emergence of the nation. Reformist cultural influences would be felt and would succeed
in leaving a tangible impact nowhere more than in modern Islamic
schools, as standardised education replaced the specific Sufi, *madhhabi* or apprenticeship training. Here, reformist ideas were put in
direct contact with reality, and visions were to acquire the power
of life and continuity. The Moroccan Free schools, the Algerian
Jam'iyyat al-Ulama schools, the Indonesian Jam'iyya Muhammadiyya schools, the Indian Muslim Aligarh college and Darul 'Ulum of
Lucknow, Maktab 'Anbar and the Kamiliyya school in Damascus,
al-Kulliyya al-Salahiyya in Jerusalem and Rida's Madrasat al-Da'wa
wa'l-Irshad in Cairo, all became fertile grounds for producing generations of influential Muslims,[64] inculcated with reformist ideas
that would enable them to transcend old loyalties and maintain a
strong sense of belonging to Islam and the wider Muslim community at the same time.

The Muslim reformists, furthermore, played a vital role in the
emergence of a new linguistic medium in society, less elitist than the
language of the traditional ulama, comprehensible to the ordinary
man and capable of carrying the novel idioms and concepts of the
modern times.[65] This remarkable outcome of the reformist project
was closely linked to the embrace of journalism as a powerful and
effective means of communication. Deeply self-conscious of their
role as a force of change, the Muslim reformists aspired through
journalism to present their case to the widest possible sections of society. Besides being critical of the traditional ulama's ambivalence to
the living demands and questions of the times, and competing with
an increasing number of publications, the Muslim reformists were
keen to discuss modern concerns and project a broad preoccupation
with Islamic (and not exclusively Islamic) issues. In other words, to
underline their self-assumed role as spokesmen of change and the
people, the reformists had to speak the people's language and relate
to their everyday situation. Reformist journals, such as *al-Manar* and
al-Fath in Egypt, *al-Hilal* in India and *al-Shihab* in Algeria, were, thus,
bound to immerse themselves in the new socio-cultural milieu, its
debates and discourses, contributing thereby to the development of
a new and ever-evolving linguistic medium that was faithful to high
cultural standards and yet meaningful to the ordinary man.

In the middle of the intellectual and social upheaval of the late nineteenth/early twentieth century, Muslim reformists represented the minority voice, the oppositional force against the established order, whether it was the alliance of the state with the traditional ulama institution in Egypt and the Ottoman lands, or the Sufi *tariqa*s, Sufi-oriented ulama and the colonial administration in North Africa, India and Indonesia. Perhaps for the first time since its classical period, Islam became a contested arena for heated socio-political debates, called upon to legitimate new ideas and conceptions, remoulded to encompass or exclude certain dogmas, and reconceived in light of established or novel systems of thought. Contrary to the Wahhabi discourse (which was also oppositional) where state and society were viewed in purely religious terms, in the reformist scheme of things, state and society acquired independent status of their own. On the fault-lines between Islam as a body of laws, beliefs, values and history, and the modern conceptions of state and society, two central questions played a vital role in the Muslim reformists' embrace of the idea of the nation: revival and identity. Search for revival and preservation of identity were both essential for the emergence of nationalism among Muslim peoples, but the magnitude of influence that each exercised differed from one place and situation to another.

Arab Muslim reformists of the late Ottoman era, resenting the Arabs', and their own, exclusion from shaping and charting the future course of state and society, began to develop a reading of history in which the Arabs were associated with the rise and glory of Islam, while the Turkish ascendance was associated with its decline. For 'Abduh, al-Kawakibi and Rida, revival of the umma became conditional upon the re-emergence of the Arabs in the leadership of Islam and its peoples. This perception of history and vision of the future provided the logical foundation for the rise of Arabism. In Algeria, where Ibn Badis's verse '*Sha'b al-Jaza'ir Muslimun wa ila al-'urubat yantasib*' (the Algerian people are Muslim and to Arabism they belong) became the motto of Algerian nationalism, it was the threat of Francophonisation to the Arab-Islamic identity which underlined the reformists' contribution to the development of the Algerian nationalist movement. For al-Khattabi, 'Allal al-Fasi and the reformist circles of Morocco, both questions of self-renewal and preservation of identity were germane to the emergence of Moroccan nationalism.

In a slightly different fashion, threats to Islamic identity and way of life, emanating from rising Hindu self-assertiveness in post-Mutiny India, were conducive to the development of the idea of a separate Muslim entity within Indian Muslim reformist circles.

Essentially, the Muslim reformists conceived of the nation in Islamic terms and for Islamic ends, but soon 'the nation' would acquire a life of its own. This crucial development in the making of the modern Muslim world was due to the intensification of the struggle against the colonial powers in the first half of the twentieth century, and to the rising role of the modern, Western-educated, secular Muslim intellectual. Yet, the Islamic dimension of the nation was never eclipsed, neither during the later stages of the nationalist movement, nor, as the last quarter of the twentieth century would testify, in the post-colonial nation-state. What is crucial for defining the position of the Muslim reformists is that their involvement in the birth of nationalism and the nationalist movement was decisive in determining the fate of their confrontation with the traditional Islamic institution. In the Arab Mashriq, the demise of the Otto-man state severely weakened traditional Islamic forces that had for long been dependent on state patronage, while in other parts of the Muslim world Sufis and traditionalists were discredited by their mild attitudes toward colonial administrations and policies. At the same time, second-generation students of the Islamic reform move-ment were proving to be more radical in their views of the West and in their confrontation with the Western imperialist presence in their countries. Once the national struggle for independence was joined, traditional Islamic forces effectively, and by and large, lost the battle.

Conclusions

It has often been said that the Islamic reformist movement failed to achieve its goals or to leave a lasting imprint on the political and cultural order of modern Islamic societies. In many instances, the modern state and its ruling elite would use, and misuse, the reform-ist mantle and figures to reach their own ends, while the reformist synthesis of Islam and the West, or tradition and modernity, frag-mented as a result of radicalisation and polarisation in the Islamic intellectual arena. The emerging 'Islamic' state of Pakistan had almost nothing to do with the legacy of Iqbal, or even of Sir Sayyid Ahmad Khan. Although he was a towering figure, 'Abduh's legacy would only be invoked by the Egyptian ruling class, from Zaghlul to Nasser, to provide a symbolic legitimation to a political order that was totally anti-reformist. After destroying the reputation of al-Tha'alibi in the 1930s, Bourguiba used al-Zaytuna reformist circles to tailor an Islamic garb for the deeply nihilist, anti-Islamic policies of the post-independence Tunisian state. What confirmed the breakdown of the reformist project was the intensified intellectual conflict between post-reformist Islamists and secular nationalists, as well as between liberals and socialists.

Yet this picture reflects only one face of reality. Without doubt, the reformists failed to advance a coherent political vision. Their largely apologetic comprehension of Western modernity, and the fragility of their eclectic system of thought, made them unable to chart a successful course amid the testing times of the colonial and post-colonial periods. Equally important was the limitation of their aspirations, arising from the centuries-old separation between 'men of the sword' and 'men of the pen', which left them content with the secondary role of advisers, educators and guides. Yet one has also to acknowledge the subtle diffusion of reformist ideas, their impact on the position of Islam in the modern world and on the development of the traditional Islamic institution itself. A reformist is by definition non-radical. The Muslim reformists, who were no exception, were not seeking a total change of the existing order. In the long term, however, reformist influences were both radical and profound.

By attempting to engage modernity on philosophical and socio-political levels, the Muslim reformists contributed in a significant measure to affirming the relevance of Islam to modern times. Even the simplistic reformist perception of a science and technology severed from their cultural underpinnings, provided the discursive sanction for the appropriation of many aspects of modernity to continue with the minimal degree of inner tension and conflict. Like most of the great intellectual movements in Islamic history, the reformist project was deeply pre-occupied with the restoration of unity and consensus, and was therefore instrumental in creating a possibility for self-revitalisation ordained by a reconstructed religious vision.

While no religious system could escape the impact of modernity unscathed, Islamic reformist thought paved the way for the assimilation of modernity with the least possible loss for Islam. In many parts of the Muslim world, where students of the Islamic reformist school, such as al-Khattabi in Morocco, al-Qassam and al-Husayni in Palestine, followers of Jam'iyyat al-Ulama in Algeria and Jam'iyya Muhammadiyya in Indonesia, became closely involved with the national struggle, the Muslim reformists succeeded in shedding their pro-Western image and in asserting the role of Islam in the forefront of the peoples' awakening and revival.

It is tempting, in light of the creative diversity and unlimited exploratory currents within modern Islamic thought, to believe that the triumph of reformist Islam over its adversaries within the traditional Islamic institution was final. The truth is that the outcome of this confrontation was manifold. The reformist challenge did break the dominance of traditional Islam, and in many parts of the Muslim world restricted the space available to it in the public sphere. But this cannot be solely attributed to the impact of the Islamic reformist movement, for it was the very alien nature of the modern condition that imposed on traditional Islam demands it could not meet. Like the Catholics during the Reformation of the sixteenth and seventeenth centuries, to survive, traditional Islamic institutions had to embark upon a restructuring and reform of their own. But the lines between reformist and traditional Islam were not so sharply drawn as the Catholic-Protestant divide; hence the later rise of students of the reformist school to the highest positions in the traditional Islamic institutions. Disciples of 'Abduh were to occupy the shaykhdom of al-Azhar and lead its restructuring for most of the twentieth century,[66] while Muhammad al-Tahir b. 'Ashur would become the most influential of all the Zaytuna scholars until well after the independence of Tunisia.[67] In other places – as in the case of the Nahdatul Ulama in Indonesia or the Indian Darul 'Ulum at Deoband[68] – the regrouping of traditional forces was so effective that the Islamic arena became indefinitely divided. *Tasawwuf* too, though never as influential as it was during the pre-modern times, would survive both the challenge of Islamic reformism and the test of modernity.

With the appearance of Hasan al-Banna and Abul al-A'la Mawdudi from under the wings of Rida, al-Khatib, Abul-Kalam Azad, Iqbal and the reformist Nadwatul Ulama, political Islam emerged from within the intellectual crucible of the reformist project. The relation between these two great movements of modern Islam was not, however, mechanical. By liberating Islam from the monopoly of the traditional institutions, the reformists prepared the ground for the laymen, the modern Muslim intellectual and the Muslim professional, to speak on behalf of Islam. In some respects, the reformist version, in which Islam was presumed to be an ideological equivalent to all aspects of modern life and the answer to economic, social and military decline, provided the canonical logic for political Islam. In other respects, Islamic political forces went much beyond the reformist project by seeking power in its ultimate manifestation: state power. Equally, political Islam was more disposed to adopting modern Western instruments of political organisation, confronting the secular Muslim state with a tool of its own nature. While political Islam is, therefore, more potent and pronounced, it is a less consensual, or inclusive, sequel of its ancestor: reformist Islam. One could conclude, perhaps, that the remarkable rise of political Islam in the second half of the twentieth century represented the end of the road for the reformist project. Yet, a closer look at various currents of modern Islamic political thought will perhaps reveal a more complex process of appropriation and reproduction of reformist ideas than initial impressions might suggest.

Notes

1. C.f. Azar Tabari, 'The Role of the Clergy in Modern Iranian Politics', in Nikki R. Keddie, ed., *Religion and Politics in Iran: Shi'ism from Quietism to Revolution* (New Haven, CT, 1983), pp. 58–59.

2. Cf. Malcolm Kerr, *Islamic Reform: The Political and Legal Theories of Muhammad Abduh and Rashid Rida* (Berkeley, CA, 1966), where ideas and creed are presented as static and to exercise, in their own right, considerable influence on the social and the political.

3. London, 1962.

4. On Ibn Taymiyya, see Henri Laoust, *Essai sur les doctrines sociales et politiques de Taki-d-Din b. Taimiya* (Cairo, 1939); Muhammad Abu Zahra, *Ibn Taymiyya: Hayatuh wa 'asruh, ara'uh wa fiqhuh* (Cairo, 1974).

5. On the impact of Ibn Taymiyya on the nineteenth-century Muslim re-

formists, see David Dean Commins, *Islamic Reform: Politics and Social Change in Late Ottoman Syria* (New York, 1990), p. 25; Khaliq Ahmad Nizami, 'The Impact of Ibn Taymiyya on South Asia', *JIS*, 1 (1990), pp. 120–149.

  6. On al-Haytami, see Muhyi al-Din 'Abd al-Qadir b. 'Abdullah al-'Aydarus, *al-Nur al-safir 'an akhbar al-qarn al-'ashir* (Cairo, n. d.), pp. 287–292; Khayr al-Din al-Zirikli, *al-A'lam* (Beirut, 1989), vol. 1, pp. 234; *EI2*, s. v. 'Ibn Hadjar al-Haytami', by C. van Arendonk and J. Schacht.

  7. On the concept of Islah and its manifestations in different Islamic situations, see *EI2*, s. v., 'Islah'.

  8. Al-Zirikli, *al-A'lam*, vol. 5, pp. 12–13. For al-Harawi's attack on Ibn 'Arabi, see Mulla 'Ali b. Sultan al-Qari, 'Risala fi'l-rad 'ala Ibn 'Arabi', ms. 199, Tasawwuf, Institute of Arabic Manuscripts, the Arab League, Cairo.

  9. On him, see Ishtiaq Husain Qureshi, *The Muslim Community of the Indo-Pakistan Subcontinent, 610–1947* (The Hague, 1962), pp. 149–163; Yohanan Friedmann, *Shaykh Ahmad Sirhindi: An Outline of His Thought and a Study of His Image in the Eyes of Posterity* (Montreal, 1971); Abul Hasan Nadawi, *Saviours of Islamic Spirit: Shaykh Ahmad Mujadid Alf Thani* (Lucknow, 1983).

  10. John Voll, 'Muhammad Haya al-Sindi and Muhammad Ibn 'Abd al-Wahhab: An Analysis of an Intellectual Group in Eighteenth-Century Madina', *BSOAS*, 38, 1 (1974), pp. 32–39; *EI 2*, s. v. 'Ibrahim al-Kurani', by A. H. Johns; Basheer M. Nafi, 'Tasawwuf and Reform in Pre-Modern Islamic Culture: In Search of Ibrahim al-Kurani', *WI*, 42, 3 (2002), pp. 307–355.

  11. Ed. F. H. Mahmud (Cairo, 1977), vol. 2, pp. 20–21.

  12. Qureshi, *The Muslim Community*, pp. 176–192; G. N. Jalbani, *Teachings of Shah Waliyullah of Delhi* (Lahore, 1967); J. M. S. Baljon, *Religion and Thought of Shah Wali Allah Dihlawi, 1703–1762* (Leiden, 1986); Sayyid Habibul Haq Nadvi, *Islamic Resurgent Movements in the Indo-Pak Subcontinent* (Durban, 1987), pp. 34–35 and 40–43.

  13. 'Uthman ibn 'Abdullah ibn Bishr, in A. al-Shaykh, ed., *'Unwan al-majd fi ta'rikh Najd* (Riyadh, 1971); Husayn ibn Ghannam, *Ta'rikh Najd*, ed. Nasir al-Din al-Asad (Beirut, 1985); 'Abdullah al-Salih al-'Uthaymin, *Ta'rikh al-mamlaka al-'Arabiyya al-Sa'udiyya* (Riyadh, 1984), vol. 1, pp. 33–56; Christine Moss Helms, *The Cohesion of Saudi Arabia: Evolution of Political Identity* (London, 1981), pp. 76–110; Esther Peskes, 'The Wahhabiyya and Sufism in the Eighteenth Century', in Frederick de Jong and Bernd Radtke, ed., *Islamic Mysticism Contested* (Leiden, 1999), pp. 145–161.

  14. John Voll, *Islam: Continuity and Change in the Modern World* (Boulder, CO, 1982), pp. 54–5, 59, 667; Stefan Reichmuth, 'Murtada Az-Zabidi (d. 1791) in Biographical and Autobiographical Accounts. Glimpses of Islamic Scholarship in the 18th Century', *WI*, 39, 1(1999), pp. 64–102.

  15. Qureshi, *The Muslim Community*, pp. 193–211.

16. B. G. Martin, *Muslim Brotherhoods in Nineteenth-Century Africa* (Cambridge, 1976), pp. 99–124; Ahmad Sidqi al-Dajani, *al-Haraka al-Sanusiyya* (Beirut, 1967).

17. On him, see 'Abbas al-'Azzawi, *Dhikra Abu al-Thana' al-Alusi* (Baghdad, 1958); Basheer M. Nafi, 'Abu al-Thana' al-Alusi: An 'Alim, Ottoman Mufti and Exegetist of the Qur'an', *IJMES*, 34 (2002), pp. 465–494.

18. 'Abd al-Mut'al al-Sa'idi, *al-Mujadidun fi'l-Islam* (Cairo, 1962), pp. 472–475; Rudolph Peters, 'Idjtihad and Taqlid in 18th and 19th Century Islam', *WI*, 20 (1980), pp. 132–145.

19. J. Spencer Trimingham, *A History of Islam in West Africa* (Oxford, 1962), pp. 195–206; Martin, *Muslim Brotherhoods*, pp. 1–12; Voll, *Islam*, pp. 135–136; Ahmad Dallal, 'The Origins and Objectives of Islamic Revivalist Thought', *JAOS*, 113, 3 (1993), pp. 351–355.

20. On the Akhbari-Usuli conflict and the role of Bihbahani, see Hamid Algar, *Religion and State in Iran, 1785–1906* (Berkeley, CA, 1969), p. 33 ff.; Juan R. Cole, 'Imami Jurisprudence and the Role of the Ulama: Mortaza Ansari on Emulating the Supreme Exemplar', in Nikki Keddie, ed., *Religion and Politics in Iran* (New Haven, CT, 1983), pp. 33–46; Juan R. Cole, 'Shi'i Clerics in Iraq and Iran, 1722–1780: The Akhbari-Usuli Conflict Reconsidered', *Iranian Studies*, 28 (1985), pp. 3–34.

21. Abbas Amanat, *Resurrection and Renewal: The Making of the Babi Movement in Iran, 1844–1850* (Ithaca, NY, 1989), p. 34.

22. On the military reforms of Salim III, see Uriel Heyd, 'The Ottoman 'Ulama and Westernization in the Times of Selim III and Mahmoud II', in Heyd, ed., *Studies in Islamic History and Civilization, Scripta Hierosolymitana*, 9 (1961), pp. 63–96; Stanford J. Shaw, *Between Old and New: The Ottoman Empire under Sultan Selim III, 1789–1807* (Cambridge, MA, 1971). On Muhammad 'Ali's reforms, see Khaled Fahmy, *All the Pasha's Men: Mehmed Ali, His Army and the Making of Modern Egypt* (Cambridge, 1997). On the Qajars, see Ann K. S. Lambton, *Qajar Persia* (Austin, TX, 1987), p. 22 ff., and 96 ff.

23. Stanford Jay Shaw, 'Some Aspects of the Aims and Achievements of the Nineteenth-Century Ottoman Reformers', in William R. Polk and Richard L. Chambers, ed., *Beginnings of Modernization in the Middle East: The Nineteenth Century* (Chicago, 1968), pp. 29–39. Cf. Hafez Farman Farmayan, 'Forces of Modernization in Nineteenth-Century Iran: A Historical Survey', in ibid., pp. 119–151; F. Robert Hunter, 'State-Society Relations in Nineteenth-Century Egypt: The Years of Transition, 1848–79', *MES*, 36, 3 (2000), pp. 145–159.

24. Charles Issawi, ed., *Economic History of the Middle East, 1900–1914* (Chicago, 1966), pp. 182, 191–193, 207, 208 ff.; Donald Quataert, 'Transportation', in Halil Inalcik and Donald Quataert, ed., *An Economic and Social History of the Ottoman Empire, 1300–1914* (Cambridge, 1994), pp. 798–823;

Roderic H. Davison, *Essays in Ottoman and Turkish History, 1774–1923* (Austin, TX, 1990), pp. 133–165.

25. On land reforms in the Ottoman empire and its consequences, see Haim Gerber, *The Social Origins of the Modern Middle East* (Boulder, CO, 1987); Kemal Karpat, 'The Land Regime: Social Structure and Modernization in the Ottoman Empire', in Polk and Chambers, ed., *Beginnings of Modernization*, pp. 69–90.

26. Davison, *Essays in Ottoman and Turkish History*, pp. 166–179; Donald M. Reid, 'Educational and Career Choices of Egyptian Students, 1882–1922', *IJMES*, 8 (1977); Dale F. Eickelman, 'The Art of Memory: Islamic Education and Its Social Reproduction', in Juan R. I. Cole, ed., *Comparing Muslim Societies: Knowledge and the State in a World of Civilization* (Ann Arbor, MI, 1992), pp. 97–132.

27. S. S. Onar, 'The Majalla', in M. Khadduri and H. Liebesny, ed., *Law in the Middle East* (Washington, DC, 1965), vol. 1, pp. 292–308; N. J. Coulson, *A History of Islamic Law* (Edinburgh, 1964), pp. 149–162; Gabriel Baer, 'Tanzimat in Egypt: The Penal Code', in Gabriel Baer, ed., *Studies in the Social History of Modern Egypt* (Chicago, 1969), pp. 109–133; Gabriel Baer, 'The Transition from Traditional to Western Criminal Law in Turkey and Egypt', *Studia Islamica*, 45 (1977), pp. 139–158; Rudolph Peters, 'Administrators and Magistrates: The Development of Secular Judiciary in Egypt, 1842–1871', *WI*, 39, 3 (1999), pp. 378–397.

28. John Robert Barnes, *An Introduction to Religious Foundations in the Ottoman Empire* (Leiden, 1986), pp. 118–153.

29. As quoted by Russell Kirk, *The Conservative Mind From Burke to Eliot* (7th edition, Chicago, 1986), p. 15.

30. Shaw, 'Some Aspects of the Aims and Achievements of the Nineteenth-Century Ottoman Reforms', p. 33.

31. Timothy Mitchell, *Colonising Egypt* (Cambridge, 1988), p. 130.

32. 'Abd al-Razzaq al-Bitar, *Hiliyat al-bashar fi ta'rikh al-qarn al-thalith 'ashar*, ed. M. Bahjat al-Bitar (Damascus, 1961–3), vol. 1, pp. 260–280; Kamal Salibi 'The 1860 Upheaval in Damascus as Seen by al-Sayyid Muhammad Abu al-Su'ud al-Hasibi, Notable and Later Naqib al-Ashraf of the City', in Polk and Chambers, ed., *Beginnings of Modernization in the Middle East*, pp. 185–202; Albert Hourani 'Ottoman Reform and the Politics of Notable', in Polk and Chambers, ed., *Beginnings of Modernization in the Middle East*, p. 73; Moshe Ma'oz, *Ottoman Reform in Syria and Palestine, 1840–1861* (Oxford, 1968), pp. 227–240; Leila Tarazi Fawaz, *An Occasion for War: Civil Conflict in Lebanon and Damascus in 1860* (Berkeley, CA, 1994).

33. Fahmy, *All the Pasha's Men*, pp. 76–111.

34. On 'Abduh and Rida, see Hourani, *Arabic Thought*, pp. 130–160 and

pp. 222–244. On al-Qasimi and al-Jaza'iri, see Commins, *Islamic Reform*, pp. 34–48.

35. The following section is based on a brief discussion of the reformist ideology published in Basheer M. Nafi, *The Rise and Decline of the Arab-Islamic Reform Movement* (London, 2000), pp. 45–55.

36. Muhammad Rashid Rida, *Ta'rikh al-ustadh al-imam* (Cairo, 1906–31). vol. 2, pp. 425–432; Jamal al-Din al-Afghani, *al-A'mal al-kamila*, ed. Muhammad 'Amara (Beirut, 1979–81), vol. 1, pp. 214–222.

37. Jamal al-Din al-Qasimi, *Tanbih al-talib fi ma'rifat al-fard wa'l-wajib* (Cairo, 1908), pp. 13–61 and 77–85.

38. Muhammad 'Abduh, *Risalat al-tawhid*, ed. Muhammad 'Amara (Cairo, 1994), pp. 61–66.

39. *al-'Urwat al-Wuthqa* (24 April 1884), '*al-Qada' wa'l-qadar*', (pp. 161–174 of the collection of reprints of 1328 AH, Beirut); Muhammad 'Abduh, *al-Islam wa'l-nasraniyya ma' al-'ilm wa'l-madaniyya* (Cairo, 1902), pp. 124–125; Rida, *Ta'rikh al-ustadh al-imam*, vol. 2, pp. 209–267 and 391; al-Afghani, *al-A'mal al-kamila*, vol. 1, pp. 306–313.

40. Al-Qasimi, *Tanbih al-talib*, pp. 38, 108–109, 118; 'Abduh, *Risalat al-tawhid*, pp. 19, 116–118; Mahmud Shukri al-Alusi, *Ma dal 'alyih al-Qur'an mima yu'adid al-hay'a al-jadida al-qawimat al-burhan* (Beirut, 1971), pp. 10–11.

41. Barbara Daly Metcalf, *Islamic Revival in British India: Deoband, 1860–1900* (Princeton, NJ, 1982), pp. 264–296.

42. Muhammad Bahjat al-Athari, *Mahmud Shukri al-Alusi wa ara'uhu al-lughawiyya* (Cairo, 1958).

43. In his highly celebrated work, *Risalat al-tawhid*, 'Abduh largely adhered to the main themes of salafi theology; he is even frequently critical of the Mu'tazilis. Yet, on the controversy of the nature of the Qur'an, he seems to accept the Mu'tazili view that the Qur'an is the creation of God (*Risalat al-tawhid*, p. 48).

44. For an examination of the reformists' attack on *tasawwuf*, see Elizabeth Sirriyeh, *Sufis and Anti-Sufis: The Defence, Rethinking and Rejection of Sufism in the Modern World* (Richmond, Surrey, 1999), pp. 86–102. See also, Rida, *Ta'rikh al-ustadh al-imam*, vol. 1, pp. 106–108.

45. Annemarie Schimmel, *Gabriel's Wing: A Study into the Religious Ideas of Sir Muhammad Iqbal* (Leiden, 1963); Javed Majeed, 'Putting God in His Place: Bradley, McTaggart, and Muhammad Iqbal', *JIS*, 4, 2 (1993), pp. 208–236.

46. 'Abd al-Hamid al-Zahrawi, *al-Fiqh wa'l-tasawwuf* (Cairo, 1960), pp. 36–37 ff.; Rida, *Ta'rikh al-ustadh al-imam*, vol. 1, pp. 557–560, 940–1; Jamal al-Din al-Qasimi, *Qawa'id al-tahdith min funun mustalah al-hadith* (Damascus, 1935), pp. 281, 323–326 (see also an extensive study of al-Qasimi's view of *ijtihad* in Commins, *Islamic Reform*, pp. 70–76).

47. On al-Shatibi and his contribution to the Islamic legal theory, see Muhammad Khalid Mas'ud, *Shatibi's Philosophy of Islamic Law* (Islamabad, 1995). According to Draz, it was 'Abduh who encouraged him to edit al-Shatibi's major work of fiqh and legal theory. See Draz's introduction to al-Shatibi, *al-Muwafiqat*, ed. 'Abdullah Draz (Beirut, 1996), vol. 1, p. 30.

48. On the deeply-rooted Islamic notion of the objectivity of the law, see Bernard Weiss, 'Exotericism and Objectivity in Islamic Jurisprudence', in Nicholas Heer, ed., *Islamic Law and Jurisprudence* (Seattle, WA, 1990), pp. 53–71.

49. *al-Manar*, 9 (1906), pp. 745–770; Malcolm Kerr, *Islamic Reform, The Political and Legal Theory of Muhammad Abduh and Rashid Rida* (Berkeley, CA, 1966), pp 81–83 and 97–102.

50. Rida, *Ta'rikh al-ustadh al-imam*, vol. 2, pp. 40–43, 166–167, 353, 505; *al-Manar*, 12 (1908), pp. 16–26; Muhammad al-Tahir b. 'Ashur, *Alayis al-subh bi-qarib* (Tunis, 1988), p. 115 ff.

51. On the Moroccan Free Schools, see John Damis, 'Early Moroccan Reactions to the French Protectorate: The Cultural Dimension', *Humaniora Islamica*, 1 (1973), pp. 31–51. On the activities of the Algerian Jami'iyyat al-'Ulama in the field of education, see Ali Merad, *Le Reformisme Musluman en Algerie de 1925 a 1940* (Paris, 1967), p. 338; Turki Rabih, *al-Ta'lim al-qawmi wa'l-shakhsiyya al-wataniyya* (Algiers, 1975). On the Indonesian Muhammadiyya Society schooling activities, see 'Abdu-l Mu'ti Ali, 'The Muhammadijah Movement: A Bibliographical Introduction' (MA Thesis, McGill University, 1957), p. 74; Deliar Noer, *The Modernist Muslim Movement in Indonesia, 1900–1942* (Kuala Lumpur, 1978), p. 83. On the reformist educational institutions in India, see Qureshi, *The Muslim Community*, pp. 234–257; Annemarie Schimmel, *Islam in the Indian Subcontinent* (Leiden, 1980), pp. 189–215.

52. Rida, *Ta'rikh al-ustadh al-imam*, vol. 2, pp. 103, 157.

53. 'Abd al-Mun'im al-Jumay'i, *Madrast al-qada' al-shar'i* (Cairo, 1986); 'Abd al-Mut'al al-Sa'idi, *Ta'rikh al-islah fi'l-Azhar* (Cairo, n. d.), pp. 86–89.

54. For example, *maslaha* (public interest) as utility; *shura* (consultation) denoted parliamentary democracy and *ijma'* (consensus) was interpreted as public opinion, Hourani, *Arabic Thought*, p. 144. See also examples of 'Abduh's fatwas in Rida, *Ta'rikh al-ustadh al-imam*, vol. 1, pp. 498–502, 648–666, 668, 762–763 and 927.

55. In an essay on the 'Advantages of the Europeans and their Detriments', Rida once wrote: 'Had not we mixed with Europeans, we would not have awakened as a nation or nations to this (virtuous) great thing, even despite its lucid and unequivocal expression in the Qur'an' (*al-Manar*, 10, 1907, pp. 282–283).

56. Characterising physical sciences as the basis on which progress, wealth

and power were built, Rida wrote that reform in the East was attainable only if the traditionalist ulama were reconciled to the introduction of these sciences (*al-Manar*, 2, 1899, p. 70). See also, 'Abd al-Rahman al-Kawakibi, *Umm al-qura* (Cairo, 1899), pp. 34–36; al-Kawakibi, *Taba'i' al-istibdad* (Cairo, 1901), pp. 37–38. On al-Qasimi's views see Commins, *Islamic Reform*, p. 86.

57. *al-Manar*, 1 (1898), p. 733; 7 (1903), p. 358; 8 (1905), p. 759.

58. Jamal al-Din al-Shayyal, *Ta'rikh al-tarjama wa'l-haraka al-thaqafiyya fi 'asr Muhammad 'Ali* (Cairo, 1951), pp. 33–38; Jack Tajir, *Harakat al-tarjama fi Misr khilal al-qarn al-tasi' 'ashar* (Cairo, n.d.), pp. 26–128. 'Abduh himself, for whom education was the chief and indispensable tool of reform, translated Spencer's *On Education*. Earlier, in 1877, a disciple of al-Afghani had produced an Arabic version of Guizot's *Histoire de la Civilisation en Europe*, a book that al-Afghani highly admired and used to read to his Azhari students in private meetings at his home. But it was Fathi Zaghlul, a disciple of 'Abduh and brother of Sa'd Zaghlul, the Egyptian nationalist leader, who embarked on an extensive effort for translation. Among the many titles he presented to the Arab readers were Rousseau's *The Social Contract*, Bentham's *Principles of Legislation*, Le Bon's *Spirit of Society and Secrets of Evolution of Nations*, and Demolin's *A quoi tient la superiorité des Anglo-Saxons*. Inspired by Demollin's ideas, Fathi Zaghlul advocated adoption of the British model in the Egyptian education system, leading through his writings to the creation of 'a cult of British education'. See Jamal M. Ahmad, *The Intellectual Origins of Egyptian Nationalism* (London, 1960), pp. 44–46.

59. Hourani, *Arabic Thought*, pp. 92, 157–158, 220–223.

60. See, for example, *al-Manar*, 1 (1898), pp. 47–48. In 1923, Rida republished some of al-Afghani's anti-imperialist articles (*al-Manar*, 24, 1923, p. 26). See also Emad Eldin Shahin, 'Muhammad Rashid Rida's Perspective on the West as reflected in al-Manar', *MW*, 78 (1989), 27–28.

61. On the theories of nationalism as a modern development, see A. D. Smith, *Theories of Nationalism* (London, 1983); A. D. Smith, *National Identity* (London, 1991); Eric Hobsbawm, *Nations and Nationalism Since 1780* (Cambridge, 1990); B. Anderson, *Imagined Communities: Reflections on the Origins and Spread of Nationalism* (London, 1983); Ernest Gellner, *Nations and Nationalism* (Ithaca, NY, 1983).

62. On the Islamic-reformist origins of Arabism, see Sylvia G. Haim, 'Alfieri and Al-Kawakibi', *Oriente Moderno*, 34 (1954), pp. 231–234; Ernest C. Dawn, *From Ottomanism to Arabism: Essays on the Origins of Arab Nationalism* (Urbana, 1973); 'Abd al-'Aziz al-Duri, *al-Takwin al-ta'rikhi li'l-umma al-'Arabiyya: Dirasat fi'l-hawiyya wa'l-wa'i* (Beirut, 1986); Basheer M. Nafi, *Arabism, Islamism and the Palestine Question: 1908–1941: A Political History* (Reading, 1998); Commins, *Islamic Reform*. On the origins of Turkish nationalism, see

Serif Mardin, *The Genesis of Young Ottoman Thought* (Princeton, NJ, 1962). On the reformist roots of the idea of Pakistan, see Qureshi, *The Muslim Community*, pp. 279–304. On the Islamic reformist movement and the making of Indonesian nationalism, see Noer, *The Modernist Muslim Movement in Indonesia*, pp. 101–161. On the Moroccan salafis and the Moroccan nationalist movement, see Jamil M. Abun-Nasr, 'The Salafiyya Movement in Morocco: The Religious Bases of the Moroccan Nationalist Movement', in Albert Hourani, ed., *St. Antony's Papers, Middle East Affairs*, 3 (London, 1963); Mohamed El Mansour, 'Salafis and Modernists in the Moroccan Nationalist Movement', in John Ruedy, ed., *Islamism and Secularism in North Africa* (New York, 1994), pp. 53–71. On the Tunisian reformist ulama and the origins of the Tunisian nationalist movement, see Arnold H. Green, *The Tunisian Ulama, 1873–1915* (Leiden, 1978), pp. 152–155, 163, 221–224, 236. On Jam'iyyat al-'Ulama' and the emergence of Algerian nationalism, see André Nouschi, *La Nasissance du Nationalisme Algerien, 1914–1954* (Paris, 1962); Merad, *Le Reformisme Musluman*; Bu al-Sufsaf 'Abd al-Karim, *Jam'iyyat al-'Ulama' al-Muslimin al-Jaza'irin wa dawruha fi tatawwur al-haraka al-wataniyya al-Jaza'iriyya, 1931–1945* (Constantine, 1981).

63. Ernest Gellner, *Culture, Identity, and Politics* (Cambridge, 1987), p. 6.

64. On the reformist education and the rise of nationalism, see Taufik Abdulla, *Schools and Politics: The Kaum Muda Movement in West Sumatra, 1927–1933* (Ithaca, NY, 1971); Martin Strohmeier, 'Al-Kulliyya al-Salahiyya: A Late Ottoman University in Jerusalem', in Sylvia Auld and Robert Hillenbrand, ed., *Ottoman Jerusalem: The Living City, 1517–1917* (London, 2000), pp. 57–62; Commins, *Islamic Reform*, pp. 95–98.

65. Ami Ayalon, *Language and Change in the Arab Middle East* (New York, 1987); Hisham Sharabi, *Arab Intellectuals and the West: The Formative Period, 1875–1914* (Baltimore, MD, 1970); Pierre Cachia, *An Overview of Modern Arabic Literature* (Edinburgh, 1990), pp. 29–58.

66. The rise of 'Abduh's students in al-Azhar is documented in Bayard Dodge, *al-Azhar: A Millennium of Muslim Learning* (Washington, DC, 1961), pp. 146–156; Kate Zebiri, *Mahmud Shaltut and Islamic Modernism* (Oxford, 1993), pp. 11–31.

67. Muhammad Mahfuz, *Tarajim al-a'lam al-Tunisiyin* (Beirut, 19??), vol. 3, pp. 355–357.

68. On the Indonesian Nahdatul 'Ulama, see Noer, *The Modernist Muslim Movement in Indonesia*, pp. 233–240. On the Darul 'Ulum of Deoband, see Metcalf, *Islamic Revival in British India*, pp. 87–263.

3

The Diversity of Islamic Thought: Towards a Typology

William Shepard

This chapter undertakes to present an overview of Muslim thinking in the twentieth century in its ideological dimension, understanding this broadly to include thinking in which a religious or philosophical world-view consciously undergirds political and social concerns. It will not attempt to deal with such areas as theology, metaphysics, *tafsir* or fiqh (in its technical aspects), although writings in these areas undoubtedly have ideological implications. Also, it will not deal with specific ideologies so much as with 'ideological orientations', a typology of which is described below. In the realm covered I have attempted to cast a very wide net, but inevitably many important individuals, movements and countries are omitted or short-changed. In particular, I have nothing to say about sub-Saharan Africa or China. For this I can only apologise and plead the limitations of space and my own knowledge.

The dominating fact of life for the Islamic world in the twentieth century as in the previous one was Western imperialism in its various dimensions, military, political, economic and cultural. Crucial for ideology is the spiritual and cultural crisis that this has provoked. Traditionally most Muslims have assumed that the truth of Islam would be reflected in the military, political and cultural success of the Muslim umma.[1] For about a thousand years this was largely true, but

today it is all too obviously not. Like other religious people, Muslims
have been able to find some theological understandings for their re-
verses. Either God was punishing them for their moral failures or was
testing their faith. But increasingly these explanations have seemed
unsatisfying in the face of the persistence and depth of the Western
challenge. Increasingly it has seemed that history has gone off the
track, that God's will is not being done in the world – an impossible
proposition for a Muslim believer. Almost fifty years ago Wilfred
Cantwell Smith described the situation in these words:

> The fundamental malaise of modern Islam is a sense that something
> has gone wrong with Islamic history. The fundamental problem of mod-
> ern Muslims is how to rehabilitate that history, to get it going again in
> full vigour, so that Islamic society may once again flourish as a divinely
> guided society should and must. The fundamental spiritual crisis of Is-
> lam in the twentieth century stems from an awareness that something is
> awry between the religion which God has appointed and the historical
> development of the world which He controls.[2]

Over the course of the twentieth century overt Western political
and military domination has largely receded and oil has allowed
some Muslim countries a strong economic role in the international,
but still essentially Western, system. What is called 'cultural imperialism', however, has increased and here the initiative has come
mainly from the Muslim side. The first generation of post-independence rulers generally worked harder to westernise their societies
than the colonialists had and today if the West sells Barbie dolls to
Muslims, for example, it is because many Muslims want them.[3] As
a result, Western norms and practices that had at the beginning of
the century characterised a small urban elite had by the end been
transmitted to virtually all areas and levels of Muslim societies.[4] This
cultural imperialism is distressing evidence that history is still off
track, and in particular it has provoked the reactions since about
1970 that are commonly labelled 'Islamic resurgence'. The shape
of imperialism has changed but its challenge is perhaps more profound now than ever.

This chapter is organised in terms of several 'ideological orientations' that can be considered different types of responses to the
challenge Smith describes. I discern three general orientations,

'secularist', 'Islamist' and 'traditionalist', with subdivisions in each case. Most of the labels that I will use are common in academic parlance today and I do not intend to use them in radically new ways, although I hope my refinements make them more precise.[5] Primarily they indicate different attitudes toward the claim that Islam is a 'total way of life',[6] and toward borrowing from the West.

The secularist orientation more or less explicitly rejects the claim that Islam is a 'total way of life'. Most or all areas of public life are to be governed not by the Islamic sharia but by human reason and initiative. In effect this usually means by norms and practices derived from the West. Often religion is seen as a conservative, even reactionary, force that has held Muslims back. Just as the West (so it is thought) has limited religion to ritual and private life, so the Muslims must do if they are to match the West's progress. Muslim history will get back on track largely by following the paths the West has pioneered.

The Islamist orientation, by contrast, insists that Islam is indeed a total way of life covering public and private areas. It is not Islamic religion as such that has held Muslims back but its stagnation and misinterpretation, and the failure of Muslims to follow it. Muslims must reinterpret the basic sources of authority, the Qur'an and Sunna, in ways that are true to the original and appropriate to the present. They are not bound to adhere to traditional practices and past consensus. Whatever is borrowed from the West must be put in an Islamic framework. The secularist approach is seen as leading to moral catastrophe, already too evident in the West, and to the loss of cultural identity. Muslim history will get back on track when Muslims return to the sources and become more truly Muslim. Islamists may be more or less extreme in their Islamism and I shall discuss them below under two headings, Muslim modernists and radical Islamists.[7]

Both secularists and Islamists are 'modern' in that they take with utmost seriousness the changes that constitute 'modernity'. Traditionalists, by contrast, are strongly loyal to the traditional practices and past consensus, finding in them a wisdom which is not to be lightly rejected. There should be no unseemly rush to abandon them. Traditionalists generally feel the crisis described by Smith less acutely than do secularists and Islamists or, if they do feel the crisis strongly, they are likely to perceive it in terms of traditional categories, such as the hope for the Mahdi. Pure traditionalists were a vanishing breed in the twentieth century, but we may discern an intermediate category, 'neo-traditionalists'.

These types may be placed on a two-dimensional spectrum, with particular individuals often located at intermediate positions, and groups covering an area of the spectrum. There is a 'vertical' continuum of 'modernity', with secularists, Modernists and radical Islamists near the top and traditionalists at the bottom. There is a 'horizontal' continuum of 'Islamic totalism' from extreme secularism at the 'left' to extreme Islamism at the 'right'. For the horizontal continuum among (neo-) traditionalists I prefer to use 'adaptationist' on the left and 'rejectionist' for those on the right.[8]

These orientations are of course only one of many factors that determine actual developments. At any given time and place, the particular experience of imperialism, the nature of traditional society, the course of economic development, the class structure, the momentary configuration of political power and much else will condition the specific positions taken by different people of a given orientation. Also, we may note that diversity within given orientations is likely to be greater toward the left and bottom of the spectrum, since secularists vary in terms of which Western ideologies they follow and traditionalists vary with the traditions of their different societies, while those at the right and top, i.e. radical Islamists, will vary less among themselves. Unfortunately, there is not space here to do more than allude to these other factors from time to time.

While I pay most attention here to politics and law, these orientations can in fact be discerned in many areas of life and a given person may be said to have different orientations in different areas, e.g. Islamist in personal dress and economics, but secularist in politics and science.[9]

Secularist Orientations

Secularist responses to Western imperialism can be found in the nineteenth century, for example, in the adoption of Western-derived commercial and civil codes in Egypt in the 1870s. The first example of a full-fledged and fully intentional secularism, however, comes with the Turkish reforms of the 1920s and 1930s, the best known and in many ways the defining case. At the end of the First World War the Ottoman Empire lay prostrate, but Mustafa Kemal, later to be known as Atatürk, led the Turks in repelling a Greek invasion and extracting a more favourable settlement from the European victors.[10] Atatürk then undertook to impose a series of reforms aiming to make the new Republic of Turkey a strong nation able to hold its own with the Europeans. Among these reforms were the replacement of sharia law with a civil code adapted from the Swiss Code, the banning of the Sufi orders, the closing of the schools run by the ulama and establishment of a secular state school system with no religious instruction, greater government control over the mosques and their activities, the adoption of the Western calendar, and the enforcement or encouragement of Western-style clothing for men and women. Islam ceased to be the religion of state and sovereignty was 'vested in the Turkish nation without reservation and condition'.[11]

The purpose of all this was to make Turkey, both materially and symbolically, as European as possible. The ideology of nationalism, in the name of which this was being done, was of course a Western import, and as often happens in the West, the nation was endowed with a degree of sacrality. The preamble to the 1982 Constitution speaks of the 'eternal Turkish nation' and the 'sacred Turkish state'.[12] The reforms were also made in the name of something called 'civilisation'. When the Sufi *tekkes* were closed, Atatürk said, 'The straightest, truest way (*tariqa*) is the way of civilization. To be a man, it is enough to do what civilization requires.'[13] Both in Turkey and elsewhere secularists have regularly invoked the name of 'civilisation' or 'modern civilisation', explicitly or implicitly identified with Western civilisation, as an almost sufficient justification for their activities, so much so that these could be said to have functioned as quasi-religious symbols for them.[14]

There have, of course, been limits to secularism. Religion was severely restricted but certainly not abolished from people's lives. Indeed, for many secularists general ethical values derived from Islam are important. It must also be noted that Islam, at least as culture and history, is an inescapable part of Turkish national identity, and this is true to some degree of most other Muslim peoples.[15] Therefore, Islam properly 'tamed' has an important contribution to make to the national venture and, partly for this reason, neither in Turkey nor in any other Muslim state does secularism mean the separation of 'mosque' and state. Particularly in Turkey, the religious institutions are firmly under the control of the state.[16]

Since the late 1940s secularism has retreated somewhat in Turkey. Religious instruction is now given in state schools, there are schools and faculties to train religious functionaries, politicians sometimes invoke God and have used religion to seek votes. Even an Islamist party has been allowed to function, but without the name of Islam. On the other hand, the sharia has not been re-established as public law, Islam is still not officially the religion of state, the state still controls the religious institution, and 'Islamic dress' for women has been strongly resisted. Turkish secularism illustrates the fact that secularism is often not democratic. It was imposed from the top and it was precisely at the time when the government became more democratic that it relented somewhat on its secularism. The retreat has been allowed to go only so far, however, since the Turkish army effectively guards the borders of secularism. The experience of the Islamist party suggests where those borders are. It was allowed to come to power in alliance with a secular party in 1995 but it was soon forced out by the army when it was seen to push its programme too far.[17]

Atatürk's reforms sent shock waves throughout the Muslim world. For some Turkey showed the way forward while for others the Turks were apostates. The new ruler of Iran, Reza Shah Pahlavi, emulated the Turks as far as he could. He introduced or expanded secular law and secular education and pushed nationalism and Persian identity. He severely curtailed the power of the ulama but could not bring them under state control in the way the Turks had, partly because the institution of *ijtihad* in its Shi'i form gave the leading scholars a level of personal authority not possessed by their Sunni counterparts. From 1907 to 1979 Iran functioned at least in theory under a constitution which recognised Twelver Shi'ism as the religion of state and described sovereignty as 'a trust confided, by the Grace of God, to the person of the Shah by the nation',[18] although it also described powers of the state as 'derived from the nation'. Iran, in fact, had a source of symbols for a secular nationalism not available to the Turks, namely the long and well-recognised period of pre-Islamic

Persian greatness. These symbols were exploited in various ways, most prominently by the second Pahlavi shah in the celebrations of the 2500th anniversary of Cyrus the Great at Persepolis in 1971. If the shahs pushed a 'statist' form of secularism, other versions were promoted by opposition groups in the 1940s and 1950s, Marxist in the case of the Tudeh party and a more liberal nationalism in the case of the National Front. Mossadegh provides a good example of a leader who was personally pious but followed a secularist ideology.

Egypt achieved a qualified independence in 1922 and adopted a constitution that located all authority in the nation but made Islam the religion of state. The religious institution, headed by the mosque-university of al-Azhar, has been under state aegis, not as tightly controlled as in Turkey but not as independent as in Iran. The substance of sharia law has been applied in 'personal status' cases, but this does not violate secularism as here defined since a significant area of public life is clearly removed from sharia control. A state-run school system, secular but including religious instruction, has developed and overtaken the system connected with al-Azhar. In 1961 al-Azhar was integrated into the state education system, but it still retains its identity and no small degree of influence. Unlike Turkey and Iran, Egypt has a sizeable non-Muslim minority in the Christian Copts, whose concerns must be taken into account. This provides an important justification for secularism, but the Christian presence also provides a focus against which Muslims may sharpen their sense of identity and hence strengthens Islamism.

While most secularist writers have been content to invoke the virtues of 'civilisation' and argue practically from the need for strength and for national unity across religious lines, some have tried to ground secularism in Islamic sources. The best known example of this is the book *al-Islam wa usul al-hukm* by 'Ali 'Abd al-Raziq, written in the context of the debate in Egypt occasioned by the Turkish abolition of the caliphate. The author tried to show that establishing a government was not part of Muhammad's divine mission. In the ensuing controversy, he was 'defrocked' as an *'alim*, which hardly encouraged others to try this route, but later writers such as Khalid Muhammad Khalid (in his earlier writings), Muhammad Khalaf Allah and Muhammad Sa'id al-'Ashmawi have attempted something of the same.[19]

Like Iran, Egypt also has a significant pre-Islamic history and an effort, known as Pharoanism, was made by some to construct a national identity out of this in the 1920s but it soon lost ground to Arab nationalism, which is friendlier to Islamic sensibilities.[20] The government of Nasser particularly stressed Arab nationalism and added a form of socialism originally derived from British Fabian socialism. While this government controlled the religious establishment quite closely, it often spoke in Islamic language and was quite willing to use Islam to defend its policies and to further its goals abroad.[21]

Along with the rise of Arab nationalism from the 1930s, the secular intellectuals began to take a greater interest in their Islamic heritage and wrote a number of books dealing with the people and events of early Islam. To the extent that these treat Islam as heritage, more as a source of identity and inspiration than specific guidance, they stay within the bounds of secularism as here defined, but it is a secularism with a large, consciously-Islamic component. I like to call this and the various government ideologies 'Muslim' secularism.[22] It is this 'Muslim' secularism, rather than the 'purer' Atatürk variety that characterised the Shah's Iran and characterises the ruling ideologies of most Muslim countries today. Turkish secularism, too, is now close to this type.

Arab nationalism fits particularly well with Muslim secularism since it shares with Islam central heroes and symbols which can be used with convenient ambiguity. Nationalists regularly use the word 'jihad' for their liberation struggles in ways that evoke its religious force in greater or lesser degree, greater when Yasser Arafat calls for 'jihad for the liberation of Palestine and the recovery of Jerusalem'.[23] Secular Arab nationalism, especially but not exclusively in its more radical forms, such as Ba'thist ideology in Syria and Iraq and the thought of Colonel Qadhdhafi in Libya, has a tendency to subordinate Islam to itself, making Islam an aspect of Arabism and Arab history. The shared symbols and terminology usually keep this from becoming too clear, but it seems likely that the force of the slogan of the Arab Ba'th Party in Syria and Iraq, 'one Arab nation (umma) with an eternal mission (*risala*)' is more to transfer sacrality from Islam to the nation than to share it.[24]

A slightly different form of secularism is found in Indonesia. Although Indonesia's population is about 87 per cent Muslim, there is a strong Christian and Hindu presence and a distinctive tradition of Javanese spirituality.[25] When independence was won in the late 1940s there was debate about the place of Islam in the future order. The result was an ideology called Pancasila, the 'five principles'. The first of these is belief in 'one supreme divinity' but not specifically 'Allah'.[26] The suggestion that Muslims be obligated to follow Islamic law was rejected, but the state Department of Religion runs a network of educational and other institutions that serve Muslims very significantly. Among the factors favouring secularism were a strong Christian presence among those who had fought for independence and a strong sense of Javanese tradition among the largest ethnic group. For all the ups and downs of Indonesian politics over the last half century, this ideological orientation of the state has remained quite stable.[27] We may describe it as 'religious secularism', rather than Muslim secularism. The use of religion rather than Islam in secularist slogans is of course found elsewhere, not least in Egypt.

The most anti-religious forms of secularism have, of course, been experienced by Muslims living under Communist regimes, which severely limited religious expression. Some degree of Islamic expression was allowed as part of ethnic expression, however, especially among ethnic groups that were entirely Muslim, for example, Kirghiz, Kazaks, Uzbeks and others. In Yugoslavia the term 'Muslim' was explicitly used as an ethnic name.[28] The absolute extreme of anti-religious secularism was represented by communist Albania, which officially abolished religion from 1967 to 1990. Today most of the ex-communist peoples live under regimes that could be described as Muslim secularist and to a considerable degree 'ethnic' Muslim. There have also been individual intellectuals who have been publicly quite anti-religious, such as Sadiq al-'Azm in Lebanon and Ahmad Kasravi in Iran and, perhaps ambiguously, Salman Rushdie.[29]

Going from left to right on the scale of Islamic totalism, we find first the extreme anti-religious secularism of Albania, then the anti-religious secularism of the other communist countries, then the secularism of Atatürk's Turkey, then the religious secularism of Indonesia, and finally the Muslim secularism of most of the other Muslim countries.

While secularism is easily seen as a copying of the West, its style does not lack significant roots in the earlier tradition. One of the strengths of Islamic civilisation has always been its ability to 'borrow' ideas and techniques from other civilisations and secularism may be considered an intensification of this. Also, although the sharia is supposed to be obeyed in all areas of life, Muslim rulers have not always in practice followed it and in many places a distinction between sharia and custom (*'urf* or *'ada*) has been recognised such that one applied to certain areas of life and the other to others.[30] Secularism could be considered a formal recognition and further extension of these realities.

Islamism: Islamic Modernism[31]

In formal contrast to secularists, Islamists insist that Islam, or more precisely the Islamic sharia, must be followed as a guide for all areas of life, public and private. Today they commonly call for an 'Islamic state' and 'the application of the sharia'. They value Islam as heritage, to be sure, but they seek more. The less extreme forms of Islamism are commonly called Islamic modernism.

Like secularism, Islamic modernism has its nineteenth-century precursors, such as the Ottoman codification of sharia law known as the Mecelle and the tendency in much reform writing to compare desired Western institutions with Islamic ones, such as parliaments with *shura* (consultation).[32] The most important early modernist was the Egyptian, Muhammad 'Abduh.[33] 'Abduh argued that Muslims need not and should not turn to secularism because Islam, properly understood, is adequately suited to modern needs. Christianity might be authoritarian, intolerant and obscurantist but Islam is rational, encourages science and learning, rejects the blind acceptance of authority and allows a wide range of interpretation.[34] This illustrates the apologetic tendency that characterises much modernism. The argument here is that the West had to sideline its religion in order to progress, but Muslims need not and thus should not do this. This argument can be seen as countering an argument sometimes presented by secularists, that if Christianity can be limited to certain areas of life, so can Islam. There is also a historical apologetic which calls attention to the past greatness of Muslims and claims that modern Western achievements are rooted in what was borrowed from Muslims. This is in part an effort to assuage wounded pride, but it also implies that what Muslims once achieved they can achieve again and suggests that in borrowing from the West they are re-appropriating lines of development that are properly their own. This historical apologetic is also used by Muslim secularists, as they defend the Muslim heritage.

The Islam of the Modernists is Islam 'properly understood', for centuries of imitation (*taqlid*) of predecessors and the effects of non-Islamic 'superstition' have taken Muslims far from the pure Islam of the early days. Muslims must return to the basic sources, the Qur'an, the Sunna of the Prophet and the best of his successors. This return to the sources constitutes the 'salafi'[35] dimension of modernism and often gives it a 'fundamentalistic' flavour, combining the rejection of traditional customs considered un-Islamic 'innovations' with the firm insistence on those considered valid. It also frees up interpretation, since the number of authoritative sources is limited. It involves a call for absolute *ijtihad*, which would seek its guidance directly from the basic sources, not being bound by the consensus of the existing systems (*madhahib*, sing. *madhhab*) of Islamic jurisprudence (fiqh). A slightly less radical form of modernist *ijtihad*, but more commonly used in practice, is *takhayyur*, which permits the interpreter to choose precedents from any of the existing *madhahib*, rather than being bound to one, as had been the case. This provides an element of flexibility which is important to modernist interpretation

The scope for flexibility is strengthened by a tendency to reject many hadith as inauthentic. A very few Modernists, such as Parvez in Pakistan, go so far as to reject the hadith entirely and accept only the Qur'an as fully authoritative.[36] 'Abduh came close to this potentially when he stated that no one was bound by a hadith he does not consider authentic.[37] Even more radical, and unique to my knowledge, is the approach of the leader of the Sudanese Republican Brothers, Mahmud Muhammad Taha, who would restrict full authority to the Meccan part of the Qur'an, which has little political or legal detail.[38] Modernists also gain flexibility by stressing the 'spirit of Islam' and emphasising general principles rather than specific prescriptions.[39] This is carried quite far in the 'neo-modernism' of Fazlur Rahman, a Pakistani scholar who spent the latter part of his career in the United States and has had considerable influence on the present generation of scholars. He would, in effect, convert all of the specific commands in the Qur'an and Sunna into general moral principles and it is these principles that would be authoritative.[40]

In fact, modernist flexibility has commonly led to interpretations that resemble existing Western ideas and practices. 'Abduh's famous Transvaal Fatwa, for example, justified the wearing of Western-style hats and the eating of meat slaughtered by Christians.[41] The identification of *shura* with democracy or parliament, already mentioned, is quite standard. The Islamic principles for society enumerated by the Egyptian politician and statesman, 'Abd al-Rahman 'Azzam, in his book, *The Eternal Message of Muhammad*, include 'justice, freedom, brotherhood of man, the value of work, religious tolerance, and the redistribution of excess wealth',[42] obviously hard to distinguish from Western liberal principles. About mid-century came 'Islamic socialism' which finds a basis for socialism in such hadith as, 'All people share in three things: water, fodder and fire'. On the basis of texts such as this Shaykh Shaltut, the shaykh of al-Azhar, justified Nasser's nationalisation and agrarian reform measures.[43] Another kind of Modernism is that of Ali Shari'ati, who interpreted Shi'i Islam in terms of a kind of Third World populism, with Western roots in writers such as Sartre, Marx, Durkheim and Fanon. He provides a striking justification of populism when he writes, 'Wherever in the Qur'an social matters are mentioned, Allah and "the people" (*al-nas*) are virtually synonymous ... "Rule belongs to God"' [means] rule belongs to the people.'[44] Likewise, Mehdi Bazargan and the Freedom Movement (Nahzat-i Azadi) represent a liberal-oriented modernism, while the Mujahidin-i Khalq represent a more Marxist-oriented modernism.[45]

Indeed, modernism sometimes seems to amount to little more than an Islamic justification of secularism. 'Azzam writes of 'the flexibility of the Islamic Shari'ah and the authority it gives to our reason and our *ijtihad*' and goes on to say, 'there is wide scope for human opinion and it is up to reason and experience to distinguish correct from incorrect action, to show the road to the general welfare and to steer clear of harm'.[46] A more extreme example is found in the writings of the Egyptian judge, Muhammad Sa'id al-'Ashmawi, who can be described as secularist in spirit and intention but at the left edge of modernism in his argumentation. He distinguishes between sharia, the values and principles ordained by God through the Qur'an and Sunna, and fiqh, the specific rules and judgements derived by scholars. Using a very flexible method for interpreting the sources, he argues that current 'secular' Egyptian law does not violate the sharia but appropriately applies its principles to the current situation.[47]

At the right edge of modernism, or even further right, is an interesting group of contemporary writers who combine flexibility and a strong futurist orientation with an equally strong desire to avoid copying the West. A good example is Ziauddin Sardar, who urges the need for Muslims to free themselves both from bondage to their past tradition and from Western tutelage at a very fundamental level, and to plan systematically for their own distinctive future.[48]

While Islamic modernism has been extremely influential among educated Muslims in the twentieth century, it has rarely characterised the ideology of Muslim governments. The main exception is the constitution of Pakistan, which asserts that 'sovereignty over the entire Universe belongs to Almighty Allah alone and the authority to be exercised by the people of Pakistan within the limits prescribed by Him is a sacred trust', and that 'the principles of democracy, freedom, equality, tolerance and social justice as enunciated by Islam shall be fully observed'.[49] The leader of the movement for Pakistan, Muhammad Ali Jinnah, with his 'two nation theory' has to be classed as a Muslim secularist.[50] By contrast, Muhammad Iqbal, the 'spiritual father' of Pakistan, with his view of *ijtihad* as the 'principle of movement', can be seen as a modernist.[51] Among later leaders Ayyub Khan and in certain respects Zulfikar Ali Bhutto can be considered modernist.[52] A number of Pakistani thinkers can be described as modernist, such as Parvez and Khalifah Abd al-Hakim.[53]

In Malaysia the close connection between Malay and Islamic identities along with the presence of a very large non-Muslim population makes for strong psychological pressure for Islamism but strong practical pressure against it. The prime minister, Mahathir, sometimes speaks in modernist terms and sometimes in Muslim secularist terms.[54] His former deputy, Anwar Ibrahim, and the student organisation which he headed in the 1970s and early 1980s, were more consistently modernist.[55]

Probably the oldest and largest modernist organisation in the world is the Indonesian Muhammadiyya, founded in 1912 and considerably influenced by the ideas of Muhammad 'Abduh. Its modernism is seen in its refusal to bind itself to the *madhahib* in fiqh, its rejection of many popular customs as un-Islamic, and its desire 'to create the true Islamic society'.[56] It has created an impressive network of educational and social welfare agencies and, though it is not a political organisation, many of its members have participated in Islamist parties.[57] Modernists today in Indonesia today usually speak of an 'Islamic society' rather than an 'Islamic state'. An interesting development in Indonesia is the emergence since about 1970 of a group of intellectuals commonly referred to as 'neo-modernists' and having links to Fazlur Rahman. Strictly speaking, however, they are better described as religious secularists, since they accept Pancasila and have a strong concern for inter-religious tolerance. They have influence in the state-run institutes that train ulama (IAIN) and the first president of Indonesia in the post-Suharto era, Abdurrahman Wahid, is generally counted among them.[58]

Both strengths and weaknesses lie in the tendency of Islamic modernism to give Islamic form and expression to ideas and practices coming from the West. Giving Islamic reasons and labels to such ideas and activities may facilitate their acceptance but will inevitably make more or less subtle changes in them. The result may be a healthy indigenisation or merely a travesty of the Western practice. The tendency to equate *shura* with parliamentary government, for example, may facilitate the actual development of democracy, may cover up the fact that there is no democracy, or may lead to forms that are not democracy in its Western form but something else that is suitable to a given Muslim situation.[59]

Radical Islamism

Radical Islamism has arisen usually out of a Modernist context but is more insistent and purist. It is at least foreshadowed in the later writings of Muhammad 'Abduh's self-appointed disciple, Rashid Rida, and found its first large-scale manifestation in the founding of the Muslim Brothers organisation in Egypt in 1928 by Hasan al-Banna, who had been influenced by Rida.[60] The Brothers called for an 'Islamic order' in society. Beginning as an educational and cultural organisation, it became involved in politics and by the late

1940s was the largest mass political and social organisation in Egypt and was spreading to other Arab countries. Its relation to secularist governments has usually been problematic but has varied. It was banned in Egypt in 1954, for example, but has had a peaceful modus vivendi with the government in Jordan. The second well-known radical Islamist organisation was the Jama'at-i Islami, founded in 1941 in India by Abul al-A'la Mawdudi, who had earlier been associated with Iqbal. It has been active in both India and Pakistan, but particularly Pakistan. Functioning as a political party it has not done well at the polls, but Mawdudi's writings have been extremely influential throughout the Muslim world and among Muslims living in the West.[61] Influenced by Mawdudi but eventually more radical was the Egyptian Muslim Brother ideologue, Sayyid Qutb, who was executed by the Egyptian government in 1966.[62] Another prominent radical Islamist group in the 1940s and 1950s was the Feda'iyan-i Islam, who participated violently in the Iranian politics of the time and had some contact with the Muslim Brothers. In Indonesia the Dar al-Islam movement of West Java, which rebelled against the central government in the 1950s, had a radically Islamist ideology, and some of leaders of the Masyumi Party appear to have moved in a radically Islamist direction after the party was banned in 1960. The small Indonesian social and cultural organisaton, Persatuan Islam (Persis), seems to me closer to radical Islamism than Modernism.[63] Mawdudi and Qutb provide probably the 'purest' examples of radical Islamism, while others are predominately so but have tendencies either toward Modernism or neo-traditionalism.

Since 1970 radical Islamist movements have become more prominent and widespread. The Muslim Brothers in Egypt were allowed to resume their activities, though without full legality, in 1971 and have participated indirectly in four elections. Under Islamist pressure a provision has been included in the Egyptian constitution that 'the principles of the Islamic Sharia are the primary source of legislation', but without removing the ascription of sovereignty to 'the people only'.[64] Today in Egypt a secularist government walks an uncomfortable tightrope between secularist and Islamist pressures. In Turkey, an Islamist party without an Islamic label has also participated in elections and even briefly come to power, as mentioned earlier. In Pakistan the military government of General Ziaul Haq allied itself for a time with the Jama'at-i Islami and sought to put into effect many of its ideas.

On the other hand, there have been bloody confrontations between secular governments and Islamists, notably in Syria in 1980, in Algeria since 1991 and in Tajikistan from 1992 to 1994, and also violence by small extremist groups, such as the assassinations in Egypt of the president in 1981 and the violent activities of the 1990s, and the 1993 bombing of the New York World Trade Center. The destruction of these same buildings in 2001 and the other activities of al-Qa'ida represent an ominous development, novel in its international basis and its use of willing martyrs, and typically Islamist in its use of the latest technology.

Undoubtedly the most dramatic and significant victory for radical Islamism and other rejectionist orientations has been the Islamic revolution in Iran in 1979. Also significant has been the strength of the Islamic-oriented resistance in Afghanistan and the success of Hizb Allah in forcing the Israelis to leave Lebanon. The Sudan has had a military government with a radically Islamist programme since 1989 supported by the Muslim Brothers.[65] A radically Islamist government has been in power in the Malaysian state of Kalantan since 1990. These developments have made it clear to all that radical Islamism is a serious contender for power in today's world.

Competition between secularists and Islamists may be less visible when Muslims are engaged in a common struggle against a non-Muslim enemy but surface after the enemy is defeated. The power struggles following the revolution in Iran involved the sidelining of secularists such the National Front and the Marxists, modernists such as the Freedom Movement and the Mujahidin-i Khalq and some traditionalists in favour of radical Islamists. Likewise in Afghanistan a very wide range of orientations participated in the struggle to expel the Russians and then struggled against each other, ending in the victory of the extremist Taliban.[66] These tensions have also been quite evident during the struggles in Lebanon and Palestine, between the secularist Amal and the Islamist Hizb Allah in the first and between the secularist PLO and the Islamist Hamas and Islamic Jihad in the second.

Radical Islamists react against certain aspects of modernism while continuing others. They explicitly object to the modernist tendency to put Western borrowings in Islamic form. Mawdudi complains of those who wish to identify Islam with 'democracy', 'communism', or 'dictatorship', seeing in this an 'inferiority complex', a 'belief that we as Muslims can earn no honour or respect unless we are able to show that our religion resembles modern creeds'.[67] Sayyid Qutb speaks of this as 'defeatism' and warns against 'putting Islamic signs over the camps of depravity and decay'.[68]

Along with this goes a demand for radical obedience to God. Khumayni insists that Islam is 'the rule of the divine law over men' and, criticising many Shi'i traditionalists, that this law is not just to be studied but put into effect.[69] Like modernists, radical Islamists accept the need for absolute *ijtihad*, but more restrictively, and are less likely than modernists to soften the interpretation of a difficult Qur'anic or hadith text. Says Mawdudi, 'The purpose and object of *ijtihad* is not to replace the Divine law by man-made law. Its real object is to understand the Supreme Law.'[70] Their attitude toward flexibility is indicated by Sayyid Qutb's view that Islam is 'flexible' but not 'fluid'.[71] They are somewhat more likely than Modernists to recognise the value of past traditions of interpretation, while still not being tied to them.[72]

Radicals are quite modern, however. They are generally no less avid for modern material technology than secularists or modernists and they make full use of modern methods of organisation and communication. They form mass organisations and political parties and print and broadcast their propaganda. Today they make liberal use of the Internet. In fact, radical Islamism appears to have its greatest appeal to people with modern and particularly scientific and technical training and their leaders are usually not ulama but people with 'secular' training and careers.[73]

They also betray their modernity in more subtle ways. Their slogans are often modelled on Western ones. Mawdudi has written of 'that International Revolutionary Party organized by Islam' and Sayyid Qutb has described Islam as 'a universal proclamation of the liberation of man'.[74] They generally accept the modern state as an entity of control that reaches more deeply into the lives of its citizens than earlier states did. Moreover, the 'application' of the sharia in the modern state will give it characteristics of Western law it never had before.[75] It has been suggested, aptly, that Modernists wish to 'modernise Islam' and radical Islamists wish to 'Islamise modernity',[76] but in fact Islamising modernity will also modernise Islam![77]

An effort to achieve Islamic distinctiveness in the face of this may be made by stressing the idea that Islam is an integrated 'system' and that it is the system as a whole that is distinctive, not every individual element within it. This view of Islam as a 'system' is itself a subtle sign of modernity.[78] Another way is to give particular stress to a few ideas and practices that are clearly and distinctively Islamic, such as the rejection of bank interest, 'Islamic' garb for women or cutting off the hand of a thief, though this approach may be seen as more traditionalist.[79]

The most popular Western-derived ideological ideas are nationalism and democracy. These are rejected by the most extreme Islamists, such as Sayyid Qutb, as giving to humans the authority and loyalty that belongs only to God.[80] Most Islamists, however, accept them so long as they are subordinated to Islam. Mawdudi rejected Jinnah's Muslim nationalism on these grounds before Partition but moved to Pakistan to continue his work afterwards.[81] Many radical Islamists, along with modernists, accept the idea of Islamic democracy based on the concept of humans as God's 'caliph', this 'caliphate' being exercised not just by the rulers but by the people as a whole. Mawdudi speaks of 'theo-democracy' in this connection.[82] Khumayni rejected both nationalism and 'democracy' but he was certainly populist if not 'democratic', and the Islamic Republic has in fact found a place for Iranian nationalism and is generally agreed to be more democratic in practice than most Muslim governments.[83] One point on which radical Islamists generally differ from secularists and Islamic modernists has been in a principled unwillingness to give non-Muslims full equal status with Muslims in an Islamic state.[84]

Differences among radical Islamists have to do more with styles, methods and strategies than ideological content and ultimate goals. One may contrast a 'top down' strategy, which concentrates first on gaining political power, with a 'bottom up' strategy, which seeks to prepare the way by first reforming other aspects of society.[85] The Jama'at-i Islami in Pakistan and the Iranian revolution are examples of the first, while the Muslim Brothers have frequently been an example of the second, giving more immediate attention to educational and social activities and even to taking over professional associations.[86] Some movements are more populist, as with both the Muslim Brothers and the Iranian revolution, while others are more elitist, as with the Jama'at-i Islami. Some are willing to accept a limited amount of Islamic legislation for a start, half an Islamic cake so to speak, while others are inclined to insist on all or nothing. Some are prepared to state in some detail beforehand what an Islamic order will look like while others say that this must wait until the Islamists come to power.[87] Some Islamists have been willing to participate in the political process in existing secular states, while others have opted for more violent methods, whether revolutions, coup d'etats or assassinations. The choice among these options probably depends less on the Islamists' principles than on their assessment of their particular situation at any time. This was particularly obvious in Algeria, where the Islamists turned violent only after they were denied the fruits of electoral victory, and among the Palestinians, where the intifada opened the way for the radical activism of Hamas and Islamic Jihad. Radical Islamists also differ in their moral analyses of existing societies. Sayyid Qutb argued that all so-called 'Muslim' societies of his time were in reality *jahiliyya*. Not many go this far but even this view does not correlate in a simple manner with violence.[88]

Although politics is usually central, Islamists are concerned with all areas of life and some of the most distinctive departures outside of politics may be described as radical Islamist even if many involved in them are not radically Islamist in politics. An obvious example is the 'Islamic' garb for women that has been so prominent for the last generation. This garb covers the body completely but in many places is sartorially different from the old, traditional women's dress. It therefore well illustrates the combination of Islam and modernity that the radicals seek. The movement for Islamic banking, especially in so far as it does not just reject interest but seeks to develop a whole system of banking based on this rejection and able to function in the modern world, can be called radically Islamist. In the area of science, the popular 'scientific exegesis' (*tafsir 'ilmi*) which seeks to find modern science in the Qur'an is best described as a form of apologetic modernism, since it gives an Islamic basis to Western results. The movement for the 'Islamisation of knowledge' associated with people such as Isma'il R. al-Faruqi, however, is more properly within the realm of radical Islamism since it seeks, at least in principle, a profound restructuring of the bases of human knowledge, upon which virtually everything in modern society depends. Al-Faruqi writes, 'As disciplines, the humanities, the social sciences and the natural sciences must be reconceived and rebuilt, given a new Islamic base and assigned new purposes consistent with Islam.'[89] Equally radical are the ideas of Ziauddin Sardar, who is discussed above but might be included here so far as his ultimate objectives are concerned. Certainly many who wear Islamic garb, participate in Islamic banking or take an interest in Islamic science are not radicals in the political realm but often their goals may be more profoundly radical that what political Islamists seek. In many cases they may be seen as examples of the 'bottom-up' approach mentioned above or their activities may be seen as an 'outlet' for radical Islamist feelings in areas where the pressure for political Islamism is great but the scope limited, as in Malaysia, and of course in Western countries.

The main strength of radical Islamism lies in its combination of modernity with a strong and plausible claim to Islamic authenticity. It seeks to be modern without being Western, a goal which may not be realistic but is enormously significant. It appeals especially to people for whom 'modernity' has corroded the traditional authorities but for whom secularism is morally unacceptable or at least unable to generate strong moral commitment. Its purist nature tends to make it intolerant and it has a worrying capacity to exacerbate inter-religious strife, but some radical Islamist movements do appear to be learning the value of religious and civil tolerance. Paradoxically, their very effort to live Islam radically in new conditions may force radical Islamists into creative developments, though they may not recognise that they are creative. Khumayni's doctrine of *vilayat-i faqih,* for example, is the one truly new political doctrine in twentieth-century Islam, while al-Qa'ida is undoubtedly creative in strategy and tactics.

Traditionalism and Neo-Traditionalism

Secularism and the two kinds of Islamism taken together comprise a scale running from anti-religious Albanian secularism at the far left to radical Islamism at the far right but all are 'modern' in the sense of either accepting Western modernity or seeking to replace it with a no less 'modern' form of Islam.[90]

Many Muslims, however, have given a lower priority to 'modernity' while at the same time have a strong loyalty to the particular religious forms they have inherited from the past. These may be labelled traditionalists and have included both conservative ulama and many members of Sufi orders. In fact, nearly all Muslims in 1900 apart from a limited urban elite would have been in this category.[91] A century later the spread of Western influence has been such that there are probably few if any pure traditionalists left.[92] We can, however, speak of neo-traditionalists, people who have taken on modern values to some degree but still value very greatly their received traditions. Traditionalists and neo-traditionalists presumably do not feel the 'fundamental malaise of modern Islam' described by Smith so acutely as the more 'modern' groups.

As mentioned at the beginning, the concept of traditionalism involves a 'vertical' scale, from extremely modern (whether secularist or Islamist) to extremely traditionalist. Also, within traditionalism there is a left to right scale, going from extreme adaptationism to extreme rejectionism, in relation to ideas and practices that may be considered un-Islamic or *bid'a*, whether from the West or from within their own societies. On both scales, most people and movements are located somewhere between the extremes.

In fact, many who initially appear as secularist or Islamist are not at the very top of the modern-traditionalist scale and some are better described as neo-traditionalist. The ulama of al-Azhar and comparable institutions who co-operate with secularist governments are in some cases Islamic modernists but more often are probably to be described as adaptationist neo-traditionalists. Their training in the past tradition inclines them to be more traditionalist, and because their tradition includes a strong element of political quietism,[93] they may find it easier to accommodate to secular regimes than do strict Islamic modernists.

Most of the grand ayatollahs in Iran at the time of Muhammad Reza Shah, other than Khumayni, also seem to have been adaptationist neo-traditionalists. Either traditionalism or neo-traditionalism seems to me to characterise most of the Muslim leaders who opposed the partition of British India.[94]

Sufi *tariqas* today, having undergone a certain amount of modernist reform, are likely to be neo-traditionalist in orientation, and also likely to be adaptationist. The Hamidiyya Shadhiliyya in Egypt, as described by Gilsenan, seems to be a particularly good example.[95] The ability of Sufis with this orientation to survive in the face of radically secularist regimes was demonstrated in the Soviet Union. In Uzbekistan it appears that the Naqshbandis are allied with a Muslim secularist government against more rejectionist tendencies.[96] In Chechenya, the struggle against the Russians appears also to have been carried out largely by an alliance of Sufis and Muslim secularists, although most recently a more rejectionist tendency appears to be dominating the resistance.[97]

The most extreme example of adaptationist neo-traditionalism that I am aware of is an Indonesian group called Permai which, according to Clifford Geertz, combined Marxism with 'original' Javanese practices purified of Islamic elements. This might almost be called an 'Albanian-style' neo-traditionalism.[98]

Probably the 'classic' example of neo-traditionalism is the Nahdatul Ulama in Indonesia, who are in fact usually labelled 'traditionalist' by observers.[99] This organisation, which is today the largest Muslim religious organisation in the world, was founded in 1926 by ulama at least partly in reaction to the activities of the modernist Muhammadiyah. They explicitly accept the traditional *madhahib* in fiqh, which the Muhammadiyah rejects, and also many local practices that the Muhammadiyah considers un-Islamic. The very fact of forming such an organisation, however, makes them 'modern' to some degree.[100] Over the years they have involved themselves in politics or not, as circumstances dictated. They have found it easier to co-operate with secularist governments than have the Muhammadiyah.[101] Abdurrahman Wahid, its leader until he became president of Indonesia, has come personally to the point where he is a religious secularist, as indicated above, accepting Pancasila and rejecting the idea of an 'Islamic state', and also articulating a very liberal position on human rights and religious dialogue. At the same time, he has a strong appreciation of the tradition, good links with more traditional people and a very 'Javanese' personal style.[102]

Saudi Arabia is best understood in terms of traditionalism. Its government is heir to an extremely rejectionist pre-modern movement, that of Ibn ʻAbd al-Wahhab, and it continues to be very rejectionist in many ways. On the other hand, its experience with Western modernity has been less difficult in crucial respects than that of most of the Muslim world. It was never politically dominated by any Western power and, thanks to oil, entered the modern world with economic strength. This makes its alliance with Western powers such as the United States easier. On matters related to ritual and family life the Saudis are extremely rejectionist and have geographically 'quarantined' the Western oil company employees and others that live there. In terms of political forms they are very traditionalist, not even strictly having a constitution.[103] In terms of political ideology, I suspect a close analysis would find almost every position, from the most rejectionist to the most accomodationist and from the most traditionalist to the most modern, among people of influence in the country. In technology and economics the Saudis have been very accomodationist to my knowledge. There have also been some strikingly rejectionist groups, however, such as those who rejected radio and later television as satanic and the group that took over the Grand Mosque in Mecca in 1979, and of course Bin Laden's al-Qaʻida.[104]

Many that are commonly called 'fundamentalist' are probably appropriately labelled 'rejectionist neo-traditionalist'. A good example is ʻAbd al-Salam Faraj, one of the leaders of the Jihad group that assassinated Anwar al-Sadat. In his tract, al-Farida al-ghaʼiba, he draws his arguments mainly from the medieval 'rejectionist', Ibn Taymiyyah, and his view of history is traditional and probably Mahdist, with little reference to the Western doctrine of progress.[105] Considerable neo-traditionalism can also be seen in the Iranian revolution, particularly in the prominence of the ulama and the presence of eschatological expectations. An interesting 'modern' expression of the latter is the phrase 'the revolution of the Mahdi (inqilab-i mahdi)' in a popular slogan.[106] Khumayni was neo-traditionalist in his connection with the ulama, his ʻirfani mysticism and much of his argumentation; but his populism was modern and his doctrine of vilayat-i faqih is, as mentioned, extremely innovative. I am inclined to place him intermediate between radical Islamism and rejectionist neo-traditionalism. The Taliban in Afghanistan are not only rejectionist but seem closer to traditionalism than neo-traditionalism. It is commonly claimed, at least, that their extreme practices reflected a particular form of Pashtun tradition more than Islam.

The Malaysian political party PAS (Pan Malaysian Islamic Party) is best seen as neo-traditionalist, with the ulama playing an important role in it. It began in 1951 in opposition to UNMO, the dominant secularist party, calling for an Islamic state but also pushing Malay ethnic concerns. Over the years it has become somewhat 'modernised' and the ethnic emphasis has decreased. The Islamist emphasis has remained strong, however, partly because it has always defined itself over against the secularist UNMO. The present PAS chief minister of Kalantan is closer to radical Islamism, perhaps about where Khumayni is on the spectrum.[107] A particularly interesting and unusual group in Malaysia was Dar al-Arqam, banned by the government in 1994. It was founded by a former member of PAS in 1968 and its members lived in semi-separatist communes. Their women were heavily veiled and their men wore Arab-style robes and turbans and they had Sufi-like rituals and Mahdist tendencies. They made considerable use of modern technology and set up schools, health clinics and successful businesses. To some extent they appealed to middle-class youth as a kind of counter-culture. They called for an Islamic state but gave priority to raising the moral level of society. This mix is clearly neo-traditionalist and extremely rejectionist in the social realm though less so politically.[108]

Neo-traditionalism has come to the West through several Sufi groups that have gained Western adherents.[109] It is also, in a distinctive and highly adaptationist form, found in the writings of certain followers of the 'perennial philosophy', such as Seyyed Hossein Nasr, Frithjof Schuon, Martin Lings and René Guénon, who stress the authority and value of tradition over against modernity.[110]

Neo-traditionalism has much to recommend it. Neo-traditionalists are generally better placed to draw on the wealth of the past, both traditions of learning and popular customs, with which the more modern groups are less in touch, and they may be in more effective contact with the masses of their society. They are likely to have a reasonable appreciation of modern innovations and may not be so mesmerised, positively or negatively, by the West as the others often are. They may therefore be able to be more appropriately selective in their borrowing.

Concluding Comments

The twentieth century began with the Western world at the height of its moral and cultural self-confidence and near the height of its military and political domination of the Muslim world. From the 1920s military and political domination receded as 'decolonisation' set in. Wars and depressions took their toll on Western cultural self-confidence and its claim to moral superiority, while the brief successes of fascism and the longer-term successes of communism for a time presented the rest of the world with competing models of society, none having the 'self-evidence' that the Western model had earlier had. More recently, the collapse of communism has left one superpower with a world dominance almost undreamed of in the past and a level of cultural confidence that has allowed talk of the 'end of history' and the victory of the 'liberal' model of society. At the end of the century the West's military power was still dominant but subject to considerable constraints, as the Gulf War and later developments well illustrate. Its 'cultural imperialism' continues to spread ever wider and penetrate ever deeper. At the same time, however, it has lost the 'taken-for-granted' legitimacy it once had for many; it is recognised as more problematic and open to challenge. Few people today equate 'civilisation' with the West quite so simply as they once did. The terms of the spiritual crisis described by Smith have changed somewhat, but the crisis itself is still with us.[111]

The Muslim responses have developed over the course of the century. At first conscious responses mainly characterised the elite, but over the course of the century the masses have increasing bought into 'modernity' and in the process become aware of the crisis. At the beginning of the century we can speak of traditionalism and modernism, the latter only beginning to divide into secularism and Islamic modernism. From the 1920s these had both developed various forms, but secularism has dominated in the ruling circles and has provided the ruling ideologies in most Muslim countries. These ideologies sought inspiration mainly from Western 'socialist' models from about 1950 to 1980 and mainly from 'liberal' models before and after that. 'Muslim secularism' was strong at the beginning and over time has gained at the expense of the more extreme secular alternatives. A new orientation, radical Islamism, came into existence in the

1920s and was presenting a political challenge, albeit unsuccessful, by the 1940s and 1950s. The increasing exposure of the masses to modernity has helped radical Islamism. It has also meant that neo-traditionalism has largely replaced traditionalism.

Since 1970 the Muslim world has experienced an Islamic 'resurgence'. Radical Islamist and rejectionist neo-traditionalist groups and movements have led the way and governments following these ideologies have come to power in Iran, Afghanistan, the Sudan and for a time at least in Pakistan. But the 'resurgence' is a broader phenomenon than this. There appears to be a greater concern with religion in all areas of life, not just politics. Many secularists have become more Islamic in their expression without becoming Islamist while others have shifted to Islamic modernism but not radical Islamism. For many, neo-traditionalism represents an alternative that seems more authentic.

While a detailed discussion of the reasons for this resurgence is beyond the scope of this chapter, three factors are worth noting. The first is the failure of secular regimes to deliver the promised degree of progress, strength and justice. The most dramatic evidence was the Arab defeat at the hands of Israel in 1967. The second is the decline of the West's moral hegemony. Not only world wars and depression but the nuclear arms race, the 'sexual revolution' and blatant consumerism have made the West morally less attractive than once was the case. The third reason is connected with one point where secular regimes generally have been successful, in educating the masses and allowing many to rise in the social scale. These people have usually brought their traditional Muslim concerns with them as they have risen and have therefore been responsive to Islamist or rejectionist neo-traditionalist options.

Secularism, once thought to be the wave of the future, has been seriously challenged but has not lost its vitality and secularist spokespeople fight more than a rear-guard action against Islamists. In fact, at present there seems to be something of a stalemate between secularism and Islamism. Islamists in most places have not been able to take over from secularists nor have secularists been able to eliminate the Islamists. They have therefore had to learn to live with each other as recognised participants in the scene. Some scholars now speak of the 'normalisation' of the resurgence as some radical Islamists become part of the 'mainstream' of society.[112] The same is true at the international level, between Islamist governments, secularist Muslim governments and the rest of the world. Coexistence at both levels is often uneasy, however. In my view the situation is far from stable and therefore far from predictable.

What of the future? The fact that Smith's statement of the situation is still relevant suggests that not enough has yet changed. In fact, to get Islamic history 'going again in full vigour' requires a degree of cultural creativity that has been little in evidence in Muslim society in the twentieth century. At most, there is perhaps more awareness of the depth of the problem now and some interesting approaches proffered, as we can see in the futurist thinking of Ziauddin Sardar and others. What influence the ideas of this group will have is hard to say since their resources to effect change appear limited, but they perhaps deserve more attention than they have received. From where else might such creativity come? The neo-modernism of Fazlur Rahman would provide receptive ground for creative departures but whether it can stimulate their occurrence is hard to say. The Indonesian form of neo-modernism, with its links to neo-traditionalism and a rich tradition and also its considerable access to the resources of the state, may be the place to look. This is especially the case if, as has been suggested, its main representatives are free of the 'inferiority complex' vis-à-vis the West which is the main symptom of Smith's 'malaise'.[113] Although Abdurrahman Wahid did not survive as president of Indonesia, what he stands for is still very much alive and we may see interesting developments there. Alternatively, having mounted a successful revolution, it may be the Iranians who have the needed self-confidence. Moreover, as mentioned above, the effort to live out a radical form of Islam in an uncongenial world may stimulate creativity. Necessity could be the mother of invention. Iran, especially if President Khatemi and his followers can moderate Khumayni's heritage and make good on his call for a 'dialogue of civilisations', may be the place to look for significant innovation. Perhaps Imam Khumayni and Abdurrahman Wahid can stand as alternative symbols of possible Muslim futures. Or, ominously, Bin Laden. The crystal ball is clouded.

Notes

1. The most commonly quoted Qur'anic passage in this connection is from Q.63:8, 'Power and glory belong to God, to his Messenger and to the believers'.

2. W. C. Smith, *Islam in Modern History* (New York, 1957), pp. 47–48. For a good critique of Smith's thesis, which points out some necessary qualifications, see Newell Booth, 'The Historical and the non-Historical in Islam', *MW*, 60 (1970), pp. 109–122.

3. Barbie dolls even in Iran! See 'Barbie Struts into an Islamic Stronghold', Scott Peterson, *Christian Science Monitor* (Feb. 19–25, 1999), pp. 1, 7.

4. Akbar Ahmed has aptly commented, 'If, for Muslims, late-nineteenth century European colonialism was a modern siege, the Western cultural campaign of the late twentieth century is a postmodernist blitzkrieg.' *Postmodernism and Islam* (London and New York, 1992), p. 157.

5. The typology used here was published in 1987 in my article, 'Islam and Ideology: Towards a Typology', *IJMES*, 19 (1987), pp. 307–336. Other writings in which I have elaborated on some aspect of the typology are: 'The Doctrine of Progress in some Modern Muslim Writings', *The Bulletin of the Henry Martyn Institute of Islamic Studies*, 10, 4 (1991), pp. 51–64; 'Modern Science: Muslim Approaches to the Cultural Challenge', *The Bulletin of the Henry Martyn Institute of Islamic Studies*, 14, 1–2 (1995), pp. 30–38; 'The Myth of Progress in the Writings of Sayyid Qutb', *Religion*, 27 (1997), pp. 255–266; 'Secularists, Traditionalists and Islamists in Southeast Asia: A Paradigm Revisited' (unpublished paper presented at the Islam, Civil Society and Development in Southeast Asia Conference, July 1998, Melbourne University). Some of the material here draws on these articles but is presented in a different form and with the addition of new material.

I believe that the typology presented here reflects a widespread consensus among contemporary scholars, although some use different labels, some slice the cake a bit differently, and few have as detailed a typology as this one. Esposito discerns 'four positions or attitudes toward modernisation and Islamic socio-political change'. These are 'secularist', 'conservative', 'neo-traditionist', and 'Islamic reformist' (along with 'modernist') These correspond essentially to my secularist, (neo-)traditionalist, radical Islamist, and Islamic modernist orientations respectively. See John L. Esposito, *Islam and Politics* (3rd. ed., Syracuse, NY, 1991), pp. 275–278. Mousalli's 'traditional *ulama*, ruling elites, modernists, and fundamentalists' correspond quite closely to my (neo-) traditionalists, secularists, and radical-Islamists, although I would not agree with all of his characterisations, e.g. that fundamentalists are more inclined to reject the older tradition than modernists. See Ahmad S. Mousalli, *Radical Islamic Fundamentalism: The Ideological and Political Discourse of Sayyid Qutb* (Beirut, 1992), pp. 213–230.

Ishtiaq Ahmed, *The Concept of an Islamic State; An Analysis of the Ideological Controversy in Pakistan* (London, 1987) provides an interesting and detailed spectrum which can be fairly closely co-ordinated with parts of that presented here. His two types of 'Sacred State excluding human will', absolutism and fundamentalism, correspond to my rejectionist (neo-) traditionalism and radical Islamism, respectively. His four types of 'Sacred State admitting human will' and two types of 'Secular State admitting divine will' correspond with various forms of my Islamic modernism, going from right to left (more to less rejectionist). His 'Secular State excluding divine will' corresponds to my secularism.

In most cases the term 'fundamentalism' (which I prefer to avoid) corresponds roughly to my 'radical Islamism', but usually includes also what I call rejectionist (neo-) traditionalism and the right wing of the Islamic Modernists. This is illustrated by Youssef M. Choueiri, *Islamic Fundamentalism* (London, 1990). The author divides fundamentalism into revivalism, reformism and radicalism. The first corresponds mainly to my rejectionist traditionalism and to some extent neo-traditionalism, the second to my Islamic modernism along with some of the less rejectionist radical Islamists (e.g. Hasan al-Banna), and the third to radical Islamism and perhaps the more modern of the rejectionist neo-traditionalists. He also links his typology more closely to particular social and historical circumstances than I do.

A writer whose categories bear a significant and interesting relation to mine is John O. Voll, *Islam: Continuity and Change in the Modern World* (2nd ed., Syracuse, NY, 1994). Voll presents four categories: 'adaptationist', 'conservative', 'fundamentalist' and a style which emphasises 'the personal and individual' (pp. 21–23). He describes these as 'styles of action' rather than 'ideological orientations', which suggests a somewhat different intent, and these categories are applied to the whole of Islamic history, not just the modern part. Still, the first three can be correlated successfully to my types: his 'adaptationist' to my secularist, some Modernists and most adaptationist neo-traditionalists, his 'conservative' to most of my traditionalist and neo-traditionalists, and his 'fundamentalist' to my radical Islamist and rejectionist (neo-) traditionalists. His fourth type seems to me relevant to a different scale from mine (see below). His typology suggests the relationship of my types to earlier historical trends. It is from him that I have taken the term adaptationist, adding to it rejectionist as a colloary. One can see secularism and Islamism as continuations in the modern period of the adaptationist and rejectionist trends of earlier times, although these terms do not capture all that is involved. See footnote 2 in 'Islam and Ideology', and my article 'Islamic Resurgence Re-Viewed', *Religious Studies Review*, 24, 1 (1998), pp. 13–16 for further comments on Voll and comments on Leonard Binder, H. Mintjes, R. Stephen Humphreys, Yvonne Haddad, Fazlur Rahman, R. Hrair Dekmejian, Ali Rahmena and Ibrahim Abu Rabi'.

The typology presented here focuses on the content of ideology and is complementary to some other typologies or distinctions, such as the distinction between 'establishment Islam' and 'populist Islam', or between 'text-oriented' and 'leader-oriented' (Voll's 'personal and individual'), or between revolutionary and evolutionary, or between violent and non-violent, or, of course, between Sunni and Shi'i. Any of my orientations is in principle capable of either of the terms of these dichotomies. For example, establishment Islam is secularist in most places but not in Iran, Sudan or Afghanistan today. See further comments in 'Islam and Ideology', pp. 308–309 and footnotes 8–10, also n. 85, below, on Kepel's distinction between 'Islamisation from above' and 'Islamisation from below'.

6. A very common claim by both Muslims and Western Islamicists, but one that has to be problematised. For a typical statement in a Western source, see Philip H. Stoddard et al., ed., *Change and the Muslim World* (Syracuse, NY, 1981), p. 2.

7. Like many, I prefer 'Islamist' to 'fundamentalist'. The term seems first to have been used in French, *islamiste*, and Olivier Roy thinks that it began among Muslims in the Maghreb around 1970. See *Islam and Resistance in Afghanistan* (London, 1986), pp. 232, 5.

8. The spectrum is diagrammed in 'Islam and Ideology', p. 321. For the more modern types I prefer to speak of the left-right continuum as 'Islamic totalism' and for the less modern types 'adaptationist-rejectionist'. For convenience I use adaptationist and rejectionist when I am discussing the modern and traditional types together. The two labels are somewhat different conceptually (e.g., a rejectionist traditionalist is less totalist than a radical Islamist), but they largely coincide in practice. Among (neo-) traditionalists the same sorts of people who are rejectionist toward earlier forms of *bid'a* are likely to be rejectionist toward the West, but Islamic modernists are generally quite rejectionist toward earlier forms of *bid'a* but relatively adaptationist toward the West. See n. 90, below, for comments on what comprises modernity.

9. This fact raises issues for the typology which are worth mentioning though there is not the space to discuss them in detail here. A woman who wears Islamic dress of the sort called for by radical Islamists but does not believe in Islamic government would, strictly speaking, have to be called a secularist, since there is a significant area of social life in which she does

not demand application of the sharia, even though her personal life-style may be radically Islamist. Politics and law may be seen as central because they, at least potentially, dictate to and control other areas. For this reason I would hesitate to include as radical Islamist anyone who does not call for an 'Islamic state' and the application of the sharia in a very totalist way, at least as a long term goal.

10. The Treaty of Sèvres, signed by the Ottoman government in 1920, left Turkey with much more restricted borders than the Treaty of Lausanne in 1923.

11. Article 6 of the Constitution of 1982. See A. P. Blaustein and G. H. Flanz, ed., *Constitutions of the Countries of the World* (New York, 1971-).

12. This was changed in 1995 to 'the eternal existence of the Turkish homeland and nation and the indivisible integrity of the Grand Turkish State'. See ibid.

13. Quoted from Bernard Lewis, *The Emergence of Modern Turkey.* (London, 1961) pp. 404–405, by Edward Mortimer in *Faith and Power: The Politics of Islam* (London, 1982), p. 141.

14. Atatürk told a journalist, 'Our aim is to establish a modern, therefore a Western state in Turkey'. See Binnaz Toprak, *Islam and Political Development in Turkey* (Leiden, 1981). Compare the statement of Abdallah Jevdet: 'there is no second civilization; civilization means European civilization, and it must be imported with both its roses and its thorns.' See Lord J. P. D. B. Kinross, *Atatürk: The Rebirth of a Nation* (London, 1964), p. 47. The Egyptian reformer, Taha Hussein, likewise said, 'In order to become equal partners in civilization with the Europeans, we must literally and forthrightly do everything that they do; we must share with them the present civilization, with all its pleasant and unpleasant sides.' See *The Future of Culture in Egypt*, tr. S. Glazer (New York, 1975) (Arabic ed., 1938), p. 15.

15. It is commonly remarked that no one is considered fully a Turk who is not in some sense a Muslim. This would be true for some others but not for all, e.g. for Malays but not for Arabs and Iranians.

16. Perhaps the most obvious example of state control of religion was the requirement, from 1933 to 1950, that the *adhan* be given in Turkish rather than Arabic.

17. It has been banned three times and each time resurfaced under a new name. Founded about 1970 by Neçmettin Erbakan, it has been called successively the National Order Party, the National Salvation Party, the Welfare Party and the Virtue Party.

18. Article 35 of the Supplementary Constitutional Law of October 8, 1907. See Blaustein and Flanz, ed., *Constitutions.*

19. For a good summary and discussion of *al-Islam wa usul al-hukm* see Al-

bert Hourani, *Arabic Thought in the Liberal Age* (London, 1970), pp. 183–188 and Leonard Binder, *Islamic Liberalism: A Critique of Development Ideologies* (Chicago, IL, 1988), ch. 4. For Khalid Muhammad Khalid and Muhammad Khalaf Allah see *The Oxford Encyclopaedia of the Modern Islamic World* (New York and Oxford, 1995) vol. 2, pp. 411–413 and the references there. For al-'Ashmawi see below.

20. Michael Wood, 'The Use of the Pharaonic Past in Modern Egyptian Nationalism', *Journal of the ARCE*, 35 (1998), pp. 179–196, argues that while Europeans appreciate it, it is the 'wrong past' for Egyptians, who have little feel for it, and it is problematic for Islam.

21. A good survey of ulama-state relations is provided by Daniel Crecelius, 'The Course of Secularization in Modern Egypt', in John L. Esposito, ed., *Islam and Development* (Syracuse, NY, 1980), pp. 49–70.

22. The Islamic works of writers such as 'Abbas Mahmud al-'Aqqad and Muhammad Husayn Haykal have been seen as a retreat from liberal secularism by Nadav Safran, *Egypt in Search of Political Community* (Cambridge, MA, 1961), but Charles Smith, 'The "Crisis of Orientation"; The Shift of Egyptian Intellectuals to Islamic Subjects in the 1930s', *IJMES*, 4 (1973), pp. 382–410 and *Islam and the Search for Social Order in Modern Egypt, A Biography of Muhammad Husayn Haykal* (Albany, NY, 1983) and quite recently Israel Gershoni, 'Egyptian Liberalism in an Age of "Crisis" of Orientation', *IJMES*, 31 (1999), pp. 551–576) have rejected this. 'Abd al-Razzaq al-Sanhouri, the great modern Egyptian jurist, provides a very good example of Muslim secularism. See Enid Hill, *Al-Sanhuri and Islamic Law* (Cairo, 1987).

23. Nels Johnson, *Islam and the Politics of Meaning in Palestinian Nationalism* (London, 1982), p. 75. Johnson quotes another person (p. 76) as saying, 'I'm proud to be a Muslim ... but jihad ... isn't part of religion to me.' There is a good but brief discussion of this and other terms in ch. 3. The Algerians, secularist and Islamist, fought the French under the label of jihad, as did the Afghans the Russians.

24. On this see, inter alia, Kamel S. Abu Jaber, *The Arab Ba'th Socialist Party: History, Ideology, and Organization.* (Syracuse, NY, 1966), esp. ch. 9–10 and Elyas Farah, *Arab Revolutionary Thought in the Face of Current Challenges* (n.p., 1973), esp. ch. 13. A particularly good example of the subordination of Islam to Arabism can be seen in the selection from the Egyptian intellectual, Ibrahim Jum'a, in Kemal Karpat, ed., *Political and Social Thought in the Contemporary Middle East* (London, 1968), pp. 48–51. Since the time of the Gulf War Saddam Hussein has made more use of Islamic symbolism, but he has also pushed the restoration of the site of ancient Babylon and made use of this symbolism, something at least superficially reminiscent of Egyptian Pharoanism. Qadhdhafi's *Green Book* (Tripoli, n.d.) speaks of reli-

gion but never of Islam, while he sees both religion and tradition (custom) and natural groupings, such as the family, the tribe, and especially the nation, but not religion, as the basis of the state (pp. 89–90). I believe he has made the suggestion that Arab Christians ought to become Muslims because they are Arabs. On Qadhdhafi see Ronald Bruce St. John, 'The Ideology of Mu'ammar al-Qadhdhafi: Theory and Practice', *IJMES*, 15 (1983), pp. 471–490, and Ann Elizabeth Mayer, 'Islamic Resurgence or New Prophethood: The Role of Islam in Qadhdhafi's Ideology', in Ali E. Dessouki, ed., *Islamic Resurgence in the Arab World* (New York, 1982), pp. 196–220.

25.   There are five recognised religions: Islam, Catholicism, Protestantism, Hinduism and Buddhism. Hindus are mainly in Bali. At one point an effort was made to have the Javanese spiritual tradition (*Aliran kepercayaan*) recognised as a religion, but this was not successful. The figure of 87 per cent comes from Greg Barton.

26.   *Ketuhanan yang maha esa*, more literally, 'absolute unity of divinity'. It is somewhat non-Islamic both in that it is rather abstract and in that it avoids Arabic words, and was apparently perceived thus by both Muslims and Christians at the time. See Alwi Shihab, 'Muslim-Christian Encounters in Indonesia', *Harvard University Center for the Study of World Religions News*, 4, 2 (Spring 1997), p. 10. The phrase *yang maha* is in fact used in the Indonesian translation of the names of God. According to R. Martin, M. R. Woodward with D. S. Atmaja, *Defenders of Reason in Islam: Mu'tazilism from Medieval School to Modern Symbol* (Oxford, 1997), pp. 195–196, Muslim intellectuals today take the phrase as an indirect reference to *tawhid*.

27.   For developments in Indonesia to the 1960s see B. J. Boland, *The Struggle of Islam in Modern Indonesia* (The Hague, 1971).

28.   In 1961 people were allowed to register as 'Muslims in the ethnic sense' and in the early 1970s there was agitation to re-designate Bosnia a 'Muslim Republic'. See Sabrina P. Ramet, *Nationalism and Federalism in Yugoslavia, 1962–1991* (2nd ed., Bloomington, IN, 1992), pp. 184–186. I do not know enough about the situation in the civil war in the 1990s to be sure, but I have the impression that this ethnic sense predominated although actors with more 'totalist' orientations were also present.

29.   al-'Azm, a Marxist, was the centre of a public furore in Lebanon in the late 1960s primarily for his book *Naqd al-fikr al-dini* (Lebanon, 1969) in which he presented Islam as an ideology of reaction and an obstacle to social progress. See S. Wild, 'Sadiq al-'Azm's Book, "Critique of Religious Thought"', *Correspondance d'Orient*, 11 (1971), pp. 507–513. Kasravi was a radical nationalist who has been described as a 'mullah turned inside out': Roy Mottahedeh, *The Mantle of the Prophet: Politics and Religion in Iran* (London, 1986), p. 104. He used to burn religious books. He was assassinated

in 1946 by a member the radical Islamist Fadayan-i Islam. For some of his writings in translation, see Ahmad Kasravi, *On Islam and Shi'ism*, tr. M. R. Ghanoonparvar. (Costa Mesa, CA, 1990.) Salman Rushdie's *Satanic Verses* is clearly radically secularist but his attitude toward the Islamic tradition is complex. He is the one prominent Muslim figure I would be inclined to call 'post-modernist'. Those Muslims who have supported him appear to be fairly radical secularists.

30. In parts of Indonesia even inheritance follows *'adat.* Evidently Abdurrahman Wahid's father, a leader of the Nahdatul Ulama, followed *'adat* at this point (personal communication from A. R. Wahid).

31. For convenience I will often shorten the term 'Islamic modernism' to 'Modernism', capitalised. The term modernism as commonly used refers to both this orientation and the secular ones. The term Reformist is sometimes used for Islamic modernists but this could be misleading since some Modernists, such as the Mujahidin-i Khalq are in some sense revolutionary.

32. Hourani, *Arabic Thought*, pp. 68, 92, 144 and passim.

33. Jamal al-Din 'al-Afghani' is commonly linked with 'Abduh, but his views are too complex, or contradictory, to be easily categorised. He adumbrated most twentieth-century tendencies and has been praised by regimes as diverse as those of Nasser and Khumayni.

34. The argument especially in *al-Islam wa'l-Nasraniyya ma'a al-'ilm wa'l-madaniyya.* On 'Abduh see, inter alia, Hourani, *Arabic Thought*, ch. 6 and Malcolm Kerr, *Islamic Reform* (Berkeley, CA, 1966).

35. From *salaf*, the respected early leaders.

36. Ishtiaq Ahmed quite appropriately finds in Parvez a 'theocratic position seeking severance with tradition'. *The Concept of an Islamic State*, pp. 128–135.

37. Abduh, *The Theology of Unity*, tr. I. Masa'ad and K. Cragg (London, 1966), pp. 155–156. See also Hourani, *Arabic Thought*, pp. 146–147.

38. See esp. Mahmud Muhammad Taha, *The Second Message of Islam*, tr. Abdullahi Ahmed An-Na'im (Syracuse, NY, 1987). There are, however, Sufi and eschatological elements in his thought that make him more neo-traditionalist. Abdelwahab El-Affendi describes his movement, the Republican Brothers, as 'a militant Sufi-fundamentalist group'. See *Turabi's Revolution: Islam and Power in Sudan* (London, 1991), p. 44. Taha was executed by the Numeiri government in 1985.

39. For example, one Egyptian modernist, when asked about the Qur'an's provision to cut off the hand of a thief, said that it symbolised a strong law and order policy (personal interview.)

40. See esp. 'Islam: Challenges and Opportunities', in A. T. Welch and

P. Cachia, ed., *Islam: Past Influence and Present Challenge* (Edinburgh, 1979), pp. 315–330; also his 'Islamic Modernism: Its scope, method and alternatives', *IJMES*, 1 (1970), pp. 317–333. Perhaps this is an appropriate place to mention Mohammed Arkoun, although I am not sufficiently familiar with his thought to try to fit it into my typology. My impression is that his work is not ideological but pre-ideological, so to speak, an effort to reformulate the epistemological and hermeneutical foundation on which ideology might be based. See Mohammed Arkoun, *Rethinking Islam Today* (Washington, DC, 1987).

41. C. C. Adams, 'Muhammad Abduh and the Transvaal Fatwa', *The Macdonald Presentation Volume* (Princeton, NJ, 1933) pp. 13–29.

42. English tr. Caesar E. Farah (New York, 1964), pp. 54ff, 90–92, 101–102. The title in Arabic is *al-Risala al-khalida*, which in my view would be better translated 'Eternal Mission'.

43. See 'Fatwa on Land Reform in the United Arab Republic', in D. E. Smith, ed., *Religion, Politics and Social Change in the Third World: A Sourcebook* (New York, 1971), pp. 211–214.

44. Ali Shariati, *On the Sociology of Islam*, tr. H. Algar (Berkeley, CA, 1979), p. 116. For a thorough recent study of Shari'ati, see Ali Rahnama, *An Islamic Utopian: A Political Biography of Ali Shari'ati* (London and New York, 1998).

45. Earlier in the century, Na'ini's justification of the Constitutional Revolution *(Tanbih al-umma wa tanzih al-milla)* can be described as modernist, using traditional Shi'i ideas about the illegitimacy of all government to justify constitutional limitations on the ruler. See Abdul Hadi Hairi, *Shi'ism and Constitionalism in Iran* (Leiden, 1977), esp. pp. 166–197. Ayatollah Taleqani, who wrote a preface to the 1955 edition of his book is also, I think, to be classed among the modernists.

46. *The Eternal Message of Muhammad*, p. 105 (English tr.); p. 212 (Arabic ed., *al-Risalah al-khalidah*, Cairo, 1964). (author's translation.)

47. Moreover, all legal systems are basically similar because human nature is the same everywhere, and, more particularly, the Code Napoleon has an indirect historical relation to Islamic fiqh via the Code of Justinian which he thinks influenced both. See inter alia W. E. Shepard, 'Muhammad Sa'id al-'Ashmawi and the Application of the Shari'a in Egypt', *IJMES*, 28 (1996), pp. 39–58 and *Muhammad Sa'id al-'Ashmawy, Against Islamic Extremism*, ed. Carolyn Fluehr-Lobban (Florida, 1998). An important difference between 'Ashmawi and 'Azzam is that elsewhere 'Azzam is at pains to make the point that Islam is comprehensive and that this distinguishes it from other religions.

48. See *The Future of Muslim Civilisation* (London, 1979) and *Islamic Futures: The Shape of Ideas to Come* (London and New York, 1985). I would call

his first book radical Islamic, but elsewhere the emphasis on flexibility and change probably puts him close to Modernism. Similar concerns are shared by many of the contributors to the periodical *Islam 21* (published five times a year in London in English and Arabic). In the same circle though with somewhat different emphases is Syed Muhammad Naquib al-Attas. In his *Islam, Secularism and the Philosophy of the Future* (London and New York, 1985), he particularly stresses the moral and intellectual training of Muslims. Sardar and others are also interested in the Islamisation of knowledge, which is discussed below under radical Islamism.

49. Preamble, Blaustein and Flanz, ed., *Constitutions*.

50. For his statement of the two nation theory see W. H. McNeil and M. R. Waldmann, ed., *The Islamic World* (New York, l973), pp. 458–460 and A. Ahmad and G. E. von Grunebaum, ed., *Muslim Self-Statement in India and Pakistan, 1857–1968* (Wiesbaden, 1970), pp. 153–155.

51. Muhammad Iqbal, *The Reconstruction of Religious Thought in Islam* (Lahore, 1971), ch.6. The following, from a letter to Jinnah, supports this: 'For Islam the acceptance of social democracy in some suitable form and consistent with the legal principles of Islam is not a resolution but a return to the original purity of Islam.' See A. Schimmel, *Gabriel's Wing* (Leiden, 1963), p. 235.

52. 'In some sense, one could argue that during the Ayub Khan and Zulfikar Bhutto years (1956–77), Pakistan was an Islamic republic with a modernist bent'. John L. Esposito and John O. Voll, *Islam and Democracy* (Oxford, 1996), p. 109.

53. See his *Islamic Ideology: The Fundamental Beliefs and Principles of Islam and Their Application to Practical Life* (3rd. ed., 2nd impression, Lahore, 1965). Ubaydullah Sindhi seems to represent a 'revolutionary' modernism, but I do not know very much about him. For an excellent study of various Pakistani thinkers, see Ishtiaq Ahmed, *The Concept of an Islamic State*. Note that most of his thinkers I would call Modernists (see n. 5, above).

54. His slogan, Vision 2020, seems both secular and technocratic, as does his statement on banking in 1991: 'Banks with a Heart', *Saudi-Malaysian Newsletter*, 3, 3 (1991), pp. 1, 4. On the other hand, a speech reprinted in 1997 seems closer to Islamic Modernism, urging that Muslims must 'return to the teachings of the Qur'an and the Sunnah of the Prophet'. 'Toward the 21st Century: Reformation and Challenges', *Islamic Future*, 12, 66 (1997), p. 8. This criticises the divisions in the Muslim world and calls for openness to new ideas.

55. He is evidently sympathetic to Ziauddin Sardar's circle. See for example Sardar's interview with him in Ziauddin Sardar and Merryl Wyn Davies, ed., *Faces of Islam: Conversations on Contemporary Issues* (Kuala Lumpur,

1989), a book which also includes an interview with Syed Naquib al-Attas.

56. *Muhammadiyah Movement in Indonesia.* (Jakarta and Yogyakarta, 1985), pp. 8–9.

57. Particularly the Masyumi, the Islamist party of the 1940s and 1950s. The National Mandate Party (PAN, Partai Amanat National), with which it was primary associated in the 1999 election, was not technically Islamist. E.g., it did not call for an Islamic state. See Chris Manning and Peter van Dierman, ed., *Indonesia in Transition: Social Aspects of Reformasi and Crisis* (Singapore and London, 2000), pp. 310–312.

58. Nurcholish Madjid, one of the most prominent of this group, has coined the slogan, 'Islam yes, partai Islam no'. See ibid., pp. 310, 313. The neo-Modernists, like Modernists, insist that Islam provides general principles, but seem even less concerned for its distinctiveness. Greg Barton says that Indonesian neo-Modernism 'does not feel the need to constantly proclaim its difference from the west, or to insist upon a wholly separate identity for itself', and that 'The neo-Modernists argue that the Qur'an and the Sunnah neither contain a blueprint for an Islamic state nor stipulate that a religious state is necessary, or even possible. All that was stipulated, they argued, were general principles by which Muslim society should be guided.' 'Nurcholish Madjid and Abdurrahman Wahid as Intellectual *'Ulama'*, paper presented at the AFAMAM and EURAMES conference, Aix-en-Provence, July 1996; copy supplied by author, p. 13. Wahid has been quoted as rejecting even an 'Islamic society', in contrast to the Muhammadiyah, but favouring 'an "Indonesian society" which the Muslims are strong'. See Greg Barton and Greg Fealy, ed., *Nahdatul Ulama, Traditional Islam and Modernity in Indonesia* (Clayton, Victoria, Australia, 1996), p. 241.

59. One way of distinguishing different forms of Modernism would be in terms of the particular Western ideologies they tend to follow, thus, Liberal Modernism, Socialist Modernism, etc. Another way of categorising modernisms would be in terms of their interpretative approach, thus, apologetic Modernism (emphasising defence against the West), 'salafi' Modernism (emphasising strict adherence to the Qur'an and Sunna), neo-Modernism (emphasising flexibility). Cf. Shepard, 'Islam and Ideology', pp. 313–314.

60. On Rida see esp. Hourani, *Arabic Thought*, ch. 9. The standard monograph on the Brothers through the 1950s is R. P. Mitchell, *The Society of the Muslim Brothers* (London, l969).

61. A good, detailed study of the Jama'at is Sayyed Vali Reza Nasr, *The Vanguard of the Islamic Revolution: The Jama'at-i Islami of Pakistan* (Berkeley and Los Angeles, CA, 1994). Among the many translations of Mawdudi's work is S. A. A. Mawdudi, *Islamic Law and Constitution* (2nd ed., Lahore, 1969). The Jama'at was founded only in 1941, but Mawdudi had already written a

radically Islamist tract, *Jihad in Islam,* in 1929.

62. Sayyid Qutb was for some time a secularist writer but he began writing Islamist work in 1948, joined the Muslim Brothers in the early 1950s and before his death had become extremely radical. On him see, inter alia, Ibrahim Abu-Rabi', *Intellectual Origins of Islamic Resurgence in the Modern Arab World* (Albany, NY, 1996), chs 4–6 and Yvonne Y. Haddad, 'Sayyid Qutb: Ideologue of Islamic Revival', in John L. Esposito, ed., *Voices of Resurgent Islam* (New York and Oxford, 1983), ch. 4. His best known and most radical work is *Ma'alim fi'l-tariq,* translated into English by S. Badrul Hasan as *Milestones* (Kuwait, 1978). The development of his thinking from 1948 can be followed with the help of W. Shepard's translation of another important work, *Sayyid Qutb and Islamic Activism: A translation and critical analysis of 'Social Justice in Islam'* (Leiden, 1996).

63. On the Feda'iyan-i Islam see F. Kazemi in Said Amir Arjomand, ed., *From Nationalism to Revolutionary Islam* (London, 1984), ch. 8. On Indonesia to the 1960s see esp. Boland, *The Struggle of Islam in Modern Indonesia.* On Persis see Howard M. Federspiel, *Persatuan Islam: Islamic Reform in Twentieth Century Indonesia* (Ithaca, NY, 1970.)

64. Articles 2 and 3, respectively. Blaustein and Flanz, *Constitutions* (author's translation). The Constitution of 1972 reads 'a primary source' and in 1980 this was changed to 'the primary source'. In view of Article 3 and of the way in which Article 3 has (or has not) been implemented, I consider the constitution still more secularist than Islamist.

65. On the Sudan see Esposito and Voll, *Islam and Democracy,* ch. 4 and Abdelwahab el-Affendi, *Turabi's Revolution.* Turabi appears to me radically Islamist but closer to Modernism on the scale than the Egyptian Muslim Brothers and Mawdudi. (See esp. el-Affendi, ch. 9.)

66. See Roy, *Islam and Resistance in Afghanistan* for a good account of the Afghan mujahidin groups other than the Taliban, including their ideological orientations. It seems to me that Gulbadin Hekmatyar's group most precisely fits the radical Islamist label. The Taliban are surely traditionalist or neo-traditionalist, as suggested below.

67. For Mawdudi, *The Islamic Law and Constitution,* tr. and ed. Kurshid Ahmad (5th ed., Lahore, 1975), p. 118.

68. E.g. W. Shepard, *Sayyid Qutb and Islamic Activism,* p. 106, 353.

69. R. M. Khomeini, *Islam and Revolution, Writings and Declarations of Imam Khomeini,* tr. H. Algar (Berkeley, CA, 1981), pp. 55, 72–6, 138–149.

70. Mawdudi, *The Islamic Law and Constitution,* p. 72.

71. 'Flexibility is not Fluidity (lit. "melting")'. *Milestones* (Beirut and Damascus, 1978), p. 197. Arabic text: *Ma'alim fi'l-tariq* (Beirut, 1973), p. 121.

72. While Modernists tend to emphasise centuries-old corruptions,

Mawdudi states that the sharia was the law of the land until the British took over. Mawdudi, *The Islamic Law and Constitution*, p 93–4.

73. See, e.g., Saad Eddin Ibrahim, 'Anatomy of Egypt's Militant Islamic Groups: Methodological Note and Preliminary Findings', *IJMES*, 12, 4 (1980), pp. 435–440. The Bandung Institute of Technology in Indonesia is a well-known centre for Islamists in Indonesia.

74. Mawdudi, *Jihad in Islam* (Kuwait, 1981), p. 5. Qutb, *Milestones*, p. 103; *Ma'alim*, p. 59.

75. Classically, both the sharia and fiqh are as much like a set of moral judgements as like law. It has been stated that the Iranian revolution 'did not mean a direct return to the rich Shi'i legal literature, but a large-scale codification of Islamic law according to Western textual forms'. Leon Buskens, 'An Islamic Triangle: Changing Relationships between Shari'a, State Law and Local Customs', *ISIM Newsletter*, 5 (2000), p. 8. Mawdudi quite explicitly recognises the need to re-edit traditional fiqh and put it 'in modern terms'. Mawdudi, *The Islamic Law and Constitution*, pp. 193–194.

76. Louis Brenner, 'The Study of Islam in Sub-Sahara Africa', *ISIM Newsletter*, 4 (1999), p. 31.

77. It has been noted that Islamic discussion on the Internet is mainly in English (and allied points) in *JAIMES*, 5, 2 (1999), p. 73. This is another example of the 'subtle' modernisation.

78. E.g. Sayyid Qutb, *al-'Adala al-ijtima'iyya fi'l-Islam* (Cairo and Beirut, 1974), p. 94; cf. Shepard, *Sayyid Qutb and Islamic Activism*, p. 106. See also Shepard, 'Islam as a "System" in the Later Writings of Sayyid Qutb', *MES*, 25, 1 (1989), pp. 31–50. W. C. Smith has noticed this in the case of Mawdudi. Smith, *Islam in Modern History*, p. 236. These points bear reflection in the light of Timothy Mitchell's remarks about the European concern for 'nizam, order and discipline' (but the word also means 'system', as used here). Mitchell, *Colonising Egypt* (New York, 1988), ch. 1.

79. More systematic is the common view that such punishments as cutting off the hand of a thief should be done only after an Islamic order, and thus true justice, has been established. (See, e.g., Mitchell, *The Society of the Muslim Brothers*, pp. 240–241.) That the symbolism may be at least as important as the reality is suggested by a debate that occurred in Malaysia a few years ago. The government of the state of Kalantan signalled its desire to put into effect the rule of cutting off the hand of a thief. This led to a lively media debate in which all sides got to make their points, but it was safe in the knowledge that the approval of the Federal government was required and there was no chance of this being forthcoming.

80. Qutb, *Milestones*, pp. 219–239, 249–252; *Ma'alim*, pp. 136–147, 153–155; Shepard, *Sayyid Qutb and Islamic Activism*, p. 108.

81. Smith, *Religion, Politics and Social Change*, pp. 114–115.

82. Mawdudi, *Islamic Law and Constitution*, p. 131–132. Cf., Hasan al-Turabi: 'an Islamic order of government is essentially a form of representative democracy. But this statement requires the following qualification. First, an Islamic republic is not strictly speaking a direct government of and by the people; it is a government of the *shari'ah*'. Hasan al-Turabi, 'The Islamic State', in Esposito, ed., *Voices of Resurgent Islam*, p. 244.

83. During the Islamic revolution in Iran, Khumayni refused to include the word 'democratic' in the name of the Islamic Republic of Iran (*Islam and Revolution*, pp. 337–338). On the later experience of the Islamic Republic see Esposito and Voll, *Islam and Democracy*, ch. 3.

84. For Mawdudi on *dhimmi* rights, see *The Islamic Law and Constitution*, pp. 177–178, 229–234, 256–278. Nasr states that since 1947 'the Jama'at has become increasingly committed to democracy and the constitutional process'. *The Vanguard of the Islamic Revolution*, p. 220.

85. Gilles Kepel distinguishes between 'Islamisation from above' and 'Islamisation from below'. *The Revenge of God* (University Park, PA, 1994), ch. 1.

86. Brothers or their sympathisers took control of the doctors', engineers' and lawyers' professional associations in Egypt in the late 1980s and early 1990s.

87. An example of the former is Shaykh al-Nabahani, founder of the Islamic Liberation Party in Palestine, who published a detailed constitution for an Islamic state. Suha Taji-Farouki, 'Islamic State Theories and Contemporary Realities', in A. S. Sidahmed and A. Ehteshami, ed., *Islamic Fundamentalism in Perspective* (Boulder, CO, 1996) An example of the latter is Sayyid Qutb, who held that detailed measures should be determined only after Islamists come to power since Islam is a 'practical' religion which provides solutions only at the time they are needed. *Milestones*, pp. 57–62, 74–77; *Ma'alim*, pp. 33–36, 44–47.

88. Qutb propounded his *jahiliyya* view most fully in *Milestones*, but there is debate as to whether he saw violence as necessary. The best known refutation of this position by a radical Islamist is Hasan Hudaybi's *Du'ah la quda'* (Cairo, 1977). A group that did accept Qutb's view was the so-called Takfir wa-Hijrah group in Egypt, who, moreover, insisted that the whole of society and not just its rulers was apostate. Interestingly, this was logically less conducive to violence in the short term than views that saw only the rulers as apostate, such as the 'Military Academy' group, and the Jihad group that assassinated Anwar al-Sadat. See esp. Ibrahim, 'Anatomy of Egypt's Militant Islamic Groups', 441–443.

89. Quoted by Ilyas Ba-Yunus in, 'Al-Faruqi and Beyond: Future Direc-

tions in Islamization of Knowledge', *The American Journal of Islamic Social Science*, 5, 1 (1988), p. 19. The International Institute of Islamic Thought in Herndon, Virginia, USA, publishes in this area and this is a concern of the Faculty of Islamic Revealed Knowledge and Human Sciences which the International Islamic University in Malaysia has recently started. See also Shepard 'Modern Science: Muslim Approaches to the Cultural Challenge'. It should be noted that, like Islamic discussion on the Internet, discussion of Islamisation of science is largely in English. *ISIM Newsletter*, 6 (2000), p. 11.

90. I take the characteristics of 'modernity' to be an acceptance of the use of modern material technologies, the symbolic valuation of this technology (e.g., an automobile as a status symbol as well as a means of transport), use of modern means of communication and organisation, and various attitudes and symbolic factors, such as a belief in 'progress', a 'Weberian' work ethic, the use of 'modern' terminology and, indeed, adherence to something that can properly be called an 'ideology'.

91. In 1899 Lord Cromer, the British Resident in Egypt, stated that there were only 7,735 students in state schools as opposed to about 180,000 in *kuttabs*, and that over 90 per cent of Egyptians were illiterate. Crecelius, 'The Course of Secularization in Modern Egypt', p. 61.

92. Dale F. Eickelman tells of an Omani village which was extremely traditional as late as 1978 but is so no more. He goes on to say that 'No Muslims – whether their outlook be deemed "fundamentalist", "traditionalist", or "modernist" – have been unaffected by the sweeping changes of recent decades.' He continues: 'Increasingly in the Muslim world, religious beliefs are self-consciously held, explicitly expressed, and systematised. It is no longer sufficient simply to "be" Muslim and to follow Muslim practices. One must reflect upon Islam and defend one's views.' 'Inside the Islamic Reformation', *Wilson Quarterly*, 22, 1 (1998), pp. 80–89.

93. Reflected in such sayings as 'Sixty years with an unjust ruler is better than one night without a ruler.' Ibn Taymiyyah, quoted by Hamid Enayat, *Modern Islamic Political Thought* (London, 1982), p. 12.

94. Including most of the more conservative ulama and political leaders such as Abu al-Kalam Azad. See Voll, *Islam: Continuity and Change*, pp. 235–237 for their orientations.

95. M. Gilsenan, *Saint and Sufi in Modern Egypt: An Essay in the Sociology of Religion* (Oxford, 1973).

96. Paul Goble, 'Fighting Fundamentalism with Sufism', Uzbekistan Daily Digest, 25 January, 2001 (<http://www.eurasianet.org/resource/uzbekistan/hypermail/200009/0030.html>, downloaded 25 January 2001). See also: Uzbek Ambassador makes official visit to Shaykh Kabbani, Naqsh-

bandi mureeds, (25 October, 2000, Naqshbandi e-mail Network <naqshnet-work-owner@listbot.com>).

97. Sometimes referred to as Wahhabi. See David Damrel, 'Religious Roots of Conflict: Russia and Chechenya', *Religious Studies News* (September, 1995), p. 10; various reports on the Naqshbandi e-mail Network (15 February–2 December, 2000); Amila Buturovic, 'Muslims of the Mountains feel a Rift over an Islam they barely knew', *Christian Science Monitor* (20 August, 1997). Amila Buturovic, 'Raduev Calls for Ban on "Wahhabism"', (9 January, 1998, email: amilab@yorku.ca); Shamil Basayev interview December 1999 <http://www.jamiat.org.za/whatsnew/basayev.html>.

98. Clifford Geertz, *The Religion of Java* (New York, 1960), pp. 112–118.

99. On the NU see, inter alia, Barton and Fealy, ed., *Nahdlatul Ulama*, also Geertz, *Religion*, ch. 12.

100. A point noted explicitly by Fealy in Barton and Fealy, ed., *Nahdlatul Ulama*, pp. 13–14.

101. They were much quicker than the Muhammadiyah, which has a history of not easily compromising on principle, to yield to the Indonesian government's insistence in the mid–1980s that all social and religious organisations adopt Pancasila as their ideology. While generally adaptionationist, it is worth remembering that NU members participated in the 1965 anti-Communist bloodletting.

102. See n. 58 above, and Gregory Barton, 'Abdurrahman Wahid, a religious liberal' (*Australia/Israel and Jewish Affairs Council Review*, 25 October, 1999). Geertz remarked, perhaps with prescience, that 'the modern-minded son of a *kolot kijaji* may end up an NU leader out of opportunity rather than out of conviction'. Geertz, *Religion*, p. 163.

103. In 1992 the king promulgated 'The Basic Form of Government' (*al-Nizam al-asasi li'l-hukm*), which has the form of a constitution, but the first article states, 'its constitution (*dastur*) is the Book of God Almighty and the Sunnah of His Messenger'. Blaustein and Flanz, ed, *Constitutions*.

104. On these, see Robert L. Lacey, *The Kingdom* (London, 1981), pp. 243–244, 369–371, 478–491. Those who took over the Grand Mosque proclaimed the coming of the Mahdi, marking them as (neo-) traditionalist, I think.

105. See esp. J. J. G. Jansen, *The Neglected Duty: The Creed of Sadat's Assassins and Islamic Resurgence in the Middle East* (New York, 1986). This includes a translation of Faraj's *The Neglected Duty*.

106. Seen by the author in Tehran in 1984 and 1999, and also elsewhere.

107. My view is based in part on an interview with him in 1992.

108. On Dar al-Arqam see, inter alia, J. Nagata, *The Reflowering of Malaysian*

Islam (Vancouver, 1984), ch. 4; Esposito and Voll, *Islam and Democracy*, pp. 25–30; N. S. Talib, 'The Banning of Al-Arqam', *Business Times* (Singapore), Oct. 29–30, 1994; my comments are also based on interviews with members of the group in 1984 and some of their literature. Dar al-Arqam definitely represented a 'bottom-up' approach to an Islamic state as opposed to the 'top-down' approach of PAS, to whom they were more opposed than to UNMO. They were banned in part because of 'Sufi'-style 'deviations'.

109. My attention has most recently been called to Naqshbandi followers of Shaykh Muhammad Hisham Kabbani, who send e-mail messages almost daily (see n. 96 above). Some Western Sufis, such as many of the followers of Hazrat Inayat Khan, reach such a degree of 'adaptationism' that they are no longer distinctively Muslim, either in their own eyes or the eyes of others.

110. These are sometimes also called 'primordialists'. See, e.g., Frithjof Schuon, *Islam and the Perennial Philosophy*, tr. J. Peter Hobson (London, 1976), and Martin Lings, *A Moslem Saint of the Twentieth Century: Shaikh Ahmad al-Alawi* (London, 1961). On Nasr see my brief discussion in 'Islam and Ideology', n. 90. For a good brief discussion of this group see Carl Ernst, 'Traditionalism, the Perennial Philosophy, and Islamic Studies', in *MESA Bulletin*, 28 (1994), pp. 176–180.

111. Sadiq al-'Azm in a recent article describes the psychological situation of the Arabs in much the same terms as Smith uses for the Muslims. For him this involves a dysfunctional self-image that must be exorcised. Arabs must recognise that the Western intrusion into their world has led to a rupture with the past as final as that effected by the early Muslims on Sasanid Persia. 'Owning the Future: Modern Arabs and Hamlet', *ISIM Newsletter*, 5 (2000), p. 11.

112. Voll, *Islam: Continuity and Change*, pp. 376–377.

113. Barton states that 'Nurcholish and Abdurrahman know nothing of the "inferiority complex" felt by so many Muslim intellectuals towards the West.' 'Nurcholish Madjid and Abdurrahman Wahid as Intellectual *Ulama*', p. 22.

4

Sufi Thought and its Reconstruction

Elizabeth Sirriyeh

The Fluctuating Fate of Twentieth-Century Sufism

In 1900 the vast majority of Muslims understood Islam as mediated to them, directly or indirectly, by Sufi shaykhs and traditional ulama who accepted Sufism as the inner, spiritual dimension at the heart of Islam. Despite critiques of their excesses and aberrations over the centuries, Sufi leaders still appeared in a strong position to confront their opponents and influence the general Muslim public. Sufis operated at all levels of society and were found among the highest ranks of the scholarly establishment through to the pious among the working class of the great cities and village shaykhs and enraptured wandering beggars. While some Sufi brotherhoods (*tariqa*s), such as the Qadiriyya, attracted members across a range of countries, racial groups and classes, others were more regionally or even locally based and might draw on particular tribes, professions or socio-economic categories.

Many ordinary affiliates of Sufi brotherhoods may not have felt themselves to be deeply involved in pursuing the mystical path to enter a special relationship of closeness to God; they may not have shared Ibn 'Arabi's understanding of Sufism as 'assuming the character traits of God'.[1] Only a few of 'God's friends' (*awliya' Allah*), the great mystic saints, could truly participate in such a level of Sufism.

So how might the great majority have viewed their enterprise? It is highly likely that many would have been in agreement with a number of Sufis interviewed in Egypt much later in the century and who responded that for them Sufism meant 'purification of the heart, sincerity of worship and renunciation of fleshly passions'.[2] All this was to be achieved by a variety of individual and collective pious exercises of prayer and meditation, cultivating remembrance of God (*dhikr*) and developing devotion to the Prophet and one's shaykh. Private and shared experiences of the miraculous, analysis of dreams and visions, visits to saintly tombs and attendance at festivals formed part of the process of engagement with Sufism.

Muslim leadership was still to a very great extent influenced by Sufi thinking as the century opened. In the major Islamic state of the Ottoman Empire, Sultan 'Abd al-Hamid II (r. 1876–1909) was prone to listen to the guidance of Arab Sufis in his entourage, including arguably his closest spiritual mentor, the Rifa'i shaykh Abu al-Huda al-Sayyadi from the neighbourhood of Aleppo in Syria.[3] The Sultan also saw the Sufi leaders as a valuable tool in promoting his pan-Islamic policy and claims to the Caliphate; he consequently gave his backing to their *tariqa*s and supported the publication of their works, while suppressing alternative viewpoints whether they were seen as issuing from anti-Sufi Wahhabism or Western rationalism. Wahhabism was temporarily at a weak point, as the second Saudi-Wahhabi state had collapsed in 1887 and the Saud family were living in exile in Kuwait, although their fortunes were about to change.

Elsewhere, in Muslim lands under the rule of European colonial powers, it was often Sufi *tariqa* heads who were being seen by those powers as crucial to maintaining harmonious relations with the Muslim communities. By 1900 brotherhoods in a number of areas were involved in some degree of collaboration with non-Muslim government, although some could prove tough negotiators on behalf of their people and cause ongoing anxiety to the occupiers. A notable example is that of Lalla Zaynab (*c.* 1850–1904), a remarkable saintly woman and powerful figure within the Algerian Rahmaniyya. She alarmed French officials with her rebelliousness and ability to drive a hard bargain, just as she was adored by the thousands of North Africans flocking to her *zawiya* in search of blessing and education. A foreign woman visitor to the district in 1912 noted: 'So beneficent had been her sway, so charitable was she that "her memory is still green in the hearts of her people".[4] This level of closeness to the people's hearts seems hardly to have been experienced by the circle of reformists around Muhammad 'Abduh in Egypt or the followers of Sayyid Ahmad Khan in India.

However, by mid-century Sufi fortunes had undergone a dramatic change in certain parts of the Muslim world. Lamenting the supposedly sad state of Sufism in 1950, A. J. Arberry remarked that it 'may now be said to have come to an end as a movement dominating the minds and hearts of learned and earnest men'.[5] For him, as a literary scholar of the classical Arabic and Persian tradition, the 'learned and earnest men' were the great intellectuals, mystics and poets, especially those of the twelfth to thirteenth centuries represented by such as Ibn al-Farid, Ibn 'Arabi and Rumi. Yet even given his personal enthusiasm for the earlier age, Arberry is willing to concede the survival of occasional spiritual figures worthy of note into the twentieth century. The latest to whom he grants some space is a Naqshabandi shaykh of Irbil in Iraq, Muhammad Amin al-Kurdi, who died in 1914.[6] But he believed that Sufism had now become the preserve of the 'ignorant masses' and was no longer relevant for the modern, educated Muslim.

Arberry's focus was on the central Middle East, the region where there was the most visible decline in Sufi numbers by the 1950s. He was certainly not alone in regarding Sufism there as appealing primarily to the traditional, working-class membership of the *tariqas* and in expecting it to lose support further and, ultimately, to disappear with increasing exposure to scientific education. A growing number of Middle Eastern Muslims held not dissimilar views, including many vociferous critics of Sufis as an anachronistic embarrassment to Muslim societies seeking paths to modernisation.

A mixed array of anti-Sufi forces had been gaining ground steadily during the first half of the century, but especially since the 1920s. Prominent among them were nationalists and secularisers, perhaps the most significant being Mustafa Kemal Atatürk, who saw the Sufi brotherhoods as a reactionary and subversive element in the newly-established Republic of Turkey and ordered their suppression in 1925, closing their centres (*tekkes*) and saints' tombs; in his eyes, there was simply no place in a land aspiring to become a secular, modern nation-state for those he deemed so 'primitive' as to turn to Sufi shaykhs for guidance. But the traditional anti-Sufism of the Wahhabis also discovered a new strength in the Arabian Peninsula with Ibn Saud's capture of the Hijaz where he became king in 1926, and the subsequent establishment of the Kingdom of Saudi Arabia in 1932. Both Atatürk and Ibn Saud had their admirers and none were friends to the Sufis. Among Ibn Saud's most ardent supporters and one who shared his suspicions of Sufism was Rashid Rida (1865–1935), a close associate of Muhammad 'Abduh and a man of immense personal influence in spreading the salafi reformists' message across the umma as far as South East Asia. He was an important influence also on Hasan al-Banna (1906–1949), himself a Sufi, but famously the founder, in 1928, of the Muslim Brotherhood, which would become the strongest of Islamist organisations in the 1950s and 1960s and, in general, virulently opposed to Sufism.

The exposure to all these powerful challenges is usually seen as sufficient explanation for a weakened Middle Eastern Sufism as the twentieth century wore on. However, an interesting alternative explanation has been offered by Charles Lindholm in comparing the state of Sufism in South Asia with that in the Middle East. He suggests that the primary cause of the Sufis losing their importance in Middle Eastern society may be due to 'the compulsive tendency of Sufi sects to exaggerate the powers of their founders, which led them to set themselves at irreconcilable odds with the ascetic and egalitarian principles that animate Middle Eastern society'.[7] By contrast, in South Asia, Sufis and their brotherhoods were to remain strong and even to gain in strength throughout the century, despite a long-established and outspoken opposition from conservative reformers, liberal thinkers and Islamists. While Lindholm notes the ability of Sufis to maintain a greater degree of autonomy and wealth, both pre- and post-independence from the British, he also remarks on the ways in which they served to provide a sense of moral security in the face of a corrupt political order and the constant threat of being overwhelmed by Hindu neighbours. Finally, he concludes that, most importantly, the authority of the Sufi pirs has found ready acceptance in a culture favourable to traditions of a sacred hierarchy, in which 'saintly, world-renouncing figures of superhuman purity and universal love' occupy a pivotal position.[8]

Perhaps this analysis is truer for South Asia than for the Middle East. Sufism does indeed seem to have fitted very well into the South Asian cultural context; but, it might be asked if one of Sufism's great strengths, that has enabled it to survive, has not been its very flexibility in adapting to different environments, yet retaining a core of perennial values and goals. Thus it could satisfy the needs of an ascetic and egalitarian society, if that of the twentieth-century Middle East were to be identified as such (which is by no means certain). Conversely, it could also flourish in societies which set little store by asceticism, as could be noted in some of the African brotherhoods, and in those with a strong anti-egalitarian heritage, as in India.

By the 1980s and 1990s the *tariqas* were continuing to defy mid-century predictions of their demise in the face of competition from more up-to-date forms of religious association, such as the burgeoning Islamist organisations and new religious political parties. In some countries, for example in Egypt, where collapse had been confidently anticipated, *tariqas* were actively fighting back, regaining lost ground and even expanding. One who viewed this with dismay was the Egyptian radical Islamist 'Umar 'Abd al-Rahman of Egyptian Jihad, currently in jail in the USA for terrorist activities including the 1993 attempt to bomb the World Trade Center in New York. Seeing himself as a defender of orthodoxy, he railed against the Sufis as 'an innovation', arguing that their 'superstitious practices' constitute unbelief. The brotherhoods' existence was symptomatic of Muslim decline and lack of true religion, which he perceived to be increasing, declaring: 'The more the Muslims decline and their faith weakens, the more numerous become these Orders, superstitions, and humbug (*shaw'adhat*) in the religion of God.'[9] For those who shared 'Umar 'Abd al-Rahman's opinion of Sufism the situation in Egypt was little short of disastrous, since by 1990 there were seventy-three officially recognised brotherhoods as well as around fifty that did not qualify for recognition.[10]

Naturally, there were obvious variations throughout the century in the fluctuations of Sufi fortunes between regions and countries. Whereas Egypt and parts of the Middle East saw Sufi thought dominant in 1900, then witnessing decline before a late revival and South Asia experienced constant Sufi success despite challenges, there were areas which followed neither pattern. For example, in most of Sub-Saharan Africa until late in the twentieth century, to think about Islam was to think about Sufi interpretations of it. In the case of Nigeria, where Sufis faced some of their fiercest opposition, it was principally from the 1970s that the ideas of the powerful Tijani and Qadiri brotherhoods were seriously called into question by Islamists, especially those of the Yan Izala movement (founded 1978) and its leader Abubakar Gumi (1924–1992).[11] In marked contrast, in North America and Western Europe both old-established *tariqas* and new groups developed and expanded their membership in the later part of the century, drawing on converts as well as members of Muslim communities settling in the West.

Preserving the Sufi Tradition

Understandably, many leading Sufi thinkers were to focus a major part of their efforts on working to preserve for their own and later generations what they saw as valuable in the Sufi tradition. At the same time they aimed to exclude perceived undesirable aspects tarnishing the pure faith and fought an ongoing battle of words with critics. Some of the fiercest controversies took place in the Indian subcontinent, which, in the late nineteenth century, had become an arena of intense debates among ulama concerned with maintaining the spirituality and moral integrity of their communities under British rule. Movements of renewal had formed around groups of like-minded scholars, who held sharply differing views from other groups of what might constitute 'true' Sufism, if indeed it existed.

One of the earliest important centres was at Deoband, about ninety miles to the north of Delhi, where a body of conservative reformers had founded their own famous school in 1868.[12] There they frequently combined the roles of teachers and spiritual directors (pirs) for their student disciples (*murids*), training them using the approaches of whichever of the major *tariqas* they judged most suited to the individual concerned. The Sufism that they set out to preserve was of an austere nature, stripped of all the accretions of custom associated with the veneration of the Prophet and the cults of saints. Their aim of rooting out unacceptable innovations was expressed through the publication of fatwas and in debate with ulama of different persuasions; the most prominent of these from the 1880s through the twentieth century were from the movement of Ahl-i Sunnat wa Jama'at, commonly known as Barelwis after the key figure in developing the movement's ideas, Sayyid Ahmad Riza Khan Barelwi (1856–1921).[13]

The Barelwis are, above all, noted for their ardent defence of the shrine-centred Sufism of India with much, but not all, its wealth of local cultural acquisitions. This has led to a widespread perception of Barelwis as representing all unreformed Sufis in the subcontinent and having a particularly close connection with an uneducated rural population. However, despite the desire of Barelwi leaders to speak for a much wider range of South Asian Muslims than the members of Ahl-i Sunnat, the mass of worshippers at the shrines have not generally associated themselves with the movement.

Ahmad Riza Khan had been admired by his followers for his extraordinary academic abilities from early childhood, reading the Qur'an at the age of four and writing fatwas from the age of fourteen. It would be through his fatwas that he would deliver his principal opinions on Sufi topics. The year 1900 marked a critical point in Ahmad Riza's achieving general recognition for his leadership role, since it was then at a gathering of Barelwi ulama in Patna that he was declared to be the renewer of the faith (*mujaddid*) of the fourteenth Islamic century. International recognition came on his second hajj in 1905–6, when he was treated as an honoured scholar by the ulama of Mecca and Medina; but for him the highest spiritual validation was granted through a waking vision of the Prophet at his tomb during a month spent in Medina. In the last years before his death in 1921 he was treated like royalty when he travelled within India.

Even though he was anxious to promote the religion of the shrines, Ahmad Riza was also a strong supporter of the sharia. He had no regard for those who held that spiritual advancement could be achieved without a need to perform prescribed religious duties. Such 'false' Sufis were, in his opinion, 'inspired by Satan'.[14] This strict view of the necessity of both sharia and *tariqa* places him in a line of mainstream Sufi thought, but also means that he cannot accept every manifestation of Sufism current in early twentieth-century India. The stress on observing the Law is an aspect of his deep devotion to the Prophet, which demands that he follow the Sunna in every detail. For Ahmad Riza, the Prophet Muhammad is higher than every other prophet, as he writes: 'Only the Prophet can reach God without intermediaries.'[15] He is created by God of His Light before all things and the World is created for his sake. He is the man of light without shadow and other prophets are his shadows. Such an exalted conception of the Prophet led the Barelwis to make his birthday (*milad*) on 12 Rabi' al-Awwal into a major occasion for celebration. Some of their most heated arguments with the Deobandis concerned their belief that he had been given knowledge of the Unseen, otherwise known only to God, and that he would be spiritually present with the worshippers who stood in his honour to hear blessings called down upon him.

These controversies over the Prophet's qualities, as well as over Barelwi support for the commemoration of saints' death days and the importance of seeking their intercession with God, continue to the present. In the second half of the century the disputes also surfaced in South Asian Muslim communities in diaspora, notably in Britain, where the Barelwis and Deobandis constitute the two largest movements.

In the Arab lands of the early twentieth century, Sufi writers found their position seriously weakened after the restoration of the Ottoman constitution in July 1908 and the subsequent deposition of their greatest supporter, Sultan 'Abd al-Hamid II, in April 1909. Among the leading figures affected by these events was Shaykh Yusuf al-Nabahani (1849–1932), who lost his post as chief judge of the criminal court in Beirut after twenty years' service. He took refuge in the more hospitable atmosphere of Medina, a number of whose ulama being those who had welcomed Ahmad Riza Khan on his hajj a few years earlier. Enemies among the salafi reformists of Syria were glad to see him lose office. In May 1909 one, Jamal al-din al-Qasimi, wrote: 'As for al-Nabahani, let him die in his rage, may God fight such a superstitious man who does harm to many simpletons with his writings ... [A] sign of this age is rejecting writings such as his, barren of knowledge and culture.'[16]

Whether he was indeed 'barren of knowledge and culture' is a matter of debate. Nabahani, to his admirers, was an accomplished poet who, like Ahmad Riza Khan, spent much effort in writing devotional poetry on the Prophet and in promoting the traditional Islamic knowledge and culture of his home region.[17] In addition to his own thousands of verses eulogising the Prophet's spiritual qualities and miracles, he also dedicated much of his life to gathering a huge corpus of pious adulatory literature on the same theme. He was also the author of a renowned collection of biographies of 'God's friends', recounting their saintly miracles.

Nabahani was also strongly committed to the defence of the Sufi intellectual heritage, especially the ideas of Ibn 'Arabi on existential monism (*wahdat al-wujud*). He also, like the Barelwis, championed much Sufi ritual practice, such as seeking the intercession of saints during visitation to their tombs. However, in order to defend his beliefs, he launched vicious verbal attacks on those he saw as working to destroy the true faith, particularly the Wahhabis and the reformists Afghani, 'Abduh and Rida, all of whom he had personally encountered, and detested. In his old age, after the First World War, he returned to his native village of Ijzim near Haifa in Palestine, where he died in 1932.

Although Nabahani was a prolific author and his works well known in Sufi circles, he appears a somewhat isolated and old-fashioned figure by the 1920s and 1930s, when the old orthodoxies of the Ottoman establishment were being swept away by the tide of reformism and nationalism. A younger contemporary, the Algerian shaykh Ahmad al-'Alawi (1869–1934), was far more successful in convincing a wide following of the timeless values of the Sufi tradition. Within Algeria itself he drew thousands to be initiated into his 'Alawi *tariqa*, derived from the Darqawiyya, itself an offshoot of the major North African brotherhood of the Shadhiliyya. He also exerted a considerable fascination for those Europeans who came into contact with him. Frithjof Schuon recalled a few months after his death: 'To meet such a one is like coming face to face, in mid-twentieth century, with a medieval Saint or a Semitic Patriarch.'[18] Schuon offers a sense of the inner, as well as the outer, man in his description:

> In his brown jallabah and white turban, with his silver-grey beard and his long hands which seemed when he moved them to be weighed down by the flow of his *barakah* (blessing), he exhaled something of the pure archaic ambiance of Sayyidna Ibrahim al-Khalil [Abraham]. He spoke in a subdued, gentle voice, a voice of splintered crystal from which, fragment by fragment, he let fall his words ... His eyes, which were like two sepulchral lamps, seemed to pierce through all objects, seeing in their

outer shell merely one and the same nothingness, beyond which they saw always one and the same reality – the Infinite.[19]

Ahmad al-'Alawi had little formal education and yet there is evidence of a formidable intellect at work, combined with mystical inspiration, in his meditations on the Qur'an and in his spiritual poetry published after the First World War.[20] Poetically, probably the strongest influence on him came from the Egyptian poet Ibn al-Farid (d. 1235), whose beautiful odes were regularly chanted by the shaykh's *murids*. Otherwise, apart from the thought of Ibn 'Arabi (d. 1240), so pervasive in later Sufism, 'Alawi had studied the work of later writers, such as 'Abd al-Karim al-Jili (d. 1408) on the Perfect Man, Ibn 'Ashur (d. 1631), author of a treatise that was required reading for Darqawis, and 'Abd al-Ghani al-Nabulusi (d. 1731), the great Sufi of Damascus. Some of 'Alawi's writings remained unpublished, notably a Qur'anic commentary of both exoteric and esoteric exegesis up to the fortieth verse of Surat al-Baqara and a book of cosmology. Among his publications an interesting early treatise is *The Unique Archetype* written about 1910 on the symbolism of letters of the Arabic alphabet.[21]

However, 'Alawi was not only conscious of a need to preserve traditional Sufi thought, but also to speak and write in its defence. He perceived the salafi reformists as posing a serious threat to the very survival of Islam as he conceived it and, from 1920 until his death in 1934, he laboured to combat their criticisms. He was particularly concerned with upholding the good reputation of Sufis and explaining the Sufi perspective on controversial issues. For example, on the question of visiting tombs, he maintained the validity of seeking the intercession of the holy dead, since many Muslims feel they have not reached a sufficiently high spiritual level to be able to dispense with mediators between them and God.[22] He is responding here to a critic from Tunis, who has used a quotation from Ibn 'Arabi to the effect that a dead man cannot help the living. 'Alawi explains that this does not refer to the practice of intercession, but of seeking guidance on the Path, and he asserts his own view that it is indeed necessary to receive training from a living shaykh. In taking this position, he is actually going against the beliefs of those Sufis, including Nabulusi, who held that dead masters might also guide.

'Alawi argued that the reformists were harming Islam with their attacks on Sufis, when westernisation in Muslim societies was a more fitting target for their attacks. He was opposed to the spreading adoption of Western ways, including dress, being concerned about the power of clothing to corrupt the soul. His essentially conservative viewpoint, lamenting a decline in spirituality in both his own and Western society, gave his teachings considerable appeal to European converts as well as North African Muslims troubled by modern threats to their way of life.

Adaptation within *tariqas*

Defence of tradition by Sufi thinkers would become increasingly robust in the later twentieth century. However, it would also frequently be linked with a consciousness of needing to help *tariqas* adapt to new circumstances and compete with the attractions of anti-Sufi movements and organisations and the continuing invasion of Western ideology. Adaptation could take a variety of forms. Some of its advocates would present themselves as reformers anxious to rid Sufism of unworthy corruptions; others would be concerned with making their message more acceptable in post-colonial conditions or allowing scope for converts to adjust to the faith.

Egypt constituted one of the most important arenas for debate about Sufi reform. This was partly because it had a particularly varied range of Sufi perspectives, represented both by the seventy-three *tariqas* registered with the Supreme Council of Sufi Orders and other unregistered *tariqas*, such as the large Burhaniyya brotherhood with over three million members.[23] Its importance was also due to Egypt's centrality in the development of reformist and Islamist critiques of Sufism, as well as its established intellectual influence in the umma. Active reforming tendencies are especially noticeable among branches and offshoots of the Shadhiliyya from the 1930s onwards, reaching greater heights of intensity in the 1970s to 1990s.

Western scholarly attention was drawn to the Hamidiyya Shadhiliyya by the work of Michael Gilsenan, who studied the brotherhood in the 1960s and 1970s.[24] Its founding shaykh was Salama Hasan al-Radi (1867–1939), a civil servant with a bureaucratic mind but also a miracle-working ascetic devoted, in the 1930s, to the welfare of the poor. Radi set out his rules, known as *The Laws*, for establishing a reformed, theologically sound and sharia-observant body of *murids*. They would be marked by their orderliness and sobriety and the readiness of officials in the *tariqa* to control any sign of excessive emotionalism in *dhikr*. In effect, the mystical aspects and much popular ritual seem to have been de-emphasised so that there was little to distinguish the membership from that of any pious, welfare association.

A similar approach to reform was to be adopted by another Shadhili branch, the Muhammadiyya Shadhiliyya and its affiliated body of non-initiated men and women, the 'Ashira al-Muhammadiyya, also dating from the 1930s. Its founder, Muhammad Zaki Ibrahim, had an Azhar education and became noted as a poet and prolific writer on Sufi affairs. He has also been perceived as an establishment figure, a member of the Higher Religious Committee and the Sufi Supreme Council, honoured by Presidents Nasser, Sadat and Mubarak, and yet an independent thinker ready to speak out on core issues of Sufi concern and to campaign for reform.[25]

Like Radi and the Hamidi Shadhilis, Ibrahim stressed obedience to sharia in an organised, socially responsible manner with the suppression of wild forms of *dhikr*, music, dance and the mixing of men and women, especially at the great *mawlid* celebrations of saints' true 'birthdays' (after their death to the earthly life). The *mawlids* were a perennial target of criticism in Egypt as occasions for immoral and lewd behaviour and it was these aspects to which Ibrahim, in common with other Sufi reformers, was opposed, while advocating a purified, spiritual participation in *mawlids* rather than the ban called for by some Islamists. Women of the 'Ashira, catered for in their own separate section, were discouraged from simply gathering at some of the most popular shrines, such as that of Sayyida Zaynab in Cairo, and exhorted instead to model their lives on those of such saintly women exemplars.[26]

Among Shaykh Ibrahim's most widely read works is one entitled *The Alphabet of Islamic Sufism*, in which he answers fifty-four key questions posed by Egyptian journalists.[27] Although this appears as an attempt to respond to common criticisms of Sufism, the 'Ashira's Editorial Committee assert that it would be a useless task to try to dissuade opponents from their attacks. 'Rather, the aim is to fortify those who have not been afflicted with their disease and to identify those who have been deceived by their confusion.'[28] A principal topic addressed is whether Sufism is truly Islamic in its origin or whether it owes its origins to non-Islamic sources such as Buddhism and Christian monasticism. Ibrahim insists on Sufism's Islamic credentials and that its aim is to seek human perfection, an essential Islamic duty. Questioned about philosophical Sufis, he does not set out to defend them, but to deflect attention away from them by claiming that they are very few in number, their writings are no longer relevant, rarely read and even unavailable. Therefore, they should be left alone. Instead, all Muslims should concentrate on pursuing true Sufism in conformity with the Qur'an and Sunna and working to eradicate the social ills of the day.

By contrast, the most prominent Shadhili intellectual of late twentieth-century Egypt, 'Abd al-Halim Mahmud, Rector of al-Azhar from 1973 to 1978, was strongly opposed to this kind of anti-intellectualism.[29] While also supporting the importance of active social involvement to help overcome contemporary problems, he did not see this as an alternative to studying the work of great Sufi intellectuals of the past. On the contrary, Mahmud held that there was considerable benefit to be gained from such as Ibn 'Arabi in moulding a spiritual and intellectual elite who would revivify true Sufism. In his opinion, it was a mistake to label al-Ghazali as the acceptable, orthodox face of Sufism and Ibn 'Arabi as its unacceptable, heterodox face; he stressed the connections and essential consistency between the two. Given his impeccable credentials in the eyes of those lobbying for a strict implementation of sharia in Egypt, 'Abd al-Halim Mahmud was a powerful champion for the Great Shaykh.

Yet, despite his image as a stern and austere intellectual, Mahmud did not confine his instruction to academic students, but included those whom he regarded as part of the potential spiritual elite, even if they were illiterate. One such illiterate shaykh claimed to have been guided on the Way by Mahmud and by his visions of the long-dead founding figure of the Shadhiliyya, Abu al-Hasan al-Shadhili.[30] In the 1980s he considered his oath to the thirteenth-century al-Shadhili far more important than what was for him a routine oath to a living shaykh.

Similar convictions of belonging to a spiritual elite, even if

illiterate, have been a hallmark of the Tijaniyya since its foundation by Ahmad al-Tijani in eighteenth-century North Africa.[31] However, for the Tijanis the whole brotherhood constituted this elite,
superior to other Sufis and Muslims in general.[32] In the twentieth
century the *tariqa* would become spectacularly successful, especially
in West Africa, but it would also face divisions and fierce confrontations with other Sufis, particularly Qadiris, and anti-Sufi Wahhabis.
The brotherhood was noted for its extravagant claims that Ahmad
al-Tijani was, like Ibn 'Arabi, the Seal of Muhammad-like Sainthood,
the pole of mystical poles (*qutb al-aqtab*), had been taught special
prayers directly by the Prophet in a vision and granted permission
from God to admit all his followers to Paradise regardless of whatever sins they had committed. Critics were further shocked by Tijani
assertions that they were actually in reception of the beatific vision
of God Himself (*ru'yat Allah*), the mainstream Islamic belief being
that only the Prophet could have such a vision in this life. How Tijanis conceive of being able to see God appears to be related to their
beliefs in the 'overflowing' (*fayd*) of the divine into the creation, as
passed to them by Ahmad al-Tijani in a simplified form of the ideas
of Ibn 'Arabi and other medieval Sufi thinkers. What they would
claim to see is, therefore, this all-pervading divine presence in the
world, supremely manifested in Prophet Muhammad as the perfect
human; Tijanis would believe the Prophet to be with them in body
and spirit at their Friday afternoon group recital of the prayer of
blessings upon him, *The Jewel of Perfection.*[33] Consequently, they lay
out a white cloth for the Prophet in their midst.

While the Tijaniyya split into different branches, the most significant doctrinal adaptation in the twentieth century was that initiated by the Senegalese shaykh Ibrahim Niass (1900–1975). He first
developed his new model of Tijanism in Senegal around 1930, but
was far more successful in spreading it outside his home country,
notably when he introduced his ideas into northern Nigeria in the
1950s. The Niassian Tijanis numbered several million by late in the
century and described themselves as Jama'at al-Faydat al-Tijaniyya
(the Community of the Tijani Overflowing) commonly known in
Hausa as Faila.

Ibrahim Niass understood himself to occupy a very special and
exalted position in the Tijani hierarchy, but it was one that would

extend great advantages to those who joined his new community.[34] In 1930 he put forward the claim to be the 'saviour of the age' (*ghawth al-zaman*). He also believed that he had received from Ahmad al-Tijani the divine overflowing and the Greatest Secret, marking him out as specially favoured by God with mystical knowledge. However, he held that this 'secret' and 'overflowing' were not for him alone, but could be transmitted to his community through training which must not be divulged to anyone outside the initiated group. In the final stage of the training, some Tijanis claim, the secret is divulged to them that Ibrahim Niass is effectively one with Prophet Muhammad and Ahmad al-Tijani.[35] Probably a major part of the appeal of Niass's teaching was the assurance that followers belonged to a privileged elite, enjoying God's favour in this world, where they were told they would prosper even in times of general hardship, as well as in the Afterlife, where Paradise was a certainty. Although the Tijaniyya as a whole was immensely successful in adapting to twentieth-century African conditions, it also won more enemies than any other *tariqa* in the region and for many Wahhabi critics became synonymous with the perceived evils of Sufism.

Outside Africa, the Tijaniyya spread briefly on a small scale to Turkey in the 1950s, where it was quickly suppressed. It found more fertile ground for propagation in Indonesia from the 1920s and 1930s, angering the well-established major brotherhoods of the Naqshabandiyya and Qadiriyya.[36] By 1957 these *tariqa*s, together with the Shadhiliyya, formed an umbrella organisation. The Tijaniyya, being regarded as not sufficiently orthodox and sharia-conscious, was excluded. In the 1980s simmering disputes flared up once again, apparently because of other Sufis' dislike of what they felt to be Tijani spiritual arrogance in laying claim to superior status and because of the Tijanis' aggressive methods of proselytisation.

Despite concerns about the poaching of *murid*s by Tijanis, it was actually the Naqshabandiyya that emerged as the most entrenched and adaptable *tariqa* in modern Indonesia. In the early twentieth century it was represented by the stern reformist Khalidi branch imported in the mid-nineteenth century from the Ottoman Empire, but was also present in an eclectic and combined form, merged with the Qadiriyya and known as the Qadiriyya wa-Naqshabandiyya founded by an Indonesian shaykh resident in Mecca. However, arguably the most successful local adaptation of the *tariqa* in the mid-twentieth century came about through the work of a modern-educated teacher, Jalal al-Din of Bukittinggi (d. 1976).[37] From about 1940 he was a prolific producer of books and pamphlets offering instruction in the Naqshabandiyya, although these were much criticised by more traditional Naqshabandis, who questioned his knowledge and pointed to numerous errors. Jalal al-Din's practice of initiation is notably unconventional, involving a symbolic death and rebirth, in which the *murid* 'is covered with a shroud and must imagine that he is dead and buried, and he is put to sleep in the position of the grave. While asleep he should have one of twenty possible dreams or visions.'[38] The procedure would be repeated, if necessary, until the desired dream occurred and this would be followed the next day by a meeting for instruction with the master.

From 1945 Jalal al-Din became actively involved in politics, forming his own religious party and militia before entering parliament in the mid-1950s. He was a devoted supporter of Sukarno, labelling his political programme the Sukarno Tariqa. Nevertheless, in spite of Jalal al-Din's dubious ability to play politics with the Way, the influence of his teaching sank into rapid decline after his death in 1976.

New Mystical Directions

Some of the most radical attempts to reconstruct Sufi thought took place outside the *tariqa*s. In certain instances, these were cases where an individual Muslim thinker with a modern education, but an interest in Sufi ideas or even a Sufi affiliation, sought to think through his own understanding of Islam for the twentieth century and drew to some extent on a base of Sufi ideas. The result could be a metamorphosis of traditional Sufi thought into a new construction that was not readily recognisable or, indeed, acceptable to adherents of mainstream Sufism.

Perhaps the most celebrated of such figures was the Indian philosopher-poet Muhammad Iqbal (1873–1938), who combined philosophical Sufism and modern European philosophy in an adventurous and original effort to address the problems of Muslim adjustment to modernity.[39] Iqbal had already received an Islamic and Western-style education in Lahore and shown his poetic and philosophical talents, before his move in 1905 to study philosophy at Trinity College, Cambridge. He went on to further advanced studies in Germany, where he presented a doctoral thesis at Munich on *The Development of Metaphysics in Persia*. This was to be a groundbreaking work for scholarship on Persian Sufism, drawing attention to important contributors to the Sufi intellectual tradition, including Suhrawardi al-Maqtul, Jili and Mulla Sadra, scarcely known in the West at the time.[40] Iqbal's admiration for the mystics in this early period of his career was to oscillate later between love and loathing. While at times he valued the great spiritual qualities of particular early and medieval Sufis, at times he abhorred the effects of obscurantist thought on later generations and the retreat from facing everyday realities. He complained bitterly of his Sufi contemporaries that 'owing to their ignorance of the modern mind' they had 'become absolutely incapable of receiving any inspiration from modern thought and experience'.[41]

Yet, if Iqbal was ambivalent in his attitude to Sufism, the same ambivalence is to be detected in his view of some of the 'modern thought' that inspired him. He was fascinated by European philosophical irrationalism, especially that of Schopenhauer, Nietzsche and Bergson. For one educated in a Sufi tradition, the irrationalists' rejection of totally rational and scientific interpretations of life had a clear appeal. But he realised that there would also be a conflict between his values as a Muslim and the moral outlook of some philosophers. Notably, Nietzsche's concept of the Superman, the superior fortified being with a relentless will to power, conflicted with his own perception of the central role of love and compassion in the perfected human being. Yet he believed that there could be benefits for Muslims in taking the best elements of each to encourage the development of a strong, but spiritual and caring, personality. In a Persian poem of 1915, *Secrets of the Self*, he writes of this new hybrid self, a cross between Superman and Perfect Man, who will become God's true vicegerent on earth. Far from pursuing the Sufi goal of weakening the desires of the human self until it is completely replaced with God-like qualities and annihilated in *fana'*, Iqbal proposes the strengthening of the self through desire. His ultimate aim was to overcome Muslim weakness by encouraging the building of strong human egos to form a powerful, assertive Muslim nation. By later generations he would be remembered and honoured as the inspirer of Muslim nationalism that would lead, after his death, to the 1947 creation of the state of Pakistan.

Iqbal's vision of the powerful, life-affirming self would exert its influence among opinion-makers of South Asia. Abul al-A'la Mawdudi (1903–1979), founder of the Jama'at-i Islami movement, was a working associate of Iqbal and himself well-educated in Sufi theosophy and poetry. Like Iqbal, he was critical of Sufis who retreated from the world and stressed the need for committed, social activism rather than the self-destruction of *fana'*. Similarly, in Shi'i circles, another enthusiastic admirer of Iqbal was the radical activist 'Ali Shari'ati (1933–1977), who was generally negative towards Sufism, but advocated his own socially responsible style of Islamic mysticism.[42]

Some other efforts at radical rethinking would lead to the creation of new Islamic movements and organisations with their roots in Sufism. In Turkey, new groups arose out of the Naqshabandiyya, one of the most successful being that of the Nurcus, founded by Bediüzzaman Said Nursi (1876–1960).[43] Nursi was interested in interpreting the Qur'an in the light of modern science and his work in this direction is entitled *The Epistle of Light* (*Risale-i Nur*), hence the name of Nurcus for his followers. However, espousal of modernity did not mean acceptance of the Turkish secular republic.

A branch of the Nurcus that attracted considerable publicity in the 1970s to 1990s was that of the Fethullahis, named after its leading figure Fethullah Gülen. Gülen's ideas were to harness the movement to the cause of Turkish nationalism, promoting a specifically Turkish Islam, while at the same time seeking closer ties with the European Union. A more radical mystical group emerging in the 1990s was the Aczmenci, that arose out of the Nurcus in eastern Turkey, but separated from them. This group was accused of involvement in the murder of secularists and its leaders were exposed on television in 1995–1996 for allegedly tricking young girls into sexual relations with them as a way of supposedly drawing nearer to God.

It is perhaps understandable that Turkey should have become such a locus of new religious movements, given its heavy exposure to secularisation and the suppression of a mainstream role for the traditional *tariqa*s. Yet, outside Turkey, especially in North America and Western Europe, there was a significant input of Turkish Sufi thought into both regular brotherhoods active in the West and neo-Sufi organisations. The Naqshabandiyya-Haqqaniyya led by a Turkish Cypriot shaykh, Nazim al-Qubrusi (b. 1922), was one regular *tariqa* that would attract members both among immigrant Muslim communities and European and American converts. Shaykh Nazim records himself how his new *tariqa* section expanded after his first visit to London:

> I came here first in 1974 and I could never find a place to pray *jum'ah* in the Turkish or Cypriot community. I prayed in the east London mosque, which was in a small house ... that first year I prayed in Kilburn with 40 English Muslims, *taraiveha* prayer.[44]

By the 1990s more than 3,000 worshippers would attend Ramadan prayers with Shaykh Nazim and his followers had grown in numbers globally, especially in the USA, and included many African-Americans. He is noted as valuing highly these African-American *murids*, saying that they 'are very spiritually powerful and ... that the Mahdi awaited by Muslims will be of African descent and will be wearing a red turban'.[45] While the practices of the brotherhood were, on the whole, standard Naqshabandi, the different ethnic origins of the members were identified by different colour turbans and there was a certain relaxation of rules for the new converts.

Other *tariqa*s were successful in spreading traditional or adapted Sufi teachings in the West in the second half of the twentieth century, but more controversial were the many groups with relatively loose connections to established Islamic Sufism. Such groups have frequently been described as 'neo-Sufi', although critics would label them as 'pseudo-Sufi'.[46] There was considerable variety, but it would not be unusual for the membership to include a number of people who did not and were not expected to convert to Islam. In some cases, the whole group would consist of non-Muslim Westerners.

The origins of these movements were often regularly Islamic Sufi, one example being that of the Helveti-Jerrahis, brought from Istanbul to the USA around 1980 by Shaykh Muzaffer Ozak (1916–1986). The order was subsequently developed by an American teacher Lex Hixon (1941–1995) in quite unorthodox and eclectic directions, since Hixon was also a prominent figure in other non-Islamic movements. Observers noted that he was an 'orthodox priest on Monday, a Buddhist lama on Tuesday' and 'Christian among the Christians, Muslim among the Muslims'.[47] However, not everyone in the order accepted such an obvious break with tradition. Also from a Turkish origin and giving rise to more unorthodox tendencies were several supposedly Mevlevi organisations, acknowledging the great popularity of Rumi's poetry in the West and of the celebrated Mevlevi dance.

By far the best-known and most often criticised of neo-Sufis was Idries Shah (1924–1996), prolific author of popular books and founder of the Society for Sufi Studies.[49] Shah claimed that Sufism was a form of universal wisdom and not Islamic, since it existed from before the historical development of Islam. It was not static in nature and could not be understood by studying past manifestations and methods of old masters. It needed to be constantly redefined for new circumstances and new environments. Consequently, he displayed a general disregard for academic descriptions of Sufism and believed that an obsession with its traditional forms might actually prevent the seeker from recognising the real thing. He expresses this succinctly: 'Show a man too many camel's bones, or show them to him too often, and he will not be able to recognise a camel when he comes across a real one'.[50]

Shah's methods for training Western followers to recognise the 'real camel' seem to have had little in common with traditional methods, but appear to owe something to the spiritual training system of the philosophical occultist George Gurdjieff (c. 1866–1949) and his Institute for the Harmonious Development of Mankind. Shah groups apparently met for study sessions to discuss Sufi teaching stories and engage in exercises to heighten personal spiritual awareness.[51] Shah was the supreme populariser of Sufism for Western consumption, but James Moore was to point eloquently to the dangers: 'that his is a "Sufism" without self-sacrifice, without self-transcendence, without the aspiration of gnosis, without tradition, without the Prophet, without the Quran, without Islam, and without God. Merely that.'[52]

These are damning words indeed and may serve as a chilling reminder that Sufism's friends, as well as its enemies, had some concerns about certain directions it was taking in the late twentieth century. Flexibility and adaptability enabled Sufi ideas to be transmitted to new audiences and break free from being labelled as the preserve of old-fashioned Muslim traditionalists. Ever wider access was granted to esoteric Sufi teaching, both mainstream Islamic and New Age, beyond the confines of carefully prepared and initiated *murid*s. By the 1990s any interested seeker, or simply the curious, could learn about supposed Sufi mysteries via a range of popular books and magazines, film and music recordings and through the great explosion of information on the World Wide Web.[53] Some groups, such as the Naqshabandi-Haqqanis, showed extraordinary readiness to disclose detailed information on what would normally in the past have been considered knowledge to be kept hidden from outside view. The result was that Sufi thought, in all its twentieth-century variations, was increasingly exposed, publicly attacked and defended on an unprecedented scale. The test of the twenty-first century will be whether traditional, adapted or radically reconstructed Sufi ideas can survive such massive exposure.

Notes

1. William C. Chittick, *Sufism: A Short Introduction* (Oxford, 2000), p. 23.

2. Valerie J. Hoffman-Ladd, 'Devotion to the Prophet and His Family in Egyptian Sufism', *IJMES*, 24 (1992), p. 618.

3. On al-Sayyadi see Elizabeth Sirriyeh, *Sufis and Anti-Sufis: The Defence, Rethinking and Rejection of Sufism in the Modern World* (London, 1999), pp. 74–80.

4. Helen C. Gordon, *A Woman of the Sahara* (New York, 1914), p. 77, cited in Julia A. Clancy-Smith, *Rebel and Saint: Muslim Notables, Populist Protest, Colonial Encounters (Algeria and Tunisia, 1800–1904)* (Berkeley, CA, 1994; 2nd ed. 1997), p. 250.

5. A. J. Arberry, *Sufism: An Account of the Mystics of Islam* (London, 1950), p. 133.

6. Ibid., pp. 129–132.

7. Charles Lindholm, 'Prophets and *Pirs*: Charismatic Islam in the Middle East and South Asia', in Pnina Werbner and Helene Basu, ed., *Embodying Charisma: Modernity, Locality and the Performance of Emotion in Sufi Cults* (London, 1998), p. 219.

8. Lindholm, 'Prophets', p. 229.

9. From an interview with 'Umar 'Abd al-Rahman published in the Egyptian Arabic weekly *al-Nur* in 1986, in Julian Johansen, *Sufism and Islamic Reform in Egypt: The Battle for Islamic Tradition* (Oxford, 1996), p. 147.

10. Tomas Gerholm, 'The Islamization of Contemporary Egypt', in David Westerlund and Eva Evers Rosander, ed., *African Islam and Islam in Africa: Encounters between Sufis and Islamists* (London, 1997), p. 138.

11. See Roman Loimeier, 'Islamic Reform and Political Change: The Example of Abubakar Gumi and the Yan Izala Movement in Northern Nigeria', in Westerlund and Evers Rosander, ed., *African Islam*, pp. 286–307.

12. On the Deobandis, see Barbara D. Metcalf, *Islamic Revival in British India: Deoband, 1860–1900* (Princeton, NJ, 1982).

13. On Ahmad Riza Khan and the Barelwis, see Usha Sanyal, *Devotional Islam and Politics in British India: Ahmad Riza Khan Barelwi and his Movement, 1870–1920* (Delhi, 1996).

14. Ibid., p. 42.

15. Ibid., p. 155.

16. Jamal al-din al-Qasimi in David Dean Commins, *Islamic Reform: Politics and Social Change in Late Ottoman Syria* (New York and Oxford, 1990), p. 117.

17. See Annemarie Schimmel, *And Muhammad is His Messenger: The Veneration of the Prophet in Islamic Piety* (Chapel Hill, NC and London, 1986) on poetry in honour of the Prophet, including mentions of Yusuf al-Nabahani's contributions.

18. Frithjof Schuon, 'Rahimahu Llah', *Cahiers du Sud* (Aug.-Sept. 1935), in Martin Lings, *A Sufi Saint of the Twentieth Century: Shaikh Ahmad al-'Alawi, his Spiritual Heritage and Legacy* (Cambridge, 1993), p. 116.

19. Ibid., p. 117.

20. See Lings, *Sufi Saint*, pp. 214–228 for translations of some of 'Alawi's poems.

21. Ibid., pp. 148–157 for a partial annotated translation.

22. Ibid., pp.100–101 for translation from 'Alawi's 1920 treatise *al-Qawl al-ma'ruf fi'l-radd 'ala man ankara al-tasawwuf.*

23. Valerie J. Hoffman, *Sufism, Mystics and Saints in Modern Egypt* (Columbia, SC, 1995), p. 14.

24. See Michael Gilsenan, *Saint and Sufi in Modern Egypt: An Essay in the Sociology of Religion* (Oxford, 1973) and his *Recognizing Islam: Religion and Society in the Modern Middle East* (London, 1982; 2nd ed. 1990).

25. See Johansen, *Sufism and Islamic Reform* for a detailed study of the 'Ashira Muhammadiyya and the Muhammadiyya Shadhiliyya.

26. Hoffman, *Sufism, Mystics and Saints*, p. 371.

27. Johansen, *Sufism and Islamic Reform*, pp. 169–198 for further discussion of this work.

28. Quoted in Ibid., p. 171.

29. Hoffman, *Sufism, Mystics and Saints*, pp. 368–370 on Mahmud's views on Sufi reform and, in more detail, Ibrahim M. Abu-Rabi', 'Al-Azhar Sufism in Modern Egypt: The Sufi Thought of 'Abd al-Halim Mahmud', *Islamic Quarterly*, 32 (1988), pp. 207–235.

30. Hoffman, *Sufism, Mystics and Saints*, p. 129 records this from her personal contact with Shaykh 'Izz al-Hawari.

31. For French and English studies of Tijanis see Jean-Louis Triaud and David Robinson, ed., *La Tijaniyya: Une Confrérie musulmane à la conquête de l'Afrique* (Paris, 2000) and on the history of the brotherhood Jamil Abun-Nasr, *The Tijaniyya* (Oxford, 1965).

32. On Tijani mystical thought, see Patrick J. Ryan, 'The Mystical Theology of Tijani Sufism and its Social Significance in West Africa', *Journal of Religion in Africa*, 30 (2000), pp. 208–213.

33. See translated text of this prayer in Ryan, 'Mystical Theology', p. 211.

34. See Muhammad S. Umar, 'Sufism and its Opponents in Nigeria: The Doctrinal and Intellectual Aspects', in Frederick de Jong and Bernd Radtke, ed., *Islamic Mysticism Contested: Thirteen Centuries of Controversies and Polemics* (Leiden, 1999), pp. 362–369 on the development of Tijani doctrines, including pp. 367–369 on the Niassian contribution.

35. Umar, 'Sufism and its Opponents', p. 368.

36. Martin van Bruinessen, 'Controversies and Polemics Involving the Sufi Orders in Twentieth-Century Indonesia', in de Jong and Radtke, ed., *Islamic Mysticism Contested*, pp. 720–721.

37. On Jalal al-Din's writings and activities see van Bruinessen, 'Controversies', pp. 722–726.

38. Ibid., p. 724.

39. See Sirriyeh, *Sufis and Anti-Sufis*, pp. 124–39.

40. Annemarie Schimmel, *Gabriel's Wing: A Study into the Religious Ideas of Sir Muhammad Iqbal* (2nd ed., Lahore, 1989), pp. 37–39.

41. Muhammad Iqbal, *The Reconstruction of Religious Thought in Islam* (Lahore, 1930; 2nd ed. 1977), p. v.

42. Sirriyeh, *Sufis and Anti-Sufis*, pp. 161–167 on Mawdudi and Shari'ati and their views of Sufism and Iqbal.

43. See Svante Cornell and Ingvar Svanberg, 'Turkey', in David Westerlund and Ingvar Svanberg, ed., *Islam Outside the Arab World* (London, 1999), pp. 132–137 on new movements arising out of the Naqshabandiyya. For a study of the Nurcus see Şerif Mardin, *Religion and Social Change in Modern*

Turkey: The Case of Bediüzzaman Said Nursi (Albany, NY, 1989).

44. Shaykh Nazim interviewed in *Muslim News* (24 May, 1991), p. 6.

45. Shaykh Abdul Rashid Matthews of Chicago in Marcia Hermansen, 'In the Garden of American Sufi Movements: Hybrids and Perennials', in Peter B. Clarke, ed., *New Trends and Developments in the World of Islam* (London, 1997), p. 166.

46. See L. P. Elwell-Sutton, 'Sufism and Pseudo-Sufism', *Encounter,* 44 (1975), pp. 9–17 for an early and influential attack on the 'pseudo-Sufi', in this case with reference to Idries Shah (see below).

47. Marcia Hermansen, 'Hybrid Identity Formations in Muslim America: The Case of American Sufi Movements', *MW,* 90 (2000), p. 164.

48. See Jeffreys Somers, 'Whirling and the West: The Mevlevi Dervishes in the West', in Clarke, ed., *New Trends,* pp. 261–276.

49. On Shah see Peter Wilson, 'The Strange Fate of Sufism in the New Age', in Clarke, ed., *New Trends,* pp. 179–209.

50. Idries Shah, *The Dermis Probe* (London, 1980), p. 18, in Clarke, ed., *New Trends,* p. 187.

51. Hermansen, 'Hybrid Identity Formations', pp. 166–167 on Shah's training methods.

52. James Moore, 'Neo-Sufism: The Case of Idries Shah', *Religion Today,* 3 (1986), p. 7.

53. See Carl Ernst, *The Shambhala Guide to Sufism* (Boston, MA, 1997), pp. 215–220 on Sufi publication of the 'secret' and Gary Bunt, *Virtually Islamic. Computer-mediated Communication and Cyber Islamic Environments* (Cardiff, 2000), pp. 58–65 on surfing Sufi cyberspace.

Nationalism and Culture in the Arab and Islamic Worlds: A Critique of Modern Scholarship

Ralph M. Coury

The Centrality of Nationalism in the Islamic World

The role of the nation-state and of nationalism has been central to the modern history of the Islamic world. This has been so to such an extent that Reinhard Schulze, who has written one of the most perceptive political overviews of the Islamic nineteenth and twentieth centuries, argues that the territorial state has been the 'invariable constant' of this history, and that nationalism has been 'confirmed as the dominant, extremely flexible' view of the world among Muslims, in spite of the passage of a succession of distinct ideological-political phases.[1] A number of powerful arguments can be adduced in support of such assertions:

1) Contemporary territorial states in the Islamic world have accepted the 'world of nations' system and the existing international economic order, in spite of the fact that the political system does not give these states any advantages over non-Muslim ones, and the existing economic order places all Muslim countries in a position of dependency in respect to the capitalist core. The principle of state sovereignty prevails in multinational organisations that contain various Muslim countries and ambassadors are exchanged in

the standard manner. Muslim states do not offer automatic political support to other Muslim states and they do not usually give other Muslim states priority in trade, investment, or importation of labour. Although Saudi Arabia has sometimes given priority to aiding Muslim states, the main bulk of Saudi and Arab aid is extended to Arab rather than Muslim countries.[2]

2) Supranational Islamic networks (the Muslim Brotherhood, the World Muslim League) have never been able to create an international policy that transcends the conflicts of interest and perspectives of regional states or ethnic groups. Individual branches have adopted local positions linked to the various contexts in which they have been operating – collaboration with the government in Kuwait and Jordan, pacific opposition in Egypt, and armed opposition in Libya and Syria. Moreover, although the Muslim Brotherhood maintains a supranational dimension, this is not true of the Islamist groups of North Africa, Afghanistan, the former Soviet Union, and Turkey, all of whose networks are even more grounded within a national framework. The Islamic Renaissance Party, for example, the only active Islamist party in former Soviet territory, itself splintered into nationalist branches, the 'Russian' section under Tartar and Northern Caucasian direction, and the Tajiki branch as an autonomous unit.[3]

Some might argue, especially under the influence of the current attention given to its allegedly world-wide sweep, that al-Qa'ida is an exception in its internationalism. Yet here, too, significant national specificities have played a central role. Al-Qa'ida is essentially Arab, and, more particularly, Saudi-Yemeni and Egyptian, and many of its allegedly 'international cells' are of purely or primarily local provenance with essentially local concerns and agendas.

3) The links between Islamists and secular nationalists are often extremely difficult to unravel. They have often drunk at the same spring and have shared certain essential aspirations, including the effort to develop national cultures and national blocs. Joel Gordon's acute analysis of the relationship between the Egyptian Muslim Brotherhood and the Free Officers provides insight into the often tangled nature of Islamist-secular nationalist interaction. Hasan al-Banna, the founder of the Muslim Brotherhood, supported a nationalist call to end the British occupation. As was true of other

extra-parliamentary groups, however, the Brothers long remained uncertain of the extent to which they should oppose the political regime. They grew increasingly disillusioned with liberalism but 'they never quite made a revolutionary leap of faith'.[4] As late as the spring of 1952, the Brotherhood was still debating whether it should form a political party. Within the context of this ambiguity the Brotherhood nevertheless provided an organisational framework for nationalist activity within the officer corps. A strong commitment to the Brotherhood's religious ideology was downplayed in an effort to attract young nationalist officers, with the result that virtually the entire leadership corps of the Free Officers joined Brotherhood cells under rubrics that did not mandate rigid religiosity. The Free Officers therefore had a unique recruiting advantage, especially after 1948 when other opposition forces had been virtually entirely suppressed by the government.[5]

4) In contexts of confessional and national-ethnic conflict, Islam often serves to articulate the nationalism of groups that are living within a political structure including Muslims and non-Muslims or different linguistic and ethnic communities.[6] This is perhaps nowhere better illustrated than in Malaysia where the most potent bonds of Malay national identity have been represented through Islamic religious symbols.[7] As a result of colonial policy, which included the importing of substantial immigrant labour, the indigenous Malay population was numerically eclipsed by Chinese and Indian fellow citizens (mostly Chinese) who, at independence in 1957, formed a collective minority of a little less than 50 per cent. In order to create a constitutional base for the affirmation of Malay political dominance in the face of this demographic challenge, the parameters of Malayness were articulated in the constitution as the practice of Malay custom (*adat*), the use of the Malay language, and adherence to Islam.[8] Until 1970, popular ideas of race (ethnicity) and language dominated the quest for Malay identity. However, once the Malay language was firmly established, to the extent that even most non-Malays had become fluent, a new basis of Malay distinctiveness had to be found. The Islamic religion, the third element of Malay constitutional identity, therefore superseded language and custom as a source of Malay domination. In the words of Judith Nagata, it became 'the core of Malay nationalism'.[9] Even new Chinese Muslims

were relegated to a marginal category of 'new associates'. They were not accepted as new Malays. Most Malays, in fact, appeared to feel a closer bond of religious solidarity with fellow Muslims from Indonesia or the Middle East than with Chinese Muslims in their own country. Protection of Malay ethnic status also exacerbated the differences between Malays and Muslim Indians, including Indians who had married into the Malay community.[10]

Malaysia may supply particularly titillating examples to those in need of showing how Islamic universalism can give way before the force of nationalism or a sense of national-ethnic identity, but examples can, of course, be found in many other areas, including Pakistan. Although this nation was supposed to unite its various ethnicities on the basis of Islam vis-à-vis secular India, once partition was achieved 'Muslim ethnicity ... outlived its original purpose'.[11] Punjabis in fact came to dominate Pakistan, while Sindis, Baluchis, Pashtuns, and Bengalis also pressed their claims. In the case of Bengali Muslims, the fragility of elitist religious identity led to the creation of Bangladesh on the basis of a separate linguistic-cultural identity.[12] Bengali separatism should not come as a surprise. No Muslim nations separated by differing ethnic-linguistic identities have attempted full mergers with one another. Such efforts have been confined to the Arab states (Egypt and Syria in 1958 and North and South Yemen in 1990).

5) The employment of religious terms or terms of religious origin, even by the most secular of nationalisms in the Islamic world, does not mean that these terms reflect a content that is necessarily religious. The Iranian revolution, for example, appeared to reject nationalism as a secular, alien, and limiting ideology, and yet if one considers the programme of Khumayni's movement before and after it seized power, one finds much in common with many nationalisms.[13] Khumayni used populist language. He spoke of the struggle between *mostaz'afin* (the oppressed) and *mostakbirin* (the oppressor); the main enemy was imperialism, described as *istikbar-i jahani* (world arrogance); his Iranian foes were 'corrupt traitors'; the Shah was called *sagi-i karter* (the running dog of Jimmy Carter). The word *taghut*, a Qur'anic term for a golden idol, was also applied to Carter, the Shah, and Saddam Hossein, and it can be seen as operating as a Persian equivalent of Mao's 'paper tiger'.[14] Much of Khumayni's

rhetoric was that of Third World radicalism, and the invocation of religious terminology finds its counterparts in the nationalisms of the Christian West. The French spoke of revolutionary France as the 'Vatican of reason', the Russians of their country during the nineteenth century as the 'third Rome' (an idea developed by a six-teenth-century Russian cleric)[15] and the *theotokos* or 'God-bearer', a traditional Orthodox phrase for the Blessed Virgin.

Significant differences certainly exist between token invoca-tions of religion by essentially secular rulers such as Nasser and the more central place given to Islam by other leaders. But even when Islam is given more prominence, the content will differ according to context, including the degree to which the state wishes to em-ploy Islam to legitimate and consolidate its position. One should here note that after coming to power, and particularly after Iraq invaded Iran, Khumayni was capable of speaking in totally non-re-ligious nationalist terms as he invoked the *mihan* or 'motherland', the *mellat-i 'aziz* or 'dear nation', and the primacy of the interests of state and society over the obligations of religious law and ritual.[16] A revolutionary state, in spite of its extra-territorial mission, may have to stress its national character in order to mobilise domestic support in times of difficult change and external threat (Stalin's in-vocation of the great warriors of Russian history during the Second World War comes to mind).[17] Moreover, and apart from reasons of state resorted to in trying circumstances, even a revolutionary re-gime of international significance is likely to 'evoke and reclaim'[18] pre-revolutionary nationalist elements that are virtually impossible to discard. As Fred Halliday observes, in spite of Khumayni's efforts to associate his movement with the struggle of all Muslims, 'there was a strong element of Persian cultural and national pride in the Iranian revolution, combined with the particular Shi'i character of the revolution and subsequent state'.[19]

In light of the above arguments and evidence, which support the idea that nationalism has been just as 'modular'[20] in the modern Is-lamic world as it has been elsewhere, how are we to understand the persistence of the widespread assumption that this world is excep-tional in its virtual immunity to nationalism or that it is only able to produce nationalisms that are grotesque parodies of what we find in the West? I believe that the answer is to be found in Orientalist perspectives that continue to shape the way in which the history of nationalism and its relation to culture within the Islamic world are understood. The remainder of this chapter, which takes the above theme as a primary focus, and which concentrates on the Arabs and their pan-Arab nationalism (also referred to as Arab nationalism or Arabism), is divided into several parts: 1) a consideration of some traditional Orientalist perspectives on the constitutive essence of Islamic societies that are relevant to the consideration of nationalism and its historiography; 2) an analysis of how theories of postmodernism and neo-modernisation have reinforced and recycled these traditional perspectives over the last thirty years, and particularly since the end of the Cold War; and 3) a critique of these perspectives and themes and an analysis of the intellectual and political uses to which they are put.

Although many of the ideas discussed have their origin in the West, they have had a profound influence on thinkers in Islamic areas, either because some of these thinkers have adopted them directly, or because they have spent an inordinate amount of time in combating or seeking to free themselves from them, or because they have been more likely to have an audience in their own countries if they are taken seriously as interlocutors in a Western-dominated global intellectual context. There is also no question that discourses of Western origin have reinforced compatible intellectual trends of a more particular Islamic specificity. This is due to the fact that metropolitan and peripheral discourses share, to varying degrees, common theoretical and historical conditions of provenance within a world capitalist system,[21] but also because the transcultural dynamics between the two universes of the West and Islam, and particularly the West and the Arab Middle East and North Africa (the Islamic areas on which I focus), continue to be a unique phenomenon.[22]

Essence as Religion and Essence as Fragmentation

The question of essence, the idea that Islamic societies have inhering, unique and exceptional features that are decisive and everywhere the same, has played a central role in these transcultural dynamics, whether in respect to nationalism or an array of other highly contested subjects. If distinction, cultural or otherwise, always needs an external other, one can argue that the Islamic world, and particularly the Arab world, has often been cast in the role of *the* world that stands opposed to everything the West holds dear. 'The uniqueness of Western modernity', Armando Salvatore writes, 'can be properly assessed only by reference to another uniqueness, represented by Islamic history'.[23] The uniquely Islamic essence has been variously defined. There are, nevertheless, two commonly posited features that have special relevance to my consideration of nationalism. The first feature is religion. Westerners have often assumed that the Islamic religion has governed the cultural, economic, social, and political processes of Islamic societies to an extent that is not true of other religions in other areas, and that it has done so in a manner that has blocked the development of institutionalised rationality.[24] In the second half of the nineteenth century, more particularly, and through the influence of Weber's study of Islam in the context of comparative sociology, Islam was transformed into a reified ideological system, what Salvatore calls a framework for common reference, and a major concern for offensive Western authors and their defensive Islamic counterparts.[25] The legacy of Weber, who believed that Islam lacked a concept of salvation in its ethical dimension, that it could not produce the spiritual inwardness (in spite of some similarity to Calvinism) conducive to the mastery of the outer world in the form of capitalism, and that this failure was linked to Islam's political and material character as a war religion, is alive among Western and Islamic contemporaries. Islam is a 'barrack room' religion, Levi-Strauss writes, appealing to 'anxious men who make up for their feelings of inferiority by jealousy, pride and heroism, the traditional forms of sublimation with which the Arab soul has always been associated'.[26]

Few Muslims would subscribe to Levi-Strauss's or Weber's view of Islam, but many have been profoundly influenced by a Weberian view of world development that conceives of societies as existing at a general civilisational level in which social life, polity, and culture correspond to one another and reflect the degree to which reason and other key traits prevail.[27] This type of thinking has involved a certain reification of religion, which was first manifested towards the end of the last century as the word 'Islam' became the subject of sentences and an adjective, and as the concept 'sharia' began to consolidate as an abstract medium of social normativity distinct from the concrete laws applied by the courts and the science of jurisprudence.[28] A second feature that is often posited as characteristic of the Islamic essence is fragmentation. Those thinking in terms of the fragmentary view Islamic societies as mosaics of eternally antagonistic, or at least profoundly disparate religious, sectarian, tribal, and ethnic groups.[29] The two features, a constitutive Islam and a constitutive fragmentation, are not necessarily conceived as being incompatible. Weber believed that Islam as a cultural religious unit rested on tribalism, and that it could not be consolidated without resorting to Oriental despotism justified in Islamic terms.[30]

These assumptions are not new. They are standard features of the repertoire of Orientalism. What *is* new is the manner in which these standard ideas have been reformulated in terms of the postmodern and neo-modernisation theories that have played prominent roles in the post Cold War period, and the particular meaning that the recycling of these ideas has had in respect to the understanding and practice of nationalism.

Postmodernism

Postmodernism appeared upon the Western intellectual scene by the end of the 1970s. If the radicals of the 1960s had emphasised the public, the heroic, the collective and universal, and grand narratives of the struggle against capitalism and imperialism, these very qualities were condemned or cast aside under suspicion by the postmodernists.[31] The postmodernists sang the praises of the playful, the hybrid, the nomadic, the migratory, the fragmented, the contingent, and of a multiple, diffuse, and de-centered self. If the radicals of a previous generation had given societies the rank of historical subjects, the postmodernists placed their emphasis on smaller heterogeneous groups conceptualised in terms of 'identities', or, à l'Americain, 'multicultural identities' upon which identity politics could be grounded.[32] The development of postmodernism cannot, of course, be separated from the politics and culture of its day. As Terry Eagleton argues, its principal features are, at one and the same time, a reflection of the success of late capitalism and the political and diplomatic defeat that can be associated with this

'success'. The subject as producer in the metropolitan areas – coherent, disciplined, self-determining – has yielded to the subject as
consumer – mobile, ephemeral, and constituted by insatiable desire.
Moreover, in a world in which many mass movements have collapsed,
is it not natural to make a virtue of necessity and to demonise the
mass, the dominant, and the consensual?[33]

This sort of thinking, in which even the determinant can be perceived as in itself dogmatic, oppressive, and totalitarian, pervades
contemporary intellectual life. Schubert, Joseph Horowitz tells us,
is less an 'ideologue' than Beethoven because his music is elusive,
with pauses and silences and unharmonised, oscillating modes. His
musical thought is not controlled by a navigating ego, there is no
wilfulness, no grand total scheme, no motivic recurrences.[34] And the
elaborative letting go of 'classical Arabic song', says Edward Said, is
part of the work of building a civil society from the ground up and
not the top down, in contrast to the 'administrative and executive
authority' of (particularly) post-Beethoven Western classicism.[35]
The political/economic implications of such remarks are obvious
enough. Postmodernists and those operating under their influence
have 'refocused attention away from the macro realm (the global
system, or the national state, or the economy) toward a 'micro politics' grounded in the immediate, local and more tangible elements
of daily life'.[36] The postmodernists assume that any efforts to unify
opposition are bound to fail or that success will come at the price
of totalitarianism (Said argues that Foucault's conception of power
leaves no room for resistance, that it is a Spinozist conception which
has drawn a circle around itself,[37] but Said also believes that 'a non-
pathological authority' is a contradiction in terms.)[38]

What this kind of postmodernism has meant for many Third
World intellectuals has been elucidated by Aijaz Ahmad who has
subjected the anti-political politics of Said to a withering critique.
As the stagnation of the Third World state has become more obvious and transnational projects like Arab nationalism have collapsed,
Ahmad argues, many Third World intellectuals have taken refuge
in a poststructuralism that debunks all collective agents. They emphasise hybridity, contingency, the collapse of the nation-state as
a horizon of politics, and a globalised, postmodern culture. First
World academics from various ex-colonial countries have been one

of the most important vehicles for this Third World poststructuralism. Many of them have been predisposed to embrace a politics and discourse that is acceptable in their new environment. Indeed, some of these intellectuals speak as if their migrancy represents a universal Utopian condition.[39]

Neo-Modernisation

The second major theory that has special relevance to issues of nationalism is neo-modernisation, or what is sometimes called neo-liberalism. It, too, emerged in the late 1970s but it received enormous reinforcement from the collapse of communism and from the success of aggressive capitalist market economies in the United States and elsewhere. The neo-modernisationists assume that there are, indeed, global narratives after all, and that the institutions of the entire world are converging. Two key factors are looked upon as necessary in the transition to democratic happiness – an emancipatory market that brings liberation through privatisation, contracts, monetary inequality, and competition, and, also, a civil society – an informal, non-state, non-economic, political zone, in which citizens compete in the market place of ideas, but in terms of a common empirical point of reference that defines the good and the bad.[40]

Postmodernists celebrate the local, the micro, and the fragmented, and neo-modernisationists celebrate the world-wide triumph of capitalism and the civil society that is supposed to accompany it. Although one might expect these orientations to be at odds they are in effect often complementary. They are complementary because the postmodern deconstruction of the macro scarcely ever applies to the structures of a system of capitalist domination in which economic and political power is concentrated in fewer and fewer hands. The postmodern critique is more likely to extend to Marxism, or to radical nationalism, or to any broad movement or transformative project that goes beyond capitalism or that threatens the political and economic domination of the largely Western nations, and particularly the United States, of the capitalist core. Postmodernist writing may reflect the disintegration of a unifying public sphere but it also easily coexists with the market system and the political structures that maintain it.[41] By often subordinating encompassing political and economic structures and forces to cultural questions, and, more particularly, to cultural questions centred on the identity of minority or subaltern groups, or in taking these encompassing structures and forces for granted as a kind of second nature, postmodernism resurrects the prejudices of an old style of cultural criticism for which politics and economics of any kind had little meaning.[42]

Islam as 'Saracen Menace'

The emphasis on an essence defined in terms of Islam as a religion, or on an essence defined in terms of fragmentation, has been strengthened by postmodern and neo-modernist discourses and by discourses within the Islamic world that provide mirror images for them. There are many diverse positions, but the tendency to demonise or discommend the macro and, more particularly, as I have said, any macro transformative project that would challenge the hegemony of the capitalist core, provides a common thread.

There is, for one, Islam as 'Saracen Menace',[43] a religion to which 'fundamentalism' is deemed inherent, and which readily fills the role (now that communism is dead) of a world historical threat to the good. 'Apparent exceptions to the trend towards secularisation in the world as a whole turn out to be special cases', Ernest Gellner writes, 'explicable by special circumstances. But there is one very real, dramatic exception to all this: Islam. To say that secularisation prevails in Islam is not contentious. It is simply false. Islam is as strong now as it was a century ago. In some ways it is probably much stronger.'[44] And, in his *Encounters with Nationalism,* in which the nationalism of the Arabs (implicitly) and the Islamic religion are denigrated, we read:

> There is a kind of Consumerist International of developed or semi-developed societies, united in placing production over coercion or honour or, at any rate, seeking power through production rather than force, and having both disassociated glory from territory, and abjured faith in a unique and obligating salvation, no longer inclined to go to war against each other. But they share the planet with other religions, in which there are societies which exemplify either the role of honour-committed coercers, or which take an absolutist Faith seriously and literally, or both of these conditions at once.[45]

Expressions of this sort of fear and contempt are common to the 'refined' and the 'popular', the 'high' and the 'low', the 'official' and the 'unofficial'. We have just heard the relatively polite Gellner, but here is the angrier and cruder Conor Cruise O'Brien: 'Arab and Muslim society is sick and has been sick for a long time. At the heart of the matter is the Muslim family, an abominable institution. It looks repulsive because it is repulsive.'[46] Or here is Sir Alfred Sherman, a former personal advisor to Margaret Thatcher: 'The gradual Moslem colonisation of Western and Central Europe owes much to social and spiritual disorientation there [the Islamic world].'[47] Or here is the United States' Pat Buchanan in 1992: 'For a millennium, the struggle for mankind's destiny was between Christianity and Islam; in the twenty-first century it may be so again.' [48]

The sense of crisis to which these remarks attest reflect the consolidation of a Western-dominated international media which, after the 1973 war and oil embargo, projected the image of Islam as a threat to 'Western values' and the world's peace and security.[49] This allegedly Islamic threat provided the occasion for a 'vengeful settling'[50] of accounts as those waiting to cry 'I told you so' rushed forth to announce that the fundamentally secular nature of the politics of the twentieth-century Islamic world had been a sham. Bernard Lewis supplied the *locus classicus* in 'The Return of Islam' (1976). There has been an historical continuity in the Islam-inspired processes of politicisation, Lewis claimed, in spite of the fact that during the 1950s and 1960s Westerners mistakenly believed that many political phenomena, especially in the Arab parts of the Islamic world, were manifestations of secular nationalism.[51]

As Salvatore remarks, the academy played more than an ancillary role in the game of projecting Islam as a global issue on the Western agenda. Yvonne Y. Haddad, a former president of the Middle East Studies Association, recalls a meeting of some of the members in October, 1990, to organise a two-week summer institute for high school teachers on the general subject of teaching about Islam and the Arab world. After choosing the over-all topics they decided to leave one day to deal with whatever might be the crisis of that period. Someone asked, 'But what if there isn't a crisis?' Such a possibility seemed quite unthinkable to most of those present. 'I'm sure there will be something', said one person. And another added, 'And if there isn't, we can make one up.' Haddad proceeds to ask, 'What is this Middle East to the study of which we have devoted our lives? Have we somehow created an entity for our own needs and purposes that may not correspond to reality?'[52]

The Bad Nationalism of Muslims and Arabs

Gellner's assumption that Islam is a bad religion because it is unsecularisable and unable to accommodate itself to the market and its civic virtues is paralleled by the idea that nationalism among Muslims, and particularly the local and pan-Arab nationalism of the Arabs, is a bad or at least ineffective nationalism. This is so because it operates as a code for a bad religion, or because it reproduces the worst features of the political culture of this bad religion in a secular form, or because, even if this nationalism were secular and good, it is not able to overcome the power of this bad religion (or, if the observer is benignly populist, the religion of 'the people', good or bad), or the inherent fragmentation of the societies over which this religion prevails.

The intellectual origins of much contemporary neo-modernisationist discourse on nationalism in the Islamic world can be found in the hoary distinction made by Acton, Kohn, and others between a benign nationalism (sometimes designated as patriotism) that is contractual, civil and liberal, and whose politics are peaceful, moderate, measured and calculating, and an organic nationalism that is based on ethnicity or race and that is prone to violence and tyranny. In the late nineteenth century Acton believed that the Teutonic countries (England, Germany and the USA) had the good nationalism and that the Latin countries had the bad, and in the mid-twentieth century Kohn believed that the Americans and English had the good nationalism and that the Germans, the Eastern Europeans, and the Africans and Asians had the bad.[53] In the 1990s and presently, it should come as no surprise that the nationalism of Arabs and Muslims is a prime and convenient candidate for demonisation. After discussing the nationalism of Russia, Germany, Romania, Syria, Iraq and the Khmer Rouge in a 1994 article which appeared in *Theory and Society*, Liah Greenfield and C. Chirot write:

The cases we discuss here show that the association between certain types of nationalism and aggressive, brutal behaviour is neither coincidental nor inexplicable. Nationalism remains the world's most powerful, general, and primordial basis of cultural and political identity. Its range is still growing, not diminishing, throughout the world. And in most places it does not take an individualistic or civic form.[54]

There are places, however, where nationalism is benign in its civility and democracy. 'The ability to compromise', Greenfield writes in *Nationalism: Five Roads to Modernity*, a 1995 book of over five hundred pages, 'is one of the distinguishing characteristics of this intensely idealistic American nation. The uniqueness of the American nation is that it has come closest to the realisation of the principles of individualistic, civic, nationalism. It stands as an example of its original promise – democracy.' Those who cannot differentiate between the bad and the good in this respect are, she contends, the victims of a 'naive' American idealism. 'There is no greater – and graver mistake', she tells us later in her book, 'than to regard all nations as created equal. Men are created equal but nations are not. Some are created as compacts of sovereign individuals and emphasise the freedom and equality of men; some are created as beautiful great individuals who may feed on man and preach racial superiority and submission to the state.'[55] Greenfield here provides a wonderful example of how 'sophisticated scholarship' contributes to the idea of chosenness or election that is fundamental to the culture of bourgeois democracies.[56] Such arguments have long provided justification for Western domination and violence, but within the context of the emergence of neo-modernisation, they are especially reminiscent of the attitudes of Cold War modernisation theorists (whose themes the neo-modernisationists have resuscitated) towards potential Third World enemies. As Tom Nairn has written, 'Third Worlders were allowed some nationalism but were expected to be careful with what they did with it.'[57] When we turn to the consideration of nationalism in the Islamic world as such, and particularly in the Arab areas, we find a comparable continuity of themes, and a comparable contemporary resurgence or echoes of these themes, and often in new sociological and historical guises.

Elie Kedourie, a scholar of nationalism in general, and of Middle-Eastern nationalism more particularly, was one of the principal founding fathers of a discourse that is alive and well. According to Kedourie, nationalism itself is an unnatural style of politics in which principle overrides compromise and divergent interests, and in which existence is envisaged as an organic whole rather than as disparate and disconnected parts. Kedourie condemns, more particularly, the German variety of nationalism, which he contrasts to the 'patriotism' of the British and Americans. Patriotism is shorn of 'a particular doctrine of the state or the individual's relation to it'. It is love of one's country and loyalty to its institutions. In fact, the label 'nationalism' should only be attached to German nationalism and its transmutations in the rest of the world. In Asian and African regions this nationalism remained entirely alien. Initiated by a handful of Western-educated young men estranged from their own society and their scrupulous European masters, this nationalism spread by imposition or imitation, with destruction, brutal murder, and persecution of minorities as the result.[58] This understanding of nationalism permeates Kedourie's writings on the Middle East and the writings of many who have followed in his footsteps. Kedourie believed that pioneer Egyptian and Syrian pan-Arabists lacked 'a sense of concrete difficulties' and possessed faith in sedition and violence and a contempt for moderation, that they dreamt of an authoritarian state 'that would transform the heterogeneous, fissiparous, skeptical populations of the Fertile Crescent [and Egypt] to the likeness of their dream, with all the differences suddenly annihilated and external unity the emblem of a deeper, still more fundamental unity: one state, one nation, one creed.'[59]

Kedourie and other authors of his generation and persuasion[60] produced their most important writing in the 1950s, 1960s and 1970s. The interpretations found therein have nevertheless never disappeared and are, as I have said, actually undergoing a contemporary revival. In *Empires of the Sand* (1999), a work that has been the subject of a promotional campaign by Harvard University Press – it was reviewed twice by *The New York Times* and given a full page review by *The Chronicle of Higher Education* – Efraim and Inari Karsh argue that European imperialism was more benevolent than threatening and that it coexisted with Ottoman, Egyptian, and Arab imperialism. The loss of Ottoman territory in the nineteenth century, the collapse of the Empire in the First World War, and the failure of

Arab nationalism during the war, were all the result of the incompetence or duplicity of local leaders who sought to play off European powers against each other and to satisfy their own ambitions. Arab nationalism was not successful because its practitioners were not really nationalists but local imperialists. Zionism, however, was a true nationalism and was successful because European imperialism, more worthy than Middle-Eastern imperialism, approved of it. Karsh and Karsh explicitly pay tribute to Kedourie, whose work, they feel, has been unjustly ignored (Charles D. Smith points out that their 'new findings' mirror Kedourie's work of forty years ago).[61] Their debt pales, however, in comparison to that of Martin Kramer, whose *The Arab Awakening and Islamic Revival* (1996) is a worthier successor to the master's hysteria and rage. According to Kramer, the Arab awakening (always spoken of in quotation marks) was a 'discontent' that owed much to 'foreign enthusiasts and romantics' and to Presbyterian missionaries who served as the 'sorcerer's apprentices'. The Arab nationalists before and during the First World War had 'a vague admiration for the liberal democracies of the West', but they had an imperfect 'understanding of the meaning behind the slogan of liberty'. Norman Thomas 'perhaps best summarised the content of Arab radical ideology as liberty, equality, and revenge'. Arab nationalism and Soviet communism 'are two great myths of solidarity, impossible in their scale, deeply flawed in their implementation, which alternately stirred and whipped millions in a desperate pursuit of power – before collapsing in exhaustion and stranding their admirers in the faculty lounges of the West'.[62]

Such views, or echoes thereof expressed crudely or subtly, are not confined to the Westerner or Easterner, the Zionistic or Orientalist, the religious or secular. They are, of course, the stock in trade of a strain of contemporary Islamism that fiercely rejects nationalism, particularly the radical Nasserist variety, as well as liberalism, constitutionalism and Marxism, as imported ideologies that threaten the cultural essence of Islamic societies. Arab nationalism was conceived in sin and born in corruption and dissolution, says 'Abdullah 'Azzam, a Palestinian-Jordanian preacher and activist of the Afghan guerrilla warfare.[63] It was concocted by Margoliouth and Brockelmann and other European Orientalists, who built on the ideas of the French Revolution to separate Arabs and Turks, thereby weakening Islam and facilitating Western takeover.[64] But the sweeping discommending of nationalism, and especially of pan-Arab nationalism, as foreign or non-representative, or as never as strong as its promoters would have had us believe, also manifests itself in scholarly secular writings where it would not be expected. In his recent *Palestinian Identity: The Construction of Modern National Consciousness* (1997), Rashid Khalidi speaks of the 'shibboleths' of pan-Arabism, a 'powerful symbolic bogeyman' in the West where its importance as 'a convenient myth' lived on after its 1967 defeat, and where it was hard for people to understand 'the multiple, layered identities so characteristic of the Arab world in general, and of the Palestinians in particular'.[65] And in *The New Mamluks: Egyptian Society and Modern Feudalism* (2000), Amira el-Azhary Sonbol contends that Arab unity or nationalism was 'an imported ideology', the creation of the culture of the *khassa* or elite that is only now giving way to the culture of the '*amma* or the masses to which Islam is so central.[66]

The disaffection of specialised scholarly works is paralleled by that of broader theoretical reflections. Bassam Tibi's well-known critiques (the mid-1960s to early 1970s) of the great theoretician of Arab nationalism, Sati' al-Husri, reflect a critical turning point. According to Tibi, the political doctrines of Arab nationalists promoted superficiality and sloganeering and did not conform to Arab experience. Al-Husri, as theorist and educator commissioned to popularise Arab nationalism in monarchical Iraq and through the Arab League, produced an apology for this nationalism rather than a serious inquiry. His organic nationalism, reliant on German sources, including Fichte and others whom he misused, testify to a kind of proto-fascism. Michel 'Aflaq, one of the founders of the Ba'th, and the most eminent theorist of a party that came to power in two countries, offers only vague and contradictory metaphysics.[67] Tibi writes in German and English but there is an array of comparable authors who write in Arabic, including Hazim Saghiyya, who displays a remarkable capacity to think the worst. According to Saghiyya's latest book, *Qawmiyyu al-mashriq al-'Arabi* (2000), or *The Nationalists in the Arab East*, both pan-Arabists and others have created a 'new paganism' that sacrilises the national community and that is enmeshed in racism and anti-Semitism, the latter mediated, in particular, by Arab Christians drawing on a tradition of anti-Semitism unknown to Islamic societies. The subtitle of Saghiyya's book, 'from Dreyfus to Garaudy', refers to the two events that provide the framing points of his narrative of shame, that is, the Islamic reformer Rashid Rida's defence of Dreyfus in the late nineteenth century, a reflection of Islamic tolerance, and the enthusiastic reception given to Roger Garaudy by Arab and Iranian intellectuals and officials in 1996–1997, a reflection of the new paganism.[68]

Many other examples of authors writing in various languages could be cited, not the least of whom is Edward Said, who has had a significant role in the transcultural dynamics to which I have referred. Said claims that nationalism is necessary for initial stages of resistance but he is otherwise so negative that it is clear that for him it is 'a god who always fails',[69] akin to the category of religion as a metaphor for dogmatism and violence.[70] 'In time', Said writes in one of his most recent books, 'successful nationalisms consign truth exclusively to themselves and relegate falsehood and inferiority to outsiders ...'.[71] And in January of 1991, in a statement that Jeffrey Alexander saw as evidence of the virtual disappearance of Third Worldism, Said denounced 'the traditional discourse of Arab nationalism, to say nothing of the quite decrepit state system', as 'inexact, unresponsive, anomalous, even comic', and spoke of a remorseless 'Arab propensity to violence and extremism'.[72]

The 'Seamlessness' of Bad Nationalism

As I have indicated, the influence of neo-modernisation theory, which draws on a long-lived intellectual tradition that differentiates between contractual and organic nationalism, is reinforced by the influence of postmodern perspectives. This postmodernism, which is particularly hostile to the 'seamless' nationalism that has allegedly been promoted by post-colonial regimes and nationalist thinkers and scholars, is widely admitted, touted, and celebrated, often with no second thoughts or any hint of the need for problematisation.

Such deconstructive penchants are fully displayed in recent remarks by Edmund Burke III who provides a self-congratulatory grand narrative of the destruction of the grand narratives of imperialism and nationalism in an introductory chapter to a collection of essays edited by Ali Abdullatif Ahmida and entitled, *Beyond Colonialism and*

Nationalism in the Maghrib: History, Culture and Politics. Histories written from the perspective of the colonialists sought to legitimise the colonial project as a world historic mission that introduced liberal and industrial values and that opened the local economy to market forces that ended centuries of stagnation. Such a version of events was challenged by national historical schools. Nationalist historians emphasised the continuities between pre- and post-colonial histories, underscoring the disruption and violence of the colonial conquest, the exploitation of resources by the Europeans, and the negative impact of the colonial system upon standards of living. In spite of its considerable achievements in exposing colonialist distortions, nationalist history was as devoid of complexity as the colonial histories it replaced. Although it claimed to speak in the name of the people, it left the rural populations, women, ethnic, religious, and linguistic minorities, and European settlers, in the shadows. Nationalist histories subsumed the dissonant voices of pre-colonialist protest into an elite nationalist master narrative. These nationalist histories rarely acknowledged that the nationalist leaders intervened on behalf of some interests and against others, that is, that they themselves had politics. It is only in the post-colonial and post-nationalist phases, facilitated by the realisation that the nationalist elites 'were no less corrupt and brutal than the officials they replaced', that a breakthrough has been possible. Nationalist and colonialist histories are homogeneous and teleological, 'whereas ours are aware of multiple causalities and multiple agencies'. The story of the Moroccan native troops, forced to enlist in the French colonial army but providing the nucleus of the liberation army of 1955, shows that even the dichotomous formulations of coloniser/colonised need to be rethought. The close link between the hostility shown to ruling elites and the hostility to the historical and cultural understanding they are taken to represent is also expressed in Ahmida's short editorial preface in which he speaks of his generation's (he is an American of Libyan origin) disillusionment with the national regimes in the Maghrib as an inspiration for his 'critical examination of nationalist theories'.[73]

James Jankowski's and Israel Gershoni's anthology *Rethinking Nationalism in the Arab Middle East* (1997) provides a worthy companion to the Ahmida book on the Maghrib.[74] The introduction by the co-editors, with repeated references to Arab nationalist 'ideologues' who projected the homogeneous and hegemonic in contrast to the polycentric and polyvalent, could have been written by Burke. Most of the articles collected for the two works conform to what we are led to expect: there are pieces on Yemeni nationalism as a shifting field of pre-Islamic, local, and regional elements, on the gradual, hesitant and only partial commitment to Arab nationalism on the part of the Nasserist regime up to 1958, on the behaviour of Arab labourers who sought, against the counsel of Palestinian nationalist intellectuals, to make common cause with Jewish labour in the Histadrut, on the need to build a post-colonial Moroccan female subject embracing 'inescapably' hybrid identities. The lust for plurality as a value in itself, at least on the part of co-editors Jankowski and Gershoni (they assure us that the 'collage of [Arab] variants of identity and loyalty' have by no means been exhausted),[75] is wonderfully representative of the Zeitgeist. As is their remark that Philip Khoury's consideration of the 'multivalent politics' of the Syrian National Bloc during the Mandate is a 'fitting note' with which to end their anthology. Khoury once thought that the National Bloc was factious but he has changed his mind to the apparent approval of the editors. He now finds that the members of the Bloc were flexible and pragmatic in contrast to their Arabist and anti-imperialist rivals.[76] The author of this chapter is not convinced. He rejects the idea of essence as religion or essence as fragmentation.

A Critique of Essence as Religion

The religion of the majority in the Islamic world is Islam but this does not mean that Islamic societies are constituted by an Islamic essence that has been everywhere decisive and the same. As Sami Zubaida argues, the effort to totalise histories and societies as Islamic just doesn't work. Iran has a totally different political and social structure from that of Turkey, Egypt or Arabia. In a number of important ways, Tunisian coastal cities share more in common with Sicily than with Arabia or Iraq. To be sure, Muslims share, as do Christians and members of other religions, a universe of discourse, institutions and doctrines that are not limited to the religious field, but these have assumed vastly different forms and social significance at various times and places. Moreover, if Islamic societies are not unique and exceptional in the way the essentialists think, their social formations and historical variations are subject to the same analyses used for Western or other societies. Ahmida, the editor of the book rejecting Orientalism and nationalist theories and histories to which I have referred, may be right in rejecting the idea of the Asiatic mode of production as Eurocentric, but is it really possible, as he seems to imply, to develop a form of 'epistemology' that would be Maghribi-specific?[77]

If the idea of an Islamic essence is false so is the idea that the development of Islamism is a return of the repressed in societies ultimately resistant to nationalism and other foreign 'imports'. Resistance to a world of radical doubt is, for one, common to both the First and Third Worlds. Sayyid Qutb's critique of the 'failures of modernity' are shared with a company of First World critics including Charles Taylor, Alisdaire MacIntyre, and John Newhouse.[78] At the same time, the nature of certain strains of political Islamism, the level of violence with which some Islamists have been associated, as victims or as perpetrators, and the prominence of their role in public political life (Charles Taylor has not been executed), relate to the specificities of socio-economic and political crises in the peripheral societies in which the majority of Muslims live. Islamic political movements are responding to the intrusion of the state into everyday life, the evolution of legal codes, external and internal political and economic domination, large and growing gaps between rich and poor, rapid urbanisation, and fierce competition for educational and employment opportunities.[79]

As Aziz Al-Azmeh points out, the Islamic acculturation of certain social groups is the manufacturing and not the recovering of an identity. This is why Islamism is weak in places like the city of Sfax, whose economic and social structures have a strong continuity with the recent past, and strong in Tunis where sections of the population have been socially traumatised.[80] What is often attributable to Islamic uniqueness is virtually a universal phenomenon in which more and more ordinary people face arcane forces intervening in the production of value, arcane forces to which they attribute their feelings of loss. None of this is new. Balzac described it for France in the 1840s, Conrad for pre-revolutionary Russia, Gluckman for colonial Africa, where he spoke of the 'magic of despair'. In our own day, the unprecedented manifestations of zombies in the South African countryside has grown in direct proportion to the shrinking labour market for young men.[81] At the same time, we should not forget the diversity of popular attitudes. As Zubaida points out, the rural masses of Iran were not known for their piety, orthodoxy, or attachment to the clergy. It is difficult to ascertain the political and religious currents of the recently urbanised inhabitants of the shanty towns. We can assume that they are volatile and changeable and susceptible to agitation by any oppositional groups that could reach them. Islamic groups have been able to do it. Comparable arguments could be made about Arab or Turkish or other Islamic areas. Moreover, and apart from the fate of Islamic politics, we must ask if it is possible to escape certain aspects of contemporary life and thought that first developed in the West but that are now virtually universal. Zubaida and others believe that there is a certain inevitable secularising process that accompanies modernity, and that even if this process doesn't evolve to the same extent and with the same uniformity everywhere, it must nevertheless evolve. They argue that political Islam is in part a defence against continuing secularisation. Even when religion has remained influential in the law it is part of codified state law subject to political and social factors. Education has been largely removed from the religious sphere. Modern economies have forced women into the labour market and public life, subverting patriarchalism and other values associated with certain traditional beliefs and practices. In Iran, Khumayni had to restore family planning, once denounced as un-Islamic, after a few years. Most of the Shah's reforms in family law have now been restored and new reforms have been introduced. Khumayni himself, faced with the difficulties of governing, ruled in 1988 that in the interest (*maslaha*) of the Islamic community, the Islamic government could suspend any provision of the sharia, including prayer and fasting, and this category of 'interest' has been written into the constitution and institutionalised. Islamists were able to reverse major secularising trends only in Afghanistan, a society that had experienced devastating upheaval, but even there the triumph of the Islamists was more a triumph of Pashtu nationalism than that of a utopian religious movement.[82]

As I emphasised in my introductory remarks on the prevalence of nationalism in the Islamic world, Islamic discourse is often primarily an outward form that does not dispose of a specific content. I tend to agree with Schulze's contention that facts do not change with their designation, that no ideological tendencies exist or could come into existence within the Islamic world that are not otherwise found in international political life, and that Islamic terms and symbols are constantly translated into European ones and vice versa.[83]

A Critique of Essence as Fragmentation

If we must guard against the essentialising of religion we must guard against the essentialising of nationalism or, relatedly, the essentialising of the fragmentary against which nationalism, and the conceptualisation and creation of a nation, are regarded as doomed to fail.

In the first place, the dichotomising between a Western civic nationalism and a non-Western organic nationalism, Arab or other, cannot bear serious scrutiny. Civil society is virtually indefinable. It is in fact very difficult to establish a clear theoretical distinction between society and the economy or between society and the political state. In capitalist societies many coercive functions that once belonged to the state have been relocated to the private sphere – in private property, class exploitation, and the market. Secondly, the characterisation of political community in the so-called civic nations as the rational and freely-chosen allegiance of individuals to a set of principles is false. The USA or other 'civic' nations took shape because of an inherited cultural baggage contingent to their particular histories and serving as the basis of their discreet identities. Even if these nations were based on shared political principles they still might exclude those suspected of rejecting these principles.[84] It is, of course, when one thinks of atrocities committed against the working class or the 'civic' nation's people of colour, or against the non-Western other, that the myth of the peaceful and humane nature of metropolitan civility is perhaps the most vulnerable. The Ba'th Party did not bring us the extermination of the American Indian, or the devastation of Vietnam, or the massacre of tens of thousands of East Timorese, or the embargo against Iraq that has resulted in the death of hundreds of thousands of children since 1990. All of this was brought to us by that naive country that remained 'loyal to its democratic idealism' and that seeks 'power through production rather than through force'.

Essentialism based on neo-modernisation's demonisation of the non-civic other is intimately linked to postmodernism's demonisation of the macro, or, more precisely, to the macro that it doesn't like or doesn't take for granted. Terry Eagleton argues that whole ways of life are celebrated by postmodernists when they are those of dissident or minority groups, that is, that postmodernists will celebrate ways of life such as lesbianism but not nationalism, or, again, to speak more precisely, certainly not the radical Third World nationalism with which they are uncomfortable (deradicalised and de-ideologised identity politics or para-nationalism, or even the nationalism of regional groups or ethnic minorities are more likely to gain their sympathies). Eagleton's remarks resonate in light of the striking and fierce resistance to the majority and the consensual found in many contemporary works on nationalism in the Arab-Islamic worlds. If we speak, more particularly, of the Arabs and their pan-nationalism, there is often little notion that the incoherent and coherent might co-exist, that we might be able to speak of Arab national movements and broad Arab realities, or that we might even be able to speak of the Arabs themselves (!) while acknowledging that these movements and realities are not seamless, that Arab identity is constructed, that it coexists with other identities, and that it does not always take priority over them.

Excessive and misleading concentration on the multiple and polyvalent is often closely linked to a form of populism in which the cultures of various subaltern groups are juxtaposed as coherent and self-contained entities against the coherent and self-contained entities of the cultures of secularising elites that are regarded as highly unrepresentative. A recent example is James L. Gelvin's *Divided Loyalties: Nationalism and Mass Politics in Syria at the Close of Empire* (1998), which treats the period between the fall of the Ottoman Empire and the beginning of the French mandate. Gelvin asserts that he does not wish to 'substitute one nationalist myth for another', that is, that he does not want to exaggerate the significance of the mobilising efforts of the popular committees who, he contends, developed a form of nationalism that was more traditionally Islamic and Syrian-oriented, and therefore more appealing to the socially and politically marginalised than the pan-Arab nationalism of the *mutanawwirun* or cultural elite backing Faysal's government. Nevertheless, although Gelvin acknowledges that the pro-government activity of the elite Arab Club of Damascus 'facilitated and informed' the activities later undertaken by the popular committees, and although he admits that components of political discourse became the common property of many or all nationalist tendencies, we are ultimately left with the impression that there were two highly self-referential groupings, and that if both of them constituted their own 'idealized founding myth', one of these myths, that of the Arabist tendency, was more constructed (that is, had less basis) than the other. Gelvin's negative terminology when speaking of the elite ('a fundamental ideological divide separated Ottomanists and Arabists and *their ilk* [my italics] from the remainder of the society'), his argument that the popular committees' call for complete Syrian independence could draw upon a notion of Syria derived from medieval times and his correspond-ing failure to note that a sense of Arab *ethnie* could be grounded in similar realities, and, finally, his assumption that the Faysali Arab gov-ernment was 'foreordained' to fail apart from imperial opposition, can be taken to reflect a (negative) deconstructive fervour towards Arabism that transcends whatever evidence is needed and/or avail-able to establish the idea of diversity or to prove that the majority of Syrians preferred the nationalism of the committees.[85]

In November of 1967, basking in the aftermath of the June War, Elie Kedourie wrote that the 'Arabs' were making 'a considerable noise in the world'. He did not mean the 'lively and interesting denizens' of Cairo and Damascus but the 'collective entity manufac-tured by the writers of books' who smothered 'the charm and variety of this ancient and sophisticated society'. As they are described by their creators, he continues, they are a 'pitiable and unattractive lot', but the ultimate insult is that the victims have come to accept 'this caricature of themselves and have come, in fact, to behave like it'.[86] The Arabs here are at once non-existent and disgusting. Kedourie was, of course, a hatchet man, and there is no reason to reject the notion of the fragmentary, and certainly not the complex, because he happened to abuse it. It is nevertheless still difficult to avoid the conclusion, apart from whatever sheer bigotry and/or reductionism might be at work, either towards Arabs and Muslims as a whole, or the political culture of their elites and these elites' nationalisms or 'nationalist historiographies', that there is a contemporary fetishisation of the fragmentary and that it comes at a terrible price.

Albert Hourani warned that one should not take to extremes the view of E. Ernest Dawn that Arabism arose out of sheer competition for power between individual members of the new Ottoman elite. The temptation to take this point to extremes, Al-Azmeh remarks, has been repeatedly taken, most notably in scholarship on Syria from the late nineteenth century to independence that credits members of the Damascene and Aleppan elites 'with a truly superhuman capacity for egotism and mendacity'.[87] What is often lacking, Al-Azmeh argues, is a sense that Arab nationalism was the expression of growing Arab social and cultural cohesion and of the need for collective defence, and that it was constructed on the basis of shared language, traditions, and customs, both popular and high, which cut across various boundaries. These shared elements might not be sufficient for the creation of a nation or a nationality but they are usually necessary.[88] If nations created nationalisms, Miroslav Hroch wonderfully asked, then we would have to explain why it occurred to nobody at the beginning of the nineteenth century to launch a campaign to persuade the Irish that they were in fact Germans or to win over the Hungarians to the notion that they were actually Chinese.[89] It is simply not true, as Sonbol argues, that Nasser imported the sense of Arab unity from abroad, certainly not if we are speaking of a sense of Arab *ethnie*. Al-Jabarti speaks of the indigenous people of Egypt as 'sons of the Arabs', and al-Tahtawi mentions the virtues of the Arabs on more than one occasion, arguing that these virtues were common to pagan, Christian, and Jewish Arabs before the advent of Islam. And Ibn Taymiyya, not an Egyptian but certainly a worthy witness to a medieval sense of Arabness, argued that the Arabs of his time could be classified as such either linguistically, ethnically, or territorially (that is, as speakers of Arabic, or descendants of Arabs, or inhabitants of the Peninsula).[90] If this sense of Arab *ethnie* has not been translated into a lasting, significant form of political and economic unity, there are causes other than a metaphysically given Islamism or fragmentation that can account for it, including the fact that none of the dominant Arab ruling classes (comprador or latifundiast bourgeoisie, followed by the state bourgeoisie) have been capable of, or interested in, bringing about such a unity, and that the imperial powers, including the United States and Israel, have been brutal in their fierce opposition to any unity achieved under independent Arab auspices and not under their aegis. That a certain form of Islam *can* play a helpful role in seeking to foster such an aegis is reflected in the first great enterprise of petrol Islam against Nasserism and Ba'thism during the 1950s, and current American and Western support of, or at least flirtation with, 'liberal' and other forms of Islamism, sometimes also petrol-drenched or petrol-inflected, and all 'soluble' in capitalism[91] and accepting of a state system of small or easily controllable entities.

As Nazih Ayubi points out, pan-Arabism's lack of success certainly cannot be attributed to European derivation, or logical inconsistency, or the intellectual poverty and shortcoming of its theoreticians, or the sheer opportunism of its leading proponents. To be sure, vitalistic, mystical, and romantic notions of political identity and nationalism have played important roles in the modern Arab and Islamic worlds, and these notions have sometimes been marked by racist dimensions. But such ideas have coexisted with positivist understandings (emphasising shared culture and interests and subordinating, or altogether eschewing, any reference to shared biology), and elements from both strains, the vitalistic-mystical-romantic and the positivistic, as has been the case with the nationalism of the 'successful' so-called 'civic' nations (think of 'manifest destiny' or America as 'mankind's last best hope'), have sometimes intermingled with one another. Even when we turn to nationalists who speak in terms of eternally inhering vocations, we often find the romantic and explicitly utilitarian, the preposterous and realistic, juxtaposed. The well-known Egyptian Arab nationalist 'Abd al-Rahman 'Azzam, who became the first Secretary-General of the Arab League, argued for the Arabness of the Egyptian people on the basis of blood and spiritual ties and their participation in a humane 'eternal mission', but also on the basis of the economic and geopolitical needs of all Arabs, including strong economic blocs in the age of the cartel and trust.[92]

In speaking of Arab unity and of many other questions relating to Arab-Islamic realities, we must remember that no developments have been born whole or impeccable, either in Europe or elsewhere. As Al-Azmeh notes, no one today would speak of the French as having a congenital incapacity for liberal democracy, in spite of the fact that France had, in two centuries, and before the relative stability of the Fifth Republic, four republics, a commune, three revolutions, a restoration, and two empires.[93] Al-Azmeh, again, is not afraid, when it comes to the Arabs, of dwelling on the positive as well as the negative, the positive consisting, over the last two hundred years, of a transformation of staggering depth, amplitude, and tempo, involving the decline of various traditional institutions such as guilds and clans, the creation of homogeneous legal systems based on principles of universality and codification, the creation of new aesthetic forms and norms, the crafting of a modern form of Arabic, the almost complete constitution of new forms of subjectivity, and the creation of a fairly cohesive, secular, pan-Arab intelligentsia and political culture that transcend Arab boundaries.[94] One aspect of these rich accomplishments has been the production of historical and theoretical works on nationalism that bear little resemblance to the ideological and dogmatic nationalist production of which Jankowski and Gershoni and Burke speak. The classic works of a number of Arab nationalists, including the Iraqi historian 'Abd al-'Aziz al-Duri, who provides a highly sophisticated analysis of how Arabism took shape through ethnic, cultural, and political stages, and of the particulars of its development in each Arab country, or of the Lebanese cleric Shaykh 'Abdullah al-'Alayili, who used the term 'imagined community' (*khayal al-jama'a al-arabiyya*) in 1941, hardly conform to the crudity that has been portrayed.[95] Youssef M. Choueiri, more particularly, has given the lie to what have become commonplace negative assessments of al-Husri's alleged organicism and romanticism. He shows that al-Husri distanced himself from Fichte's ideas apart from linguistics, that he always cited Herder with qualification, and that his early romantic view of language gave way to seeing it as a practical instrument forged to create effective modes of communication in a state that treated all equally.[96]

The Positive Role of the State in Arab Nationalism

That al-Husri was an employee of the Iraqi government – Director General of Education, Dean of the Law College, and then Director of Antiquities – reminds one of the centrality of the state in the transformation of the last two hundred years to which I have referred. Arab nationalism was the product of an acculturation that was effected, to a significant degree, by the reforms of the Ottoman state during the nineteenth century, reforms to which the Arab successor states in the Mashriq, and the modern states in the Maghrib under analogous European influence, are heir.[97] The development of cultural and then political Arabism was an uneven process but this unevenness can be explained, in part, by either the absence or presence of Ottoman reforms or direct European rule.[98] In this respect, the local patriotism of individual Arab states, even when not also strongly pan-Arab, drew upon a common heritage of Arab culture, values, and history that could be associated with the national territory and whose influence was enhanced, either directly or indirectly, by various state institutions, and in particular by the new secular educational systems.[99] Although the high culture supported by such institutions has been associated with elite privilege, its content is not necessarily any more conservative or reactionary than that of the culture celebrated by the champions of subaltern populism. 'High culture is not some ruling-class conspiracy', Eagleton writes, and 'if it sometimes fulfils this cognitive function, it can also sometimes disrupt it'.[100] One here thinks of Ahmida's speaking of how his education in the social sciences, made possible by a Libyan state scholarship, contributed to the development of his critical attitude towards the post-independence regimes and their nationalism.

There are, clearly, a number of local causes that account for the widespread denigration of the Ottoman state and its successors, including certain tyrannical aspects of late Ottoman rule and disillusionment with the nation states that followed. The record of these states has certainly been flawed. They have been the vehicles of class, gender, and minority oppression, and the captives of neo-colonial relationships with which they have been complicit or that they have been unable to break or renegotiate. Nevertheless, I believe that the negativity towards these polities, and particularly the summary dismissal of their real achievements, cannot be isolated from a universal intellectual and political assault upon states and their nationalisms as such, and this returns me, by way of conclusion, to some of the broad themes with which I began.

The Demonisation of the State and Attendant Imperialist Agendas

If demonisation of the macro is a feature of both contemporary neo-modernisationist and postmodernist thought, or at least the demonisation of the macro in the form of any institution or project associated with the possibility of radical transformation, perhaps no institution has been as vilified or dismissed as the state. Many communitarian, feminist, and other theorists condemn the state and then banish it from discussion as they rush to embrace a minimalist approach to governance based on participation and participatory democracy at the micro, 'grassroots' level.[101] Numerous examples can be given: the development of a global economy, of capital without borders, Michael Sandel argues, spells the demise of the 'procedural republic'. Nation-states, the traditional vehicle for government, will find it difficult to bring their citizens' judgements to bear on economic forces. We must therefore foster local and not nationalist allegiances. The liberal state is inimical to communitarian citizenship, says Benjamin Barber. By aggregating people into one representative we reinforce their anonymity. We need new methods of communication, including electronic town hall meetings to bring people together and improve the circulation of civic information. The liberal state is an inadequate vehicle for citizenship, Mary Dietz argues, inasmuch as it sees citizenship as a state or a status, and not as an activity. It does not provide for self-government.[102] In the Middle East, Mohammed A. Bamyeh writes, solutions to conflicts require more regional integration, diffuse statehoods and sovereignties, and the 'pursuit of common prosperity rather than "ideology"'.[103] By weakening the nation-state, globalisation offers the opportunity to activate sources of social life long suppressed by nationalism.[104]

The tendency to confuse the cultural and the political through the invocation of the standard mantra of the hybrid, etc., is often, yet again, central to these and related intellectual strategies. In

Representations of the Intellectual, Said examines the works of Arab intellectuals in the West in the wake of the Gulf War in an effort to reveal the harm that results when an intellectual commits himself to the service of any sacrosanct identity. The disabling problem is that 'because you serve a god uncritically, all the devils are always on the other side'. Said recommends a critical thought that goes beyond sides. Instead of binary oppositions, one should 'think of politics in terms of interrelationships or of common histories such as, for instance, the long and complicated dynamic that has bound the Arabs and the Muslims to the West and vice versa'. He then adds, 'Real intellectual analysis forbids calling one side innocent, the other evil. Indeed, the notion of a side is, where cultures are at issue, highly problematic, since most cultures aren't watertight little packages, all homogeneous, and all either good or evil'. As Jonathan Arac points out, the complexity of culture is here invoked to criticise a political choice, with no sense that culture might more readily allow for ambivalence or polyphony than politics.[105] Whether one speaks of 'radicals' who emphasise public participation without a radical reconfiguration of the state itself, or 'radicals' who are uneasy with hard and fast positions in relation to the state or politics itself, we are left with a legitimisation of the liberal state as it currently exists and, more particularly, of the hegemony of the American state and its metropolitan allies.[106] 'In speaking of the weakening of the nation-state', Fredric Jameson asks, 'are we not actually describing the subordination of the other nation-states to American power, either through consent and collaboration, or by the use of brute force and economic threat?'[107] The answer is 'yes'.

In an article in *The New York Times* of 18 April 1999, Fareed Zakaria, the managing editor of *Foreign Affairs*, writes that the state has had a 'good run' since the Treaty of Westphalia. Nevertheless, in recent years the modern national leader has had to navigate through such restraints as interest rates, advocacy groups, and the international media, to say nothing of the broader realities attendant upon the end of the ideological conflicts of the twentieth century:

> There is one ideology left standing, liberal democratic capitalism, and one institution with universal reach, the United States. Not since the waning of Catholic power in the seventeenth century has one entity spread its values so widely. If the past is my guide, America's primacy will provoke

growing resistance. The twenty-first century may well bring a struggle between yet another universal system of values and national power.[108]

Here, the United States does not have 'national power'; it is not a 'nation-state'; it is an 'institution', an 'entity'. The terms 'nation-state' or 'national power' are reserved for others, the recalcitrant or those who might become so. There is not, of course, the slightest hint that democracy and capitalism, regarded as a single phenomenon and the primary ingredients of the 'universal system of values' promoted by the American 'entity', could ever find themselves at odds.

I was deeply disturbed to read the speech of the Secretary General of the United Nations, Kofi Annan, given on 7 April, 1999, and meant, obviously, to justify NATO's attacks against Yugoslavia, in which he argued that the rights of the world's peoples take precedence over those of sovereign states.[109] It does not take much political acumen to guess whose sovereignties – those of First or peripheral Third World states – are likely to be more expendable in the future. Nor should it take much political acumen to understand the extent to which American effort in support of liberal democracy and civil rights, often made selectively (congressmen are exercised over the rights of Christians in Egypt and the Sudan but not of Muslims and Christians in Israel), can contribute to, or be complicit with, the weakening of the sovereignty of the states of the periphery or even of the First World.[110] Such operations are part of a larger strategy in which, as I have indicated, a safe Islamism, liberal and/or of the petrol variety, coexists with communal fragmentations of other sorts. It is an old story, as a comparison between the views of Stratford Canning, British ambassador to Istanbul in the mid-nineteenth century, and a contemporary American diplomat in Europe, reveals. Canning was always demanding privileges for groups he was trying to constitute as para-national minorities while he was calling for equality before the law.[111] 'The religious field is now a priority of the US Government's private auxiliaries', says the US heir to Canning, 'because it offers doubly useful levers of influence. They [religious movements supported by the United States] are, on the one hand, powerful vectors for diffusing the principles of the market economy. Except for the old Catholic distrust of the accumulation of capital, most contemporary spiritual groups are objective allies of capitalism.

In addition the geo-political translation of religious beliefs suggests the atomisation and fragmentation of the arbitrary statist-nationalist configurations from the old colonial empires."[112]

The Continuing Relevance of Old Categories; the Continuing Relevance of Arab Nationalism

It is, as I have said, an old story, for which the old categories, capitalism, imperialism, the First World, the Third World, are as relevant as ever, despite all of the contemporary efforts to prove the contrary. In the so-called Gulf War, which could have been prevented if the United States had not decided to destroy Iraq's military and economic infrastructure, the allied coalition had about three hundred and fifty military casualties and Iraq between seventy thousand and a hundred and fifty thousand.[113] The OECD North, including, to be sure, Japan, still accounts for 85 per cent of world production and trade and that proportion is increasing. From 1975 to 1995, the world economy, East Asia apart, was in near stagnation. The contrast between Southern reality and the aspirations of all neo-liberal ideologies of development could hardly be starker.[114] Twenty million men, women and children are still dying every year of hunger and curable diseases. Some wealthy nations have an eighty-year life expectancy while poor ones have hardly forty.[115] There is nothing hybrid or ambiguous about these facts. Nor is there anything hybrid or ambiguous about some of the old solutions, the news of whose death, I trust, has been greatly exaggerated. I turn once again to Eagleton who, in this case as in so many others, can hardly be improved upon:

> If you do not know who you are in the West, postmodernism is on hand to tell you not to worry; if you do not know who you are in less well-heeled areas of the globe, you may need to create the conditions in which it becomes possible to find out. One traditional name of this inquiry has been revolutionary nationalism, which is not at all to the taste of postmodern theory. It represents, so to speak, particularity without hybridity, rather as cosmopolitanism might be described as the converse. There are some, in short, who can buy their anti-foundationalism on the cheap, just as there are some who, having worked their way through the agenda of modernity, can afford to be rather more sardonic about it than those who have not.[116]

There is no question that Arab nationalism has been seriously weakened in recent years, and that there are no prospects for significant institutional unity to be achieved in the near future. The traditional state structures remain standing, and the coherence of even these structures is, in some cases, being challenged by newly discovered ethnicities, localisms, and other group identities which are often celebrated as offering a liberating diffusion.

However, even if Arab nationalism were now truly dead, its sheer longevity at both a popular and ruling class level, and its contributions to eminently rational and progressive integrative and modernising achievements, provide powerful support to the contention (with which I began) that nationalism has been as modular in the Islamic world as it has been anywhere else, and that it has not differed essentially from the contractual, civic nationalism that is said to characterise the nationalism of the West.

Nevertheless, and apart from our evaluation of the significance of Arab nationalism in the past, the truth is that Arab nationalism is *not* dead. The factors making for Arab unity, and a unity that could be drawn upon for a truly transformative project, are far from spent, and these include the growing multi-level and intense interconnectedness of the Arab core.[117] As the popular support shown to Iraq at the time of the Gulf War or to the second Palestinian intifada demonstrates, the Arab system is 'a vast sound chamber in which information, ideas, and opinions have resonated with little regard for state frontiers'.[118] Within this vast chamber, one is struck by the extent to which a sense of common Arab identity, and the belief in the potential of unitary movements based on this identity, retain a central place among a great many Arab intellectuals and activists. The well-known Syrian theorist Burhan Ghalyun, for example, does not believe that the establishment of democracy will have truly important results if it does not transcend local entities and serve to create a link between a common cultural identity and polity. And another eminent theorist, the Moroccan Mohammed 'Abed al-Jabiri, also believes that democracy will facilitate Arab unity in that most Arab citizens, given their growing cultural and economic ties, would choose to create a larger and more viable state. Whatever one thinks of the various arguments of these and other contemporary Arab nationalists (a number of them, alas, are not immune

to their own fetishisation of the 'civic'), the fact remains that Arab
nationalism is very much alive. As Ahmed Abdalla notes, the question to be asked about Arab nationalism is not its date of death but
rather its interactive relationship with pan-Islamism and forms of
local nationalism. Many Arab Islamists, nationalists who place primary emphasis on the nationalism of individual Arab countries,
and pan-Arab nationalists, are highly conscious of the 'composite'
dimensions of character, but not in such a way as to accept the fragmentation of their world as a given of nature or fate.[119] One should
here also note that once the effects of the petroleum era have declined, and the structural adjustment programmes promoted by the
American-dominated IMF and World Bank have taken their full toll,
class realities and contradictions (and the global socio-economic
structures behind them) are bound to become more distinct, and
may inspire, once again, political struggles that give priority to issues
defined in socio-economic rather than cultural and religious terms.
One cannot discount the possibility of the revival of significant left
national movements which position themselves against liberal and
petrol-Islam but which are committed to democracy and a secularism that is nevertheless inclusive and sensitive to cultural (including
Islamic) environments.[120]

The works of theorists such as Ghalyun and 'Abed al-Jabiri, but
also the works of more specialised academic scholars, do not lose
sight of two persisting Arab realities: one constant and homogenising
and arising from within, and the other decentering, more episodic,
often supported by foreign favour, and, more recently, by structural
conditions that contribute to transforming sectarian and ethnic differences into communal incompatibilities.[121] If greater economic and
political unity have not been achieved, this does not mean that the
significance of the homogenising trend has been exaggerated. In a
recent work on the relationship of Arabism and Islamism to the Palestinian cause from 1908 to the early 1940s, Nafi illustrates the way in
which a divided Arab leadership identified more and more intensely
with individual regional states, to the point that the Arab unity movement came to imply regional state ambition and self-affirmation.
At the same time, however, he recognises that 'imperialist interests
were decisive' in preserving the post-First World War Arab order, that
the 'versatility and resources of the Arab interwar generation were

certainly beyond doubt', and that their achievements in reconstituting an Arab entity and expressing a fairly defined Arab national voice after the collapse of the Ottomans were 'no less impressive'.[122] In an effort to show that the later split between Arab nationalism and Islamism was not foreordained, Nafi may have underplayed the role of Christians among the Arabists (he does not mention, for example, the Coptic Wafdist leader Makram 'Ubayd, a pioneer of Arab nationalism in Egypt during the 1930s and 1940s). Nevertheless, Nafi has been able to accommodate both the homogenising and the decentering because he has not essentialised either, whether in terms of an eternally constituted Islam or an eternally constituted mosaic. He and many others resist the powerful intellectual fashions of the moment, the powerful influence of certain contemporary realities that give force to these fashions and their neo-Orientalist content, and the imperialist interests, regardless of the conscious intentions of individual scholars, that these fashions serve.

Notes

1. Reinhard Schulze, *A Modern History of the Islamic World* (New York, 2000), p. 7.

2. This section on the Islamic territorial states as part of a world of nations system is based on Nazih Ayubi, *Political Islam: Religion and Politics in the Arab World* (London, 1991), p. 122.

3. Olivier Roy, *The Failure of Political Islam*, tr. Carol Volk (Cambridge, MA, 1994), pp. 129–131.

4. Joel Gordon, 'Secular and Religious Memory in Egypt: Recalling Nasserist Civics', *MW*, 87, 2 (1997), p. 98.

5. Ibid., pp. 94–99.

6. Fred Halliday, *Nation and Religion in the Middle East* (Boulder, CO, 2000), p. 133.

7. Judith Nagata, 'Islamic Ethnonationalism versus Religious Transnationalism: Nation Building and Islam in Malaysia', *MW*, 87, 2 (1997), p. 130.

8. Ibid., p. 134.

9. Ibid., pp. 134–135.

10. Ibid., p. 139.

11. Hamza Alavi, 'Ethnicity, Muslim Society, and the Pakistan Ideology', in Anita M. Weiss, ed., *Islamic Reassertion in Pakistan: The Application of Islamic Laws in a Modern State* (Syracuse, NY, 1986), p. 43, quoted in Dale F. Eickel-

man and James Piscatori, *Muslim Politics* (Princeton, NJ, 1996), p. 103.

12. Akbar S. Ahmed and Donnan Hastings, *Islam, Globalization, and Post-Modernity* (London, 1994), pp. xi–xii, quoted in Eickelman and Piscatori, *Muslim Politics,* p.103.

13. The remarks within this section are deeply indebted to Fred Halliday, *Revolution and World Politics: The Rise and Fall of the Sixth Great Power* (Durham, 1999), and Halliday, *Nation and Religion.*

14. See, in particular, Halliday, *Nation and Religion,* pp. 49–50.

15. Halliday, *Revolution and World Politics,* pp. 150–151.

16. Halliday, *Nation and Religion,* pp. 49–50; and *Revolution and World Politics,* pp. 148–149.

17. Halliday, *Revolution and World Politics,* p. 149.

18. Ibid., p. 150.

19. Ibid., p. 151.

20. Halliday, *Nation and Religion,* p. 33.

21. Aziz Al-Azmeh, *Islams and Modernities* (London, 1993), p. 24.

22. Armando Salvatore, *Islam and the Political Discourse of Modernity* (Reading, 1997), pp. 67–79.

23. Ibid., p. 67.

24. See Halim Barakat, *The Arab World: Society, Culture and State* (Berkeley, CA, 1993), pp. 13, 119–147.

25. See Salvatore, *Islam and the Political Discourse,* especially pp. 97–112.

26. Claude Levi-Strauss, *Tristes Tropiques,* tr. John and Doreen Weightman (New York, 1992), pp. 344–345.

27. Salvatore, *Islam and the Political Discourse,* p. 97. Salvatore is particularly indebted to Bryan S. Turner, *Weber and Islam: A Critical Study* (London, 1974).

28. Salvatore, *Islam and the Political Discourse,* p. 48.

29. For a discussion of the 'mosaic' model, see Barakat, *The Arab World,* pp. 6–11.

30. Salvatore, *Islam and the Political Discourse,* p. 21.

31. Jeffrey C. Alexander, 'Modern, Anti, Post, Neo', *New Left Review,* 210 (1995), pp. 80–84.

32. See Carl Boggs, *The End of Politics: Corporate Power and the Decline of the Public Sphere* (New York, 2000), pp. 208–243.

33. Terry Eagleton, 'Where Do Post-Modernists Come From?' *The Monthly Review,* 47, 3 (1995), pp. 59–70.

34. Joseph Horowitz, 'A Journey through the Bleakest of Winters', *The New York Times* (12 December, 1999), pp. 52–53.

35. Quoted by Lindsay Waters, 'In Responses begins Reponsibility: Music and Emotion', in Paul A. Bove, ed., *Edward Said and the Work of the Critic:*

Speaking Truth to Power (Durham, 2000), pp. 105–106. The reference comes from Edward W. Said, *Musical Elaborations* (New York, 1991), p. 105.

36. Boggs, *The End of Politics,* p. 209.

37. Bill Ashcroft and Pal Ahluwalia, *Edward Said: The Paradox of Identity* (London, 1999), p. 72. The quote is from Edward W. Said, *The World, the Text, and the Critic* (Cambridge, MA, 1993), p. 245.

38. From an interview with Jacqueline Rose, 'Edward Said Talks to Jacqueline Rose', in Bove, ed., *Edward Said,* p. 23.

39. Aijaz Ahmad, *In Theory: Classes, Nations and Literatures* (London, 1992), p. 113.

40. Alexander, 'Modern, Anti, Post, Neo', pp. 84–90.

41. Boggs, *The End of Politics,* pp. 209–222.

42. Terry Eagleton, *The Idea of Culture* (Oxford, 2000), p. 43.

43. See Al-Azmeh, *Islams and Modernities,* pp. 122–145.

44. Ernest Gellner, *Postmodernism, Reason, and Religion* (London, 1992), p. 5.

45. Ernest Gellner, *Encounters with Nationalism* (Oxford, 1994), p. 180.

46. Conor Cruise O'Brien, *The Times* (May 11, 1989), quoted in Akbar S. Ahmed, *Postmodernism and Islam* (London, 1992), p. 188.

47. Quoted in Fred Halliday, *Islam and the Myth of Confrontation* (London, 1996), p. 184.

48. Pat Buchanan, 'Rising Islam May Overwhelm the West', *New Hampshire Sunday News* (20 August, 1989). Quoted in Halliday, *Islam and the Myth of Confrontation,* p. 183.

49. See Salvatore, *Islam and the Political Discourse,* pp. 133–163.

50. Al-Azmeh. *Islams and Modernities,* p. 20.

51. Bernard Lewis, 'The Return of Islam', *Commentary* (January, 1976), p. 49, quoted in Salvatore, *Islam and the Political Discourse,* p. 142.

52. Yvonne Y. Haddad, 'Middle East Studies: Current Concerns and Future Directions', *MESA Bulletin,* 25:1–12. Quoted in Salvatore, *Islam and the Political Discourse,* p. 145.

53. For a discussion of Acton and Kohn, see Youssef Choueiri, *Arab Nationalism: A History* (Oxford, 2000), pp. 1–14.

54. Liah Greenfield and C. Chirot, 'Nationalism and Aggression', *Theory and Society,* 47, 3 (1995), pp. 59–70.

55. Liah Greenfield, *Nationalism: Five Roads to Modernity* (Cambridge, MA, 1992), p. 484.

56. For an engaging discussion of the role of election in bourgeois democracies, see Peter Gran, *Beyond Eurocentrism: A New View of World History* (Syracuse, NY, 1986), pp. 52–54.

57. Tom Nairn, 'Breakwaters of 2000: From Ethnic to Civic Nationalism',

New Left Review, 214 (1995), pp. 91–103.

58. This summary of Kedourie is based on Choueiri, *Arab Nationalism,* pp. 6–8.

59. Elie Kedourie, 'Pan-Arabism and British Policy', in Kedourie, *Chatham House Version and Other Middle Eastern Essays* (London, 1970), pp. 218.

60. See, for example, P. J. Vatikiotis, *The History of Modern Egypt* (Baltimore, MD, 1992), p. 244.

61. For a superb review of the book by Karsh and Karsh, upon which my summary relies, see Charles D. Smith, 'A Review of Karsh, Efraim, and Karsh, Inari, *Empires of the Sand: The Struggle for Mastery in the Middle East, 1789–1923* (Cambridge, MA, 1999) in *IJMES,* 32, 4 (2000), pp. 559–564.

62. See Martin Kramer, *Arab Awakening and Islamic Revival* (New Brunswick, NJ, 1996), pp. 3–5, 9, 23, 45, 48.

63. From audios by 'Abdullah 'Azzam, quoted in Immanuel Sivan, 'Arab Nationalism in the Age of Islamic Resurgence', in James Jankowski and Israel Gershoni, ed., *Rethinking Nationalism in the Arab Middle East* (New York, 1997), p. 211. Mustafa al-Fiqi argues that the split between Arabists and Islamists can be traced to the anti-nationalist positions of the Egyptian Sayyid Qutb and the Pakistani Abu al-A'la Mawdudi. See Mustafa al-Fiqi, *Tajdid al-fikr al-qawmi* (Cairo, 1995), pp. 11–18.

64. From audios by Yusuf al-'Azm quoted in Sivan, 'Arab Nationalism', pp. 211–212.

65. Rashid Khalidi, *Palestinian Identity: The Construction of Modern National Consciousness* (New York, 1997), pp. 182–184.

66. Amira el-Azhary Sonbol, *The New Mamluks: Egyptian Society and Modern Feudalism* (Syracuse, NY, 2000).

67. See Bassam Tibi, *Arab Nationalism: A Critical Inquiry* (New York, 1981), and 'On Contemporary Arab Thought: Descriptive Writing and Revolutionary Writing', *Mawaqif,* 3 (1969), pp. 96. Quoted in Fouad Ajami, *The Arab Predicament: Arab Political Thought and Practice since 1967* (Cambridge, 1981), pp. 28–29.

68. Hazim Saghiyya, *Qawmiyyu mashriq al-'Arabi: min Durayfus ila Gharudi* (Beirut, 2000). Many examples of Saghiyya's determination to think the worst on the basis of unconvincing evidence and interpretations could be cited. He argues, for example, that the Christian liberal Arab nationalist Constantine Zureik exaggerated Jewish and Zionist power in the United States in 1948 and that this exaggeration is reflective of an alleged anti-Semitic strain in his thought. Saghiyya maintains that Zureik did not take note of the anti-Semitism that existed in the United States, particularly in the post-Second World War period, when it was linked to anti-communism (Saghiyya cites the Rosenberg case). This is not much of an argument at

all, for anti-Semitism and Jewish and Zionist power can clearly coexist. A large number of studies, by Zionists and non-Zionists, testify to the strong influence of the Zionist lobby, mediated through financial contributions and the promise of electoral support, on Truman in 1948. See, for example, Michael Cohen, *Truman and Israel* (Berkeley, CA, 1990).

69. William D. Hart, *Edward Said and the Religious Effects of Culture* (Cambridge, MA, 2000), p. 42.

70. Ibid., p. 61.

71. Edward W. Said, *Reflections on Exile and Other Essays* (Cambridge, MA, 2000), p. 176.

72. Alexander, 'Modern, Anti, Post, Neo', pp. 92–93. The quote from Said is taken from 'A Tragic Convergence', *New York Times* (11 January, 1991).

73. Ali Abdallatif Ahmida, ed., *Beyond Colonialism and Nationalism in the Maghrib: History, Culture and Politics* (New York, 2000), p. 1.

74. James Jankowski and Israel Gershoni, ed., *Rethinking Nationalism in the Arab Middle East* (New York, 1997).

75. Ibid., p. xxiv.

76. Ibid., pp. xxiii–xxiv.

77. See Sami Zubaida, 'Muslim Societies: Unity or Diversity?' *ISIM Newsletter* (October, 1998), p. 1, and Ahmida, *Beyond Colonialism*, p. 6.

78. See Roxanne L. Euben, *Enemy in the Mirror: Islamic Fundamentalism and the Limits of Modern Rationalism, a Work of Comparative Political Theory* (Princeton, NJ, 1999).

79. See Halliday, *Islam and the Myth of Confrontation*, pp. 107–132.

80. Al-Azmeh, *Islams and Modernities*, p. 32.

81. Jean Comaroff and John L. Comaroff, 'Millennial Capitalism: First Thoughts on a Second Coming', *Public Culture*, 12, 2 (2000), pp. 291–343.

82. See Schulze, *A Modern History*, p. 289. He discusses the way the Taliban were able to overcome the internal tribal segmentation and fragmentation of the Pashtus to forge a unity against all non-Pashtu groups, especially the Dari and Tadzhik speakers. Success was guaranteed whenever 'the population could conform to a Pashtu group identity'.

83. Ibid., p. 3, and Zubaida, 'Muslim Societies', p. 1.

84. This discussion of civil society and civic nationalism is indebted to Ellen Meiksins Wood, *Democracy against Capitalism: Reviewing Historical Materialism* (Cambridge, 1995), and Bernard Yack, 'The Myth of the Civic Nation', *Critical Review*, 10, 2 (1996), p. 208. For discussion of the concept with particular reference to the Arab-Islamic context, see 'Azmi Bishara, *al-Mujtama' al-madani: dirasa naqdiyya* (2nd ed., Beirut, 2000); and Nayif Salum, 'al-Mujtama al-madani: al-mafhum wa awdatuh', *al-Nahj*, 26 (2001), pp. 244–252. Salum neatly summarises the influence of the various theoretical

perspectives I have discussed, including the idea of the end of history and ideology (which means the end of practice and a philosophy of change or transformation), the idea of a conflict of civilisations (instead of classes), and the idea of a 'civil society' (instead of a bourgeois one).

85. James L. Gelvin, *Divided Loyalties: Nationalism and Mass Politics in Syria at the Close of Empire* (Berkeley, CA, 1998), pp. 11, 16–17, 159–160, 218, 290 and 295.

86. Elie Kedourie, 'Not So Grand Illusions', *The New York Review of Books,* 8–9 (23 November, 1967), pp. 31–32.

87. Aziz Al-Azmeh, 'Nationalism and the Arabs', *Arab Studies Quarterly,* 17, 1–2 (1995), p. 5.

88. Ibid., p. 4. For a fine overview of the common components of Middle Eastern popular culture, see Sami Zubaida, *Islam, the People and the State* (London, 1989), pp. 99–120.

89. Miroslav Hroch, 'Real and Constructed: The Nature of the Nation', in John A. Hall, ed., *The State of the Nation: Ernest Gellner and the Theory of Nationalism* (Cambridge, 1998), p. 9.

90. 'Abd al-Rahman al-Jabarti, *'Aja'ib al-athar fi'l-tarajim wa'l-akhbar* (Beirut, n.d.), vol. 1, pp. 14–15 and 440–466, and Ibn Taymiyya, *Iqtida' al-sirat al-mustaqim* (Beirut, n.d.), p. 145. Cited in Choueiri, *Arab Nationalism,* pp. 67 and 74. In the 17th century a struggle broke out between Egyptians and Turks over the control of guilds. In the course of the struggle, which we know of from an Egyptian manuscript from the period, the Egyptians argued that the shaykhs of the guilds should be from the 'sons of the Arabs' (*abna' al-'Arab*) because they are 'superior' and 'only the Arabs possess learning and eloquence'. See Gabriel Baer, *The Egyptian Guilds in Modern Times* (Jerusalem, 1964), pp. 14–15.

91. See Richard Labeviere, *Dollars for Terror: The United States and Islam,* tr. Martin de Mers (New York, 2000), for an overview of American efforts to create, support, and manage Islamic and other religious movements and identities to the US' advantage. One should here note that the attraction of 'liberal Islam' is widespread in various contexts. In the Islamic world there are intense intellectual efforts being made to disassociate Islam from utopian and revolutionary claims, to construe a cultural Islam in which free markets, media interlinks, civil rights defined in bourgeois terms, and the rule of law and 'civil society' are institutionalised. See Schulze, *A Modern History,* pp. 281–292.

One Western scholar of 'Islamic liberalism' apparently feels that it is the best Westerners can hope for from a world so terribly unwelcoming to liberalism as such: 'It is impossible to isolate the middle classes from the impoverished, traditional and ignorant mass upon whom they depend for vital and daily services ...'. The lowest class weighs upon Middle Eastern society heavily, and so it is difficult to escape 'their massive, glacial and pitiable presence'. However, the further development of the Muslim bourgeoisie, the elaboration of 'Islamic liberalism', and the 'attrition of state autonomy', provide hope. See Leonard Binder, *Islamic Liberalism: A Critique of Development Ideologies* (Chicago, 1988), p. 359.

Contemporary flirtation with liberal and other forms of Islamic politics is not unrelated to American policy towards Arab integration more generally. While the United States offers mild support for co-ordination among the small and vulnerable 'good guys' of the Gulf, its general preference is for small separate units, among the good as well as the 'rogues'. See Michael Hudson, 'Arab Integration: An Overview', in Michael Hudson, ed., *Middle East Dilemmas: The Politics and Economics of Arab Integration* (New York, 1999), p. 18.

The abandonment of revolution among a large number of Islamists has its parallels among secular Marxists. For many of the latter, whatever hope they may still harbour for the distant future, the idea of eliminating the capitalist mode of production has given way to controlling and mitigating its effects by working through its civic institutions (the trade unions, professional syndicates, and the universities and schools). A telling example is perhaps provided by the Syrian Sadiq Jalal al-Azm in his recent *Ma hiya al-'awlama?*: 'Those who have attempted to change the world among us are many but it appears to me that what is necessary at this point is to understand the world and interpret it in a better way, perhaps before it is too late.' Hasan Hanafi and Sadiq Jalal al-Azm, *Ma hiya al-'awlama?* (Damascus, 1999), p. 61.

For a brilliant discussion of why significant Arab political unity has not been achieved, see Nazih N. Ayubi, *Over-stating the Arab State: Politics and Society in the Middle East* (London, 1997), pp. 135–158.

92. See Ralph M. Coury, *The Making of an Egyptian Arab Nationalist: The Early Years of Azzam Pasha, 1893–1936* (Reading, 1998), pp. 407–472.

93. Aziz Al-Azmeh, 'Populism contra Democracy: Recent Democratist Discourse in the Arab World', in Ghassan Salamé, ed., *Democracy without Democrats? The Renewal of Politics in the Muslim World* (London, 1994), pp. 112–129.

94. See Al-Azmeh, 'Nationalism and the Arabs', *passim.*

95. 'Abd al-'Aziz al-Duri, *al-Takwin al-ta'rikhi li'l-umma al-'Arabiyya: dirasa fi'l-huwiyya wa'l-wa'i* (Beirut, 1984), and al-Shaykh 'Abdullah al-'Alayili, *Dustur al-'Arab al-qawmi* (2nd ed., Beirut, 1996), first published in 1941. Choueiri, *Arab Nationalism,* provides an informative overview of these and comparable works. See, also, Wajih Kawtharani, *al-Ta'rikh wa madarisuhu fi'l-gharb wa 'inda al-'Arab: madkhal ila 'ilm al-ta'rikh.* (Beirut, 2000), vol. 1, pp. 115–120.

96. Choueiri, *Arab Nationalism,* pp. 100–124. Al-Azmeh, too, points to al-Husri's positivism and his critique of 'Aflaq's metaphysics. See Al-Azmeh, *Islams and Modernities,* p. 43.

97. Al-Azmeh, 'Nationalism and the Arabs', p. 6. See also, Wajih Kawtharani, *al-Ittijahat al-ijtima'iyya wa'l-siyasiyya fi Jabal Lubnan wa'l-mashriq al-'Arabi: min al-mutasarafiyya al-'Uthmaniyya ila dawlat Lubnan al-kabir* (Beirut, 1986), and *al-Sulta wa'l-mujtama' wa'l-'amal al-siyasi: min ta'rikh al-wilaya al-'Uthmaniyya fi Bilad al-Sham* (Beirut, 1988); and Mahmoud Haddad, 'The Rise of Arab Nationalism Reconsidered', *IJMES,* 26, 2 (1994).

98. Choueiri, *Arab Nationalism,* p. 66.

99. Ibid., p. 25.

100. Eagleton, *The Idea of Culture,* p. 150.

101. These observations, and several of the examples that follow, are based on Keally McBride, 'Citizens without States? On the Limits of Participatory Theory', *New Political Science: A Journal of Politics and Culture,* 22, 4 (2000), pp. 507–527.

102. Ibid., pp. 513, 515, and 525. Works by Sandel, Barber, and Deitz, as well as many others, are described in McBride's article.

103. Mohammed A. Bamyeh, *The Ends of Globalization* (Minneapolis, 2000), p. 153.

104. Ibid., p. 151.

105. See Jonathan Arac, 'Criticism Beyond Opposition and Counterpoint', in Bove, ed., *Edward Said,* pp. 68–69. The passage from Said comes from Edward Said, *Representations of the Intellectual* (New York, 1994), p. 119.

106. See McBride, 'Citizens', pp. 526–527, for this legitimisation. McBride does not deal with the international dimension.

107. Fredric Jameson, 'Globalization and Political Strategy', *New Left Review,* 4 (2000), p. 4.

108. Fareed Zakaria, 'The Empire Strikes Out: The Unholy Emergence of the Nation State', *The New York Times Magazine* (April 18, 1999), p. 99.

109. *Watchlist* (16 April, 1999).

110. For the implications of a law passed by the United States Congress allowing the American government to place penalties on foreign governments that do not guarantee religious freedom, see Basheer M. Nafi, 'Nizam jadid li'l-'alaqat al-duwaliyya aw imbiriyaliyya bi wajh mubtakar', *al-Quds al-Arabi* (May 26, 1999), p. 19. See also, Bruno Fouchereau, 'Au nom de la Liberté religieuse: Les sectes cheval de Troie des Etats-Unis en Europe', *Le Monde diplomatique,* 48, 566 (2001), pp. 1 and 26; and Samir Murqus, *al-Himaya wa'l-'iqab: al-Gharb wa'l-mas'ala al-diniyya fi'l sharq al-awsat* (Cairo, 2000).

111. Al-Azmeh, 'Nationalism and the Arabs', p. 14.

112. The anonymous diplomat is quoted in Labeviere, *Dollars for Terror*, p. 197.

113. See Norman G. Finkelstein, 'Middle East Watch and the Gulf War', *Z Magazine* (September, 1992), pp. 15–19.

114. See Michael Manning, 'As the Twentieth Century Ages', *New Left Review*, 214 (November/December, 1995), pp. 116–120.

115. Fidel Castro, 'Speech to the U.N. General Assembly, October 22, 1995', *Covert Action Quarterly*, 55 (1995–96), p. 40. Discussions of globalisation as an enhancement of the imperialism of the capitalist core are common to contemporary Arab and Muslim criticism. See Jalal Amin, *al-'Awlama wa'l-tanmiyya al-'arabiyya min hamlat Nabulyun ila jawlat al-Urughway 1798–1998* (Beirut, 1999), and *al-Tanwir al-za'if* (Cairo, 1999); and Mahmud Amin al-'Alim, *Min naqd al-hadir ila ibda' al-mustaqbal: musahama fi bina' al-mashru' al-nahdawi al-'Arabi* (Cairo, 2000).

116. Eagleton, *The Idea of Culture*, pp. 75–76.

117. See Bahgat Korany, 'The Arab World and a New Balance of Power', in Hudson, *Middle East*, p. 57.

118. Paul Noble, 'The Arab System: Pressures, Constraints, and Opportunities', in Bahgat Korany, et al., ed., *The Foreign Policies of Arab States* (Boulder, CO, 1991), pp. 47–48. The passage from Noble is quoted in Korany, 'The Arab World and a New Balance of Power', p. 57.

119. For an array of views on future Arab nationalist possibilities, see Burhan Ghalyun, *al-Mihna al-'Arabiyya: al-dawla did al-umma* (Beirut, 1994); Muhammad 'Abid al-Jabiri, *Mas'alat al-huwiyya: al-'uruba wa'l-Islam wa'l-gharb* (Beirut, 1997); Choueiri, *Arab Nationalism*, pp. 205–218; Butrus al-Hallaq, ed., *Mas'alat al-qawmiyya 'ala masharif al-alf al-thalith: dirasat muhdah ila Antun Maqdisi* (Beirut, 1988); Ahmed Abdalla, 'The Egyptian National Identity and PanArabism: Variations and Generations', in Roel Meijer, ed., *Cosmopolitanism, Identity and Authenticity in the Middle East* (Richmond, UK, 1999), pp. 171–182; al-'Alim, *Min naqd*; al-Fiqi, *Tajdid al-fikr*. The publications of the Markaz Dirasat al-Wahda al-Arabiyya (Beirut) offer rich and detailed records of contemporary thinking.

120. A broader discussion of these possibilities is found in Ayubi's finely wrought study of political Islam. See Ayubi, *Political Islam: Religion and Politics in the Arab World*, *passim* and especially pp. 214–238; see also 'Abd al-Ghaffar Shukr, ed., *al-Yasar al-'arabi wa qadaya al-mustaqbal* (Cairo, 1998).

121. Al-Azmeh summarises the two trends with characteristic intelligence. See al-Azmeh, 'Nationalism and the Arabs', p. 16.

122. Basheer M. Nafi, *Arabism, Islamism, and the Palestine Question, 1908–1941* (Reading, 1998), pp. 395–396.

On the State,
Democracy and Pluralism

Abdelwahab El-Affendi

Modern attitudes towards democracy and pluralism in the Muslim world have been shaped by a series of seminal debates that erupted early in the twentieth century. These debates, many of which are still ongoing, had been provoked by major events and developments in Muslim political life, including Iran's constitutional revolution (1905–1911), the Young Turks revolution in Turkey (1908) and its sequel, the Kemalist revolution of 1919–1923, and the abolition of the *khilafa* (caliphate) in 1924. The *khilafa* debate was, in a sense, 'the mother of all debates' in modern Islamic political thought, marking what one writer described as 'the apogee of a long period of intellectual ferment among Muslims which had started at the end of the eighteenth century'.[1] Like other debates, it has taken place against the background of certain 'facts on the ground' regarding the emergence of national movements, political feuds, democratic aspirations, new institutions and rival reform projects. This is a pivotal factor that is often neglected when Islamic thinking on democracy is being discussed and evaluated. The *khilafa* debate in Egypt, for example, could not be isolated from ongoing contests over the status of the monarchy, Egypt's own transitional status following its separation from the Ottoman Empire and its quest for full independence from Britain, and the evolving alignment of rival political and social forces.[2] In India, it became intertwined with nationalist agitation and later the debate over Pakistan. The Palestinian struggle also played a pivotal role in these debates, and the personalities and movements engaged in the struggle were also key players in other contests.[3]

The conception actors had of democracy had also been directly influenced by the historical context. Early activists were impressed by the perceived achievements of Western democracies, especially when compared to their own experience of despotic rule at home. Thus while the precise parameters of democratic governance may have not been fully grasped, the early and intuitive inclination of most reformers was to champion democratic (or, to be more precise, constitutional) reforms. However, the resulting ferment released centrifugal forces and tendencies that came into conflict, in particular generating the tension between democracy and secularism that remains the dominant feature of Muslim politics to this day.

Constitutionalism

Early debates and political experiments in Muslim lands were focused more on constitutionalism than on democracy. The concern was not to effect the widest political participation, but to limit the authority of rulers, establish the rule of law and ensure that influential groups in society were incorporated into the governing system. (This, incidentally, was the same trajectory that democratisation had taken in Europe and the United States.) The common denominator of early experiments with constitutionalism (Tunisia in 1861, Egypt in 1868, the Ottoman state 1876) was that they were imposed from above, did not involve any real transfer of power, and were often very unpopular or soon became so.[4] The Constitutional Revolution of 1906 in Iran, by contrast, involved the first modern-style mass action any Muslim country has experienced, with agitation from below, not reforms from above, dictating the pace of change. It featured a grand coalition of the indigenous business community (the bazaar), modern intellectuals, and the ulama.[5] The nature of this alliance was reflected in the new constitution, modelled on the Belgian one, but incorporating provisions recognising Twelver Shi'ism as the official religion and stipulating a five-man committee of 'supreme *mujtahids*'

to scrutinise all legislation passed by the National Assembly and ensure conformity to sharia.[6] However, rifts soon began to appear in
this coalition, as the liberals who took control of the assembly alienated the masses by harsh economic measures and the promotion of
an overt secularist agenda. Misgivings over such provisions as the
equality of all citizens, the drive towards women's education and
secularist reforms caused some conservative ulama, led by Shaykh
Fazlullah Nuri, to reverse initial support for the constitutional movement and rise up against the Assembly.[7] Although the constitution-
alists managed to keep enough popular support to win the civil war
and secure the constitution, foreign intervention and national disintegration put an end to this pioneering experiment.

The Iranian revolution set the agenda and the main themes that
would characterise the ensuing debates on democracy and pluralism. Support for constitutionalism from the ulama, in particular
among the *usuli* tendency that emphasised reason and *ijtihad*, was
both genuine and indispensable for the success of the revolution.[8]
Ulama support declined, however, when democratic themes came
to prominence and pluralism, especially religious pluralism, began
to be championed by secular forces. As the National Assembly began
to justify its authority as 'the representative of the whole People',
and to make proposals for electoral reform to widen the franchise
and include representatives of religious minorities,[9] the fragility of
the initial consensus became apparent.

The *khilafa* Debate

Nationalism, rather than democracy, was the dominant theme of
the Young Turk revolution of 1908, and the cause of the alienation
of sections of the traditional elite in non-Turkish regions who wanted to safeguard the Ottoman Empire as a constitutional polity, but
were put off by the aggressive nationalism of the Young Turks.[10] The
resultant collapse of the empire was the trigger for the debate on
the *khilafa*, as the Khilafat Movement, established in India in 1919,
was joined by others in the campaign against the Grand National
Assembly's decision to depose the Sultan and establish a papal style
non-executive caliphate in 1922. The tone of the debate was set in a
1922 book published by the Grand National Assembly entitled 'The

Caliphate and the Authority of the Community', and a subsequent lengthy intervention in the Assembly by Mustafa Kemal himself.[11] The argument was that the *khilafa* was not a religiously sanctified institution, but a mere expedient and context-dependent form of governance, which existed most of the time as a fiction camouflaging despotic rule. It is impossible to revive, as Muslim unity is no longer feasible, while a properly qualified caliph would be difficult to find or to accept as ruler. In any case, the idea of one-man absolute rule is no longer appropriate, as the people insist on a popularly legitimised and accountable authority and reject autocratic rule. Mustafa Kemal added that the Turkish nation could not be expected to shoulder the burden of a pan-Islamic institution on its own and against its own interests in the absence of support from other Muslims.[12]

For the pro-*khilafa* campaigners, Muhammad Rashid Rida (1865–1935) sought to refute these claims in a riposte serialised in *al-Manar* and later published as a book. The *khilafa*, Rida argued, 'is the greatest interest for the umma as a whole, and does not exist without the sword and power'. Its establishment is a religious obligation on all Muslims, and not merely a rational and utilitarian expedient, as the Mu'tazilites and others had earlier argued.[13] Rida concedes the Kemalist point that the genuine *khilafa* had existed only for a very brief period (the thirty years of the Righteous Caliphate), leaving the field for the '*khilafa* of necessity', or of 'coercion'. But this did not justify the scrapping of the institution altogether, as the system has its own inbuilt corrective mechanisms, mainly the proactive role of *ahl al-hall wa'l-'aqd* (community leaders, those who 'loose and bind'), whose central role must be revived as the electors of the caliph, guarantors of people's freedoms and rights and guardians of the implementation of sharia. The debate was later joined by many others. The contribution of shaykh 'Ali 'Abd al-Raziq (1887–1966), an Egyptian sharia judge and Azhari graduate, received great attention because of the status of his 1925 book *al-Islam wa usul al-hukm* as a cause célèbre, but his input was not that significant. 'Abd al-Raziq argued the caliphate was on the whole a despotic and repressive institution harmful to the umma, which could not be justified by reference to basic Islamic teachings or texts.[14] The Prophet's mission was a purely spiritual one, and his political experience and that of his successors need not be regarded as normative or indicative.

Muslims should thus be free to adopt whatever system of governance reason and the experiences of other nations suggest is the best and more suitable.[15] In spite of the storm 'Abd al-Raziq's work provoked (he was condemned by al-Azhar and stripped of his status as *'alim*, which meant the automatic loss of his job as judge),[16] the main contribution of his work was to restrict the debate and reaffirm the traditional stance with minor modifications, and thus contribute to the ongoing intellectual stagnation.[17] Dwelling as he did on dubious theological arguments and questionable historical assertions,[18] 'Abd al-Raziq actually wanted to make the simple point, made earlier more coherently by the Turkish Grand National Assembly, that Muslims were free to choose the form of government they wanted, which should preferably be democratic. This was not entirely clear from his book, but one could infer this from later remarks, like his praise of King Fuad I as 'the first Muslim king in Egypt to become a constitutional monarch, and [to support] the principles of freedom in his country'.[19]

The Indian philosopher and poet, Muhammad Iqbal (d. 1937), presented the case even more coherently when he commended the Turkish move to vest the *khilafa* in an elected assembly rather than an individual as a 'perfectly sound' *ijtihad*.[20] While Iqbal did express misgivings about Western democracy and its suitability for Muslims, or for multi-cultural societies in general, he argued that the 'republican form of government was not only thoroughly consistent with the spirit of Islam, but has also become a necessity in view of the new forces that are set free in the world of Islam'.[21] The road to the restoration of the *khilafa*, and with it the unity of the umma must come at the end of a quest for national independence and identity, and take the form of a 'league of nations', a commonwealth of autonomous national entities.[22]

From *khilafa* to Islamic State

It is ironic, as has been noted by many observers, that the critics of both the Grand National Assembly and other opponents of immediate restoration of the *khilafa* have actually conceded many of their arguments. In particular they conceded the point that the *khilafa* that existed for most of Islamic history was not what it claimed to be, and had become almost impossible to revive under the prevalent circumstances.[23] Most critics also conceded the necessity of incorporating democratic principles in the revived *khilafa*, mainly by institutionalising *shura* (consultation) and the authority of *ahl al-hall wa'l-'aqd*. The sovereignty of the umma was emphasised against early opinions that suggested that the authority of the caliph derived from God or from the Prophet. Even later neo-traditionalists influenced by Islamism offered a prescription that reiterated Iqbal's prescription of a commonwealth of democratic nations states modelled on the United Nations.[24] (The European Union did not exist then.) But this convergence did not entail complete agreement. For, as Rida noted, already a polarisation had begun to take shape between two tendencies: one that wanted to follow the Turkish model of separating religion and state, and another trend that was working to revive the *khilafa*. Rida also issued the fateful judgement, which would be reiterated by many of his successors: since the establishment of the *khilafa* was an inescapable religious duty, the Muslim community does not exist as a community unless and until the caliphate is restored.[25]

At this stage in the debate, a major shift also began to occur: the idea of the restoration of the *khilafa* was beginning to be replaced by a new concept, that of the 'Islamic state' (as opposed to the secular one established by the Turks).[26] While for Rida this state (or states) still involved at least the re-establishment of a symbolic *khilafa*, the stage was set for the post-caliphate order. But this shift now raised new problems, chief among which was the problem of religious authority, thought in the past to reside in the *khalifa* or imam (for the Shi'a). In the ensuing contests, many rival centres arose to compete to fill this authority vacuum.

The Rise of Islamism

A major premise behind the attempts to revive the *khilafa* was the belief that existing Muslim communities were already imbued with the Islamic spirit, making their free self-expression as nations a legitimate reflection of their Islamic identity. All that was needed in order to restore the worldly presence of Islam and the integrity of the Muslim community was to unite Muslims around a legitimate and effective authority. These assumptions began to be contested by a new breed of thinkers and activists, whose common premise was that re-Islamisation needed something more than a new government. The people themselves need to be guided back to Islam. Advocates of this view were new contenders for the mantle of supreme religious authority, led by self-styled intellectuals influenced by modern learning, but also conversant with traditional learning and committed to a neo-traditionalist stance. They were more modern than traditional, however, and no longer content with the traditional approach of preaching, gathering disciples and giving advice to rulers, or acquiescing in the authority of the ulama. Significantly, these actors proceeded to form modern-style organisations that were in themselves a major departure from informal traditional networking.

The first and most influential of these was the Muslim Brotherhood (al-Ikhwan al-Muslimun) set up in Egypt in 1928 by a charismatic schoolteacher, Hasan al-Banna (1907–1949). Combining the organisational structure of modern elite parties with the mass appeal of the mainstream parties, the emergence of these movements was a reaction against the de facto triumph of the secular tendencies, where sharia has preceded the *khilafa* on the way out, and westernisation was gathering pace. It was also a reflection of the perception that traditionalism, even though it had appeared to win the argument against men like 'Abd al-Raziq, was incapable of stemming the tide of secularisation. Al-Banna was assassinated in 1949 before the group could develop a clear vision of the Islamic polity he sought to establish. However, his expressed opinions favoured the parliamentary system as the closest one to the Islamic ideal, even though he suggested some reforms to the system, including the abolition of the party system, which he found divisive and corrupt. A proper Islamic parliament, he suggested, reiterating Rida, should include all *ahl al-hall wa 'l-'aqd*.[27]

The concept of the Islamic state was elaborated in great detail on the Indian subcontinent, where the *khilafa* debate became an integral aspect of the nationalist struggle and later with the idea of Pakistan,[28] by Sayyid Abu al-A'la Mawdudi (1903–1979), founder of another new group there, Jama'at Islami. Mawdudi condemned the emerging 'Muslim nationalism' encouraged by his mentor, Iqbal. Far from being a living embodiment of Islam's 'ethical ideal', so-called Muslim communities had 'reached the lowest point of moral decline'.[29] It was ridiculous to claim that basing a state on these entities under the slogan 'free Islam in free India' was going to be the first step towards creating an Islamic state. A democratic polity where the public has not acquired adequate Islamic awareness and commitment would only bring to power those who care little for Islam, and thus become an obstacle to the true Islamic state, not its harbinger.[30] To form a Muslim community, one has to go back the starting point, as we are now back to a period of *jahiliyya* (pre-Islamic barbarism), where no genuine Muslim community existed, and create a genuine Muslim community from scratch. Only with a group committed to the principles and values of Islam and nothing else, would a genuine Muslim community emerge which would lead the revolution needed to set up a state in its own image.[31] Such a state would not be democratic, since democracy and its secular connotations is anathema to Islam. But it would not be despotic either. The polity would be governed by Islamic law, the sharia, and its leader would be elected by the community. He will also have to consult with community leaders through formal procedures that could include an elected assembly. However, while he is incumbent, he has absolute powers, and can disregard the wishes of the assembly and everyone else for that matter. Mawdudi calls this system a theo-democracy (a democracy governed by divine law).[32]

The Ikhwan were more inclined to accept the traditional position espoused by Rida and others that political reform was the key factor in the re-Islamisation drive. However, a shift towards Mawdudi's stance, led from the early 1960s by Sayyid Qutb (1906–1966), called not only for the rejection of democracy, but of politics as such. Even theoretical debates over how to resolve the problems facing modern societies were redundant, he argued, since such problems may not exist in a truly Muslim society. The believers must therefore concentrate on creating this society, and not be sidelined into contemporary politics.[33] While Qutb's prescription meant the deferral of all politics until the vanguard community was established, some Islamic groups that emerged from the 1970s claimed to be precisely this community, and decided that they had the legitimacy and authority to impose their vision by force on society. Egyptian groups such as Islamic Jihad, al-Jama'a al-Islamiyya and Jama'at al-Muslimin (also known as Takfir and Hijrah) rebelled against the regime's repressive apparatus, but also rejected democracy and targeted hostile secularist intellectuals. In the process, they also supplied a pretext for existing despotic regimes to cling to power in the face of this 'menace'.

Anti-Democracy Views

Some critics have argued that anti-democracy tendencies are inherent within Islamism, which is by nature illiberal.[34] Others, however, argue that anti-democratic views are only supported by a marginalised minority and are of fairly recent origin, emerging in the past two decades or so in reaction to severe government repression.[35] The dominant trends have been supportive of democracy, and the early writings of both traditionalist and modernist Islamists 'reveal no noticeable conflict with democracy or the Western liberal project as a whole'.[36] While this is largely true, Islamist attitudes have been characterised by ambivalence towards democracy. The central point is the one already made by Mawdudi: that the Muslim polity cannot be subject to popular will alone, but must be governed by sharia as well. In addition, others have remarked that the 'people' or *demos* in an Islamic polity have to be the Muslim community as a whole, and not just the nationals of one country.[37] Al-Banna's endorsement of the parliamentary system and constitutionalism was also coupled with misgivings about popular attitudes and 'the trend of degeneracy spread in personal attitudes, in opinions and in ideas, in the name of the freedom of thought, and in behaviour, morality and actions in the name of personal freedoms'.[38] His demand was therefore for a patronising state to enforce conformity to Islamic values and 'implement Islam's rules and social system, and propagate its principles to the people'.[39]

In later decades of the twentieth century, this ambivalence became untenable and a clear polarisation emerged, with one trend moving decisively towards support for democracy, simultaneously with the rise of groups opposed to democracy on principle. Most of the latter belonged to ultra-conservative groups influenced by salafi ideology, rejecting foreign concepts such as democracy and calling for violent action to establish the Islamic order.[40] The salafi trend bases its objection to democracy on the argument that the objective of the state is to worship God and implement the sharia. Consensus-building and other devices are a means to this end, and not an end in themselves. The will of God as embodied in the principles of the sharia should be the final arbiter of the way the state is run, and not the will of the people. And this divine will can only be ascertained by ulama, not by parliament or public opinion.[41]

But the most vocal and articulate on anti-democracy views among these groups is Hizb al-Tahrir, founded in Palestine in the 1950s but currently active internationally, in particular in Britain, Pakistan and some Arab countries. All these groups criticise the 'moderate' Islamic groups such as the Muslim Brotherhood (Egypt, Jordan, etc.) or the Islamic Front for Salvation (Algeria) for agreeing to participate in the political process in their countries. Their critique is both one of principle (that democracy is anti-Islamic because it vests sovereignty in the people, not God) and of expediency (the so-called democratic processes are a fraud anyway). The solutions they offer differ, though. The armed groups call for a 'jihad' to overthrow incumbent governments and establish proper Islamic rule. Hizb al-Tahrir, by contrast, calls for a campaign of education and intellectual debate which would lead to the re-establishment of the *khilafa*. While employing the concept of the 'Islamic state', Hizb al-Tahrir espouses the traditional belief that the restoration of the *khilafa* is both necessary and sufficient to resolve the problem of governance. Even Hizb al-Tahrir, however, could not resist the seduction of democratic procedures. The *khalifa* has to be elected, and consultative councils form part of the structure of power.

The founder of Hizb al-Tahrir, Taqi al-Din al-Nabahani, avoids the problematic term 'sovereignty of God', employed by Mawdudi and Qutb, using 'sovereignty of sharia' instead, adding that 'authority' is vested in the umma. This fine distinction between sovereignty and authority is not fully elaborated, but it soon appears redundant, since the power to determine sharia law is said to devolve on the *khalifa* alone.[42] Thus the sovereignty of sharia ends up as 'the dictatorship of the *khalifa*', a term al-Nabahani does not use, of course. According to his proposed constitution of the Islamic state (the idea of the 'constitution' itself cannot of course be traced to any authentic Islamic source) the *khalifa* is to be elected by a majority vote from candidates proposed by a consultative assembly. Once elected, however, the *khalifa* cannot be deposed by the people (but he can by a special court), and he can impose his authority by force not only against the minority that did not elect him, but also on the populations of other countries. In fact, it is his duty to do so, since the Muslim umma can have but one ruler (Articles 3, 24, 26–29, 33, 34). The *khalifa* not only rules on behalf of the umma, but he 'possesses all the authority of the state' (Article 35). The Islamic state, in the final analysis, is the *khalifa*.[43]

A number of intellectuals also took the line that Islam and democracy were incompatible. Sayyid Muhammad Husayn Tabatba'i in Iran was categorical in rejecting democracy, citing the Qur'an in support of the argument that the 'whims of men' are not a reliable guide to the truth, which has to be sought in revelation.[44] However, most of these condemnations often present philosophical arguments against the normative and conceptual presuppositions of democratic thought, while conceding that democratic procedures (voting, debating, representative institutions, etc.) are perfectly acceptable as consensus-building mechanisms and could be adapted to use in Islamic governments. One thus notices important ambiguities and lack of clarity about what democracy is, and which aspects of it are to be rejected. Some commentators have put this down to the fact that democracy itself is a contested and imprecise term, but it certainly goes beyond this.

While Islamic critiques of democracy made it clear that the problem with democracy is a fundamental one, hinging on the perception that popular will is too volatile to be entrusted with final authority,[45] they also do not hesitate to cite critiques that Western democracy as practised today is not the genuine rule of the people, since oligarchies appear to usurp this power. This position has recently received a boost from Western sources. A prominent American political theorist, Louis Cantori, recently argued that Western political theory (and Western democracy), which represents a 'combination of the idealisation of Enlightenment theory and of the American democratic experience', is completely inappropriate for Muslims societies in view of its elitism, ethnocentrism, individualism and secularism.[46]

Pluralism and the Human Rights Debate

In contrast, many other voices continued to advocate democracy and refute claims that it was incompatible with Islam.[47] In the early 1960s a new and even bolder line of thought began to emerge, calling for a firmer and unequivocal commitment to democratic values.[48] In a 1961 book, Fathi Osman called for the espousal of pluralism and human rights, especially the rights of women and religious minorities.[49] This call was followed and accompanied by many others, while regional and international trends towards democratisation influenced many Islamic leaders who began to address the issues of human rights more specifically. Even Mawdudi made a contribution to this debate in a 1975 lecture, where he put forth the argument that human rights are regarded in Islam as God–given, which meant that no earthly authority could abrogate or curtail them.[50] In 1981, a group of Muslim intellectuals and activists published the 'Universal Islamic Declaration of Human Rights', a move that was emulated by the Organisation of the Islamic Conference (OIC),[51] which adopted the Cairo Declaration of Human Rights (1991). Attempts were also made to elaborate a more cohesive Islamic vision of human rights, based on the belief that such a conception must be different from the Western 'anthropocentric perspective'. The latter views rights merely as 'expedient modes of protecting the individual from ... the state's coercive power', while, 'Islam ... formulates, defines and protects these very rights by inducing in the believers the disposition to obey the law of God ... By accepting to live in Bondage to this Divine Law, man learns to be free.'[52] In the Islamic context, where the idea of justice is central, duties have priority over rights, and the main reference of morality is the total social order, and not the individual.[53]

Others denied the Western origin of modern human rights, or claimed a decisive Islamic influence in their emergence and elaboration. For Hasan al-Turabi, modern constitutional thought can be traced to Islamic precedents: the idea of the social contract, on which modern democratic thought is based, can be traced to the idea of *bay'a*. Similarly, the idea of natural law is merely what divine law becomes when it is severed from its religious moorings.[54] Like Brohi, Turabi holds that since Western norms are derivative rather than original, they exhibited and continue to exhibit many basic flaws and contradictions, while the Islamic vision remains superior, since it holds that it is the believer's duty to God to protect the rights of others, while it is also his moral duty to exercise his rights.[55] Moham-med 'Abed al-Jabiri in turn argues that the values underlying the modern notion of human rights, far from being specifically West-ern, were actually 'a revolution in – and against – this very (West-ern) culture, and a call for the abandonment of the behavioural, intellectual, social and economic norms that this culture embodied'. The Declaration of Human Rights could thus be seen, from this per-spective 'as a truly universal declaration, proclaiming a new basis of legitimacy in place of the dominant one'.[56] The basic principles on which modern human rights are based can be perfectly reconciled with Islamic doctrines. The idea of 'social contract', for example, can be compared to the Islamic idea of covenant, while the concept of an original, ideal condition, is also present in Islam which claims to be the religion of *fitra*, or unspoiled human nature.[57]

These endeavours were, however, criticised as representing largely a negative conservative reaction to the model of freedom in Western societies and the scope of rights protection afforded by the interna-tional declaration of human rights.[58] More importantly, the authors of these schemes, it was argued, tended to 'think in terms of two conflicting models simultaneously. Even while promoting Islamic versions of human rights, they seem to regard international human rights norms as the standard against which all rights schemes must eventually be measured and from which they fear to be caught de-viating.' [59] The Islamic pedigree of these schemes is 'dubious', and they do not 'represent the outcome of rigorous, scholarly analyses of the Islamic sources or a coherent approach to Islamic jurispru-dence'.[60]

While this criticism is not wholly justified, there is no doubt that Islamic human rights schemes remain plagued by their lack of originality and defensiveness. This problem can also be seen in Islamic misgivings about pluralism, which appeared harder for Is-lamic thought to accommodate than democracy. In particular the accommodation of non-Muslims as equals in a Muslim polity and the acceptance of multi-party politics continued to face stiff resistance. During the early stages of agitation for political reform in the Ottoman state and Iran, pluralism was advocated as the only viable way of maintaining the unity of a multi-ethnic and multi-religious empire. In India, Muslim leaders like Muhammad Iqbal and Abu al-Kalam Azad espoused national unity in the struggle against British colonialism. As mentioned above, however, cracks began to appear in all these coalitions, ultimately leading to the disintegration of the Ottoman Empire, the collapse of the Iranian constitutional experiment and the division of India. But what is interesting is that this fragmentation did not in the end lead to the creation of any 'purely' Muslim polity where citizenship was based on religion alone.

Traditional Islamic polities accepted ethnic pluralism as well as (within limits) religious pluralism. However, the modern reconstitution of the world into territorial nation-states made the conception of a political community based on religion alone rather problematic. Attempts to resolve the matter through mass migration, as was the case with Pakistan, or a sort of 'ethnic cleansing', as was the case in Turkey, did not seem to resolve the problem conclusively. Nationalist ideologies were proposed as a remedy, but they in turn created new problems of ethnic minorities, as is the case with Kurdish minorities in Turkey and Iraq. Some de facto compromises did evolve in this regard, and attempts were made to legitimise them from an Islamic perspective. Later, Islamist positions began to evolve slowly as the call for Muslims to transcend the old categories and classifications denoted by the term *dhimmi* (member of a protected or covenanted minority) and accept non-Muslims as full citizens was taken up by a rising number of Islamic thinkers.[61] Within the current global setting, it has been argued, Muslims cannot escape interacting with non-Muslims on the world stage, whether as minorities in non-Muslim countries or as a 'minority' on this planet. In this context, reciprocity and a common stance against discrimination is an absolute necessity.[62]

In Muslim countries, a new formula of coexistence needs to be developed on the basis of the 'legitimacy of liberation' as opposed to the 'legitimacy of conquest'. The traditional Islamic polity dealt with non-Muslims as a conquered people, since that state incorporated non-Muslims within its borders mainly on the basis of conquest. However, modern Muslim states have come into being as a result of a liberation struggle in which non-Muslims participated equally. They have thus earned their right as full citizens, and the old formulas no longer applied.[63] The fact that modern nation-states have been established as a partnership between Muslims and non-Muslims means that the religious basis of traditional Muslim political communities is no longer tenable or necessary. When religious and political community coincided, religious affiliation became the equivalent of citizenship in modern nation-states. In both cases, the exclusion of non-citizens was seen as legitimate and inherent in the very nature of the polity.[64] However, in modern nation states, where Muslims are a dominant majority, and have no reason to fear the full participation of non-Muslims who share their loyalty to the country in administering the affairs of the state, exclusion on the basis of religion is no longer necessary to safeguard the polity. Executive posts in the modern state do not hold exclusive and unchallenged power. Consequently, all posts in the modern Islamic state should be open to non-Muslim citizens, who should have full citizenship rights, having earned it by their role in the struggle to liberate the country and safeguard its independence.[65] While these novel ideas (and similar ones by thinkers and activists such as shaykh Rashid al-Ghannushi of Tunisia)[66] were welcomed as bold attempts to redefine doctrine to accommodate the modern demands for equal citizenship, a significant gap still remains between Islamist conceptions of citizenship and the emerging consensus among democratic theoreticians, as well as the demands of non-Muslim minorities.

The practical implementation of Islamist ideas has revealed some additional problems as well. The constitution of the Islamic Republic of Iran pays homage to the unity of Muslims (Article 11), but bases citizenship exclusively on Iranian descent, not on religion. As such, its provisions restrict the rights of Muslim and non-Muslim citizens alike by restricting participation in the name of Shi'i doctrine, but simultaneously excluding non-Iranian Shi'a from citizenship, the worst of both worlds. The problem is similar in Sudan, where the 1998 constitution provided for inclusive citizenship without reference to religion, but non-Muslims complain of provisions that may compromise this theoretical equality. Muslims also protest that the military regime puts many restrictions on political participation for all, including dissident Islamists.

Islamic Governments

The 'Islamic states' which emerged in Iran, Sudan and Afghanistan have faced other difficulties too. In Iran, modern Islamist movements like the Feda'iyan-i Islam or Mehdi Bazargan's Freedom Movement,[67] were eclipsed by a figure who appeared to come from the past: Ayatul-lah Ruh-Allah Khumayni (1902–1979) who came to dominante post-revolutionary Iran. In his book, *al-Hukuma al-Islamiyya*, first published in 1971, Khumayni pioneered a revolution in Shi'i thought by in-sisting on the absolute necessity of establishing a government even in the absence of the infallible imam. And since the ulama are the guardians of the heritage of the imam, it is their duty to step in and fill the authority vacuum.[68] The resulting Islamic government will not be a tyranny, Khumayni argued, but 'it is also not constitutional in the current sense, that of being based on approval of laws in ac-cordance with the opinion of the majority. It is constitutional in the sense that the ruler is subject to a set of conditions ... set forth in the Qur'an and the Sunna.'[69] While adopting this theory of *vilayat-i faqih* (the authority of the jurist) as its central principle of govern-ment the Iranian constitution also enshrined popular sovereignty as a major principle, allowing for direct and indirect elections of all officials, including the Leader of the Revolution. At the same time, the Leader and a number of other institutions, including the Coun-cil of Guardians, were empowered to overrule or pre-empt popular will in the name of the sharia. In 1988, Khumayni went further and expounded the principle of the 'absolute jurisdiction of the *faqih*', whereby the supreme leader could overrule even the provisions of sharia in the interest of preserving the Islamic state.[70]

Opposition to these doctrines came from secularists like the mili-tant Mujahidin-e Khalq, from traditionalists unhappy about Khu-mayni's innovations in Shi'i thought and practice, and from Islamic liberals like the Freedom Movement (Nahzat-i Azadi) which wanted less ulama influence. More significantly though, the 'jurist' in ques-tion, whose authority is deemed decisive in theory, did not appear as easy to designate as the theory implied. The traditional system of designating such an authority had a democratic component to it: in addition to peer recognition, the *'alim* who enjoyed the widest popular support was considered the most senior authority or *marja'*.

But Khumayni bypassed this tradition, relying more directly on specifically political popular support, and using it to marginalise and even ostracise some of the senior ulama who opposed his doctrine. In the past few years, the liberals appeared to be on the ascendant as indicated by the landslide election victory of President Muhammad Khatami on a platform of radical reform in 1997 and again in 2001. Khatami is surrounded by liberals, even pro-secular intellectuals. The liberal trend was also promoted by a new breed of intellectuals, most prominent among whom is Abdolkarim Soroush.[71] The conservatives, however, have succeeded in exploiting their entrenched positions in the judiciary, the military and elsewhere to frustrate, and even reverse, reforms. For example, the judiciary managed to silence the bulk of the outspoken liberal publications.

Hasan al-Turabi's perception of political authority was in theory, more democratic. He reiterated the traditional Sunni view that the community as a whole was the repository of authority. But he rejected both the notion that this authority could be mandated to a *khalifa* or monopolised by the ulama. The authoritative consensus stipulated by sharia is not the consensus of the ulama, but of the community 'enlightened by its ulama'.[72] In addition, the concept of *'alim* should not be restricted to those steeped in traditional learning, but must incorporate scientists, economists, social scientists and other experts.[73] The role of the vanguard movement is also one of facilitator, not of guardian. When Turabi attempted to implement his ideas as he became the architect of the new regime following the coup of June 1989 in Sudan, the result was not only a disappointment to those who pinned their hopes on his preaching of Islamic democracy, but to Turabi himself, who had suffered at the hands of the regime he had established. Part of the flaw emanated from the vision itself. An attempt to evolve popular consensus through the institution of 'non-party' democracy ran into problems as most people either refused to participate or maintained loyalty to their old parties. There were also serious questions about the genuine intentions of respecting even this limited concept of democracy.[74] Later, Turabi was converted to multiparty democracy, with some reservations, but by then the whole system had become unworkable, and serious rifts developed, resulting in Turabi himself being kicked out of power in December 1999 and placed under arrest from February 2001.

In both Sudan and Iran, the personal authority of the leader permitted nation (or even party) very little input, if at all, in the governing process. The way things evolved here (and later Afghanistan under Taliban rule) gave a new impetus to the 'debate about the debate', or what Kramer called the 'Islamism debate'. Put in a nutshell, this debate hinges on the question: 'are Islamist groups an obstacle to, or an indispensable component of the democratic transformation in Muslim countries?' Various answers continue to be given,[75] although in practice one consistent answer given by the incumbent regimes and their Western backers is 'no' to both democracy and Islamism.

Conclusion

The debate over democracy has been one of the most important debates in the Muslim world this last century. The fact that it is still continuing without a resolution is an indication of a serious crisis in the Muslim world. As we have noted, the overwhelming consensus of Muslim opinion has tended towards the practical adoption of democratic procedures, but found difficulty in reconciling traditional Islamic thinking and democracy. We can discern three main trends as far as Islamic attitudes to democracy were concerned: those who enthusiastically espoused the idea and worked to promote it and to prove its compatibility with Islam; those who were inclined to accept democratic procedures, but voice conceptual and philosophical objections to democracy and propose certain procedural limits on the democratic process to ensure conformity to sharia; and, finally, those who reject democracy root and branch. As mentioned above, the debate on Islam and democracy was conducted against the background of other related debates: the debates on the *khilafa*, Muslim unity versus nationalism, the contests within the anti-colonial movements, the debates over secularisation, the contests over power, borders, ideologies and sectarian and religious rivalries. Above all, there were unavoidable contests over what is meant by democracy itself. Those who rejected democracy categorically usually focused on its ideological and philosophical justifications. Those who supported it emphasised its procedural aspects.

The system established by Khumayni points to a convergence

between various Muslim positions on democracy, as it appears close to the blueprint elaborated by Rida in the 1920s. In both models, the ulama were designated as guardians of the system. This role for the ulama was not conceded by Islamist leaders such as Hasan al-Turabi or Mawdudi. For the latter, it is the new vanguard community that is collectively the repository of authority. By implication, this means the organised Islamist group, a point that is explicitly made by Sa'id Hawwa, who equates the Muslim Brotherhood with the genuine Muslim community, and argues that all Muslims must adhere to it.[76] The convergence between the rival positions, including secularists and Islamists, has prompted some analysts to regard the differences between these groups as 'a conflict between two factions of the intellectual elite'.[77] Others put it as the sign of a pathological hegemony of Islamic discourse, propelled by populism and the prevalent muddle in Arab and Muslim thinking about democracy and pluralism.[78] This convergence, however, is deceptive. The various groups may agree on such ideas as the 'authority of the umma' and the value of democratic consensus. They may also tend to express reservations about democracy here and now. But their projects pull in different directions. For the Islamists, the umma may not be ready for democracy because it is not Islamic enough; for their opponents, because it is too Islamic.

Enayat argues that Islam, like any religion, is fundamentally incompatible with democracy, because religion is based on a minimum of unquestionable tenets, while democracy invariably involves 'ceaseless debates and questioning'.[79] As a result, Enayat praises Tabatba'i's rejection of democracy as 'courageous and sincere', as contrasted with those who attempt artificial integration of Islam and democracy.[80] In this, Enayat misses the point in the same way as Mawdudi and Qutb do when speaking of the Sovereignty of God, or Brohi does when he refers to the primacy of duties over rights. In all these cases, the writers make the wrong assumption of politics being about the relations between man and God, when the issue is man's relation to man. Democracies, like all other human co-operative endeavours, are also based on basic principles that are not open for questioning. On the other hand, religion is also dependent on human consent, starting from its adoption and ending with its interpretation. It is therefore misleading to contrast the alleged absolute fluidity of democratic systems with the presumed rigidity and lack of human input in religious-based systems. This is to commit the same fallacy Binder ascribes to the Islamist vision of an 'ideal Islamic government', in which 'law may be determined with absolute certainty, so that Muslims are left in no doubt about what they must do'.[81] In fact the problem in Islam has always been the near impossibility of institutionalising religious authority in a way that would enable the state (or any other agency) to impose what it deems to be the correct interpretation of Islam. This problem has been most acute in countries that have engaged in re-Islamisation, as we have seen. The modern debate on democracy has demonstrated the great diversity of views, while the modern experience in the Muslim world has shown that whatever is holding up democratic advances in the Muslim world, it is not religious doctrine.

Notes

1. Hamid Enayat, *Modern Islamic Political Thought* (London, 1982), p. 52.

2. See Muhammad 'Amara, *Ma'rakat al-Islam wa usul al-hukm* (Cairo, 1989), and Diya' al-Din al-Rayyis, *al-Islam wa'l-khilafa fi'l-'asr al-hadith* (Beirut, 1973).

3. Basheer M. Nafi, *Arabism, Islamism and the Palestine Question, 1908–1941: A Political History* (Reading, 1998).

4. Elie Kedourie, *Democracy and Arab Political Culture* (London, 1994), pp. 13–23.

5. Ervand Abrahamian, *Iran Between Two Revolutions* (Princeton, NJ, 1982), pp. 81–92.

6. Ibid., p. 90.

7. Ibid., pp. 93–95.

8. Enayat, *Modern Islamic Political Thought*, pp. 164–169.

9. Abrahamian, *Iran Between Two Revolutions*, pp. 88–89, 92–96.

10. Albert Hourani, *Arabic Thought in the Liberal Age: 1789–1939* (Cambridge, 1989), p. 280 ff.

11. Enayat, *Modern Islamic Political Thought*, pp. 53–57.

12. Ibid., pp. 53–54; Hourani, *Arabic Thought*, pp. 183–184.

13. *Al-Manar*, 23 (1922), pp. 775–776; and M. Rashid Rida, *al-Khilafa aw al-imama al-'uzma* (Cairo, 1925).

14. 'Ali 'Abd al-Raziq, *al-Islam wa usul al-hukm* (Cairo, 1925), pp. 13–33.

15. 'Abd al-Raziq, *al-Islam wa usul al-hukm*, pp. 102–103.

16. 'Amara, *Ma'rakat*, pp. 52–60.

17. For a detailed account of the controversy, see 'Amara, ibid., and Hourani, *Arabic Thought*, pp. 182–192. See also Leonard Binder, *Islamic Liberalism: A Critique of Development Ideologies* (Chicago, IL, 1988), pp. 128–169.

18. Binder, *Islamic Liberalism*, pp. 131–132.

19. Quoted in 'Amara, *Ma'rakat*, p. 19.

20. Muhammad Iqbal, *Six Lectures on The Reconstruction of Religious Thought in Islam* (Lahore, 1930), p. 220.

21. Ibid., p. 220.

22. Ibid., pp. 222–223.

23. Hourani, *Arabic Thought*, p. 184; Enayat, *Modern Islamic Political Thought*, pp. 55–56.

24. al-Rayyis, *al-Islam wa'l-khilafa*, p. 383 ff.

25. 'Amara, *Ma'rakat*, pp. 16 and 54.

26. Enayat, *Modern Islamic Political Thought*, p. 69 ff.

27. Hasan al-Banna, *Majmu'at rasa'il al-imam al-shahid Hasan al-Banna* (Beirut, 1974), pp. 162 ff. and 357 ff.

28. Enayat, *Modern Islamic Political Thought*, pp. 58–59.

29. Abu al-A'la Mawdudi, *Minhaj al-inqilab al-Islami* (Cairo, 1977), pp. 21–23.

30. Ibid., pp. 20–28.

31. Ibid., p. 28 ff.

32. Abu al-A'la Mawdudi, *Islamic Law and Constitution* (Lahore, 1967), pp. 147–149; Mawdudi, *Tadwin al-dustur al-Islami* (Cairo, 1991), pp. 25–50.

33. Sayyid Qutb, *Ma'alim fi'l-tariq* (Beirut, 1978), pp. 34–37.

34. See John Waterbury, 'Democracy without Democrats?: The Potential for Political Liberalisation in the Middle East', in Ghassan Salamé, ed., *Democracy Without Democrats? The Renewal of Politics in the Muslim World* (London, 1994), pp. 39–42.

35. Fahmi Huwaydi, 'al-Islam wa'l-dimuqratiyya', in Magdi Hammad et al., ed., *al-Haraka al-Islamiyya wa'l-dimuqratiyya* (Beirut, 1999), pp. 46–48.

36. Ibid., p. 40.

37. Ibid., pp. 41–43. Cf. Haydar Ibrahim 'Ali, *al-Tayyarat al-Islamiyya wa qadiyyat al-dimuqratiyya* (Beirut, 1996), p. 139 ff.

38. Hasan al-Banna, *Mudhakkirat al-da'wa wa'l-da'iya* (Cairo, 1966), p. 43.

39. al-Banna, *Majmu'at rasai'l*, p. 225.

40. J. J. G. Jansen, *The Neglected Duty: The Creed of Sadat's Assassins and Islamic Resurgence in the Middle East* (New York, 1986); Gilles Kepel, *The Prophet and the Pharaoh: Muslim Extremism in Egypt* (London, 1985).

41. Sa'ad al-Faqih, 'Tahaffuzat al-salafiyyin 'ala al-dimuqratiyya', a paper

presented to the 11th conference of the Project for the Study of Democracy in the Arab world, Oxford, 1 September, 2001.

42. Taqi al-Din al-Nabahani, *The Islamic State* (London, 1998), pp. 221–222 and 240.

43. Cf. Suha Taji-Farouki, 'Islamic State Theories and Contemporary Realities', in Abdelsalam Sidahmed and Anoushiravan Ehteshami, *Islamic Fundamentalism* (Boulder, CO, 1996), pp. 35–40.

44. Enayat, *Modern Islamic Political Thought*, pp. 135–138.

45. Mawdudi, *Islamic Law and Constitution*, pp. 147–149.

46. Louis J. Cantori, 'The Limitations of Western Democratic Theory: The Islamic Alternative', a paper prepared in the panel, 'Religion, Islam and Democracy in the Contemporary Middle East', MESA Conference, 17 November, 2000, Orlando, FL.

47. Hammad et al., ed., *al-Haraka al-Islamiyya wa'l-dimuqratiyya*, pp. 31–46, 63–77. See also Muhamamd al-Ghazzali, *Azmat al-shura fi'l-mujtma'at al-'Arabiyya wa'l-Islamiyya* (Cairo, 1990); Ahmad Shawqi al-Fanjari, *al-Hurriya al-siyasiyya* (Kuwait, 1973); Rashid al-Ghannushi, *al-Hurriyyat al-'ama fi'l-dawla al-Islamiyya* (Beirut, 1993).

48. See Abdelwahab El-Affendi, 'Reviving Controversy: Islamic Revivalism and Modern Human Rights', *Encounter*, 6 (2000), pp. 117–150.

49. Fathi Osman, *al-Fikr al-Islami wa'l-tatawwur* (Cairo, 1961). See also 'Ali 'Abd al-Wahid Wafi, *Huquq al-insan fi'l-Islam* (Cairo, 1967).

50. Abu al-A'la Mawdudi, *Human Rights and Islam* (Lahore, 1977), p. 39.

51. See 'Wathiqat huquq al-insan fi'l-Islam', in *al-Muslim al-mu'asir*, 13, 50 (1987), pp. 171–174.

52. A. K. Brohi, 'The Nature of Islamic Law and the Concept of Human Rights', in International Commission of Jurists, *Human Rights in Islam* (Kuwait, 1982), p. 60.

53. Brohi, 'The Nature of Islamic Law', pp. 44–51.

54. Hasan al-Turabi, 'al-Usul al-fikriyya li-huquq al-insan', an address delivered at the Conference on Human Rights in Islam, organised by the Sudanese Bar Association, 12–14 February, 1993, Khartoum, p. 1.

55. Ibid., pp. 2–5.

56. Muhammad 'Abid al-Jabiri, 'Min ajl al-ta'sil al-thaqafi li-huquq al-insan fi'l-fikr al-'Arabi al-mu'asir', *al-Sharq al-Awsat* (25 February, 1993), p. 22.

57. Ibid., p. 20.

58. Ann Elizabeth Mayer, *Islam and Human Rights: Tradition and Politics* (Boulder, CO, 1991), p. 207.

59. Ibid., pp. 52–53.

60. Ibid., p. 207.

61. El-Affendi, ed., *Rethinking Islam and Modernity*, pp. 84, 124–128. See also Osman, *al-Fikr al-Islami wa'l-tatawwur.*

62. Fathi Osman, 'Islam and Human Rights: The Challenge to the Muslims and the World', in El-Affendi, ed., *Rethinking Islam and Modernity*, pp. 47–56

63. Salim al-'Awa, *al-Nizam al-siyasi li'l-dawla al-Islamiyya* (Cairo, 1989).

64. Tariq el-Bechri, 'Participation of non-Muslim', in El-Affendi, ed., *Rethinking Islam and Modernity*, pp. 68–73.

65. Ibid., pp. 80–83.

66. al-Ghannoushi, *Al-Hurriyyat al-'amma.*

67. Enayat, *Modern Islamic Political Thought*, pp. 93–99; Said Arjomand, *The Turban for the Crown* (Oxford, 1988), pp. 91–102.

68. Ayatullah Ruhullah Khumayni, *al-Hukuma al-Islamiyya* (Beirut, 1979).

69. Quoted in V. Martin, *Creating the Islamic State: Khomeini and the Making of a New Iran* (London, 2000), p. 122.

70. Arjomand, *The Turban for the Crown*, pp. 182–183.

71. Abdolkarim Soroush, *Reason Freedom and Democracy* (Oxford, 2000).

72. See Abdelwahab El-Affendi, *Turabi's Revolution: Islam and Power in Sudan* (London, 1991), pp. 159–162.

73. Ibid., pp. 170–173.

74. Abdelwahab El-Affendi, *Al-Thawra wa'l-Islam al-siyasi fi'l-Sudan* (London, 1995), pp. 31–43.

75. Martin Kramer, ed., *The Islamism Debate* (Tel Aviv, 1997); John Esposito and John Voll, *Islam and Democracy* (Oxford, 1996).

76. Abdullah al-Nafisi, 'al-Fikr al-haraki li'l-tayyarat al-Islamiyya', in Hammad et al., ed., *al-Harakat al-Islamiyya wa'l-dimuqratiyya*, pp. 187–212.

77. Binder, *Islamic Liberalism*, pp. 157 and 244.

78. Aziz Al-Azmeh, 'Populism Contra Democracy: Recent Democratist Discourse in the Arab world', in Salamé, ed., *Democracy Without Democrats?*, pp. 112–129.

79. Enayat, *Modern Islamic Political Thought*, p. 126.

80. Ibid., p. 137.

81. Binder, *Islamic Liberalism*, p. 131

7

The Development of Islamic Economics: Theory and Practice

Rodney Wilson

The emergence of Islamic economics as a distinct branch of economics can be seen as one manifestation of the Islamic revival of the late nineteenth century. Sayyid Jamal al-Din al-Afghani, arguably the most influential pioneer of Islamic modernism and anti-imperialism from the 1880s, sought to change Islam from a religious faith into a politico-religious ideology.[1] Much of the effort of the Islamic modernisers was in legal reform and *ijtihad*, reinterpretation of the sharia.[2] The reformist agenda of al-Afghani and his followers, Muhammad 'Abduh and Rashid Rida, was essentially political, as their concern was with strengthening Islam so that it could meet the challenges posed by the Western powers. These reformers had only a limited knowledge of and interest in economics however, either as a discipline or as a subject area.

It was not until the post-colonial era of the second half of the twentieth century that politics in Muslim states became increasingly about economic and developmental issues. Given this new emphasis it was perhaps inevitable that an attempt should be made to re-evaluate contemporary economic theories from an Islamic perspective. The self designated Islamic economists who undertook this re-evaluation saw themselves as modernisers in the mould of Afghani, whose pioneering efforts they viewed with much respect. Despite Afghani not being an economist, his views on the need for pan-Islamic unity resonated with Islamic economists who saw their type of economics as applicable to all Muslim societies.

There were scattered writings on economic issues throughout the Muslim world in the early decades of the twentieth century, including contributions by Seoharwi Muhammad Hifzur Rahman in India,[3] Shaykh Mahmud Ahmad in Pakistan[4] and Yaqut al-'Ashmawi in Egypt.[5] These authors were working in isolation however, and with their writing in Arabic and Urdu they lacked international links. Furthermore they did not have followers who could have undertaken continuing research in Islamic economics. It was not until the 1970s that their work was brought to the attention of a wider community of Muslim scholars when Muhammad Nejatullah Siddiqi published his survey of contemporary literature on Islamic economics for the First International Conference on Islamic Economics held in Mecca in 1976.[6]

The Pioneering Work in the 1940s of Sayyid Abu al-A'la Mawdudi

The first influential writer in the twentieth century was Sayyid Abu al-A'la Mawdudi, an ideologist from the Indian sub-continent and head of the powerful Jama'at-i Islami, who popularised the term 'Islamic economics'.[7] A seminal collection of his writings, most of which were in the form of pamphlets and tracts, was first published in Urdu in Lahore in 1947, and was only translated into English in 1975.[8] Mawdudi was a populist, who attracted a growing number of followers amongst the young generation of economists in the Indian sub-continent, before and after the establishment of Pakistan as an independent state. Many of these economists had undertaken postgraduate degrees in economics in the United Kingdom, and were later to become significant contributors to the literature themselves.

It was Mawdudi's critique of practical economic issues from the perspective of Qur'anic teaching and the hadith that attracted widespread attention. Mawdudi was not an economic theorist, but he was concerned with the economic injustices arising from inequitable land holding and the indebtedness of many poor Muslims. For Mawdudi such injustices facing Muslims could only be solved in the context of an Islamic state where the sharia was enforced. Mawdudi was opposed to Jinnah's concept of Pakistan as a separate secularist state, but rather believed Islam should be central to the new state's political and economic system.[9]

Mawdudi was however cautious in his interpretation of the sharia, as he disagreed with another Muslim reformer, Nasir Ahmed Sheikh, who argued that Qur'anic teaching was opposed to private ownership of land beyond that which the owner could personally cultivate.[10] For Mawdudi the problem was with the sharecropping system that was widely used in the Indian sub-continent. He drew parallels between the uncertainty facing the tenants who were obliged to hand over much of their crops even when harvests were bad, and the evils of *riba*, which resulted in debtors paying interest on their loans when they were already facing hardship. The solution for Mawdudi lay in the application of sharia law to tenancy agreements, not in the confiscation and nationalisation of vast tracts of privately owned land.

The Islamic Economics Movement in the 1960s

Despite his undoubted intellect and his superb grasp of economic issues, Mawdudi was primarily a sharia scholar who did not have the benefit of a formal training in mainstream economics. Nevertheless his writings and speeches profoundly influenced a new generation of professional economists on the Indian sub-continent, who sought to reconcile Islamic teaching with the ideas and concepts they had acquired through their economics training. This new generation, all of whom were born in the 1930s, included amongst its most notable contributors Muhammad Abdul Mannan,[11] Muhammad Nejatullah Siddiqi,[12] M. Umer Chapra[13] and Syed Nawab Naqvi.[14] These writers had all a good knowledge of Western neo-classical economics through their undergraduate and postgraduate degrees and professional training.

There were parallels between their experience and that of classical Islamic writers on economic issues in the thirteenth and fourteenth centuries such as Ibn Taymiyya[15] and Ibn Khaldun[16] who were influenced by Greek philosophy. Ibn Khaldun was able to construct a moral theory of the business cycle based on a fusion of Islamic ethics and classical Greek interpretations of the rise and decline of civilisations. Similarly these contemporary writers drew on the Islamic concepts of *tawhid* (the unity of God), *khilafa* (vice-regency or responsibility) and *'adala* (justice)[17] and the secular social democratic ideas of distributive justice and co-operation in the interests of social welfare.

Muhammad Abdul Mannan was born in East Bengal in 1938 in what was subsequently to become East Pakistan after partition and Bangladesh after the secession from Pakistan. After working in the government economic service in Pakistan, Mannan enrolled at Michigan State University where he completed a taught MA in economics and a PhD.[18] Mannan's major accomplishment was to write the first English-language textbook on Islamic economics. This was organised by topic in a manner that was similar to that of contemporary mainstream textbooks, with chapters on consumer behaviour, the organisation of production, distribution of income and wealth, price theory, money and banking and fiscal policy. The book had a major impact on Muslim economists, and was reprinted twelve times in the first ten years after its initial publication and translated into Arabic, Turkish and Bengali.

Mannan saw Islamic economics as being both a positive and normative science, concerned not only with what existed, but rather with what ought to exist. It was in other words prescriptive, with the rules ultimately determined by the sharia. Even though no actual Islamic economy existed according to Mannan, merely states with Muslim rulers where the sharia was applied imperfectly or not at all, this did not imply that Islamic economics was unnecessary. Indeed this absence of a properly functioning Islamic economic system highlighted the need for Islamic economists to analyse the gap between the Islamic ideal and the secularist structures under which Muslims were forced to live. For Mannan the implementation of sharia law would bring greater social harmony and ensure religious aspirations could be translated into all aspects of everyday life.

Mannan saw Islamic economics both as a system and a science, his definition of science being an organised body of knowledge formed through human attitudes and methods. His definition is therefore of economics as a behavioural science, with the behaviour of Muslims shaped by their religious beliefs. The system is based on revealed knowledge from the Qur'an, the Sunna and hadith, as well as through the consensus of sharia scholars (*ijma*'). The system is not static however as the economy changes and fresh thinking (*ijtihad*) is needed.[19] Siddiqi, Naqvi and Chapra were in agreement with these premises regarding the basis of an Islamic economic system, but each built on the foundations, as outlined by Mannan, in distinctive ways.

Muhammad Nejatullah Siddiqi was perhaps the most influential writer of the first generation of modern Islamic economists. He was born in Gorakhpur in 1931, and went to the Muslim University in Aligarh, which was central to the Muslim reawakening on the Indian sub-continent, as many theological scholars there were concerned with how modern society could be governed under the sharia law. Siddiqi became well versed in sharia law, but his real interest was economics. Unlike Mannan, however, he did not define Islamic economics as a separate science, but rather emphasised that its central concern was the behaviour of economic agents. He was prepared to accept much of the analytical framework of conventional neo-classical economics, but suggested that an Islamic strategy for organising the economic system must be based on three main ideas. First clearly specified goals, second well-defined moral attitudes by economic agents and thirdly specific laws, rules and regulations derived from the sharia and enforced by the state.[20]

Siddiqi explains how the system of education inherited by Muslim states from the imperial powers did not lend itself to the study of Islamic economics as secular and religious education were compartmentalised.[21] The essentially secularist institutional framework which was developed in the colonial era in much of the Muslim world continued after independence. This was unhelpful as it meant there was no testing-ground for the hypotheses being formulated by Islamic economists and no empirical evidence that could be used in making theoretical formulations. Islamic economists through their writings hoped to influence governments to abandon secularist positions and to convince their readers of the desirability and viability of an economic system based on Islamic injunctions.

The Emergence of Islamic Economics as a Discipline in the 1970s

Although Mawdudi had coined the term 'Islamic economics', it was really only from the 1970s that the subject took on some of the characteristics of an academic discipline. By then it had its own group of scholars engaged in academic debate and a growing literature of books and journal articles. By the late 1970s there were dedicated conferences and journals, partly as a result of the growing respectability of Islamic economics. This was helped at the institutional level by the newly formed Organisation of the Islamic Conference (OIC). The governments participating in this provided much momentum to the Islamic finance movement when they agreed to sponsor the Islamic Development Bank in 1973, even though most of those taking part in the conference represented secularist governments.[22] The newly oil rich states of the Gulf were much more sympathetic to an Islamic agenda however, and to a large extent the outcome of the 1973 conference represented their triumph over Arab socialist philosophy and nationalist secularism.

The First International Conference on Islamic Economics held in Mecca in 1976 under the auspices of King Abdulaziz University of Jeddah was an important milestone in the emergence of Islamic economics as a discipline. Most of the leading economists working in the field attended, and the conference coincided with the opening of the research centre for Islamic economics in King Abdulaziz University, where some of these scholars, notably Nejatullah Siddiqi, were subsequently to be employed.

At the conference it was evident that there remained differing views amongst Muslim academics on whether Islamic economics was a distinct or independent discipline or simply conventional economics with some of its morally objectionable features from an Islamic perspective filtered out with sharia-compliant practices substituted. Some critics of Islamic economics, notably Timur Kuran,[23] tended towards the latter view, but 'mainstream' Islamic economists such as Nejatullah Siddiqi or Umer Chapra would reject any attempt to define their field of study as a type of appendage. What Siddiqi and Chapra stressed was that Islamic economics had economic justice at its core, in terms of both fair transactions and distributive justice. There was thus emphasis on both means and ends, as transparency and honesty in transactions can be regarded as a means, and efforts, justified at least in part by material reward, can be regarded as an end.

Economics can be defined with respect to its subject matter or in terms of its methodology. Islamic and neo-classical economists are generally in agreement about what areas their subject covers, but there are differences over methodology, although these occur within each school of economists, and are not necessarily the defining feature of each school. Amongst Islamic economists Syed Naqvi went furthest in deriving a distinctive definition of his discipline, as he saw human behaviour at the core of economics, and Islamic economics concerned with the behaviour of *homo islamicus* in Muslim society, rather than *homo economicus* in secular society. Methodologically Naqvi proposed an inductive approach, in which the axioms of Islamic economics should be derived by generalising from the actual behaviour of representative Muslims, whether in managing their household finances, in running a business, or in their workplace decisions as employees. Others however, including Baqir al-Sadr whose work will be discussed presently, were prepared to accept a deductive approach, derived ultimately from both natural laws, such as those governing supply, demand and price, and the sharia law, which provides moral guidance for market participants.

Islamic economists are more concerned with means than material ends however, as writers such as Chapra see wealth as a means of realising human well-being and facilitating spirituality.[24] In this Chapra cites the position of classical Muslim scholars, notably the tenth and eleventh-century theologian al-Ghazali, who stressed that every human action, including economic behaviour, must be guided by faith.[25] Economics is often defined to students in the West as the 'science concerned with the allocation of scarce resources that have competing ends'. For Chapra, however, claims on resources must be limited by the obligations of universal brotherhood (based on the concept of *khilafa*), which implies that the basic needs of all members of society must be met. For Chapra need-fulfilment can include comfort, but not waste and snobbery about material position in society.[26]

Islam and Marxism

Although the Islamic economists from the Indian sub-continent were primarily reacting to both mainstream neo-classical economics and imperialist and capitalist structures, there was an influential group of Muslim scholars who reacted first and foremost to communist ideology. Baqir al-Sadr in his work, *Iqtisaduna*, written in the 1950s and first published in 1961, provided perhaps the most important Islamic critique of Marxist thinking.[27] Al-Sadr was a Shiʻi living in Najaf who was trained in Islamic jurisprudence rather than economics, but he was widely read, and although he wrote in Arabic, he could read English and French and was conversant with the writings of Marx as well as numerous Marxist scholars. The communist party was gaining strength in Iraq in the 1950s and those who saw a political role for Islam felt more isolated than ever. In Iran the Tudeh party, although officially outlawed, had much popular support amongst the Shiʻa, and many felt it was as much a threat to the political ambitions of the mullahs as the Shah's regime.

Baqir al-Sadr's motivation in writing *Iqtisaduna* was to demonstrate the incompatibility of both Marxism and capitalism with Islam.[28] He correctly saw Marxist analysis as being primarily concerned with the forms of production and distribution, but he rejected the class categorisation as simplistic, as capitalists and workers are not just products of a system of production but are also human beings with moral responsibilities. Material consumption and having power over resources may be one factor motivating men, but for Marxists this is the end while for Muslims this is only the means. For Baqir al-Sadr the ends are spiritual, submission to the will of Allah, but power over resources gives men, as vice-regents of Allah on earth, the ability to carry out Allah's commands and create a better society.

Although Baqir al-Sadr vehemently rejected the basic assumptions of Marxist analysis, notably the material determinism of history and social relations, he employed Marxist arguments in his denunciation of capitalism. The exploitation involved in capital accumulation was seen as socially unjust, and there was a concern with the plight of workers that was taken up by other Shiʻi writers, notably Abol Hasan Bani Sadr, who was to become the first President of the Islamic Republic of Iran,[29] although it would be incorrect to identify concerns with labour issues solely with Shi'i writers.[30] In some respects the work of Baqir al-Sadr provided the basis for the short-lived alliance between leftists and the mullahs prior to and immediately after the Islamic revolution in 1979, even though his work also demonstrated how such an alliance might be doomed to failure. The work of Baqir al-Sadr was much respected by Ayatullah Khumayni who spent most of his years in exile in Najaf. This, and the high regard in which Baqir al-Sadr was held amongst his fellow Shi'is in Iraq, resulted in his persecusion and eventual execution in 1980 on the orders of Saddam Hussein.[31]

Siddiqi suggests that communism is in conflict with 'the basic requirements of the moral and spiritual growth of the human personality' which in the economic sphere requires private property and freedom of enterprise.[32] He believes the methodology of change adopted by communism inevitably leads to a coercive regime, and that exploitation of man by man cannot be eliminated by merely changing the hands that control the means of exploitation. Rather, what is needed is a moral reorientation of individuals that makes them servants of society and workers for the social good. Siddiqi cites Mawdudi's view that although centralised planning removed unemployment, this was only achieved at the cost of liberty and denied moral values.[33] Corruption was rife in communist countries, and a sizeable proportion of the social surplus had to be spent on internal security and defence as repression increased.

Islam and Capitalism

At first sight it might appear that Islam has more in common with capitalism than with communism. The recognition of private property and the legitimacy of markets are inherent to both. However, Muslim writers see a lack of balance and moderation in capitalism. Mawdudi saw capitalism as extreme, with excessive emphasis on the rights of individual ownership and freedom of enterprise that caused suffering and privation for those who owned little.[34] Undue emphasis on self-interest and the profit motive resulted in a society devoid of human character, brotherhood, sympathy and co-operation.[35]

The private ownership of property was legitimate for Baqir al-Sadr who rejected the Marxist notion of the desirability of state ownership of all productive resources. Al-Sadr believed that it was just to acquire property through work or by inheritance, provided this was in conformity with the sharia law. These were matters for families, not the state. Al-Sadr saw a role for the state, however, as he advocated state ownership of natural resources in the public good rather than control by individuals. Where there were natural monopolies, as in the case of utilities such as electricity distribution, Al-Sadr supported the principle of state ownership. Al-Sadr described his own position as favouring a multifaceted ownership pattern, in the context of what could be described as a mixed economy, where both private business and the state play an important role.

By the 1980s it became apparent to Islamic economists, as to most other analysts, that communism was in crisis, even though none predicted its sudden demise as a significant force in 1989. Marxist teaching was, however, seen as a diminishing challenge to Islam, and the influence of secularist socialists to be in decline throughout the Muslim world. Ba'thist socialism survived in Syria and Iraq, but any ideological fervour had disappeared as economic policy responded to the pragmatic realities of the international economy and local vested interests. Nasser's Arab socialism was all but dead in Egypt, where an uneasy tension also existed between national vested interests wanting economic protection and the desire, often by the same interest groups, to profit from the opportunities available through the global economy.

With the collapse of communism there appeared to be a capitalist hegemony for a brief period in the early 1990s. The assumption in the West was that developing countries, including the states of the Muslim world, would eventually promote the opening of markets, de-regulation, privatisation and economic restructuring more generally. This would result in a greatly diminished role for the state in economic affairs. These developments presented both a challenge and an opportunity for Islamic economists, the challenge being to provide a critique of capitalism and the opportunity to present a sharia-based economic system as the only real alternative to capitalism for the Muslim world.

Islamic economists such as Syed Naqvi and Umer Chapra eagerly took up the challenge that the new circumstances brought, both making perhaps their most important contributions to the literature on Islamic economics to date. Naqvi believed Islam shared capitalism's emphasis on accumulation as an essential part of the overall dynamics of economic advance. He noted that both Islam and capitalism reject feudalism as anti-progressive, and instead believed that both systems favoured a fluid social structure.[36]

The proponents of capitalism, Naqvi argued, insisted on the moral invulnerability of self-interested behaviour. In an Islamic economy self-interest is recognised as a motivating force, but its sovereignty cannot be unquestioned. Whereas capitalism is possessive with respect to the ownership of wealth, Islam emphasises a more generous attitude. Being widely read Naqvi was aware of the Western literature on the link between Protestant ethics and capitalism, and cited economists such as Viner who wrote about it.[37] Naqvi quotes how the unremitting industry of the capitalist, concentration on business affairs and restraint on personal consumption all drive the system forward. These are qualities he applauds, but he is critical of the capitalists' neglect of human relations and in particular their exploitation of labour.

Although it is clear that Naqvi and other Islamic economists approve of some of the outcomes of the Protestant ethic, they are reluctant to get involved in the debates by economic historians over the role of the Reformation in the industrial revolution in the West. There is no attempt to draw explicit parallels between traditional Catholicism and unreformed Islam, which were both arguably associated with static feudal systems. Implicitly, however, there is the suggestion that the interpretation of religious teaching must change as productive relations and societies evolve, which in Islamic terms can be described as *ijtihad*, the notion of reinterpretation that implied free thinking.[38]

Much of Umer Chapra's work in the 1970s and early 1980s was focused on monetary issues and examining finance in an interest-free Islamic economy,[39] by the late 1980s, however, he was turning his attention to the conflict of economic systems, the demise of socialism and the limits of capitalism.[40] He had much experience of monetary systems in his role as a special advisor to the Saudi Arabian Monetary Agency. Nevertheless he felt compelled to pursue a broader theme given the changing global economy, and the need to define how Islamic society might be accommodated within it.

Islam and Development

Islamic economists such as Chapra saw capitalist and communist models as being at best of limited relevance to Muslim economies, and at worst unacceptable in terms of the excesses that both systems produced. Objectively he recognised that most Muslim economies could be classified as underdeveloped, or perhaps in some cases developing, rather than developed. Despite this categorisation Chapra had severe reservations about the sub-discipline of development economics, as he saw this as being inherently and universally unsatisfactory, and not just inapplicable in the Islamic world.

Development economics emerged as a sub-discipline in the mid-twentieth century around the same time as Islamic economics. It could be argued that they are competing paradigms, one based on a supposedly scientific interpretation of economic indicators that may be neither reliable or meaningful, the other on the revelation of divine truths, and a belief that a central facet of development is personal and social-moral regeneration. Indeed it can be debated whether the latter is a prerequisite for development or the most important manifestation of the development process itself, which Islamic economists see as a qualitative rather than a quantitative process, involving changes in human attitudes.

Chapra's major critique of development economics was not written until the late 1980s by which time there was much self-criticism from within the sub-discipline. Chapra was aware of this, and some of his views in fact mirror those of economists with whom he would not want to be identified. He asserts that development economics has been subject to fashion, moving from being *dirigiste* and in favour of the state playing a major role in resource allocation to a position where free markets with minimum regulation are thought to be essential for successful development. He suggests that in contemporary development economics there is a strictly 'this worldly perspective' which justifies 'materialism and social Darwinism' with no attention to social interest except in so far as it is served by self-interest.[41] Chapra was particularly critical of the neglect of equity by Western development economists, such as those who supported the accelerated growth approach of Kuznets who postulated that inequity could bring faster growth as the richer saved and invested more.[42]

Chapra sees Islamisation as the way forward for Muslim countries, but he acknowledges that this cannot be 'an antidote to all the problems of Muslim countries'.[43] As these have resulted from what he asserts were centuries of socio-economic, political and moral degeneration, he believes that misguided domestic policies and unhealthy external shocks are likely to persist for many years to come. In other words, socio-economic reforms that promote justice in accordance with Muslim teaching will inevitably be a long haul. Exactly what is implied by Islamisation is not fully spelt out by Chapra, but he concurs with the earlier views expressed by Khurshid Ahmad which have done much to influence the development debate amongst Islamic economists.

Khurshid Ahmad has been more of a speaker and organiser than a prolific writer, but he more than anyone else identified the key concepts from religious writing that most Islamic economists now accept as of fundamental significance for meaningful development in the Muslim world. As a former minister of development and planning in Pakistan in the 1970s he had first-hand experience of policy dilemmas, but he believes Muslim countries should draw on their Islamic inheritance rather than simply import Western models and concepts.[44]

Ahmad saw his task as being to 'clearly identify the Islamic ideal of economic development (and) to measure the distance between this ideal and the present day reality of the Muslim world'.[45] This did not imply that there was only one Islamic road to economic development, as Ahmad stresses the need to distinguish between an Islamic economy and an *Islamising* economy, the latter being a process involving a multiplicity of approaches and models. There is in other words an agreed end, but diverse means of getting there. Ahmad, like Chapra, is critical of the application of conventional neo-classical development approaches in Muslim countries, as he asserts that imitation of the West 'has failed to deliver the goods'.[46]

The core message from Ahmad is that human values are the crucial element in any development process. The major defect of Western approaches is their 'pseudo-value neutrality' as development economists using neo-classical analysis mistakenly assume their analysis is purely objective. Ahmad believes that values should be recognised and enhanced rather than being assumed away, and he stresses the need for 'value commitment' and ultimately 'value ful-filment'.[47]

Ahmad sees development in terms of the Islamic concept of *taz-kiya*: purification plus growth. This results in *falah*, prosperity in this world and the hereafter, where prosperity is defined in both mate-rial and spiritual terms. The notion is of a wider or comprehensive interpretation that involves the moral as well as the material, the social in addition to the economic and both the spiritual and the physical. The focus is on man, within and without, and development with justice, *'adl*, rather than injustice, *zulm*. Development is desir-able, and indeed imperative, as it makes believers better equipped to carry out the will of Allah.[48] At the same time, it brings a better level of understanding of what serving Allah involves. In contrast to some Christian thinking there is no virtue in poverty, as if Muslims are constantly thinking of ways to simply survive there is less space for the spiritual.

Unfortunately, Ahmad's own country of origin, Pakistan, has proved to be a poor example of how Muslim economies should have developed in the twentieth century. Even Ahmad himself does not see any positive lessons emerging, although most Pakistani econ-omists assert that the failure was in no way due to Islam. The real problem was the poor situation that the country inherited when the sub-continent was divided following the war between Muslims and Hindus after the end of British rule. In contrast Islamic economists often cite Malaysia as an example of successful development, even though it had its own ethnic and religious divisions between the ethnically Malay, Chinese and Indian communities.

Malaysian economists have made a substantial contribution to the Islamic economics literature on development. This is not surprising given the rapid economic change that occurred in Malaysia in the second half of the twentieth century. The country has moved from being a predominately primary resource based economy exporting rubber and palm oil to a newly industrialising country that has a substantial electronics sector and even a competitive car industry. Malaysia's political leaders have also paid lip service to Islamic eco-nomics, including Mahathir Mohammad who has served as prime minister since 1981, and to an even greater extent his now impris-oned former deputy, Anwar Ibrahim.[49] For over twenty years the

International Islamic University in Kuala Lumpur has been a major centre of research and teaching on Islamic economics, playing a comparable role in East Asia to that of the Centre for Islamic Economics at King Abdulaziz University in Jeddah for West Asia.

Aidit Ghazali was and remains one of the leading Malaysian writers on Islam and development with his major work published in 1990.[50] He agrees with Khurshid Ahmad's position that the central issue is *tazkiya*, purification and growth. Ghazali sees conventional economics as being 'man-thought' in origin whereas Islamic economics is divine in nature. The former, he observes, is 'based on scientific observation, economic realities and the use of logic (whereas) in Islam reasoning and the faculty of reasoning do not supersede values, principles and belief that cannot be explained through reason'.[51] In other words, Islamic approaches to development have to be based on religious values and principles, but that does not imply that development theories and policies advocated by Western development specialists have to be rejected. Indeed Ghazali sees much in both capitalism and socialism that is consistent with Islamic teaching. Ultimately, however, he believes that development cannot be achieved by man's efforts alone, as spiritual guidance is needed.

Ghazali is well versed in contemporary writing on economic development, and attempts to position Islamic approaches in relation to this literature. He sees some parallels between the human capital approach to development and the thinking of Islamic economists that also emphasises the human element rather than the merely mechanical physical capital formation associated with traditional capitalism and the Marxist analysis of industrial development. He also suggests there are some parallels with basic need approaches that stress that everyone has to have a certain level of minimum provision to preserve human dignity.

According to Ghazali the justification for such approaches differs between Islamic economics and the Western secularist literature. In the latter case the emphasis on human capital formation is justified pragmatically, whereas in Islamic economics it contributes to spiritual enlightenment. Similarly, whereas the basic need approach is justified in secularist writing with respect to income distribution and social equity arguments, in Islamic economics the issue is that severe poverty prevents believers carrying out their religious duties effectively. Where believers lack resources and are distracted by hunger and the worries associated with insecurity of income, spiritual matters may not receive the attention they deserve.

Islamic economists and Muslim development specialists were realistic about the enormous disparities between most Muslim economies and the advanced Western economies as measured by conventional development indicators such as per capita gross national product.[52] The gap between the rich Western nations and the poorest Muslim economies increased significantly in the second half of the twentieth century. There were several reactions to this. One was to suggest that quantitative development indicators were meaningless, as development was about qualitative change, not merely rises in material living standards. A second was to acknowledge the disparities, but suggest that they resulted from Western exploitation of the Muslim world, and a failure of political independence to result in real economic independence. A third reaction was to blame internal factors, not least secularist governance, and the failure of any Muslim country to adopt an Islamic economic system. This was the position of Ahmad, Chapra and Ghazali, that seemed to gain increasing support as leftist colonialist and neo-colonialist arguments became less convincing as the century progressed.

Islamic Finance in Theory and Practice

Although Islamic development theory was still in its infancy as the twentieth century drew to a close, Islamic theories of finance had reached a much more mature stage. Indeed Islamic banking and monetary theory is arguably the most developed area of the subject, where real progress has been achieved in terms of implementation, both within and outside the Muslim world. Publications on interest-free Islamic banking started to appear from the 1950s, a notable early contributor being the Pakistani sharia scholar, Muhammad Uzair who wrote an influential book on the subject that appeared in 1955.[53]

The prohibition of *riba* is of course explicit in the Qur'an,[54] as is the call for the lenient treatment of debtors,[55] but how this should be applied to mid-twentieth-century banking practice was much more a matter of debate. There was in particular the question of whether *riba,* an addition to a loan, constituted usury, excessive and exploitative interest, or any kind of interest. The consensus amongst Islamic economists from the 1960s was that it should be applied to all interest, which meant alternatives to interest-based banking had to be found.

Baqir al-Sadr also made a notable contribution with a book on interest-free banking in Islam that was first published in Kuwait in 1970[56] and later translated into Urdu.[57] He distinguished between a client depositing money with a bank and the bank advancing funds to a client. Both transactions could be covered by *mudaraba,* with the depositor sharing in the bank's profits and the bank sharing in the profits of the enterprises it supported. The assumption was that deposits would come from private citizens and business, but that there would be no personal lending, only advances to profit generating businesses. Personal advances could be covered by *qard hasan,* interest-free beneficent advances, but these were strictly non-commercial.

The major practical problem with *mudaraba* was the asymmetrical nature of the risks involved. For the bank depositor the major risks were of bank failure and the uncertainty regarding the level of profits to be shared. With effective bank regulation the risk of bank failure was minimal however, and uncertainty even applies to variable interest returns, so this was unlikely to deter depositors, indeed it was the slight risk they took that justified their reward. The more serious problem with *mudaraba* arose with bank advances, as this form of financing businesses meant that there was no guarantee that the bank could get their funds repaid. Furthermore, the risk of getting no profits was considerable, especially with the type of small businesses that characterised many Muslim economies. There were also moral hazard problems, as businesses could potentially disguise the profits they made to minimise the profits shared, especially where full audits were not required.

This problem was addressed by Sami Homoud in the 1970s. He believed that *murabaha,* or mark-up trade financing, could play an important role in an Islamic banking system.[58] *Murabaha* is much less risky than *mudaraba* as the mark-up is agreed in advance between the bank and the trader, and the period until the trader has to repay the bank is also stipulated at the outset.[59] The mark-up should reflect the bank's true costs plus an agreed profit, and if the cost calculation is incorrect, the client has the right to cancel the contract.[60] There is still business risk associated with *murabaha* as the bank that purchases the good on behalf of the trader may find it is unable to resell the good at the end of the contract period if the trader's financial circumstances have changed. It is this risk which justifies part of the mark-up the bank charges. According to the Maliki school of Islamic jurisprudence it is also legitimate for the bank to add to the mark-up to cover its legitimate expenses involved in the trade transactions.[61]

Murabaha was arguably one of the factors that enabled Islamic banking to take off in the 1970s and prove a viable alternative to conventional banking in many Muslim countries. The earliest modern Islamic banks that were started in Pakistan in the 1950s did not need to use *murabaha* as they were little more than credit unions, where members pooled their savings and drew out funds when needed. This was also how the Mit Ghamr Savings Bank that opened in Egypt in 1963 functioned.[62] In many respects these institutions were early precursors of the Grameen Bank that expanded in Bangladesh following its independence from Pakistan in 1972. Such institutions can play an important role in the finance of smallholder farming and handicrafts, but they are best classified as micro-financing institutions rather than commercial banks. Even so, in the case of Egypt, President Nasser saw the Mit Ghamr Savings Bank established by Ahmad al-Naggar as a threat because of its support from Islamists in many of the rural areas in the Delta. Consequently it was taken into state control in 1972, and renamed the Nasser Social Bank.[63]

The Islamic Development Bank, which was founded in 1975, used *murabaha* for most of its oil financing operations in the early years even though it was a development assistance agency rather than a commercial bank, as this meant its capital was less at risk.[64] Its example influenced the practice of the newly founded Islamic commercial banks, notably the Dubai Islamic Bank (founded 1975), the Kuwait Finance House (1977), the Faisal Banks of Egypt and the Sudan (1977), the Jordan Islamic Bank (1978) and the Bahrain (1979) and Qatar (1981) Islamic banks.[65]

Although the spread of Islamic banking was welcomed by Islamic economists, there was much criticism of their financing methods.

Ibrahim Warde expressed concern that too much of the financing was short-term *murabaha* and there was relatively little long-term funding of projects that might contribute more to development.[66] The over-dependence on *murabaha* was not what Islamic economists had envisaged, and many were disappointed with the banking practice and the lack of partnership financing.[67]

To counter these criticisms many Islamic banks, having built up confidence through *murabaha,* were prepared to offer their clients longer-term finance, usually through *ijara,* which was a leasing contract, or in some cases through *ijara wa-iqtina',* a hire purchase contract.[68] This became popular in the 1980s and remains important. Such financing applied to purchases of major items of capital equipment, where the goods themselves served as collateral, and the payment was by instalment, usually monthly or quarterly, up to a period of five years. Where manufacturing was financed, *istithna'* was used, whereby the bank made advances which could enable suppliers to be paid at each stage of the manufacturing process. This method could also be used for project financing of large-scale infrastructure developments.[69]

Although there was diversification in the methods of Islamic financing used in the 1980s and 1990s *mudaraba* profit sharing was only applied to investment deposits with Islamic banks rather than bank financing. *Musharaka,* where the bank forms a partnership with an entrepreneur, was also little used, as it was deemed too risky. Islamic banks which received most of their funds through current account deposits, on which no return was payable, were often accused of accepting free money and making profits for themselves out of virtually risk free operations. As the century drew to a close Islamic banking had become a $150 billion industry, but questions were still asked if it was different only in the legal designation of the financing instruments used or if it really was a genuine alternative to conventional banking.

Similar criticisms were also made of the Islamic investment fund movement that emerged in the 1980s and 1990s. These funds were criticised for investing mostly in the West rather than in the emerging stock markets of Muslim countries, with investment decisions influenced largely by risk assessment rather than any notion of Islamic solidarity. Nevertheless those who manage the funds see parallels

with the Western ethical finance movement, as although the criteria for acceptable investments differ from what is *halal* under sharia
law, there has been much scope for a cross fertilisation of ideas over
managerial practices.

Islamic Taxation

At the close of the twentieth century there were even more unan-
swered questions regarding Islamic taxation. Although the principles
had been understood for over fourteen hundred years, the application of these taxes was at best problematic.[70] Most Muslim states
raised their finances through secular taxes such as import tariffs or
business taxes, rather than through *zakat* and other religious taxes,
and there was debate over whether states (rather than the religious
authorities) should be collecting *zakat* in any case. The crucial principle is that *zakat* has to be collected and the proceeds distributed in
accordance with sharia law, and as long as this is observed, it is un-
important who administers the tax.[71] However, the issue still remains
how far the governments of Muslim states respect Islamic law.

There was much written on *zakat* in the late 1940s in newly independent Pakistan, most notably by Shaykh Ataullah,[72] but the most
comprehensive modern treatment was by Nicolas Aghnides. He was
born in 1883 in India, and wrote pamphlets and papers on Islamic
taxation during the 1920s and 1930s, many of which were rewritten
for his major work, which finally appeared in 1961.[73] Aghnides, citing
the Qur'an,[74] stresses how the payment of *zakat*, a tax on property,
results in purification from sin.[75] It is one of the five pillars of faith
cited in the Sunna, the notion being that if an owner sees the value
of his property increase, then he should share some of this growing
prosperity in this world to gain favour in the next. *Zakat* is applied to
a productive minimum of property (*nisab*) but real estate is typically
excluded, as there are separate land taxes, the *kharaj*. Productive
property is defined to include, according to Aghnides, gold or sil-
ver, farm animals and goods intended for trade. The annual liability
is calculated as one-fortieth of the value of these productive assets,
regardless of whether they are actually productive during the year
when the payment is made.[76] Any debt relating to the productive
assets is subtracted when the net liability is calculated.

Aghnides also did much to clarify the liability to *kharaj* or land tax and *jizya* or poll tax. *Kharaj* can be applied on a fixed or proportionate basis, the rate depending on the quality of the land, the kind of crop grown, the type of irrigation and the distance from markets.[77] In no case can it represent more than half the value of the crops. There is more discretion over *kharaj* than over *zakat*, the crucial factor being what the land can bear. *Jizya* is a type of security tax paid by non-Muslims living in Muslim lands. This is, in many respects, the most controversial of taxes, but there are no direct guidelines on how much is payable, though it can be regarded as a substitute for *zakat* and *kharaj*. Aghnides' treatment of these taxes tends to be factual rather than assertive, with the positions of the major schools of Islamic law explained.

Despite the efforts of writers such as Aghnides the debates on *zakat* have made much less progress in the twentieth century than those on Islamic banking issues. S. A. Siddiqi, the Military Accountant General for Pakistan attempted to build on the early work of Aghnides. Siddiqi had his work published in English in 1948, well in advance of Aghnides, although he generously acknowledges his debt to the latter.[78] Siddiqi's work is considerably shorter, but unlike Aghnides, he tries to compare Islamic to conventional taxation. The discussion of *zakat* in the light of Adam Smith's four canons of taxation is instructive.[79] The first is that each citizen should contribute to the cost of government in relation to ability to pay, which implies that taxation should be progressive. Siddiqi argues that *zakat* would be proportionate if applied to income, but as it is levied on wealth, this makes it progressive, as the poor have no wealth to tax, and wealth itself increases progressively with income. Smith's second canon, that taxes should be certain rather than arbitrary, is also met by *zakat*, as Siddiqi points out that the rate is fixed by divine sanction and cannot be altered by government. The third canon, that taxes are levied at a time when it is convenient to pay is also met by *zakat*, as in the case of agricultural produce, it is collected after each harvest, although Siddiqi does not discuss how the tax is applied in the case of manufacturing. Smith's fourth canon is that administrative costs should be minimal, which Siddiqi argues applies in the case of *zakat*, as payment is the second most important of the five religious duties for Muslims. Hence there is little attempt at evasion or concealment of assets, as payment is a matter of conscience for believers regardless of their views of the state.

S. A. Siddiqi's discussion of customs duties also reveals considerable knowledge of international practices.[80] He asserts that the Islamic economic system favours free trade that promotes specialisation rather than tariffs or quotas. However, he points out how during the early years of Islam the Caliph 'Umar introduced countervailing duties for imports from outside of the Muslim world, in retaliation for the 10 per cent tariff levied by *harbis* (neighbouring non-Muslim authorities). The *harbis* were accorded protection during their stay in the Islamic state, arguably justifying the tax collection. Siddiqi points out that the Shafi'i school of Islamic jurisprudence condemns the application of import duties on non-Muslims who are engaged in trade between Muslim states, the implication being that there should be no discrimination between traders, but rather what matters is the origin of the merchandise.

Not all taxes in an Islamic state are religious, as Siddiqi makes the distinction between these and secular taxes (*fay* revenues).[81] The latter are subject to the discretion of the ruler, and are to meet general expenses rather than, as in the case of *zakat*, being earmarked for social purposes such as the care of the needy. The burden of secular taxes, and the extent of the state's involvement in economic activity more generally, may vary from country to country, but Siddiqi argues that decisions on such matters should be taken by the Muslim community at large, that implies some form of democratic accountability. Siddiqi discussed the remuneration of rulers, believing that they should be paid an adequate amount so that they are not distracted by material concerns from their duty to serve wholeheartedly the Muslim community. Similarly those employed in the military, the particular concern of Siddiqi, should be paid sufficient so that they do not have to seek outside sources of income for their subsistence. Those with larger families and more horses to maintain should be given higher pay, as should those stationed where living costs are higher.[82]

There were some useful papers presented at a seminar on monetary and fiscal economics of Islam in Mecca in 1978, notably the contribution by Abdin Ahmed Salama, who concluded from the Saudi Arabian experience, and in line with the thinking of S. A. Siddiqi, that *zakat* had to be supplemented by conventional taxation in any modern state.[83] This work, however, was not followed up by studies of *zakat* in other countries, although a Syrian Islamic economist, Muhammad Anas Zarqa, estimated that *zakat* in his home country redistributed two per cent of national income to the poor.[84] Others, notably Mohammad Metwally, have attempted to develop macroeconomic models of a highly technical nature exploring the effects of *zakat* on consumption, investment and other variables, but the results, as with most macro modelling, depend on the assumptions made.[85] More promising was an attempt by T. I. Tag al-Din to explore the implications of *zakat* for poverty reduction and macroeconomic stabilisation.[86] *Zakat* can arguably play an important role in the former, but its favourable stabilisation effects are far from proven.

A more recent study by an Arab author, Abdullah Juma'an Saeed al-Sa'adi, covered much of the same ground as S. A. Siddiqi. Originally submitted as a thesis to al-Azhar University in Cairo in 1983, it was subsequently translated into English and published thanks to the generosity of the ruler of Qatar, al-Sa'adi's home state. [87] Al-Sa'adi's major contribution is to ask whether Islamic taxes can be classified as direct or indirect, the former being paid by an individual, whereas the latter, such as value added or purchase taxes, are passed on to others. For al-Sa'adi, Islamic taxes are direct, including not only *zakat*, but the poll tax, *jizya*, as although the latter can be collected by central government at community level, each individual in the community has to pay the tax at local level, and the collection and payments' transfer have to be separated.[88]

Unanswered Questions

It is clear that much progress has been made in the twentieth century in defining Islamic economics as a distinct branch of economics and in establishing a research agenda. There has been some success in devising an Islamic economic alternative to communism and capitalism, and although there are disagreements over development policies and strategy, some consensus has emerged over the common features of the model such as the recognition of private property and the role of markets. Islamic finance has taken off as an industry, and there has been more work on this than in any other area.

Despite these often dramatic developments, there are many un-answered questions, and it is far from clear where Islamic economics is heading. There is no consensus on the boundaries of what Timor Kuran has described as a sub-economy.[89] Few Islamic economists are explicit about their political agenda, but as the implementation of an Islamic system implies a greatly changed role for the state, it is clear their subject is more about political economy than economic analysis. Most Islamic economists feel frustrated that outside the financial field there is so little state commitment in Muslim countries to implementing the sharia law in the economic sphere. Few see Iran as a model for an Islamic economy, and most are critical of the attempts to Islamise in Pakistan and the Sudan.

Some core topics have largely been neglected, notably the institution of the *hisba*, that is concerned with the regulation of markets. Islamic economists have preferred to leave this field to legal scholars. One author, Muhammad Bashar, writes about price controls in an Islamic economy without even mentioning the *hisba*.[90] The only significant contribution was the translation of Ibn Taymiyya's work on the *hisba* written in the fourteenth century into English.[91] Furthermore there has been little attempt to see an Islamic economy in a broader context. The question of whether there is space for civil society in an Islamic economy has not been addressed, 'civil' not necessarily implying 'secular'. The position of Muslim states in the global economy has also not been discussed, or even the relationship with the contemporary literature on economics and religion more generally.[92] There is clearly much scope for work on Islamic economics in the new century, as the subject, if that is the best term to use, is still in its infancy.

Notes

1. Nikki R. Keddie, 'Sayyid Jamal al-Din al-Afghani', in Ali Rahnema, ed., *Pioneers of the Islamic Revival* (London, 1994), pp. 11–29.

2. John L. Esposito, *Islam: The Straight Path* (3rd ed., Oxford, 1998), pp. 126–132.

3. Seoharwi Muhammad Hafzur Rahman, *Islam ka iqtisadi nizam* (Delhi, 1942).

4. Shaykh Mahmud Ahmad, *Economics of Islam: A Comparative Study* (Lahore, 1947).

5. Yaqut al-'Ashmawi, *al-Khutut al-kubra li'l-nizam al-iqtisadi fi'l-Islam* (Cairo, 1959).

6. Muhammad Nejatullah Siddiqi, *Muslim Economic Thinking: A Survey of Contemporary Literature* (Leicester, 1981).

7. Seyyed Vali Reza Nasr, 'Mawdudi and Jama'at-i Islami: The Origins, Theory and Practice of Islamic Revivalism', in Ali Rahnema, ed., *Pioneers of the Islamic Revival*, pp. 98–124.

8. Sayyid Abul A'la Mawdudi, *The Economic Problem of Man and its Islamic Solution* (Lahore, 1975).

9. Farhad Nomani and Ali Rahnema, *Islamic Economic Systems* (London, 1994), p. 113.

10. Maxime Rodinson, *Islam and Capitalism* (Harmondsworth, 1977), pp. 19–20.

11. Muhammad Abdul Mannan, *Islamic Economics: Theory and Practice* (Lahore, 1970; Sevenoaks, 1986).

12. Muhammad Nejatullah Siddiqi, *Muslim Economic Thinking* (Leicester, 1981).

13. M. Umer Chapra, *Islam and the Economic Challenge* (Leicester, 1992).

14. Syed Nawab Naqvi, *Islam, Economics and Society* (London, 1994).

15. Ibn Taimiyah, *Public Duties in Islam: The Institution of the Hisba* (Leicester, 1992).

16. Ibn Khaldun, *The Muqaddimah: An Introduction to History*, tr. Franz Rosenthal (Princeton, NJ, 1958).

17. Chapra, *Islam and the Economic Challenge*, pp. 199–212.

18. Mohamed Aslam Haneef, *Contemporary Islamic Economic Thought* (Kuala Lumpur, 1995), pp. 13–14.

19. Mannan, *Islamic Economics: Theory and Practice*, p. 14.

20. Siddiqi, *Muslim Economic Thinking*, p. 12.

21. Ibid., p. 2.

22. Rodney Wilson, 'The Islamic Development Bank's Role as an Aid Agency for Moslem Countries', *Journal of International Development*, 1, 4 (1989) pp. 444–466. Reprinted in Tim Niblock and Rodney Wilson, ed., *The Political Economy of the Middle East* (Cheltenham, 1999), vol. 3 'Islamic Economics', pp. 478–500.

23. Timur Kuran, 'Islamic Economics and the Islamic Sub-economy', *Journal of Economic Perspectives*, 9, 1 (1995), pp. 155–173.

24. Chapra, *Islam and the Economic Challenge*, p. 8.

25. Abu Hamid Muhammad Ghazali, *al-Mustasfa* (Cairo, 1937), pp. 139–140.

26. Chapra, *Islam and the Economic Challenge*, p. 210.

27. Muhammad Baqir al-Sadr, *Iqtisaduna* (Beirut, 1961; repr. 1968). Origi-

nal English translation by Tehran World Services, 1981. A more recent and better translation has been made by Kadom Jawad Shubber, *Our Economics: Iqtisaduna* (London, 2000). There is also a German translation by Andreas Rieck, *Unsere Wirtschaft: Eine Gekürzle Kommentierte Übersetzung des Buches Istisaduna von Muhammad Baqir as-Sadr* (Berlin, 1984).

28. Rodney Wilson, 'The Contribution of Muhammad Baqir al-Sadr to Contemporary Islamic Economic Thought', *JIS*, 9, 1 (1998), pp. 46–59.

29. Abdol Hasan Bani Sadr, *Work and the Worker in Islam* (Tehran, 1980). Originally published in Persian (Tehran, 1978).

30. Hakim Mohammed Said, *The Employer and the Employee: Islamic Concepts* (Karachi, 1972), pp. 53–58.

31. Hanna Batatu, 'Iraq's Underground Shi'a Movements: Characteristics, Causes and Prospects', *Middle Eastern Journal*, 35, 4 (1981), pp. 578–594.

32. Siddiqi, *Muslim Economic Thinking*, pp. 52–53.

33. Sayyid Abul A'la Maududi, *Islam aur jadid m'ashi nazariyat* (Delhi, 1969), pp. 52–83.

34. Ibid., pp. 26–51.

35. Siddiqi, *Muslim Economic Thinking*, p. 46.

36. Naqvi, *Islam, Economics and Society*, p. 76.

37. Jacob Viner, *Religious Thought and Economic Society* (Durham, NC, 1978).

38. Naqvi, *Islam, Economics and Society*, p. 100.

39. Chapra, *Towards a Just Monetary System* (Leicester, 1985).

40. Chapra, *Islam and the Economic Challenge*.

41. Ibid., p. 149.

42. Simon Kuznets, 'Economic Growth and Income Inequality', *American Economic Review*, 45 (1955), pp. 1–28.

43. Chapra, *Islam and the Economic Challenge*, p. 353.

44. Khurshid Ahmad, *Economic Development in an Islamic Framework* (Leicester, 1979), pp. 10–13.

45. Ahmad, *Studies in Islamic Economics* (Leicester, 1980), p. 171.

46. Ibid., p. 173.

47. Ibid., p. 175.

48. Ahmad, 'Some Thoughts on a Strategy for Development under an Islamic Aegis', in Mustapha Filali, ed., *Islam and the New International Economic Order: The Social Dimension* (Geneva, 1980), pp. 134–136.

49. Rodney Wilson, 'Islam and Malaysia's Economic Development', *JIS*, 9, 2 (1998), pp. 259–276.

50. Aidit Ghazali, *Development: An Islamic Perspective* (Selangor, Malaysia, 1990).

51. Ibid., p. 17.

52. Khalid M. Ishaque, 'The Islamic Approach to Economic Activity and Development', in Salem Azzam, ed., *The Muslim World and the Future Economic Order* (London, 1979), pp. 78–81.

53. Muhammad Uzair, *An Outline of Interestless Banking* (Karachi, 1955).

54. Q.2:275.

55. Q.2:280.

56. Muhammad Baqir al Sadr, *al-Bank al-la-rabawi fi'l-Islam* (Kuwait, 1970).

57. Tr. Ali Jawadi, *Islamic Bank* (Bombay, 1974).

58. Sami Hasan Homoud, *Tatwir al-a'mal al masrafiyya bi-ma yattafiqu wa'l-shari'a al-Islamiyya* (Cairo, 1976). See also Sami Hasan Homoud, *Islamic Banking* (London, 1985), pp. 238–241.

59. Nabil A. Saleh, *Unlawful Gain and Legitimate Profit in Islamic Law: Riba, Gharar and Islamic Banking* (Cambridge, 1986), p. 89.

60. Ibrahim Kamel, 'A Summary of the Day to Day Working of an Existing Islamic Bank', in Muazzam Ali, ed., *Islamic Banks and Strategies of Economic Co-operation* (London, 1982), pp. 65–66.

61. Saleh, *Unlawful Gain and Legitimate Profit in Islamic Law*, p. 95.

62. Rodney Wilson, *Banking and Finance in the Arab Middle East* (London, 1983), pp. 75–79.

63. Ann Elizabeth Mayer, 'Islamic Banking and Credit Policies in the Sadat Era: The Social Origins of Islamic Banking in Egypt', *Arab Law Quarterly*, 1, 1 (1985), pp. 32–50.

64. S. A. Meenai, *The Islamic Development Bank: A Case Study of Islamic Co-operation* (London, 1989), pp. 57–59.

65. Seddik Taouti, *Vers un système bancaire conforme a la chari'a Islamique* (Algiers, 1986), pp. 199–223.

66. Ibrahim Warde, *Islamic Finance in the Global Economy* (Edinburgh, 2000), p. 175.

67. Frank E. Vogel and Samuel L. Hayes, *Islamic Law and Finance: Religion, Risk and Return* (The Hague, 1998), pp. 135–136.

68. Luay Allawi, 'Leasing: An Islamic Financial Instrument', in Butterworths Editorial Staff, *Islamic Banking and Finance, Economics* (London, 1986), pp. 120–127.

69. Muhammad Anas Zarqa, '*Istisna* Financing of Infrastructure Projects', *Islamic Economic Studies*, 4, 2 (1997), pp. 67–74.

70. Roger Arnaldez, 'Sur une interprétation économique et sociale des théories de la zakat en droit musulman', in François Perroux, ed., *Cahiers de L'Institut de Science Economique Appliquée, l'Islam, l'economie et la technique* (Paris, 1960), pp. 65–86.

71. Abdel Qadeem Zalloom, *Funds in the Khilafah State* (London, 1988), pp. 155–157.

72. Shaykh Ataullah, *Revival of Zakat* (Lahore, 1949).

73. Nicolas P. Aghnides, *Mohammedan Theories of Finance* (Lahore, 1961).

74. Q.87:14 and Q.9:2.

75. Aghnides, *Mohammedan Theories of Finance*, p. 208.

76. Ibid., pp. 210–212.

77. Ibid., pp. 376–396.

78. S. A. Siddiqi, *Public Finance in Islam* (Lahore, 1948), p. v.

79. Ibid., pp. 18–24.

80. Ibid., pp. 89–94.

81. Ibid., pp. 169–175.

82. Ibid., pp. 178–186.

83. Abdin Ahmed Salama, 'Fiscal Analysis of *zakat* with Special Reference to Saudi Arabia's Experience in *zakat*', in Mohammad Ariff, ed., *Monetary and Fiscal Economics of Islam* (Jeddah, 1982), pp. 341–364.

84. Muhammad Anas Zarqa, 'Islamic Distributive Schemes', in Munawar Iqbal, ed., *Distributive Justice and Need Fulfilment in an Islamic Economy* (Leicester, 1988), p. 182 and p. 204.

85. M. M. Metwally, 'Fiscal Policy of an Islamic Economy', in Mahamoud A. Gulaid and Mohamed Aden Abdullah, ed., *Readings in Public Finance in Islam* (Jeddah, 1995), pp. 297–326.

86. S. I. Tag al-Din, 'Allocative and Stabilisation Functions of *zakat* in an Islamic Economy', in Guliad and Abdullah, ed., *Readings in Public Finance in Islam*, pp. 327–353.

87. Abdullah Juma'an Saeed al-Sa'adi, *Fiscal Policy in the Islamic State* (Newcastle-under-Lyme, Staffordshire, 1986).

88. Ibid., pp. 194–196.

89. Timur Kuran, 'Islamic Economics and the Islamic Sub-economy'.

90. Muhammad Lawal Ahmad Bashar, 'Price Control in an Islamic Economy', *Journal of King Abdulaziz University, Islamic Economics*, 9 (1997), pp. 29–52.

91. Ibn Taymiya, *Public Duties in Islam: The Institution of the Hisba* (Chicago, IL, 1982).

92. Rodney Wilson, *Economics, Ethics and Religion: Jewish, Christian and Muslim Economic Thought* (London, 1997).

8

On Gender and the Family

Hibba Abugideiri

As a general survey of Islamic discourses on gender and the family produced by various twentieth-century Muslim thinkers, this chapter argues that such discourses have been constrained by certain thinking about the Muslim family that gives primacy to motherhood, at the expense of woman's spiritual and legal rights. Such primacy is drawn from an essentialist understanding of woman as a relational being. To demonstrate, this chapter isolates the texts of various thinkers who reaffirm and validate in modern terms an historical trope of the Muslim family, and by direct implication, that of the Muslim woman. In the process, woman, family, and by logical extension, society, become inextricably tied by these discourses in ways that foreclose the possibility of expanding definitions of womanhood. Such interplay culminates in woman's legal place in family law. Scholarship has increasingly exposed how such laws have afforded Muslim women a more visible role in public, yet paradoxically, women have been accorded more restrictive rights within the home. Part of the problem is that twentieth-century Islamic discourses uphold a system of law that has ultimately petrified the very process of interpreting gender roles vis-à-vis the institution of family in ways that prevent their redefinition (not to be misread as reinterpretation), precisely because the paradigm of family used to guide the interpretive process renders the Islamic values of family and a traditional understanding of gender roles, synonymous. A change in either fosters a looming fear of familial, and by direct implication, societal dismemberment. What is important about this study is not simply its discourse analysis of gender and the family in the modern period, which has been dealt with extensively.[1] Rather, it is in its specific critique of how gender, family-society and culture are discursively tied together in ways problematic for Muslim women, particularly as manifest in family law.

Because their works have had a far-reaching global impact on notions of gender and family through their multiple translations, speeches and/or world-wide public appearances, Sunni Muslim thinkers, like Abu al-A'la Mawdudi, Khurshid Ahmad, 'Abd al-Halim Abu Shuqqah, Yusuf al-Qaradawi, and Jamal Badawi, to name a few, will be consulted.[2] The focus, however, is less on the Muslim thinkers themselves, whether prominent or lesser known, than on the nature of their religious discourse, or, more specifically, on a certain grid of conceptual thought about gender and the family that has proven historically resilient, paradoxically, because of societal and globalising change. This analysis clearly cannot mirror the breadth of writings by the most influential or even exceptional twentieth-century Muslim thinkers, though a few are discussed. The goal here is not to target the personal beliefs of a particular group of preeminent thinkers but to deconstruct a pervasive way of thinking about gender and the family, one that is taken-for-granted by most Muslims and typifies much of the Islamic literature on this topic. Yet, this discourse requires critical and immediate redress, especially in the face of rising debates and legitimate criticisms concerning Islam, gender justice and human rights. In this way, this chapter hopes to join a very important debate about Islamic self-definition and Muslim self-reflexivity.

Discourse Analysis: Deconstructing the Framework of Family

Because much of the Islamic interpretive process has historically been a male preserve, it is not surprising that the most influential religious texts of the twentieth century have been authored by men. In attempting to differentiate between these texts, scholars typically use an analytical spectrum of religious thought to describe them as liberalist, traditionalist or Islamist, the latter with its own spectrum of moderate to radical thinking. Yet, as rightly noted by Stowasser, despite what are marked distinctions between these discourses, Muslim thinkers have historically converged on issues of gender.[3] Specifically, as a 'literature of faith', Muslim writers address women's concerns within an idealistically Islamic framework; 'accordingly, this literature lacks local specificity and consistently speaks to the problematic of "the Muslim woman", not that of the Egyptian or the Jordanian or the Turkish Muslim woman'.[4] What variances exist concerning 'the Muslim woman' relate to the degree of her seclusion or public responsibility; her maternal and domestic roles are never in question. Notwithstanding important ideological differences between Muslim thinkers, this study argues that it is their shared paradigm of the Muslim family, and thus the role of the Muslim woman within it, that renders their discourses a single discursive body. It is not the Islamic idioms that shroud their writings that make them religious, but the way in which these idioms are foregrounded in the sacred texts themselves. This analysis asserts that it is due both to the *explanatory potential* of particular analytic strategies employed by such writing, and to their *political effect* in the context of the hegemony of Islamic discourses by Muslim male thinkers (e.g., their production, publication, distribution and the consumption of ideas), that such discourses can be collectivised as a whole.[5] Islamic scholarship, like most other kinds of scholarship, is 'not the mere production of knowledge about a certain subject; it is a directly political and discursive practice in that it is purposeful and ideological'.[6]

With this in mind, certain discourses that rely on a shared 'Islamic' framework of gender and family should collectively be read as a single cultural discourse, as they produce a shared practice in the legal interpretive process: women's roles are interpreted as necessarily and exclusively relational to men, with the ontological category of Mother serving as its single most important and defining referent. Because of the interpreted meanings assigned to woman's reproductive capacity – one that is thought to be at once inherently biological and predispositionally ideological, and because her principal relationships are consequently thought to rest largely, if not exclusively, on wifehood-motherhood, the Muslim woman within the family unit ultimately becomes the cultural authenticator of society. That is, female relationality has been justified and legitimated by a specific understanding of marital 'complementarity', hence motherhood, in ways that foreclose a woman's right to her sense of personhood and spiritual individuality (not to be misread as personal account-ability). Such a narrow understanding of female relationality, e.g., as wife-mother within the family, would not be problematic except that it *fixes* definitions of womanhood within rigid categories that coalesce around maternity at the expense of other legitimate Islamic roles. More than this, the Muslim mother's very rights are eclipsed by such definitions. Unsurprisingly, her public rights outside the home are also circumscribed by her maternal relationality.

Public Versus Private: Women Outside the Home

Before delving into discourse analysis of the family, this brief but necessary detour discusses how women's rights and roles outside the family were historically deliberated by modern Muslim think-ers. From the late nineteenth/early twentieth century, as a result of increased politicisation of 'the woman question' preceding independ-ence from colonial rule, women's participation in society became a highly contestable topic in competing discourses in the independent Middle East. We now learn that women were among the interlocutors in these debates about nation building and modernisation.[7] There-fore, the role that women's issues, and indeed women themselves, played within civil society, as evidenced by these discourses of *tajdid* (renewal) and *islah* (reform), should not be overlooked. Neverthe-less, the nineteenth century set up some significant links between women and society that constitute an important backdrop to the subsequent century's discourse of family. How did twentieth-century thinkers come to view women's agency within society as, arguably, secondary to her role as Mother within the family, when in the late nineteenth century, Muslims were debating ways in which to 'liber-ate' Muslim women in both these spheres? Take, for instance, the ideas of Muhammad 'Abduh, one of the most influential reform-ers of women's issues of the time. This Azhari shaykh articulated a discourse of Islamic modernism by advocating a return to the prac-tice of *ijtihad* (individual inquiry), which invited Muslims to look to the scriptural sources of their religion for fresh inspiration. In fact, 'in the late nineteenth century and for two-thirds of the twentieth century, the reforming, revitalising doctrine of Islamic modernism accorded space for a feminism within the framework of the religious culture and provided a congenial climate for its evolution.'[8] 'Abduh was indeed unconventionally farsighted in his interpreted view of women's public rights. For one, he advocated for female education, arguing that:

> Anyone who knows how all nations before Islam gave preference to the man, and made the woman a mere chattel and plaything of the man, and how some religions give precedence to the man simply because he is a man and she a woman, and how some people consider the woman as incapable of religious responsibility and as possessing no immortal soul – anyone who knows all this, can appreciate at its true value this Islamic reform in the belief of the nations and their treatment of women ... To be sure, the Muslims have been at fault in the education and training of women, and acquainting them with their rights; and we acknowledge that we have failed to follow the guidance of our religion, so that we have become an instrument against it.[9]

To 'Abduh, then, the basic right of education was a means of restoring women's Qur'anic rights, which was key to regenerating Islamic society.

While the woman-society link is maintained in 'Abduh's discourse, it is not women's participation *per se* that 'Abduh saw as the source of regeneration; rather, he saw (re)education of all its members, including women, in the basics of Islam as the critical pivot point of societal renewal. There is no difference between men and women with regard to humanity, he argues, and no superiority of one over the other in works.[10] 'Abduh's starting point, then, is not gender or biological difference, but rather humanity, whose collective works contribute to the strengthening of society. He conceptualised women as social, not exclusively domestic agents. Women's education consequently is not solely linked to their maternal-domestic roles, it is linked to societal regeneration, which justifies, even necessitates, their participation in society, in the same way that it necessitates the involvement of males. In fact, the centrality of Islamic (re)education, the historical bedrock of *tajdid*, explains 'Abduh's rulings on marriage and divorce. He located the 'backward' and 'degraded' customs that had led Islamic nations into a deplorable state of ignorance, within the corruptions and misinterpretations of Islam, which were visibly manifest in the practices of marriage and divorce. A return to Islam's basics would make evident that 'such matters as divorce, polygamy, and slavery do not belong to the essentials of Islam'.[11] He therefore opined that polygamy was obsolete since its conditions were no longer manifest; besides, it was necessary to pursue reforms that would correct such harmful practices that had developed.

A generation later, Muslim thinkers would reverse such forward thinking in reform by deregulating such marriage practices, re-infusing the androcentric bias 'Abduh intently sought to eliminate. There are noted exceptions, however, such as Hasan al-Turabi. Like 'Abduh, Turabi views Islamic society's renewal as contingent on educated women's active participation within society, not only the home. He too starts with woman's humanity, her vicegerency, as a way of speaking about her necessary societal involvement.[12]

> In the religion of Islam, a woman is an independent entity, and thus a fully responsible human being ...The greatest injustice visited upon women is their segregation and isolation from the general society ... She was so isolated on the pretext that she might devote herself exclusively to the care of her children and the service of her husband. But how could she qualify for attending to domestic family affairs or to the rearing of children in a satisfactory manner without being herself versed through education or experience, in the moral and functional culture of the wider society?[13]

Using the early community as a model, Turabi strongly upholds the public rights of women, including prayer in the mosque, military warfare, full freedom of expression of her views, engaging in business and appointing public affairs officers.[14] Family laws follow a similar progressive approach so that a woman could propose marriage, choose her suitor, consent or refuse marriage 'on her own authority', and divorce.[15] What unifies the view of Turabi and 'Abduh is a certain hermeneutical approach to the Qur'an, deeply rooted in the notion of *tawhid* (absolute monotheism), that consequently inspires their emphasis on women as vicegerents whose social agency is not precluded by maternity.

Nevertheless, though gender issues were hotly debated between competing reform schemes, in 'Abduh's reform, women were the beneficiaries of a larger, legal reform that was targeted at more critical areas of societal degeneration, like ignorance, superstition and misappropriation of the sacred texts, as informed by his Qur'anic interpretive approach. His conceptual grid of society that informed his view of family was tied not to establishing gender roles based on a designated sexual division of labour or sexual difference, but rather to reforming rights of men and women as equal members of both society and family. Put differently, while 'Abduh's reforms were certainly gendered, his approach to reform was informed by a Qur'anic understanding that prioritised principles of interaction founded on mutual rights rather than gender difference.

With the rise of the Muslim laymen, the reformist discourse was taken a bit further. This development is illustrated in the contribution of the French-educated lawyer and Muslim judge, Qasim Amin. Since they met in Princess Nazli Fazil's salon, we know that 'Abduh influenced Amin in issues of gender reform and there is even speculation that 'Abduh edited, if not composed, parts of Amin's landmark, *The Liberation of Women* (1899).[16] Like 'Abduh, Amin called for an end to female seclusion, which he argued was not tied to Islam. He also advocated, like 'Abduh, the abolition of polygamy and for the abuses of divorce to be curtailed. Finally, women needed to be educated.[17] Despite the controversy and heated debates following the book's publication, Amin's ideas reverberated across Egypt and beyond and were eventually heralded by some as Egypt's founding feminist text. Recently, historians like Leila Ahmed, Margot Badran and Beth Baron have challenged Amin's historical standing as the 'father of Egyptian feminism', Ahmed's scathing critique of him as the 'son of Cromer' echoing the loudest.[18] At the core of these critiques is the view that Amin's gender reform was not derived from Islamic modernism, but was secular reform shrouded with Islamic idioms that ultimately tied woman to nationalist discourses of modernity. An explicit question posed by this view is whether or not, and to what degree, Amin mimicked Western notions of nation-building, culture and gender norms. Ultimately, Amin's discourse constituted a woman-society link that was engendered by Egyptian nationalism, not Islam. What gains women made in both the public and private spheres in Islamic modernist discourse were challenged, and in some places supplanted, by the dominant discourse of secular nationalism and its accompanying discourse of (middle-class) domesticity, which became pervasive in the first two decades of the twentieth century across the Middle East. This was most evident in Egypt, Iran, Turkey, and later in Algeria and Palestine.

In this secular discourse, women's societal role was reduced to motherhood, yet was glorified as the greatest role a woman could undertake for the emerging nation, on the condition that she was educated – a prerequisite for her children's *tarbiya* (moral upbringing). Given the strict prescriptive of how to be a modern Muslim mother, the discourse of domesticity advocated by the likes of Amin upheld the restricted space of maternity advocated similarly by Islamic discourses from which women were expected to perform their national, not Islamic, duty. Secular nationalist discourse, then, proved no more liberatory for women than some types of its Islamic competitors, since at their core both discourses upheld woman as essentially maternal, rendering her relationality pivotal to societal rejuvenation. Fittingly, the education Amin supported was secular, primary education, not (re)education in her Islamic rights, as advocated by 'Abduh. In Amin's words:

> A woman is the yardstick of the family. If she is vulgar, she will be despised by her husband, her relatives, and her children ... Their habits and morals will be corrupt. On the other hand, if the woman is cultured and intellectually able, she can instruct all the members of the family and will be respected by everyone ... The family will be united, and will gain strength through its unity. These traits which will characterize the family will also characterise the country. Our behaviour on a national level will therefore reflect the way we act within the family ... To summarize: the development of a country depends on numerous factors, the most important of which is the development of women. Similarly, the underdevelopment of a country is a product of numerous factors, the most important of which is the inferior position of women.[19]

In sum, both 'Abduh and Amin, in different ways, attempted to 'liberate' Muslim women through education in both society and the family. As articulators of modern discourses – one Islamic modernist and the other secular nationalist – both Muslim thinkers saw woman as instrumental to society's rejuvenation. The major difference, however, lay in the way in which each conceptualised society – a notion that was certainly in flux during this period. 'Abduh drew on a pan-Islamic framework that saw society as part of a larger Muslim community, or umma. For Amin, whose prominence was attributed to the rise of the Western-educated Muslim intellectual, society was an imagined nation, with real territorial borders, that modernised and nationalised women's maternity-domesticity as her primary identity marker. For both discourses, women at the turn of the century became the modern signifiers of societal survival and the degree of its strength.

Turning to the family, discussed as the next section, we find that twentieth-century Muslim thinkers reappropriated and Islamised the nationalist thesis of female domesticity, particularly during the last quarter of the century when Islamic discourses experienced a widespread resurgence. Women's agency outside the family consequently was made secondary to her role within it. Issues debated about women's public rights, like education, employment and political participation, were directly related to, indeed determined by, a belief in woman's nature as relational. Islamic discourses of women's public and private roles were derived from a single view of woman's primary function as Mother. Women's domestic roles, then, assumed greater importance within twentieth-century society, since their biological and ideological reproductive capacity was conceptually tied to the preservation and regeneration of Muslim society at a time when Western cultural influences intensified across the Muslim world. As woman's religious significance and roles are tied to culture – since she is uniquely viewed as the purveyor of cultural authenticity – it is no wonder that such discourses accord her the role of moral protector of the family, against the threat of cultural poisoning, moral contamination and even societal change. However, the inextricable linking of woman to family-society, and of both to culture, as understood by these Muslim thinkers, legitimates what are ultimately socially constructed gender roles as absolute and normative, and hence difficult to contest. A closer look at this discourse illustrates this argument.

The Twentieth-Century Template of the Muslim Family

The institution of family is viewed in Islamic thought as the most central unit of societal relations. In fact, the family is often referred to as the building block, the very core, of the larger unified Muslim umma. Whatever affects the microcosmic unit certainly and necessarily impacts on the macrocosmic one. One need only recall the centrality of family ties to the formation of the first Muslim community in Medina – the very blueprint of the umma. In the words of one scholar, the family is a 'society in miniature'.[20] Few Muslims, if any, deny the centrality of the family as the bedrock of Islamic society, and therefore Islamic law. Not surprisingly, one third of the Qur'an's legal injunctions relate to the family and its regulation.[21] Yet, the conceptualisation of the Muslim family by twentieth-century thinkers, especially in the last few decades, has not been one that enjoys much variation, despite the changing times and contexts from within which these scholars originate. Rather, the family in Islam is believed to be a divinely-inspired and ordained institution, characterised by a necessary sexual division of labour. Instead of viewing gender roles as socially constructed, and thus necessarily prone to change, the self-identifying Islamic framework employed essentially constructs an impermeable template of the Muslim family that renders the Islamic values of family commensurate with traditional gender roles.

Such religious thinking does not discount Islam's inherent adaptability to contextual change. In fact, much of this discourse claims legitimacy by showing how highly adaptable its interpretations are to modern challenges and exigencies. Yet, on issues of gender and family, there has been a stubborn subscription to a normative view of the Muslim family that hinges on the over-idealised role of Mother, in order to shield this template of the family from any outside, threatening change. What is striking about this body of Islamic literature is that it premises its interpretive view of gender and the family on the notion of spiritual equality. Man and woman are created from the same 'divine breath', invested with inherent dignity, equally responsible for the first human sin, and endowed with the same moral duties and responsibilities as God's appointed vicegerents.[22] 'The full equality of all human beings is beyond doubt.'[23] When discussing actual roles, however, the message of equality is overshadowed by the view that gender roles are contingent on the Muslim family in ways that make gender complementarity a means of safeguarding its institutional integrity. Consequently, woman's spiritual equality with man's translates, through the interpretive process, into a practical hierarchy of gender roles, in the name of conjugal harmony and family unity. What follows details how these scholars conceptually assimilate this spiritual value of female equality to her actual roles – a view that reaffirms and ossifies the historical trope of the Muslim woman.

Marital Complementarity as Hierarchical Difference

Gender equality, Muslim thinkers argue, 'does not entail non-differentiation of their respective roles and functions in society'.[24] Spiritual equality should not be confused with role differentiation 'in the spirit of co-operation and complementarity'.[25] It is precisely this notion of marital complementarity that provides the basis for the discursive link between the Islamic normative value of duality ('And have we not created you in pairs', Q.78:8) and the wifely-maternal role within the home, or, put differently, between the *absolute* (value) and the *particular* (role). Complementarity, in a word, constitutes the Qur'anic pretext on which traditional gender roles are assigned to the conjugal couple. It is certainly the basis on which marriage manuals discuss gender roles within the Muslim family.[26] Such differentiated roles also explain the common use of the term 'equity' over 'equality', in order to convey the idea of differentiated equality, not to be confused with absolute or identical equality.[27]

In this conceptual grid, based on a 'functional distribution between the sexes', the husband is responsible for the economic maintenance, protection, and overall leadership of the family (understood as *qawama*, or protection and guardianship, Q.4:34).[28] This degree of male advantage, asserts a marriage manual, derives from the biological differences between the sexes.[29] Accordingly:

> Islam regards [woman's] role in society as a mother and a wife as her most sacred and essential one. Neither maids nor babysitters can possible take the mother's place as the educator of an upright, complex-free, and carefully reared child. Such a noble and vital role, which largely shapes the future of nations, cannot be regarded as 'idleness'.[30]

This quotation about woman's role in society not only appears in a 1980 pamphlet written by Badawi, but also reappears, verbatim, fifteen years later in his published book on gender equity. Clearly, little had changed in this conceptualisation of the Muslim family. By extension, the Muslim mother is viewed as making her most 'sacred' contribution by becoming a mother.[31]

Abu Shuqqah confirms these marital roles by citing various hadiths (Prophetic traditions), though it is worth mentioning that his voluminous work is more of a guide of scriptural references to women than his personal commentary about gender roles in Islam. Abu Shuqqah's *Tahrir al-mar'a* is worth including in this survey for its renowned importance, being based on a thorough, comprehensive study of women in the Prophetic *sira* (biography), aspects of which, to his surprise, had completely changed his thoughts about women and gender relations.[32] His text, however, does not fit too comfortably with those analysed here. Because his focus is not on exegetical commentary about women in scriptural texts, his inclusion of Prophetic traditions that discuss the spectrum of women's public and private roles during the formative period of Islam serves as a refreshing reminder of how involved Muslim women once were in Islamic history. The impact of rediscovering these ignored traditions, nevertheless, is limited since many of them – in content or by their framing (e.g., by subject headings and categorisation) – ultimately re-inscribe the conventional view of female domesticity tied to complementarity, categorised under the heading, 'the distribution of mutual responsibilities between marriage partners'.[33]

Marital complementarity is achieved because the man's role in the family is secondary to the woman's, in the same way that the woman's role in society and the economy is secondary to man's.[34] Seyyed Hossein Nasr states it with greater precision:

> In the home the woman rules as queen and a Muslim man is in a sense the guest of his wife at home. The home and the larger family structure in which she lives are for the Muslim woman her world. To be cut off from it would be like being cut off from the world or like dying. *She finds the meaning of her existence in this extended family structure which is constructed so as to give her the maximum possibility of realizing her basic needs and fulfilling herself.* The *Shari'ah* therefore envisages the role of men and women according to their nature which is complementary. It gives the man the

privilege of social and political authority and movement for which he has to pay by bearing heavy responsibilities, by protecting his family from all forces and pressures of society, economic and otherwise. Although a master in the world at large and the priest of his own family, the man acts in his home as one who recognizes the rule of his wife in this domain and respects it. Through mutual understanding and the realisation that God has placed on each other's shoulders, the Muslim man and woman are able to fulfil their personal lives and create a firm family unit which is the basic structure of Muslim society.[35]

Interestingly, Nasr's language here echoes Mawdudi's representation of the husband-wife duo as the 'governor' and 'queen of the house'.[36] The reader is constantly reminded that these different functions are 'uniquely suited to their nature and physical structure' in order to create a domestic environment based on respect, honour and love.[37] Indeed, this envisioned sexual division of labour is presented as the single normative model for the optimal functioning of the home, familial well-being and societal health. Evidence of the moral superiority of *this* referential model of gender complementarity is typically illustrated by a comparison with the West. Mawdudi, for example, states that the problem with Western society is its definition of absolute spousal equality.

> This wrong concept of equality led women astray and made them unmindful of their natural functions on the performance of which depends the very existence of human race and civilization ... The bringing up of children and the organization and care of the home ceased to be her special care ... The result is that home life on which depends man's efficiency is fast disappearing in the West.[38]

The result, in other words, is the 'licentiousness' and 'sexual anarchy' of Western society, brought necessarily by the women's emancipation movement. Al-Qaradawi and Rahman agree.[39] The Western woman, represented as single and economically independent, necessarily becomes the 'spinster mother' with her 'illegitimate child'.[40]

In fact, the Western woman represents, as a categorical model, all that could potentially go wrong if Muslim women were to be left unmarried – a rationale that explains justifications for polygamy, discussed below. If women are not married, al-Qaradawi argues, the three possible alternatives that exist are: to pass their whole lives in

'bitter deprivation'; to become 'sex objects and playthings for lecher-
ous men'; or, to become co-wives to men who will support and treat
them kindly. 'Unquestionably, the last alternative is the correct solution.'[41] In other words, if Muslim women are left unmarried, this
necessarily leads to societal disharmony, Western women providing
the most glaring proof of such wisdom. Such an either/or interpretive view of women is characteristic. This discourse, for instance,
discusses Muslim women as either married (including divorcees),
or as daughters, who are consistently urged to seek an education as
a way to prepare for their future role as mothers.[42] There is no grey
area, no discussion of the roles that unmarried females, for instance,
could undertake for Muslim society as educated independents, or
her Islamic duties as such, like whether attendance of Friday prayers
should be made mandatory since she is free of family responsibilities. Because her social function is non-relational, because she has
not (yet) realised her natural capacity, the single, financially independent Muslim woman is not recognised as a legal category worthy
of elaboration within this discourse (unless, of course, one counts
'spinster'). Subsumed under the category of daughter, the single
woman is viewed as either too young for marriage or a woman about
to inherit social meaning upon becoming a wife.

What is problematic when analysing the rhetorical strategies and
conceptual framing of this discourse, is that, while complementarity
or gender equity may be the intended Islamic value, the interpreted
gender roles rest on a 'natural' hierarchy, where the woman, 'the
weaker sex' to quote one scholar, defers to the authority of the man
in the pursuit of familial harmony.[43] Ironically, despite the wife-mother's greater responsibility *within* the family, the husband has greater
authority *over* it – a gender dynamic mirrored in the contemporary
family law of many Muslim countries. In a word, with woman's nature interpreted as innately relational, it is not surprising that her
role, particularly as a mother, is moulded by her 'natural' ability to
nurture family cohesiveness, even at the expense of her already restricted rights. Some illustrative examples are appropriate.

A woman who wants to work, according to Badawi, 'must secure
her husband's consent', despite her Islamic right of employment.[44]
The more conservative Mawdudi disagrees and states that, 'the
most appropriate place for her, according to the Islamic law, is her

home'.[45] If she does work, continues Badawi, she should choose a profession that '[fits] her nature best and in which society needs her most', like nursing, teaching (especially children), medicine, and social and charitable work.[46] Mawdudi adds a caveat, asserting that Islam has not approved that a woman should leave her home 'without a genuine need'.[47] He is quick to remind the reader that, 'genuine need', which does include female employment, 'cannot alter the basic principles of the Social System of Islam which restricts the woman's sphere of activity to her home'.[48] Both of these views run counter to the fact that no jurist has been able to point to an explicit text in the Qur'an and Sunna (Prophetic model and traditions) that categorically excludes women from any lawful type of employment, to which Badawi himself admits in making his interpretation, clearly without consequence.[49] Despite her Qur'anic rights, woman is viewed here as predisposed exclusively to motherhood and therefore her rights are framed, but more importantly, *sacrificed*, to fit into the larger, more important, framework of gender complementarity and family cohesion.

Therefore, when considering women's ability to hold political positions, despite the clear evidence of woman's equality with man in political rights, she cannot be a head of state, since 'some decisions require a maximum of rationality and a minimum of emotionality – a requirement which does not coincide with the instinctive nature of women'.[50] Besides, given that 'she is not found suitable even for the headship of the household because of her natural temperament and aptitude', she is certainly 'not at all competent and suitable for the office of head of the state'.[51] A similar line of reasoning is used to justify why in war, women are not to take up arms as recruited soldiers, but only for self-defence, since 'woman was created for motherhood and not for killing and shedding blood'.[52] Her home is 'the battleground of her trial'.[53] If they insist, however, women should aid the wounded, take water to the thirsty, and cook food for the soldiers – roles that coalesce around the presumed nature of woman as nurturing and maternal.[54] Mawdudi explains: because of Eve, woman, who is naturally emotional, sensitive and inclined to extremes, is 'created by Allah with that nature and this is her merit, not her demerit' for 'this trait of her character can be usefully employed in the service of humanity'.[55] Al-Qaradawi echoes this view in calling

a woman, 'a human being with natural imperfections', while Rahman more generously describes her as born with 'the gift of unique
emotion of motherly affection'.[56] Her service, then, is consistently
reduced to maternity-domesticity, in tandem with her interpreted
nature. Within this framework, the primacy of motherhood frames
what rights women do have while also precluding any other or additional possibilities of female 'service' to Muslim society.

In fact, woman's maternal service even shapes her Islamic duties
to God. Some Muslim scholars, for instance, state that the best prayer
for males is offered in congregation in the mosque:

> But for the females, on the other hand, the prayer offered in seclusion is
> of greater worth than the prayer in congregation; *so much so that a prayer
> offered in seclusion by them has been regarded as of greater value and worth than
> even the greatest blessing for a Muslim, that is, a prayer offered in congregation
> in the Mosque of the Prophet under the leadership of Muhammad himself* (may
> Allah's peace be upon him), the greatest of the Prophets of Allah. The
> question is: What is the reason for this discrimination? Obviously, noth-
> ing than this, that the Law-giver has disapproved women's coming out of
> the houses frequently and mixing with the males in congregations.[57]

Despite Muslim mothers being given the legal option of attend-
ing Friday prayers, this option, articulated here in such emphatic
and idealist terms, is reconstituted as a prescriptive that expects the
mother to restrict her own religious duties to and within the home.
Her right to express and nurture her own spirituality as God's vicegerent is not at all considered here. In fact, this paradigm of the Muslim family is one that is premised on the natural self-sacrifice of the
good wife-mother. In special circumstances, for instance, she may

> ... find it is necessary to spend from her earnings or saving to provide
> the necessities for her family. While this is not a legal obligation, it is
> consistent with the mutuality of care, love and co-operation among fam-
> ily members.[58]

In cases of divorce, it is similarly rationalised that, 'to provide for the
stability of the family', and 'in order to protect it from hasty decisions
under temporary emotional stress', both men and women should
observe a waiting period. Yet, 'considering the relatively more emotional nature of women, a good reason for asking for divorce should

be brought before the judge.'[59] One of the few examples of a 'good reason' provided by al-Qaradawi is ill treatment. There are basically no restrictions placed on the husband's reasons for divorce.[60] Such exclusive conditions certainly were not placed on those women who unilaterally divorced their husbands during the formative period.[61] To be sure, Islamic family law makes divorce extremely easy for men, regardless of the Prophet's hadith that describes divorce as 'abhorrent' to God, and makes it extremely difficult for women, disregarding the Qur'anic stipulation, 'Do not retain them [your wives] by force, to transgress [against their rights]' (2:228).[62] Again, it is the conceptual framing of such legal sacrifices expectant of the mother in the name of family unity that give these particular interpretations of domestic duty their normative, and thus problematic, nature.

Or, despite the caveat that 'the mutuality and complementarity of husband and wife does not mean "subservience" by either party to the other' or a 'loss of her freedom of action and will', the wife is consistently told to seek her husband's permission, for instance, to fast (should he desire sexual relations, which is prohibited during fasting), work, travel, leave the home, or even wear makeup.[63] In fact,

> because of his natural ability and his responsibility for providing for his family … [the husband] is entitled to the obedience and co-operation of his wife, and accordingly it is not permissible for her to rebel against his authority, causing disruption. Without a captain the ship of the household will flounder and sink.[64]

Nowhere in these writings is the husband's behaviour contingent on wifely permission in the larger pursuit of conjugal equity and harmony. In fact, the husband is endowed with the 'responsibility' to correct his wife's 'bad behaviour', certainly not by abusing or physically harming her, but through 'corrective measures' taken to 'try to keep the family unit together'.[65] Those pages dedicated to the interpretation of the Qur'anic verse treating spousal lewdness (4:34) discuss the wife's dishonour, disobedience and rebellion at length; not a single page addresses the husband.[66]

This interpretation of wifely obedience, importantly, is not far from the modern understanding of *ta'a* (the institution of wifely obedience) embodied in modern personal status laws. In Egypt, for instance, the way *ta'a* has been legally institutionalised has been to give the husband, in exchange for *nafaqa* (financial support of the wife), an absolute right to *ta'a*:

> whereby a woman is required to surrender herself or be forced by the police to 'surrender herself' to her husband, even if he is abusive and she is living under the constant threat of violence and intimidation. And although the husband has the right to demand *ta'a* from his wife, she cannot sue for divorce even for abandonment until she has gone through long procedures demanded by the court to ascertain her husband's unwillingness to support her.[67]

Here, the husband has full right to his wife's 'person', physically, sexually and mentally.[68] Both these interpretations – one found in the discourse of the family, the other in family law – share their basis in an understanding of woman as exclusively relational. She is endowed with greater responsibility to uphold mutual complementarity through her actions *because* of her nature: she seeks permission from and gives obedience and shows honour to her husband, whose 'governing' duties as the guardian-protector 'entitle' him to what are privileges, passed off here as wifely obligations. These discussions are consistently shaped by Islamic ideals of mutual tolerance, equity and love, yet these same Islamic values do not limit the husband's rights and behaviours in ways parallel to women.

Finally, when considering polygamy, although the general rule is monogamy in Islam, polygamy is rationalised as a viable option, ostensibly for the Islamic goal of 'preserving the marital relationship', establishing 'a respectable family', and for the 'cohesion of family'.[69] Yet, it is the man who reaps greater privilege from these interpreted justifications, not the woman, who, psychologically speaking, 'is monogamous by her very nature' anyway.[70] If the wife is barren or fatally ill, for instance, the man, who will 'suffer the deprivation of fatherhood for life', is allowed to marry another.[71] Polygamy here becomes a way to resolve the threat to the family unit by allowing for children by another wife, since, after all, polygamy is a male-interpreted Qur'anic right to begin with. Or, despite the slight disagreement about sexual desire being a basis of polygamy, all unanimously agree that, 'the second wife legally married and treated kindly is better off than a mistress without any legal rights or security'.[72] Or, in the face of a societal imbalance brought by war, polygamy becomes necessary.[73] Otherwise, 'some women must remain perpetual spinsters and/or live in sin.'[74] Al-Qaradawi agrees but words it more gently:

> In such a situation, it is in the interests of the society and of women themselves that they become co-wives to a man instead of spending their entire lives without marriage, deprived of peace, affection, and protection of marital life and the joy of motherhood for which they naturally yearn with all their hearts.[75]

In these cases, scholars present polygamy as an either/or situation. In the former, the choice is either to marry a second wife or the man will live in sin; in the latter case, it is the woman who will live in sin.

What is problematic here are the presumptions inherent to these justifications. Within the model of the Muslim family, all rationalise polygamy as a way to protect monogamy, yet never challenge the male privilege inherent in these rationalisations, e.g., the option of fatherhood in cases of female infertility, stronger male sexual drive and women's necessary protection by men (or else suffer the fate of being either a 'spinster' or immoral). That women are not presented with any real recourse in these marital scenarios other than the highly discouraged one of divorce is not reason enough to limit how these male-privileged options are justified as Islamically plausible, in the name of gender equity. Instead, accommodating polygamy rather than further restricting and enforcing its regulations (advocated by 'Abduh), is viewed as a means to familial-societal stability.[76] Repeatedly, this discourse finds religious justification and rationales for woman's exceptionality and difference, one consistently located in her body: her reproductive capacity, her maternal instinct, her innate ability to sacrifice, her over-emotionality, her natural monogamy. Under 'woman's rights', Mawdudi acknowledges this methodology outright in saying that, 'biological and psychological differences between the man and the woman do exist' and Islam 'employs those differences for determining their place and responsibilities in the social system'.[77] This body-based methodology for defining sexual difference, in turn, justifies the gendered roles that uphold the 'natural' hierarchy of the Muslim family, which, again, ostensibly maintains men and women as gender complements within the family. In actuality, however, given the interpreted meanings assigned to these differences, this methodology ultimately upholds a hierarchy of gender inequality. Indeed, the socially-constructed meanings assigned to gender roles within this discourse translate into institutionalised gender difference within the family unit. This is precisely the crux of the interpretive quandary faced by discourses on gender and the family. That is, twentieth-century Islamic discourse has been riddled with the same challenges and conceptual issues plaguing other competing discourses of modernity – how can (Muslim) society understand and articulate *difference*, the very premise of marital complementarity, to ideally mean social equality, without institutionalising a legal hierarchy of inequalities?

To recap, the notion of marital complementarity, as conceptualised by twentieth-century Muslim thinkers, has, ironically, reified the notion of hierarchical gender difference, and thus gender inequity. Complementarity, as interpreted by this discourse, provides the Islamic pretext to duly restrict female legal rights within the family and expect the wife-mother to sacrifice those rights in the name of family cohesion. The conceptual foregrounding of such an interpretation is found in woman's biological nature, viewed as essentially relational. Because of the sacred position of family as an ordained Islamic institution, the gender roles thought to uphold this idealistic vision are sanctified, and thus more difficult to contest. The Islamic values of family and the roles that embody them become so tightly synonymous that, to even attempt to redefine these roles would, on some level, bring into question, even challenge, the entire ideological framework on which the Muslim family rests within Islamic thought. What further yokes Islamic family values to their traditional sex roles is, in a word, culture.

'Relations of the Womb': Female Relationality and Cultural Authenticity

According to this discourse, it is woman's responsibility to carry out specific tasks, like the children's *tarbiya* (moral upbringing) and domestic duties, for the natural and contingent male-female pair to maintain its delicate balance of complementarity. Similarly, it is her responsibility to safeguard the public morality of the larger Muslim

community through her behaviours and regulated physical presence. It is her role, in sum, to protect the family and society from
any moral decay or corrupting threat. What is striking about these
roles is that they do not apply to the husband-father. He, quite simply, is not viewed as physiologically equipped to handle such tasks.
On the other hand, if the wife-mother, endowed with 'her natural
gifts', fails to undertake her roles as the Muslim woman, this potentially has crippling effects on the Muslim family, and even worse, on
all of Muslim society.

> The destiny of the future generations of man has been put into the hands
> of woman. She is responsible for the building of the further generations
> of mankind. It is a huge, difficult and responsible job, and any careless-
> ness, negligence or neglect on the part of woman can do irreparable
> damage to the nation. It is therefore very vital that woman should give
> her sole attention to her work at home and never let any secondary mo-
> tive intervene or interfere in her important function.[78]

The threat alone is enough to assign to her such strict roles, the most
daunting of which is sustaining an envisioned Islamic civilisation. It
is within this matrix of gender, family and culture that woman's relationality becomes intimately ensconced in Islam's very survival.

After all, 'the key role in the proper development of the family is
played by the woman', and the family, in turn, 'initiates the new generations into the culture, tradition and further evolution of their civilisation'.[79] Al-Qaradawi adds that, had there been no family system,
there would be no society through which mankind would be able to
progress toward perfection.[80] Ahmed refers to the family as the self-
sustaining mechanism that ensures the cultural stability of society,
for all times.[81] As the physiological life-giver, the Muslim woman is
also the lifeline of Islamic culture. She is not only responsible for
fostering her children's Islamic character-building through their *tarbiya*, in order to be loving, compassionate, sacrificing, tolerant and
kind, 'emotions without which a cohesive society cannot come into
being'.[82] Children, after all, are considered to be 'the future guardians of the [Islamic] nation'.[83] She should also provide the relational
support base for 'all the dependant relations in the family', or family
members who are 'relations of the womb' – an expression derived
from a Qur'anic verse (Q.4:1), interpreted to mean all those family

members for whom the male is responsible.[84] It is her role to weld
the ties between these members, often including the extended family, into a system of mutual support, while the husband provides the
economic support and security.[85] Though these family members do
not originate from her womb, she is given responsibility over them
since she relates to them through her husband, and as the 'queen
of her home' that he maintains, she is obliged to maintain this extended family unit. With the woman assigned this unity-fostering role
in the family-society, clearly issues of modesty become central to this
discourse, since, after all, the 'Islamic system of *hijab* [Islamic dress]
is a wide-ranging system which protects the family and closes those
avenues that lead towards illicit sex or even indiscriminate contact
between the sexes in society'.[86] Flirting and sexual promiscuity are so
destructive, reads one marriage handbook, that they render a Muslim woman incapable of fulfilling her role as the basic foundation
of family and society.[87] Accordingly, countless pages of these writings are dedicated exclusively to the rules and regulations regarding
Muslim women's dress and behaviour, its implicit objective being to
reconcile the problematic place of woman's physical body in society,
given the centrality of her relational role within the family.

The consensus of these thinkers, like those before them, is that,
other than the woman's face and hands, 'her body is regarded as
'awra (that which should be covered)'.[88] Such an interpretation is
derived, yet again, from a larger model of family based ideally on
gender complementarity, where the woman is accorded greater responsibility over marital, domestic and societal harmony, despite
the rigidified space from which to achieve this. To be sure, Muslim
women, especially mothers, are entrusted most emphatically as the
moral protectors of Islamic society from any kind of corrupting
threat, including any threat that their own bodies and behaviours
may pose. One scholar, for instance, states:

> ... some Muslims emulate non-Islamic cultures and adopt their modes
> of dress, unrestricted mixing, and behavior, which influence them and
> endanger their families' Islamic integrity and strength.[89]

Though this view is cited as an extreme case of cultural practice of
Muslims around the world (the other being the excessive restriction
and seclusion of women), it is important here because it reveals, as

an extreme view, the point of reference for how Muslims, and the Muslim family, should *not* behave, precisely because such conduct leads directly to family disintegration.

> We are living in a period of cultural crisis. It seems as if the very foundations of contemporary society are being threatened from within and without. The family, as a basic and most sensitive institution of culture, is being undermined by powerful and destructive forces. All the symptoms suggest that the crisis in general is deepening and the institution of the family is, in particular, weakening, even disintegrating in Europe and America. It is time to pause for a while and re-examine the foundations on which family life is built in the contemporary West and also to study alternative foundations and structures in other cultural traditions.[90]

The moral laxity of culture, as demonstrated by Western culture, is seen as the most glaring threat to the Islamic family-society, which explains why Muslim mothers are endowed with the crucial role of cultural gate-keeping.

That is, as the character-builders, and thus identity-givers of the Muslim family-society, Muslim women ultimately become the purveyors of Islamic cultural authenticity. The profound concern and anxiety over any change to the Muslim woman's role, explains one thinker, is therefore understandable, especially when these changes emanate from the West, and especially given the fundamental position occupied by the family in Muslim society.[91]

> The demise of the family is tantamount to the demise of the whole society. And of course central to the family matrix is the wife and mother. If Western cultural domination succeeds in alienating the Muslim woman from her cultural values, the whole society will be profoundly transformed. If there is a mastermind, a malignant genius who is bent on undermining and destroying the Muslim societies, then he could not do better than concentrate his efforts on uprooting woman for her cultural identification with Islamic social values and norms of conduct.

To be sure, this unique gendered role of the Muslim woman assumes more than passing importance within this discourse and explains the greater, more focused scrutiny placed on female dress, behaviours and movement than her marital complement. Islamic culture, then, confirms the gendered role of the Muslim woman in ways that are difficult to disentangle without first understanding the centrality of woman's interpreted nature, argued here as relational, to Islamic cultural authenticity. It is no wonder that more and more scholarly studies on Muslim women, taking their epistemological cues from postcolonial cultural studies, are interrogating this vexed relationship, namely between 'the woman question' and the language of cultural authenticity versus foreign influence within political and ideological discourses in the Muslim world.[92]

As one scholar rightly argues, the effort to define an authentic identity in postcolonial Muslim societies has consequently given culture and heritage a more important and prominent role than they might otherwise have had.[93] The greater importance placed on cultural authenticity in the face of Western-led globalisation, has led, in turn, not to a redefinition of family and gender guided by the Qur'an that seriously considers these daunting inequalities, but rather a stubborn adherence to this longstanding paradigm of the Muslim family, *as a form of active resistance to such change.* Better put by Leila Ahmed, Islamic civilisation has intransigently and dogmatically clung to old values perhaps the more obstinately because it is reaffirming them against an old enemy – the West.[94] Consequently, in the effort to adapt to change on its own terms, and in hopes of remedying rising gender inequalities, women's roles have been reinterpreted. However, this process has taken place within a problematic framework of family. Problematic is that these inequalities are created by the very family laws supported by this framework – an argument angrily resisted by many Islamic thinkers. We learn from scholars like Amira el-Azhary Sonbol how modern personal status laws, in ultimately confirming the power of state patriarchy, have undermined the flexibility of the sharia; therefore, family laws have not optimally served Muslim women.[95]

Instead of protecting Muslim women, family law across the Muslim world has, to varying degrees, sacrificed women's Qur'anic rights for the Muslim family unit. Ironically, the family, as Islam's most sacred institution, has compromised gender justice for family-societal unity. This is a harsh and disillusioning reality that Muslims must acknowledge if an *effective* Islamic reform is to take place. In sum, modernity, postcoloniality, globalisation and Western cultural hegemony have all served as pretexts for the reinscribing of traditional notions of

family, and thus women's roles, within Islamic thought.[96] To compli-
cate this, Muslim women, especially mothers, also subscribe to this
paradigm of family. They find in it a way in which they can anchor
their social status as Muslim women, namely, by investing in the same
Islamic ideal of marital complementarity that defines the restricted
ontology of motherhood to begin with. It is in this way that the Islamic discourse of gender and the family are no different from other
modern discourses found in the Muslim world, be they nationalist,
secularist or otherwise. For better or for worse, Islam has its own
hegemonic cultural 'totalisation', an idealism that casts values and
practices that pertain to specific privileged groups within the community as values of the culture as a whole.[97] This means that some
ontological categories are invariably privileged over others within
Islamic culture. The framework of family deconstructed here constitutes the basis on which this hegemonic view has historically been
laid, so that while women have held the keys to Islamic regeneration,
they have played a marginal role as subjects in determining which
doors they may open.

While women appear to hold a significant place within these
competing discourses, very often what is truly at stake goes beyond
gender in the pursuit of a higher, more important principle or value.
Gender, but specifically woman, becomes central because of the type
of mediating role she is assigned in the establishment of these absolute values. At the core of these roles is an understanding of woman
as relational, as the cementing agent that uniquely holds together
family, society and culture, while also giving them Islamic legitimacy.
Accordingly, those who benefit from this particular paradigm of family, like mothers, do not challenge it, and often constitute its most
passionate defenders. As many women 'consent' (in classical Grams-
cian terms) to this framework of family, some of their own writings
echo in verse this Islamic discourse.[98] At stake is a mutually exclusive
choice between rights or respect, specifically between

> ... the *rights* given to women and the *respect* given to them. Confusion
> ensues because the two distinct factors are erroneously used interchange-
> ably, when in reality they are often inversely correlated. Thus, women
> receive great respect in certain societies that give them few rights; they
> receive equality of rights in societies in which they compete with men
> but have relatively low respect.[99]

Muslim women have prided their social status on their motherhood, despite this often being at the expense of their legal rights, precisely because they find in motherhood their ontological importance as Muslims. Muslim women, after all, are presented with a model, not of the Prophet when learning how to be good *khulafa'* (vicegerents), but rather of his wives, 'the Mothers of the Believers', or Maryam, the mother of Jesus – all of whom constitute maternal archetypes.[100]

This is not to suggest that motherhood in Islam is demeaning or that Muslim women should not genuinely love being mothers. If misread, this analysis could easily, and wrongly, be interpreted as an argument for an absolute female individuality or independence, or even as a call to break away from motherhood. Any number of sentences read in isolation could be misconstrued as an attack on the family as a fundamental and ordained institution. This is categorically not the intent. The Qur'an has beautifully articulated the spiritual equality of man and woman and their necessary and natural contingency:

> And among His Signs is this, that He created for you mates from among yourselves that ye may dwell in tranquillity with them, and He has put love and mercy between your (hearts): Verily in that are Signs for those who reflect (Q.30:21)

Other verses (e.g., Q.7:189; Q.2:187) equally reflect this harmonial conjugal pairing. Further, the Qur'anic importance given to parenthood, and specifically motherhood, is without doubt and God clearly has provided mothers with a unique source of honour, brought by the physiological toils and pain of pregnancy. The institution of family and motherhood are not in question here. Rather, the particular and subjective meanings that have been assigned to motherhood by this discourse have over-determined the category of Mother, at the expense of women's Qur'anic rights – as mothers or otherwise. Yet, these subjective meanings are equated with, and passed off as, the single, normative possibility of Islamic female behaviour. What is contested, therefore, is the lack of conceptual space allowed for expanding and redefining gender roles within and outside the virtuous family. While this historical framework does make some space for reinterpreting gender roles in light of modern exigencies, these superficial changes ultimately reaffirm, not reform, the essentialist view of woman's nature, thus the nature of her roles. For, such re-interpretations do not challenge the constructed roles assigned to the absolute Islamic values of family, since they refuse to challenge the essentialist nature of woman.

It is in this way that such thinking has consequently hamstrung the redefining of gender roles according to a modified or new matrix of Islamic justice, rights and freedoms, as well as to global standards of human rights – a critique expressed by a growing number of Muslim thinkers, many of whom are women. The overarching critique is less the legitimacy of the interpreted view of gender and the family as a historical discourse than one with *continued* application in a reality it does not effectively or justly redress. Its sustained relevance has meant that Islamic reformers must work from within very limited space in their attempts to expand women's rights, and thus Islamic meanings of womanhood. Such efforts at reform, albeit quite challenging, have not always proven Sisyphean.

A Reformed Grid of Islamic Thought: The New 'Gender Jihad'

In any attempt at religious rethinking, deconstructing thought is always easier than reconstructing. As reconstruction has been a gradual process, there has not been a single, coherent discourse to speak of that remedies the problematics posed by the paradigm of family. This is not to say that there is no critical mass. Attempts have been focused on rethinking, even redefining the interpretive process, by focusing not only on family law, but more importantly on Qur'anic hermeneutics, with the goal of gender justice. Amina Wadud's *Qur'an and Woman*; *'Believing Women' in Islam* by Asma Barlas, and Khaled Abou El Fadl's *Speaking in God's Name*, are pioneering works in this direction.[101]

Female inclusiveness within the interpretive process is a critical first step in achieving gender equity in family law, since including female subjectivities is seen as a way to balance out the dominant male view within this process. Characteristic of this reformed grid of Islamic thought is that it accepts as its epistemological cue that the interpretive process is invariably a human endeavour and consequently that gender roles are cultural constructs. After all, twentieth-century discourse of gender takes a normative-moralistic approach to analysing the family structure within Islam – an approach typically critiqued for its failure to consider the actual historical roles that women and men have actually undertaken. This critique, however, does not make this approach less effective. Again, such discourses are discursive *practice* because they are 'ideological and purposeful'.[102] This discourse, after all, is not without its direct implications. Badawi, for instance, illustrates how such an approach can be made effective:

> The *normative*, or ideal, relating to gender equity in Islam … may serve as a yardstick against which the *reality* of present-day Muslims should be evaluated. It serves also as the objective toward which any Islamic reformation and renewal should be directed, reformation of wrong practices and renewal of adherence to the Islamic ideal.[103]

While such longstanding notions of *tajdid* and *islah* are not problematic in themselves, they become so when we consider what is presented here as the normative view, the direction in which reform should take. What Badawi means by 'Islamic ideal' above is certainly problematic since it implies a perceived objectivity and timelessness – a view that denies the inherent context specificity that *should* inhere in the interpretive process.

That is, to assume that human bias within the religious interpretive process is wrongly placed is to discard the very nature of Qur'anic interpretation as necessarily subjective and context-specific. An interpretive method that considers the cultural values of a society should be embraced since it forces a continual process of redefinition that considers, not resists, change from context to context over time in the pursuit of justice. Why else would the Qur'an depend on the culturally relative term *ma'ruf* (conventionally attempted or well known) as a mechanism to uphold societal justice? Yet, the interpretations advanced by twentieth-century thinkers studied here are presented, with the help of normative language and rhetorical strategies, as *the* single objective truth, since, after all, the family as an Islamic institution is understood as timeless in both belief and manifestation. It is to this particular problematic that many Muslim thinkers are currently responding and contesting, as the new 'gender jihad', to borrow a term from Wadud. Based on this problematic, scholars are rethinking, even contesting, not the fundamental belief in marriage and family values as Islamically normative, but the Islamic rationalisations that bolster the gendered roles that have historically been assigned to the husband-wife team.[104] By starting with Qur'anic hermeneutics, such scholars are formulating an Islamic response that situates itself within a legacy of Qur'anic exegesis, thereby neutralising any Muslim critiques that attempt to dispel such rethinking as 'feminist', thus culturally polluted by the west, and by implication Islamically inauthentic.

Indeed, the very authenticators of Islamic culture are increasingly voicing their views of how cultural authenticity itself needs to be re-imagined for Islam to remain relevant to modern living, particularly to groups that have historically been represented, rather than self presenting. Again, while modest, this growing body of scholarship is a significant step in contesting, indeed reforming, a longstanding discourse derived from what Abou El Fadl calls 'authoritarian hermeneutics', namely, a methodology that usurps and subjugates the mechanisms of producing meaning from a text to a highly selective subjectivity and selective reading', which he argues became pervasive after 1975.[105] Such a methodology has corrupted the integrity of the Islamic texts and muted their voice.[106] Clearly, the androcentric textual intent that is reified by twentieth-century thinking about the family has not only discredited things feminine within orthodoxy, but has misrepresented, even corrupted the sacred texts themselves. It is these scriptural corruptions that these reformers seek to redress and purge.

Conclusion

Twentieth-century Muslim thinkers have inherited and bequeath to the reader of their writings a problematic conceptual grid of gender and the family that is encoded with male privilege. It makes invisible the very possibility that male privilege might inhere in their Islamic paradigm of family, since this institution is based on ideals, like marital complementarity, family cohesiveness and societal harmony – ideals that are inherently non-gendered. This explains how these thinkers do not see their own contradictory and subjective logic when reasoning that male authority brings no advantage before the law or that differences do not imply supremacy of one sex over the other.[107] Because the objective of these gender roles is the safe-guarding of the family, which, in turn, seeks to embody the Islamic values of unity, equality, harmony and justice, the gender and sexual difference that premise these roles are consequently understood as complementary, without necessarily being understood as subordinate. Yet, interchangeable notions like complementarity, gender equity and a sexual division of labour are rationalised in ways that obscure what is ultimately male privilege *within*, not before the law. For these religious scholars, the interpretation assigned to the differences between the sexes is based on what are ultimately subjective understandings of gender difference, presented as natural and binding. This explains why they speak in terms of 'natural constitution', 'innate dispositions' and 'the natural ordering of things'. Because their framework is pan-Islamic, the Muslim woman that they envision is rendered an idealised trope of Islamic maternity. Yet, while there are certainly real and obvious physiological differences between man and woman, how these differences are understood, what meanings – legal and social – are assigned to these ontological categories, are interpreted acts that are necessarily subjective and context-specific. Yet, they are presented as normative and everlasting.

Furthermore, we cannot view this Islamic discourse of gender and the family divorced from a larger movement that has spanned the entire twentieth century in the Muslim world, namely a movement that seeks Islamic authenticity and cultural revival in the face of Western hegemonic imperialism. As such, Muslim women as objects of this discourse reside at the very centre of this movement of Islamic orthodoxy as the unique purveyors of a perceived authentic civilisational identity. As long as Western imperialism proves problematic for the Muslim world, women's issues, indeed the very identity of Muslim women, will reside at the centre of Islamic discourses of societal change, reform and cultural authenticity.

In the Islamic thought of this century, then, like centuries before, women's roles have been constituted through a reified discourse of motherhood and Islamic culture. Strictly conceptualised as a wife-mother and as the identity-givers of the family-society, and thus as cultural authenticators, the Muslim woman as a separate identity finds her own religious meaning in her biology, e.g., her creation, her reproductive capacity, and her bodily modesty and behaviour, *not* in her independent spirituality and right to self-governance inherent in the notion of vicegerency – her first and foremost duty, not right, on earth. What twentieth-century discourses teach us, in sum, is that when the conceptual grid of family has focused on Qur'anic rights, as evidenced by 'Abduh's approach in the late nineteenth and early twentieth centuries the notion of humanity's vicegerency is the pivot point on which societal renewal and regeneration becomes contingent. In this grid, women and men, along with their legal rights as *necessary* members in both the family and society, are viewed as more equitable spiritual and social equals. When the framework is focused on interpreted roles, which is characteristic of twentieth-century thinking, the Islamic view of gender is based on biological difference that ultimately institutionalises a gender hierarchy within the family, and hence society. In this framework, woman as *khalifa* is based solely on her ontology as Mother.

It is not surprising, then, that the rising counter-discourse of the late twentieth century that seeks, as an *islah* movement, to reform these gender inequalities, are reclaiming the right of *ijtihad* and going back to the Qur'an through hermeneutics, as was done a century earlier, to reassert the importance of (re)educating all Muslims in Qur'anic rights and principals, so that they can realise their individual and collective potential. Certainly, when one thinks of the last verse God chose to reveal to mankind in the Qur'an, which addresses men and women as gendered beings, the acts we are invited to do *collectively* in the formation and sustaining of a Muslim society revolve around the genderless notion of vicegerency:

> The Believers, men and women, are protectors, one of another: They enjoin what is just, and forbid what is evil; they observe regular prayers, practice regular charity, and obey Allah and His Messenger. On them will Allah pour His Mercy: for Allah is Exalted in power, Wise. (Q.9:71)

Indeed, this is for those that reflect.

Notes

1. See Abdullah Omar Naseef, ed., *Today's Problems, Tomorrow's Solutions* (London, 1988); Hammudah Abd al 'Ati, *The Family Structure in Islam* (Indianapolis, IN, 1977); Yvonne Yazbeck Haddad, 'Traditional Affirmations

Concerning the Role of Women as found in Contemporary Arab Islamic Literature', in Jane I. Smith, ed., *Women in Contemporary Societies* (London, 1980), pp. 61–86; Mervat Hatem, 'Toward the Development of Post-Islamist and Post-Nationalist Feminist Discourses in the Middle East', in Judith E. Tucker, ed., *Arab Women* (Bloomington, IN, 1993), pp. 29–48; Nadia Hijab, 'Islam, Social Change, and the Reality of Arab Women's Lives', in Yvonne Yazbeck Haddad and John L. Esposito, ed., *Islam, Gender, and Social Change* (New York, 1998), pp. 45–55; Amira el-Azhary Sonbol, ed., *Women, the Family and Divorce Laws in Islamic History* (Syracuse, NY, 1996); and, Barbara F. Stowasser, 'Women's Issues in Modern Islamic Thought', in Judith E. Tucker, ed., *Arab Women: Old Boundaries, Old Frontiers* (Bloomington, IN, 1993), pp. 3–28.

2. See Abd al-Halim Abu Shuqqah, *Tahrir al-mar'a fi 'asr al-risala* (Kuwait, 1991); Khurshid Ahmad, *Family Life in Islam* (Leicester, 1974); Jamal Badawi, *Gender Equality in Islam: Basic Principles* (Plainfield, IN, 1995); Jamal A. Badawi, *The Status of Woman in Islam* (Plainfield, IN, n.d.); Abu al-A'la Mawdudi, *Purdah and the Status of Woman in Islam* (Lahore, 1972); Abu al-A'la Mawdudi, *Towards Understanding Islam* (Riyad, 1960); Yusuf al-Qaradawi, *The Lawful and the Prohibited in Islam* (Indianapolis, n.d.).

3. See Barbara Stowasser, 'Liberated Equal or Protected Dependent? Contemporary Religious Paradigms on Women's Status in Islam', *Arab Studies Quarterly*, 9, 3 (1991), pp. 260–283.

4. Ibid., p. 262.

5. Chandra Talpade Mohanty, 'Under Western Eyes: Feminist Scholarship and Colonial Discourses', in Mohanty, ed., *Third World Feminism and the Politics of Feminism* (Bloomington, IN, 1991), p. 55.

6. Ibid., p. 53.

7. See Beth Baron, *The Women's Awakening in Egypt* (New Haven, CT, 1994); Margot Badran, *Feminists, Islam, and Nation* (Cairo, 1996); Margot Badran, ed., *Opening the Gates* (Bloomington, IN, 1990). On Syria and Lebanon, see Elizabeth McKee, 'The Political Agendas and Textual Strategies of Levantine Women Writers', in Mai Yamani, ed., *Feminism and Islam* (New York, 1996), pp. 105–140. On Turkey, see Deniz A. Kandiyoti, 'Emancipated But Unliberated? Reflections on the Turkish Case', *Feminist Studies*, 13, 2 (1987); Yesim Arat, 'Women's Movement of the 1980s in Turkey: Radical Outcome of Liberal Kemalism?' in F. Gocek and S. Balaghi, ed., *Reconstructing Gender in the Middle East* (New York, 1994), pp. 100–112. On Iran, see William Darrow, 'Woman's Place and the Place of Women in the Iranian Revolution', in Yvonne Y. Haddad and Ellison Banks Findley, ed., *Women, Religion and Social Change* (New York, 1985).

8. Badran, *Feminists, Islam, and Nation*, p. 11.

9. Cited in Leila Ahmed, *Women and Gender in Islam* (New Haven, CT, 1992), pp. 139–140.

10. Cited in Ibid., p. 139.

11. Ibid., p. 140.

12. Vicegerency, or *khilafa*, refers to the creative purpose of humankind, as stated in the Qur'an, namely to worship God and act as His vicegerent, or appointee, on earth, to establish His Will. Vicegerency is an ungendered notion in Islam, as it refers to an undifferentiating *nafs*, or entity, that each human – male and female alike — is endowed with, as the Qur'anic verse makes clear: 'It is He Who hath made you (His) agents, inheritors of the earth... .' (Q.6:165)

13. Hasan Turabi, *Women in Islam and Muslim Society* (London, 1991), pp. 5, 43.

14. Ibid., pp. 13–20.

15. Ibid., pp. 17–25.

16. See Qasim Amin, *The Liberation of Women*, tr. Samiha Sidhom Peterson (Cairo, 1992).

17. Ibid., pp. 11–34.

18. Ahmed, *Women and Gender in Islam*, p. 163. Also see Beth Baron, *The Women's Awakening in Egypt* (New Haven, CT, 1994), and Margot Badran, *Feminists, Islam, and Nation* (Cairo, 1996).

19. Amin, *The Liberation of Women*, p. 72.

20. Ahmad, *Family Life*, p. 16.

21. Ibid., p. 16.

22. Badawi, *Gender Equity*, pp. 6–10; Ahmad, *Family Life*, pp. 8–11; Mawdudi, *Purdah*, p. 146; Afzular Rahman, *Role of Muslim Woman in Society* (London, 1986), pp. 17–18; Abu Shuqqah, *Tahrir al-ma'ra*, vol. 1, p. 70.

23. Badawi, *Gender Equity*, p. 13.

24. Ahmad, *Family Life*, p. 17, 34; see also Mawdudi, *Purdah*, p. 160; Rahman, *Role of Muslim Woman*, pp. 17–18.

25. Badawi, *Gender Equity*, pp. 13–14.

26. See Abdullah Muhammad Khouj, *Handbook of Marriage in Islam* (Washington, DC, 1992).

27. 'The term "equity" is used instead of the more common expression "equality", which is sometimes misunderstood to mean absolute equality in each and every detailed item of comparison rather than overall equality. *Equity* is used here to mean justice and overall equality in the totality of rights and responsibilities of both genders and allows for the possibility of variations in specific items within the overall balance and equality.' Badawi, *Gender Equity*, p. 47.

28. Mawdudi, *Towards Understanding Islam*, p. 165; Abu Shuqqah, *Tahrir*

al-mar'a, p. 127.

29. Khouj, *Handbook of Marriage*, p. 23; Rahman, *Role of Muslim Woman*, pp. 22–25.

30. Badawi, *Gender Equity*, pp. 18 and 24.

31. Badawi, *The Status of Woman in Islam*, pp. 21–22; Ahmad, *Family Life*, p. 34; Mawdudi, *Towards Understanding Islam*, pp. 164–165; al-Qaradawi, *The Lawful and the Prohibited*, pp. 193–194; Rahman, *Role of Muslim Woman*, pp. 1–2.

32. Abu Shuqqah, *Tahrir al-mar'a*, vol. 1, p. 28.

33. It is the subheadings that the hadiths are listed under which reveal the author's view; for instance, the subheadings for those Prophetic traditions that confirm the marital sexual division of labour are 'The Husband's Responsibilities', which include *al-qawama* and *al-infaq* (financial support), while under 'The Wife's Responsibilities', the care and upbringing of the children as well as domestic duty are listed. Both of these subheadings fall under the heading, 'The Distribution of Family Responsibilities between Marriage Partners'. Abu Shuqqah, *Tahrir al-mar'a*, vol. 1, pp. 127–128.

34. Ahmad, *Family Life*, p. 17.

35. Seyyed Hossein Nasr, *Ideals and Realities in Islam* (London, 1966), p. 113 (emphasis added).

36. Mawdudi, *Purdah*, p. 147.

37. Khouj, *Handbook of Marriage*, p. 24.

38. Mawdudi, *Purdah*, pp. 12–13.

39. al-Qaradawi, *Lawful and the Prohibited*, p. 193; Rahman, *Role of Muslim Woman*, p. 27.

40. Mawdudi, *Purdah*, p. 14.

41. al-Qaradawi, *The Lawful and the Prohibited*, p. 193.

42. 'A crucial aspect in the upbringing of daughters that greatly influences their future is education.' Badawi, *Gender Equity*, p. 22; Mawdudi, *Purdah*, pp. 155–156.

43. Badawi, *The Status of Woman in Islam*, p. 18.

44. Badawi, *Gender Equity*, p. 18.

45. Mawdudi, *Purdah*, p. 148; Mawdudi, *Towards Understanding Islam*, p. 166.

46. Badawi, *Gender Equity*, p. 18.

47. Mawdudi, *Purdah*, p. 148.

48. Mawdudi, *Purdah*, pp. 150 and 206.

49. Badawi, *Gender Equity*, p. 18. The exception to any lawful type of employment for a woman is as the head of state, though this view is modified slightly in his discussion on pp. 38–41.

50. Badawi, *The Status of Woman in Islam*, pp. 24–25. See also Rahman,

Role of Muslim Woman, pp. 292–299.

51. Rahman, *Role of Muslim Woman*, p. 295.

52. Mawdudi, *Purdah*, p. 213.

53. Rahman, *Role of Muslim Woman*, p. 3.

54. Mawdudi, *Purdah*, p. 213.

55. Mawdudi, *Purdah*, p. 158.

56. al-Qaradawi, *Lawful and the Prohibited*, p. 204; Rahman, *Role of Muslim Woman*, p. 28.

57. Mawdudi, *Purdah*, pp. 206, 207–208; Rahman, *Role of Muslim Woman*, p. 2.

58. Badawi, *Gender Equity*, p. 16.

59. Badawi, *The Status of Woman in Islam*, p. 19.

60. al-Qaradawi, *Lawful and the Prohibited*, pp. 207 and 219.

61. The example of 'Amra Bint Yazid al-Kilabiyya.

62. Najla Hamadeh, 'Islamic Family Legislation: The Authoritarian Discourse of Silence', in Yamani, ed., *Feminism and Islam*, p. 334.

63. Badawi, *Gender Equity*, p. 24; Mawdudi, *Purdah*, pp. 145 and 152; Khouj, *Handbook of Marriage in Islam*, p. 19.

64. al-Qaradawi, *The Lawful and the Prohibited*, p. 205.

65. Khouj, *Handbook of Marriage*, pp. 24–25.

66. Khouj, *Handbook of Marriage*, pp. 24–27; al-Qaradawi, *The Lawful and the Prohibited*, pp. 205–207; Badawi, *Gender Equity*, pp. 25–26; Mawdudi, *Purdah*, p. 159; Rahman, *Role of Muslim Woman*, pp. 400–411.

67. Amira el-Azhary Sonbol, 'Law and Gender Violence in Ottoman and Modern Egypt', in Sonbol, ed., *Women, the Family, and Divorce Laws in Islamic History*, p. 282.

68. Amira el-Azhary Sonbol, '*Ta'a* and Modern Legal Reform: A Rereading', *Islam and Christian-Muslim Relations*, 9, 3 (1998), p. 293.

69. Jamal Badawi, *Polygamy in Islamic Law* (Plainfield, IN, 1972), pp. 7, 9, 11.

70. Ibid., p. 9. Importantly, Badawi's view is modified in his *Gender Equity in Islam* (published in 1995, many years after the cited pamphlet), which does not include these cases that justify male polygamy and, concerning polyandry, he does not make any statements about woman's natural monogamy, but instead states that it raises 'thorny problems' with respect to children's lineal identity and the laws of inheritance – a more plausible rationale for explaining why polyandry is not Islamically ordained. Badawi, *Gender Equity in Islam*, pp. 28–29.

71. Badawi, *Polygamy in Islamic Law*, p. 7; al-Qaradawi, *The Lawful and the Prohibited*, p. 192.

72. Badawi, *Polygamy in Islamic Law*, p. 11; al-Qaradawi, *The Lawful and the*

Prohibited, p. 193; Ahmad, *Family Life*, p. 24; Khouj, *Handbook of Marriage*, p. 43.

73. Badawi, *Polygamy in Islamic Law*, p. 9; al-Qaradawi, *The Lawful and the Prohibited*, p. 193; Khouj, *Handbook of Marriage*, p. 43.

74. Ahmad, *Family Life*, p. 24.

75. al-Qaradawi, *The Lawful and the Prohibited*, p. 193.

76. Other than the condition that the husband should be just to all co-wives, a subjective determination, there is very little discussion of how to institutionally regulate the practice of polygamy.

77. Mawdudi, *Purdah*, p. 152.

78. Rahman, *Role of Muslim Woman*, p. 1.

79. Ahmad, *Family Life*, p. 27.

80. al-Qaradawi, *The Lawful and the Prohibited*, p. 149.

81. Ahmad, *Family Life*, p. 18.

82. al-Qaradawi, *The Lawful and the Prohibited*, p. 149; Ahmad, *Family Life*, p. 20.

83. Mawdudi, *Towards Understanding Islam*, p. 165.

84. This verse reads: 'O mankind! Reverence your Guardian-Lord, who created you from a single person, created, of like nature, his mate, and from them twain scattered like seeds countless men and women – fear Allah, through Whom Ye demand your mutual rights and reverence the wombs that bore you: for Allah ever watches over you.' Ahmad, *Family Life*, p. 23; Mawdudi, *Towards Understanding Islam*, p. 167.

85. Ahmad, *Family Life*, p. 27.

86. Ibid., p. 35; Mawdudi, *Towards Understanding Islam*, p. 171; Khouj, *Handbook of Marriage*, pp. 40–41.

87. Khouj, *Handbook of Marriage*, p. 40.

88. Jamal Badawi, *The Muslim Woman's Dress* (Plainfield, IN, 1980); Ahmad, *Family Life*, p. 35; al-Qaradawi, *Lawful and the Prohibited*, pp. 154 and 159; al-Mawdudi, *Purdah*, p. 177; Rahman, *Role of Muslim Woman*, pp. 421–423.

89. Badawi, *Gender Equity in Islam*, pp. 31–32.

90. Ahmad, *Family Life in Islam*, p. 7.

91. Zakaria Bashier, *Muslim Women in the Midst of Change* (Leicester, 1980), p. 9.

92. See Lila Abu-Lughod, 'The Marriage of Feminism and Islamism in Egypt: Selective Repudiation as a Dynamic of Postcolonial Cultural Politics', in Abu-Lughod, ed., *Remaking Women: Feminism and Modernity in the Middle East* (Princeton, NJ, 1998), pp. 3–31.

93. Nadia Hijab, 'Islam, Social Change, and the Reality of Arab Women's Lives', in *Islam, Gender, and Social Change* (New York, 1998), p. 47.

94. Cited in Hijab, 'Islam, Social Change, and the Reality of Arab Women's

Lives', p. 48.

95. See Amira el-Azhary Sonbol, ed., *Women, the Family and Divorce Laws in Islamic History.*

96. Such re-inscribing, however, should not be confused with the call for the 'retraditionalisation' of women's status and roles made by certain twentieth-century Muslim reformers. This particular discourse of religious reform, articulated by the likes of Qasim Amin, did not accept the Qur'an as its starting point, as do the Muslim thinkers treated by this study. Rather, these reformers assimilated a Western-informed nationalist vision of women's domesticity to 'tradition' and tried to find Islamic bases for it, while vilifying as foreign the other side of what being a Western emancipated woman might mean. These 'so-called reformers', asserts Mawdudi, were bewitched by the West and consequently put forth a call of female emancipation to 'hoodwink the common Muslims', but, in the end, it was 'a great hoax'. If Mawdudi's writings are an example, the Islamic discourse being deconstructed here certainly lays claim to a pure indigenous tradition that is not spurious, but Qur'anically rationalized. Abu-Lughod, 'Feminism and Islamism in Egypt', p. 255; Mawdudi, *Purdah*, p. 22.

97. Uma Narayan, *Dislocating Cultures* (New York, 1997), p. 15.

98. See, for example, Maryam Jameelah, *Islam and the Muslim Woman Today* (Lahore, 1976); Fatima Umar Naseef, *Women in Islam: A Discourse in Rights and Obligations* (London, 1999).

99. Hijab, 'Islam, Social Change, and the Reality of Arab Women's Lives', pp. 45–46.

100. See Allama Saiyid Sulaiman Nadvi, *Hadhrat Ayesha Siddiqa: Her Life and Works* (Kuwait, 1986).

101. See Khaled Abou El Fadl, *Speaking in God's Name* (Oxford, 2001); Asma Barlas, *'Believing Women' in Islam* (Austin, TX, 2002); Amina Wadud, *Qur'an and Woman* (Oxford, 1999).

102. Mohanty, 'Under Western Eyes', p. 53.

103. Badawi, *Gender Equity in Islam*, p. 43 (emphasis in original).

104. See Haleh Afshar, 'Islam and Feminism: An Analysis of Political Strategies', in Yamani, ed., *Feminism and Islam*, pp. 197–216; Asma Barlas, *'Believing Women in Islam'*; Ziba Mir-Hosseini, 'Stretching the Limits: A Feminist Reading of the *Shari'a* in Post-Khomeini Iran', in Yamani, ed., *Feminism and Islam*, pp. 285–319; Amina Wadud, *Qur'an and Woman.*

105. Abou El Fadl, *Speaking in God's Name*, p. 5.

106. Ibid., p. 6.

107. Badawi, *Gender Equity*, p. 33; Badawi, 'The Status of Women in Islam', p. 25.

9

Reflections on the West

Jacques Waardenburg

Introduction[1]

If the East has enjoyed a symbolic value in European culture, the West has had intense symbolic meanings in the Muslim world. The associations accompanying these terms have differed, however. From the eighteenth century onwards (and deep into the twentieth century), the East tended to evoke for Europeans the land of the rising sun with a piercing light, access to the sources of life and the universe, and enhanced spirituality. With the exoticism of mystical poetry and wisdom, the East represented for the European cultural public the region of soft souls. In contrast, the West traditionally suggested to Muslims the land of the setting sun (if not death). While for a younger generation it would raise the hope of a new kind of life and future, during the nineteenth and twentieth centuries it became increasingly associated with power and riches, and with a corresponding aggression and greed. The Western mind had developed rationality, resulting in scientific knowledge and technology, material empiricism, and a critical attitude toward metaphysics and religion. With its destructive powers and desire to dominate, the West represented for a more informed Muslim public the region of tough minds.

If these are the mutual symbolic meanings of East and West, what have been the actual historical, socio-cultural relations between

the West and the Muslim world?[2] Until the Second World War, the
Muslim discovery of the West was largely a discovery of Europe, or
at least of certain European countries and cities.[3] In the course of
the nineteenth century, Europe was gradually discovered as a civilisation, rather than solely as a power that made itself felt through
the occupation of Muslim land.[4] Students travelled to study and be
trained in Europe, specifically France and Britain. Works from the
main European languages, including Russian, were translated into
Arabic, Ottoman Turkish and Persian. In the opposite direction,
European writers and scholars visited Muslim countries. Quite a
few of them were genuinely interested in archaeology and history,
but also in the present-day living conditions of the people. Some of
them devoted themselves to academic studies as Orientalists. Some
taught at educational institutions in centres of Muslim culture such as
Cairo and Lahore. Others lived and worked in places of Muslim-European encounter, like Paris or St. Petersburg. Muslim authors wrote
about various aspects of European culture during the nineteenth
century, generally with admiration, upholding some of its elements
as an example to be followed in their own countries. Other views
and judgements also developed, however. An important example
of more critical Muslim views of the West is the monthly periodical
al-Manar, edited from 1898 in Cairo by Muhammad Rashid Rida,
until his death in 1935. This gives interesting accounts of the ways in
which the encounter between Islam and the West took place in the
heyday of European colonial rule, from a salafi point of view.[5]

'The West' was, and remains, an idea subject to discourse. The
first kind of discourse, conducted by Westerners (especially those
representing the West to non-Westerners elsewhere) describes it with
pride. This imagined West, with its civilisation, is held up as an example to non-Westerners (or at least it was in the colonial period).
The second kind of discourse about the West (generally conducted
by non-Westerners among themselves) is charged with a range of
emotional responses. Most of those subscribing to this discourse had
never been to the West. They felt its power directly or indirectly, and
allowed their imagination to develop concerning it. Their discourse
was linked to certain reported experiences, and offered an interpretation of these. The imagination it encapsulated was the result
of the feelings and emotions evoked by such experiences. The same

remark applies to specifically Muslim discourses about the West. Around the Mediterranean and in the Middle East, Muslims knew about Christians. They had their own history and experience with them, as subjected populations inside, and as enemies outside, their borders. After the expulsion of the Moriscos from Spain (1529) and with the exception of the Ottoman conquerors on their way to Vienna (1683), up until the 1820s Europe did not hold any particular attraction for Muslims. It was a region peripheral to what in their view was the central band of the world, stretching from Morocco to Indonesia. The Muslim discourse about the West (which began in the nineteenth century) was concerned mainly with Europe up until the Second World War.[6]

The Problem under Study

The following discussion explores some major orientations developed by Muslim intellectuals toward 'the West' as an idea (and as a reality) during the twentieth century. Whether appreciative or critical of the West, these orientations implied (and sometimes developed explicitly) articulations both of their own identity, and of Islam as their specific cultural legacy and normative system. Whereas Westerners mostly ask 'how does Islam relate to the West?', the interest here is how Muslim intellectuals (in the wider sense of the word) perceived, digested, and constructed 'the West'. There is also a consideration of whether there were certain links between their constructions of the West, and the ways in which they identified with Islam.

It is taken for granted that Muslim views and judgements of the West developed largely in terms of internal exchanges and debates in Muslim countries. The Muslim discourse about the West has been fundamentally a discourse among Muslims, and is part of the social and intellectual history of Muslim societies. Yet the West itself had a direct impact on this discourse in colonial times when the debate concerned the direct military and political power of the (European) West, and the question of how to remove it. Following de-colonisation and during the Cold War, Western power in Muslim countries has been indirect, and exercised largely through economic processes. Since the end of the Cold War, however, the (American) West has been exercising more direct power, with a corresponding impact on the Muslim discourse about the West.[9] This has been the case especially since the Gulf War of 1991, the Afghan war of 2001, and the 'War on Terror' declared after 11 September 2001.

Perceptions (certainly those of other cultures) are rarely immediately given. Instead, they are embedded in discourses of a cultural and ideological, but also of a socio-economic and political, nature. Muslim discourses about the West developed in particular historical contexts and situations, in which certain Muslims and certain Westerners encountered each other. While the resulting Western views and practices are more or less known, what were the Muslim perceptions, seen not from a Western but from their own point of view, and according to their own intentions? The following exploration, which concentrates especially on the Middle East, addresses this question.

Different 'Wests' Perceived and Experienced by Different Muslim Groups

Of course, not only one and the same 'West' existed for all Muslims, just as there was not one and the same 'Islam' for all Westerners. At different times and in different places there were different 'Wests', with different connotations, for different Muslim societies and groups. Moreover, the historical context in which encounters between Muslims and Westerners have taken place has undergone immense changes during the nineteenth and twentieth centuries. Muslim discourses on the West have changed accordingly in the course of time.

In the pre-colonial period, the West did not pose an immediate danger for Muslims, except for incidental wars and conquests, as in the Balkans and earlier in Russia, Spain and Italy. In the colonial period, which extended for different durations and with different impact for different Muslim countries, 'the West' (identified with Europe) was the place of origin of foreign occupants and colonisers. When Muslims wrote about the West or Europe at that time, they meant in particular the country that ruled them, and with which they had some direct experience. Between the two world wars, Europe as a whole might be seen as an aggressive military and political entity (with the exception of Germany, Scandinavia, and most of Eastern Europe).

In the post-colonial period, Europe lost its power over most Muslim territories, while the USA was able to impose its growing hegemony over the Muslim part of the world. It appears that in the 1960s, use of the expression 'the West' in Muslim countries began to refer primarily to the USA. Like the Second World War, the Cold War gave the West a new meaning as the 'Free World', while the presence of the USSR helped to keep its power within certain limits.[10] This period ended with the demise of the USSR, especially when a New World Order was imposed with the Gulf War of 1991. 'The West' as military and political power was now practically identified with the USA. The capital of the West became Washington, DC, and the American war against the Taliban in Afghanistan (October–December 2001) accentuated this fact.

Muslim discourses on the West also show a great variety in accordance with countries and their experiences with the West. The geographical area of the Muslim world is vast, and there are great differences between countries. In the Middle East, for example, the Iranian revolution changed the official pro-Western discourse at the time of the last Shah, into a virulent anti-Western and especially anti-American discourse (from 1979). The growing Islamisation in Pakistan, especially after Zia ul-Haqq's rise to power in 1977, could have led to a growing distance from the West, were it not for the fact that Pakistan and the USA needed each other during the first Afghan war against the Soviet invaders (1979–1989). Similarly, Turkey, which had been indispensable for the West during the Cold War, enjoyed broad NATO support. For its part, it has felt itself to be part of the West, to the extent that it has sought to be accepted into Europe (as a potential member state of the European Union [EU]). Its alignment with the West has increasingly become a subject of debate in Turkey. Discourses on the West in the Arab countries of the Middle East have depended to a large extent on a series of issues. These include commercial ties with the USA or its financial backing; open or tacit support from the West (i.e., the USA) for Israeli policies, and the strategies of particular Arab rulers (those of Nasser or Sadat, for example). In general, Middle Eastern Muslim discourse on the West is critical, especially of the USA for its backing of Israel. However, public statements naturally follow the official political guidelines of the countries concerned. Since its attack on Kuwait in 1990, Iraq has been practically ostracised by the West, as was Libya after the Lockerbie episode.

Outside the Middle East, Muslim encounters with the West have been varied. Muslims in India (a secular state) live under pressures magnified by tensions with Pakistan; they are very much involved in their own minority problems, and may look with certain hopes to the West. In Indonesia, where Pancasila is the official state ideology, there is an official Islam regulated by the state, and direct political expressions of Islam have been suppressed for decades. Defenders of civil society and democracy look to the West for moral and practical support (the same is the case in other Muslim countries with undemocratic regimes). Economically, Indonesia is very dependent on the USA (and on Australia). Malaysia, with its Tiger ambitions of becoming a major economic power, has its own internal problems. Islamist pressure there seeks increasing Islamisation and an orientation toward other Islamic countries, rather than the West. The Central Asian Republics still stand very much under Russian influence, and look for economic support from the West.

In North Africa, Libya has never had a very positive experience with the West; under Qadhdhafi, it became for a time a proponent of resistance against American influence. Its relations with the West, like those of other oil-producing Muslim countries that do not want Western ideological influence, seem to remain restricted to economic and financial spheres. For the other three Maghreb countries, France represented 'the West' for a long time; this has now broadened to Southern Europe and the EU. After a promising start, and notwithstanding great potential, Tunisian social and cultural openness to European values has been blocked by the current regime. Algeria has become submerged in its internal problems since the repression of Islamist advances in 1990. Only Morocco, since the death of Hasan II, seems to be opening up to more constructive relations with the West, while adapting its cultural heritage along more liberal lines. For the last few years it has implemented policies in favour of human rights. It also participates actively in international efforts to improve the situation of the countries of the South.

Muslim countries further south see the West primarily from an

African perspective. In West Africa, Islamist pressures (apparently supported by Saudi Arabia and Libya) seek to create a greater distance from the West. However, all these countries (as most countries elsewhere) are economically dependent on the West. During the last thirty years of turbulence, in spite of being repeatedly called to order by the West on issues of human rights and democracy, Nigeria has chosen its own path. Several northern provinces have declared themselves 'Islamic', and have adopted the sharia. In 1999, a more democratic regime came to power; this is renewing older links with the West, and trying to revive democracy and the country's older, more liberal cultural and political tradition. In contrast, the current regime in Sudan resists all Western influence, including efforts to help end the civil war. Its official line is Islamist, and constant reference is made to the sharia (this has been imposed on the whole country, including the South). Muslim East Africa has not experienced the West as directly as North or West Africa. Islamist pressures there (apparently supported by Saudi Arabia and Pakistan) call for a greater distance from the West.

Evidently, many 'Wests' are perceived by Muslims. The term itself requires some delineation.

The Term 'the West'

Muslim intellectuals (rather than political or religious leaders) are the focus of interest here. This is because, among them, a kind of critical reflection about the West and Islam has been taking place. In addition, it is among the intellectuals that one finds a number of individuals who, thanks to their education (often at Western institutions), know more about the West than others. That said, just as Rashid Rida wrote much about the West without any knowledge of European languages, we also find in the later twentieth century individuals who offer their ideas about the West without any detailed knowledge of it. What presents itself is thus more of an ideological discourse about relations between the West and Islam, than a precise study of the human realities indicated by the two terms (particular Western and Muslim peoples and groups, with their specific societies and histories). In short, in most Muslim discourse the West is a construct, just as the East is a construct in most Western discourse.

In Muslim usage in the second half of the twentieth century, the term 'the West' appears to have acquired a greater importance than earlier terms used to indicate non-Muslim blocs, like 'Christianity', 'Franks', or 'Europe'. The West suggests a geographical area, but the term has been used with meanings that are loaded with value and emotion. Five meanings (or images) can be identified.

One meaning, current for a long time, was that of the opposition Orient-Occident, as East-West. The 'Orient' represents the lands of the rising sun to which 'Eastern spirituality' and life are ascribed, while the 'Occident' stands for the lands of the setting sun, with the suggestion of a fatal materialism and death. The fallacy of this essentialist scheme of interpretation has been exposed in a range of critical publications. A second (and currently more important) meaning of 'the West' is political. It is a political concept in which the aspect of power typically predominates (in contrast, Christianity indicates more the aspect of religion, and Europe nowadays more that of culture). The old colonial powers (in particular Britain and France but also Russia and the Netherlands) represented 'the West' during the colonial period. The Pan-Islamic movement arose as a resistance to the West's advance.[11] In the context of the Cold War, 'the West' stood for North America and Western Europe, combined as a power bloc in the 'East-West' conflict. It held negative connotations for those who declared themselves progressive. This 'West' was seen as the political force supporting Israel, without which the latter would have succumbed. In this sense, the West, as a power, is a potential enemy.

A third meaning of 'the West' is linked to modernity. Some have seen Europe as a modern civilisation; on this basis it has been an object of admiration.[12] By definition, the West is 'modern', i.e., endowed with technological progress, economic development, scholarly knowledge, and the use of reason. This evidently also represents power, but not in the brutal sense. In this meaning, the West has positive connotations for those who want to develop society along 'modern' (and mostly 'Western') lines, but negative connotations for those who want to adhere to tradition, and older ways of life. The direct link between modernity and the West is severed by those who make a clear distinction between modernisation in general, and Western models of modernisation in particular, and between the use of reason in general, and its use in the service of specific Western interests.

A fourth meaning of 'the West' indicates a particular 'way of life' in its ordinary external aspects, without showing much concern for its traditions, lasting values, or more fundamental problems (in contrast to more complex ways of life that do carry such a burden). A fifth and final meaning has a much more symbolic and radically normative character. Here, 'the West' represents a world that can perhaps best be described as barbarian (a modern *jahiliyya,* from an Islamist viewpoint). In this meaning, the West stands for a dis-integrating society in which egoism and human solitude prevail. It is the land of loss of mind, where materialism reigns and where people are imprisoned by their desire for goods and money. It is the land of loss of soul, where a secular way of life dominates, and people drift without deeper norms and higher values. It is the land of loss of true feelings, where changing appetites are the norm, and people fall victim to desire and lust. It is the land of loss of human dignity, with a value system based on economics, and where people aggressively exploit each other. Finally, it is the land of metaphysical alienation and loss of God, with man-made idols and people who have no relationship to Being, nature, history and each other. This barbarian West is seen not only as destructive to itself, with violence flaring in bitter economic, social and political conflicts, but also as a real danger for the rest of the world, and especially the Muslim part of it. Its deep aggression has been demonstrated in its policies of colonialism, economic exploitation, and political domination over the rest of the world. At the same time, it seduces people to imitate it, and to be utterly dependent on it. Once seduced by the system or forced to surrender to it, they gradually lose their identity and authenticity. In contrast with the image of the West as exemplary in nineteenth-century modernising circles or in twentieth-century republican Turkey and Pahlavi Iran, this image of the West (as pre-sented by Abu al-A'la Mawdudi and Sayyid Qutb, for example) is utterly grim, inhuman, and repulsive.

These disparate images of the West appear in Muslim writings from the second half of the twentieth century. They convey messages (mostly warnings) to the reader. Of course, large parts of 'Western' reality fall outside the scope of Muslim observers. Countries like

Greece, Austria, Switzerland, Belgium, or those of Scandinavia are rarely discussed or even mentioned. Continental European art, literature and cultural history (perhaps with the partial exception of France) appear to be poorly known. Discussions between European thinkers and changes in the self-view and self-evaluation of Europeans that occurred before, during, and after the period of the Iron Curtain are rarely taken into account. Those currents in Europe that argue against Western domination, and that show solidarity with so-called 'Third World' countries, are mostly unknown or neglected. There is hardly any understanding of the reasons behind the various (at times ambiguous) attitudes toward Islam that have prevailed in European societies, and that cannot be reduced to wilful distortions. In brief, the factual knowledge that exists in Muslim countries about Europe and the West in general is still rather poor, and insight into Western civilisation and religion is largely lacking.

For Muslims, the impact of the West (both as a reality and as an idea) has been tremendous during the twentieth century. Muslims thus feel that 'the West' has imposed itself forcefully on their societies, just as non-Muslim minorities in the Muslim world feel that 'Islam' has imposed itself forcefully on them. Apparently, both the West and Islam represent oppression for those who do not belong to them. One should note that a number of intellectuals who studied in the West in the course of the twentieth century overcame the enthusiasm of their youth for French, British, German or American culture, and later reverted to a more distanced attitude, sometimes stressing their Islamic identity. Taha Husayn (1889–1971),[13] who once had pleaded for Egypt's Greek heritage and its belonging to Europe, later saw it primarily as part of the Muslim world. Others opted for a Muslim-Western dialogue. The more personal the responses to the West, the more striking they are. Fazlur Rahman (1919–1988)[14] analysed the transformation of Islam's intellectual tradition. Ali Shari'ati (1933–1977)[15] articulated the social and political message of Islam, specifically in the Iranian context before 1979. Mohammed Arkoun[16] stresses the need to learn from critical Western science and culture. Abdallah Laroui[17] notes the complementarity of Islam and Europe. Mohamed Talbi[18] insists on the necessity of dialogue across the Mediterranean, and within societies on both sides. Tariq Ramadan[19] defends the possibility and the good right of Muslims to pursue modernity to a certain extent. Farid Esack[20] calls for a theology of liberation, and a common effort toward it. Nasr Abu Zayd[21] develops a criticism of current religious discourse.

A number of intellectuals have begun to take active part in Euro-Arab, Christian-Muslim, and other inter-cultural and inter-religious dialogues with Westerners and others, pleading for more communication, co-operation, and dialogue beyond political or ideological barriers.[22] All of them stress their Muslim identity and emphasise their intention to sustain it, if not always religiously, then at least socially, based on moral standards largely derived from Islam. These intellectuals advocate 'modernising' society, but object to being labelled 'Westernised'. Iranian intellectuals in particular have been alert to the danger of being 'contaminated' by Westernisation, and defend Iranian culture and Islam.[23]

Islamist Views of the West and the Secular Order

Among the many responses of Muslim thinkers to Western influences on their societies, the 'Islamist' ones distinguish themselves through an ideological militancy, constructed on the basis of Islam. In Egypt and Pakistan, Sayyid Qutb[24] and Abu al-A'la Mawdudi[25] generated a specific image of the West as an enemy and danger. Especially since the 1970s, Muslims joining Islamist groups have affirmed anew their Islamic identity, largely rejecting Western criticisms of Islam or of particular situations in Muslim countries, and passing judgement on values and practices in Western countries. In contrast to what is perceived (particularly since the end of the Cold War) as the prevailing hegemonic 'Western' model of society, Islamist authors claim that Islam offers a viable (superior?) alternative model. They contend that Islam itself is able to provide the true solution to the problems of the modern world.[26] Islamist critics see both Western political and economic liberalism and Marx-inspired socialism and communism as variants of one Western 'secular' model of society. They perceive this secular model as a conscious project on the part of the West to 'Westernise' the world by means of a total 'secular' colonisation of all aspects of society. The creation of Israel is seen as a tool in this larger project, putting a foreign and inimical entity in the heart of the Arab-Muslim East, in order to divide and subdue it.

Such Islamist literature is conflict-oriented, and stresses the persistence of a continuous ideological conflict that has existed between Islam and the West throughout history. On the part of the West, it perceives from the very beginning a project to 'Westernise' the world, whether via a more religious 'Christianisation', or by a more cultural 'assimilation'. In the latter case, they attribute to the West an image of the East and Islam constructed specifically to serve Western political interests, while the West has presented itself as promoting human values and cultural progress. This literature sees in Islam, from its beginnings, a project to 'Islamise' the world. It holds that this should now be brought to fruition, in opposition to 'Westernisation'. Muslims who happen to be fascinated by the West should be 'de-Westernised', and Muslims in general should be defended against the temptations of Christianisation. On the other hand, wherever possible, Christians should be de-Christianised and Islamised. Western civilisation should be de-mystified, and its negative effects exposed, while the truth of Islam should be continuously demonstrated. In this great ideological conflict, the West has been trying to understand Islam from the medieval period, whereas Islam developed an interest in knowing the West only much later.

For Islamists, the opposition between Islam and the West essentially goes back to the conflict between Islam and a secular order. Islamists interpret the secular order, and particularly the ideology of secularism, arising from the West, as the real enemy of Islam. In Paul Khoury's view,[27] Islamism began to develop as a mode of self-defence against the activities of Christian missions, and the encroachment of the West in general on the Muslim world. It then became highly critical of the claims of Western modernity, and especially the imputed project of 'Westernising' Islam and Muslim societies. Finally, it took the shape of an active project to Islamise the world. This conflictual process took off at the very same time that Western societies began to question their own philosophical foundations. Islamism itself constitutes an internal movement within Muslim societies. It has to do with a broader process of redefining what it means to be Muslim; as a movement, it is part of the recent social history of Muslim societies. In the Arab-Muslim world, Islamism manifests itself in an increasing attachment both to the Islamic religion as an all-encompassing normative system, and to the Arab-Muslim cultural heritage. Whereas Western colonisation is categorically rejected and fought against, modernisation as such is not rejected. On the contrary, Islamists call on Muslim societies to adopt from Western civilisation its science, technology and organisation of public services. However, they reject the West's ideology and its basis: secular materialism. Indeed, they insist that Muslim individual and social life should be ever more (re-)Islamised.

Within the Islamist trend, some thinkers have made a conscious effort to develop an Islamic epistemology, distinct from the epistemology of typically Western scholarship.[28] In nineteenth and early twentieth-century Europe, some Catholic and Protestant thinkers developed a Catholic or Protestant world-view, on the basis of the data of faith. They established denominational universities to apply such world-views in teaching and scholarship. In a similar vein, in the 1970s some Muslim thinkers sought to apply an Islamic epistemology in various disciplines, producing Islamic social sciences, Islamic economics, etc. Together with the system itself, these disciplines would be taught at the new International 'Islamic' universities founded in Islamabad, Kuala Lumpur, and elsewhere. The final aim of these efforts was to carry out an 'Islamisation of knowledge', a term coined by Isma'il R. al-Faruqi[29] and worked out by a group of Muslim thinkers at the beginning of the 1980s. This project also implies a critical view of the West, and efforts to arrive at a new kind of knowledge. It imputes false claims of universality and materialist presuppositions to Western scholarship, and seeks to maintain a distance from this. However, just as with denominational teaching and scholarship claiming to be 'Catholic' or 'Protestant', an 'Islamic' epistemology turns out in fact to be acceptable only to its own adherents. It runs the risk of becoming simply a 'sectarian' way of obtaining knowledge, outside of the general criteria for ascertaining whether a given claim of knowledge is viable or not. The price of Islamism is that it develops its own ideological discourse not only in Islamic religious, social and political matters, but also in its perception, interpretation and study of reality outside Islam. It cannot be described as research scholarship; it rather becomes *Weltanschauung*, ideological world-view affirmation.

Political Discourse on the West and its Impact on Muslim Societies and Countries

The Muslim political discourse on the West is based on the experience of the West as a power, and its main concern is how to respond to it. In its critical form, it perceives the West as the origin of forces destructive of the Muslim world. In the past, colonialism was the most obvious form of the imperialist policies of the West. Nowadays, the latter imposes itself through economic, political and cultural imperialism. It supports regimes that act in conformity with its interests, and opposes those that do not recognise a Western-centred world order. It continues to support Israel and its policies. It imposes an economic open-market system that is catastrophic for most developing countries. This critical political discourse against the West focuses on the hegemonic behaviour and claims of the USA. It often takes ideological forms, with recourse to Islamic legal rules. In extreme cases, a jihad has been proclaimed.

A milder strain of this political discourse does recognise the value of certain Western democratic institutions, and of efforts to sustain social and economic development, especially those undertaken by NGOs. It appreciates the initiatives of the Red Cross/Red Crescent, Amnesty International and human rights organisations to combat abuses. Certain norms and values formulated in the West but deemed to be of a universal nature have also been accepted in Muslim countries. These include freedom of conscience and religious freedom (although Islam retains its claim to be the absolute religion, from which no departure is allowed). There is a general view that norms and values that are valid in themselves can be (and are) politically misused, and that the application of accepted rules is not always guaranteed in Western countries either. It is often said that democracy in practice has certain drawbacks, and that Muslim states are not bound to follow Western models.

Current Muslim discourses on the political impact of the West are replete with remnants of traumatic experiences from the past. Examples are experiences of colonial wars and oppression, forced labour and migration, the direct and indirect effects of the Cold War, oppression and conscious destruction in occupied territories and discrimination in Western societies. There is a revolt against the

Western tendency to identify any Muslim or Palestinian resistance to American or Israeli abuse of power with so-called 'terrorism'. At the same time, 'state terrorism' of Israel, of undemocratic regimes in Muslim countries, and of the USA after 11 September, 2001, is denounced. Samuel P. Huntington's theory of a pending clash of civilisations is utterly rejected in Muslim quarters,[30] while initiatives for Euro-Arab and Euro-Muslim dialogues are welcomed. A number of dialogue meetings between Muslims and Christians have been organised in Muslim countries, as well as in Western ones.[31] If it is not possible in Muslim countries to organise open political protests against the government, or criticise practices of state officials, such matters can be formulated in terms of norms imposed by Islam. The attentive listener (or reader) can recognise political messages in what appear at first sight to be purely religious discourses.

Socio-economic Discourse on the West and its Impact on the Muslim World

Given the imperative of development in Muslim countries, one of the main subjects of debate is the form that a just society should take in a Muslim context. During the Cold War, the ideological, economic and political confrontation between capitalist 'liberal' and socialist 'guided state' models of development were much discussed. Most current socio-economic Muslim discourse stresses the need to re-alise social justice, but rejects materialist assumptions and practices as violating Islamic norms. Certain authors reject in principle the idea of orienting oneself toward foreign models, while some claim that the sharia contains all the necessary elements to realise a just socio-economic order.

In its critical forms, the current Muslim socio-economic discourse denounces and rejects poverty, injustice, oppression and corruption. It defends the rights of the poorer nations of the South, over and against the self-enriching practices of those of the North. It can extend to broader discussions about human rights, democracy and civil society, and it may support the emancipation of women, in, for example, the right to work.[32] Criticism is directed against lack of control over trans-national corporations, and the effects of economic globalisation for the weaker nations in the South.[33] What is subject to attack is not only the West, but the current economic world order supported by the West. There is also a more moderate variety of this socio-economic discourse on the West. One finds, for example, a clear appreciation of some NGOs that assist needy Muslim populations and countries. These work at a grass-roots level, and tend to be appreciative of agriculture, small enterprises and handicrafts, and the contribution of peasants, entrepreneurs and craftsmen (who can often be looked down upon).

The impact of the West on socio-economic realities in Muslim countries is seen in terms of a necessary modernisation process. Accordingly, the question is raised as to what models are followed, and to whose advantage the process works. Some of the discourses discuss bitterly the exploitation of oil, water and other natural resources, without adequate distribution of the benefits. (Besides their economic benefits, nationalisations also have great symbolic value for the populations concerned.) Most economic discourses are concerned with the increased poverty of large parts of the population, the increased indebtedness of the countries concerned, and the growing dependence on foreign banks and investors to extricate economies from financial crises. Surprisingly, the immense costs involved in government armaments' procurement are rarely mentioned.

Cultural Discourse on the West and its Impact on Culture in Muslim Societies

Practically all Muslim discourse about the West has a cultural dimension, since it deals specifically with human and moral issues that result from the cultural encounter between Muslim societies that have their own cultures, and a technologically superior West with its own civilisation.[34] The West is perceived here first of all as representing 'modernity', as a rationalist force exercising an onslaught against existing forms and ways of human life that do not conform to rational demands.[35] The problem is then how to preserve fundamental Islamic values and culture in face of the devastation wreaked by those who might be considered technological or economic 'barbarians' from the West.

Whereas early enthusiasts endeavoured to imitate Western ways of life as much as possible, later (and especially after independence) a more self-assertive trend has insisted on the need to adopt from the West only what is of real use to Muslim societies. According to this, Muslims can (and should) adopt technology and science from the West, but they should not adopt those Western (i.e., non-Muslim) norms and values that contradict fundamental teachings of Islam. The existence of certain positive cultural forces and achievements in the West that are of general validity is recognised, however, and Muslims are encouraged to discover and study these for their own benefit.

A critical version of such a cultural discourse maintains that the West has fundamentally surrendered itself to material gain and rational modernity, implying a life according to secular principles, and the loss of certain norms and values.[36] This has been to the detriment not only of Westerners themselves (and their culture); it also represents a real danger for Muslims, inasmuch as the West is spreading and propagating its secular programme to the whole world (and, moreover, is acquiring substantial economic and political benefits from this). Consequently, Muslims should protect themselves against this programme and outlook. One way of doing this is by passing on a good Islamic education to children and youngsters, and providing good instruction to adults. When Muslims adopt cultural achievements from the West, these have to be measured and purified according to Islamic standards. In this critical view, there is a certain diffidence about non-Islamic cultural expressions in the West. In a more positive view of Western culture, however, its expressions of full humanity and its search for beauty, goodness, and truth are recognised, although Muslims should not study its literature, art and thought without a critical sense. Here we find a positive appreciation of efforts certain circles in the West are making toward co-operation and dialogue. In this kind of discourse, it is precisely obscurantism, isolationism, and an incapacity to co-operate and engage in dialogue with others that are seen as major handicaps for a common future.

Muslim discourses on the impact of Western culture on Muslim societies have been complex. Once this impact is acknowledged, the foremost problem is how to distinguish its good and undesirable aspects. Education is a good example. During the colonial period, several Western countries attached much importance to educating sectors of the younger population in various Muslim countries in accordance with a particular model of French, British, or American training.[37] At private schools (Christian or otherwise), and at public schools, teachers from abroad went to great pains to conduct classes as they would have done back home. Some countries established research institutes that allowed Western scholars to acquire knowledge of the country on site, and provided local scholars with access to Western publications. These institutes also spread knowledge of the language, history, and culture of these countries to a prospective elite. Study fellowships, practical training courses, and cultural exchange programmes brought promising young people from these countries to the West. From a Western point of view, the resulting cultural impact of the West on the Muslim world through education, study, and training was beneficial. Cultural distances were bridged, and people of different cultures could meet and co-operate.

The post-colonial Muslim cultural discourse on the West has seen this spread of Western (mainly European but also American) culture as a mixed blessing. Besides the older Western countries with their national interests in the region, international bodies began to play an increasingly important role: a lot of cultural exchange and assistance currently takes place through international channels. However, certain problems generated by the educational system have persisted. On the one hand, Muslim students became familiar with a Western language and certain aspects of European culture. On the other, during the colonial period schools implemented a Western-type programme and paid relatively little attention to the Muslim people's own language and literature, history and culture. These subjects, moreover, were mostly taught from a 'colonial' perspective. After independence, most of the cultural and educational institutions came under government auspices, and were re-oriented along more national and Islamic lines. Questions arose concerning how the curriculum should be organised, and in what language it should it be taught. Debates on the 'Arabisation' of education and culture that began in post-colonial North Africa continue to today. Indeed, the notion of culture itself has become a subject of debate.

The consequences of the debate on the impact of Western culture have perhaps been most immediately felt in the fields of school education, higher education, and research (and the broader area of the arts and sciences). Without access to educational technology such as computers, students will remain far behind their Western counterparts. Without an adequate knowledge of English and access to materials in English, future generations will be isolated from the international arena. Muslim countries need experts in all fields, but also a qualified leadership, to represent them on an intellectual level. On the other hand, pupils and students should be familiar with (and remain loyal to) their own cultural heritage, including Islam. They should not become alienated from their own country, risking disappearance in the 'brain drain' to the West.[38]

Whatever the points of view taken, however, education and culture constitute, first and foremost, a practical problem in Muslim countries. There is a lack of good libraries and Western books; books from abroad are terribly expensive, and only a few have been translated into Arabic, Turkish, or Persian. Intellectuals (including teachers) have to live under financial and other stress. For intellectuals (or those who aspire to become intellectuals), the West represents a paradise primarily because of its schools, universities, bookshops, and libraries. In the long term, this may remain the real attraction of the West for Muslim elites. The debate on education in Muslim countries is in reality a debate about the future of culture there. This cannot be well envisaged in separation from the West. When there is no knowledge of a Western language, when ideological barriers narrow people's horizons, when the conditions of living do not permit minds to develop, and when there are serious economic constraints, a particular cultural tradition is likely to disappear. Some countries (and international organisations and foundations) offer grants to students to study in the West. Some Near Eastern intellectuals have suggested developing a discipline called 'Occidentalism', to provide students with a critical knowledge of the West.[39] This has led to debates but no visible results. Curiously, the West (or in this case Europe) has not yet stepped in. Various measures could be suggested, including the creation of 'Euro Fellowships' by the EU to allow creative minds (especially from the southern and eastern shore of the Mediterranean) to study or carry out research in member countries of the EU. The EU might establish chairs of European Studies at universities in chosen Arab countries around the Mediterranean. A further initiative would be to inaugurate courses at universities in Muslim countries on relations between Western and Muslim cultures. One should also think of more regular cultural exchanges between Europe and the Muslim world. Such projects would all require political will and sizeable support from the EU or other European institutions and foundations.

In the Muslim world, and specifically the Middle East, there have been many internal debates on subjects of immediate relevance to the encounter of Western and Muslim cultures. One, for example, concerns the possibility (and desirability) of cultural exchange and dialogue of Muslims with representatives of other civilisations, including the Western one.[40] Another concerns the relationship between what is deemed universally valid, and what is held to be typically Islamic. Must cultural affairs necessarily always be cast in an Islamic perspective? There are now 'Islamic' declarations of human rights, 'Islamic' universities, and a programme for the 'Islamisation' of knowledge. The discussion here addresses the place of typically Islamic institutions in the broader international cultural world.[41] A third topic concerns the realisation of rights and duties of persons and groups in Muslim societies. To what extent, in a given Muslim country, can a civil society be realised; to what degree can human rights be applied, and in what ways can legal protection be effectively guaranteed to women? There have been intense debates on these matters in several Muslim countries, all incorporating references to the West, and it is important to detail their concrete results.[42] The fourth topic, that of the ideal Islamic state based on the sharia, might be considered an internal Muslim affair.[43] However, the results of the vigorous debates on this subject do touch Muslim relations with the West. For example, the Taliban experiment was hardly condemned by Muslim religious authorities. What are the limits of claims to establish an Islamic order that potentially violates fundamental human rights? This question is particularly relevant in the case of minorities that have special links with the West. In an era of globalisation, states can no longer permit themselves to retreat fully from the rest of the world, and to neglect its judgements.

These four topics (and many others in the cultural sphere) have been discussed intensely in Muslim societies during recent decades. This discussion has taken place more or less in the West's shadow, or at least with the West ever on the horizon, even if the debate has

not always referred consciously to the West. If there is no reference
to the West, might this indicate the narrow horizon or the provincial
character of the debate? If the West is referred to, in what sense is this
done? If a specific Islamic orientation is sought, what does this imply
not only for future relations with the West, but also for participation
in the broader international debate on the issues in question?

All in all, the impact of Western culture did not end with independence, and it does not restrict itself to information technology
or abstract science. It is no longer primarily transmitted through foreign schools and foreign language books, but through the media, the
Internet, and socially. Turkish students discuss religious taboos with
German counterparts, Iranian researchers discuss Heidegger in the
Islamic Republic, Pakistani intellectuals discuss postmodernism in
an Islamic state, and many Muslim critical minds practice a Marxist
analysis of society. Current Western philosophies touching upon textual interpretation, dialogue, social justice and human rights are far
from unknown in Muslim intellectual quarters. Indeed the Western
impact on thought throughout the Muslim world is ongoing, not
only in the case of so-called liberal, but also in so-called fundamentalist and other forms of thought. With a healthy natural curiosity,
Muslim students are interested in history, literature, sociology, and
recently also the history of religions as practised in the West. Even
Western 'Orientalism' attracts those interested in 'other' points of
view. In cultural matters, 'Islamic' and 'Western' are stamps, rather
than identities.

It is fair to say that, following the ideological opposition proclaimed between Islamism and the secular order (with the West represented as hell and Islam as heaven on earth), the tendency is now
towards a more intellectual stand. For reflecting Muslim intellectuals,
the very reality of 'the West' has become an intellectual problem.
How did the West become what it is now, in its many European and
North American varieties? What have been the forces at work in
Western civilisation, strengthening or weakening it? Do a certain
individualism, social disintegration, and secularisation (visible in
the contemporary West) constitute a unique Western case, or are
they part of more general processes, that occur in all 'modernising'
societies? How can the impact of faith and religion in Western and
Muslim societies be assessed? On this level, the very relationship

between 'Islam' and 'the West', and between Muslims and Westerners, can be discussed as an intellectual and ethical problem for
both sides. In fact, a number of Iranian intellectuals have wrestled
with such problems for half a century.[44] Their debates cannot be
seen independently of their views of the West, its civilisation and
its religion. [45]

The Spiritual Discourse on the West and its Religion

A more 'spiritual' Muslim discourse on the West concerns the foundations of contemporary Western life and culture, i.e., its ontological
basis and metaphysical assumptions.[46] In its critical, pessimistic form,
such discourse holds that the West has paid too high a price for the
particular development of thought that gave rise to its technology
and scientific thought. This price was the severing of its civilisation
from its very source: from Being. Floating mainly on rational, material and secular interests, Western society is doomed to collapse. In
the course of the twentieth century, its internal tensions and conflicts became manifest in the rivalries of imperialism and colonialism, most notably in the two world wars, and the following Cold War.
They are indications that Western civilisation is falling apart. In its
positive variant, however, this philosophical discourse admits that,
although weak, spiritual forces are present in the West, and these
resist the downward movement. The final outcome of the battle of
these positive forces with those of materialism and the secular order
is uncertain, however. In fact, this metaphysical discourse about the
West tends to assume a basic dualism between an Islam connected
with a particular metaphysics, on the one hand, and a West lacking
such a metaphysics, on the other.

Until the mid-twentieth century, Muslim discourses on Western
religion were preoccupied with the presence of Christian missions
in Muslim territory: they were intent on refuting Christianity. This
trend is weaker now, and Christianity is seen less as an aggressive enemy. Muslim reports on and from Europe indeed mention the fact
that religion is weakening there, and even disappearing from public
life.[47] Muslim discourse has critically described the rise of a secular
view of life, first originating in Western Europe, then spreading all
over the West and finally extending to the East, including Muslim

countries. Subsequently, this discourse focused on the struggle against secularism (the doctrine bringing about a secular order), including in Muslim societies, considering it an all-pervading subversive influence from the West. A huge corpus of Muslim religious writings has been devoted to the task of combating secularism as an ideology, and to re-instilling religious faith and practice in Muslim societies. Faced by the demon of secularisation, this discourse implies a certain willingness to recognise the positive role of Christianity in the battle against it, as it threatens Western society and people as well. In its critical view, this discourse affirms (as indicated) that the West is losing its religious and moral foundations. A secular attitude to life is taking the place of religion, and secularism (as a negative ideological force) is spreading from the West to Muslim countries, like a kind of disease. By implication, it is the West that is finally responsible for any secularisation that may take place in Muslim societies. For the West itself, this negative course furnishes proof that Christianity is not the right religion.

In contrast, the more moderate Muslim discourse on Western religion in decline tends to recognise the persistence of a basic theism and morality in the West. This is then viewed as a step toward the Muslim demand to recognise Islam as a valid faith and religion, and ultimately as religious truth. The Islamic recognition of Jesus as a prophet, and of Christianity as a revealed religion, is then used as an argument for the mutual recognition of Islam and Christianity (and their communities) as valid religions (and religious communities).

There is a remarkable alertness on the part of Muslim intellectuals to denounce influences from Western secular philosophies as well as religious doctrines in Muslim societies. The thought of Kant and Hegel, Feuerbach and Marx, Husserl and Wittgenstein, Heidegger and Ricoeur, may be known and respected, but their views should not be adhered to as absolute truth. Muslim discourses on the West's religious impact on Muslim societies, in particular through the missions, require separate study. There have been polemical writings against Christianity since the beginning of Islam, but from the nineteenth century a special genre has developed. This consists of publications addressed specifically against Christian missions (Catholic and Protestant) that began to appear on the Muslim scene. Their educational activities, medical care and charitable work in general was surely appreciated by the local people enjoying their benefits. It contrasted with the military and administrative rule imposed by Western governments, and with the economic interests pursued by Western colonialists and traders. The Christian call to convert, however, has always been received with mixed feelings, and has sometimes caused friction. Conversions implying apostasy from Islam could result in uproar.

Actual Muslim perceptions of Christian missions (and responses to them) up to the 1920s deserve careful scholarly research. This must seek beyond the generally negative stereotypes that were later developed, in particular after the First World War. Only by looking at the Muslim side will it be possible to arrive at a better insight into the ways in which Christian missions worked and were actually perceived and received in Muslim societies.[48] It might be suggested that, at least in Egypt, public attacks on the work of Christian missionaries paralleled the rise of organised national and Islamic movements: incidents that disprove this hypothesis should be identified. The activities of missionaries from the West were generally seen as 'Western' Christian activities: they were not perceived as possibly connected with the older, local 'Eastern' Christian communities. However, the latter were also subjected to Western missionary work, especially when missions among Muslims did not bear fruit. With independence, the work of existing Christian missions in Muslim countries was mostly limited to educational, medical, and social activities. It was carried out mainly by Christians from within the country concerned. In many respects, Christian missionaries and their communities were now freed from the burden of supposed complicity with foreign political and economic interests. Their communication with Muslim people may have become somewhat easier, and certainly less paternal and hegemonic. The Muslim discourse on Christian missions thus slowly makes way for a discourse on the possibilities of dialogue. In some Muslim countries, however, 'sectarian' hard-line missions from North America continue to work.

Muslim Discourses on Muslim Minorities in the West

The problem of relations between Islam and the West, and thus of Muslim perceptions of the West, has become more complex through the presence of minorities on both sides. In fact, all Muslim countries now have communities of Westerners and Christians of different origins. All Western countries today have Muslim minorities. The old rule that Muslims should not live under non-Muslim governments lost its sense when the right of religious freedom allowed them to practise their religion in Western countries.

Three different groups of Muslims living in Europe can be distinguished: (1) older communities that have been living for centuries in south-eastern and Eastern Europe; (2) immigrants from Muslim countries who settled in Western Europe and in North America; (3) indigenous converts to Islam. There are no reliable figures about the number of Muslims in Europe, but a rough estimate would be more than 30 million, including European Russia and the Caucasian republics.

The Bosnian war (1992–1995) drew attention to the presence of Muslims in the former Yugoslavia, which may have had some four million Muslims by the end of the 1970s, or one-fifth of the total population at the time.[49] Muslims in south-eastern Europe had lived as quite traditional communities until the Second World War. They were largely marginalised during the following half-century, in part under the pressure of communist regimes, that sought to extirpate Islam along with other religions, and in part due to economic development and social changes that took place in these societies after 1945.

Anti-Islamic campaigns arose in the nationalist anti-Turkish measures implemented in Bulgaria in the 1980s. Such campaigns assumed an extremely violent character in the nationalist radically anti-Albanian and anti-Bosnian measures adopted by Serbia (in the latter case also by Croatia) and Bosnian Serbs since the late 1980s.[50] The ensuing war between Orthodox Serbians (assisted for some time by Catholic Croatians) and Muslim Bosnians led to an ethnic cleansing and exodus from Bosnian territories, oppression with sexual violation and even genocide of Muslim groups, wilful destruction of Islamic monuments, and an extended siege of Sarajevo. Bosnian

Muslims have an intellectual history going back to fifteenth-century Sarajevo; from the end of the nineteenth century, their intelligentsia (living in Vienna and Sarajevo) was oriented toward an enlightened humanist culture. Sarajevo has continuously had important Muslim cultural institutions, including an Institute of Oriental studies, an Islamic theological faculty, and *medresses* for the education of future imams.

Looking at the situation of Muslims in both Western and Eastern Europe, the Bosnian scholar Smail Balic suggests that Muslims in contemporary Europe cannot keep to those patriarchal and oriental ways of life that have found their way into Muslim communities, but are not an intrinsic part of Islam. In the non-Muslim European context today, he contends, Muslims are put to the test; they must give meaning to their religious practices and give shape to Muslim life in a non-Muslim context. They must adapt themselves to democratic structures of living together, and be open to democratic processes. Balic complains about the inadequate understanding so many Muslims have of their own religion, an understanding that does not correspond with the conditions of the new context in which they live. Under the general term 'Islam', a number of antiquated models and structures of thinking that do not belong to the core of Islamic doctrine continue to exist. Looking at Islam in present-day Western Europe, he sees its fundamental weakness in its uncritical adherence to ancient authorities, and the resulting alienation from reality. Islam for Balic is a continuous task that emerges from daily reality.[51]

In Muslim publications, concerns about co-religionists in Europe have become greater over the last decades.[52] A number of reasons for this can be identified: (1) The 'ethnic cleansing' experienced by Muslim Bosnians, the oppression experienced by Muslim Albanians in Serbian Kosovo, and by Muslim Chechens in Russian Chechenya; (2) Growing xenophobic trends in Europe over the last twenty years, which are directed against foreigners in general and Muslim foreigners in particular; (3) The consequences of an existing Islamophobia that has been strengthened by Western fears of terrorism in the wake of the events of 11 September, 2001; (4) The repercussions of the Palestinian-Israeli conflict for Muslims (and Jews), including those living in the West.

These concerns should be seen within the broader context of European countries' increasingly restrictive immigration policies, and the EU's attention to its prospective member countries in Central and Eastern Europe, rather than to the Muslim countries around the Mediterranean. There is a manifest worry among Muslims that Europe will distance itself from the Muslim countries surrounding it, and may prefer to receive needed immigrants from elsewhere.

As for what Muslim communities living in Europe themselves say about their situation (and about European or Western culture in general), this must be left open. However, they do not necessarily share the ideal of an enlightened, liberal, European Islam. A few observations must suffice here. Islamic movements in Europe (as elsewhere) cultivate a growing concern among Muslims about their Islamic identity. They want this to be recognised in the public sphere; they also seek a formal recognition of the right of Muslims to practise their religion, and to maintain their language and culture. In view of cases of discrimination against Muslims and Islam in European countries, Muslim organisations stress the need for anti-discrimination legislation there. A practical problem in this area is the need for sufficient proof for legal action. Discriminatory behaviour toward people who migrated from Muslim countries to Europe has mixed ethnic (racial), ideological (objections against the Islamic social system), and religious (denigration of faith) aspects, in addition to others. Moreover, there is an ongoing concern in Western public opinion about the situation of Muslim women and about contemporary issues of human rights and democracy in Muslim countries, including immigrants' countries of origin. This weakens the force of Muslim complaints about conditions in Europe, even were these conditions to deteriorate under the impact of rising right-wing movements throughout the continent.

The Muslim demand for the equal treatment of Muslims and adherents of other religions (i.e., Christianity) is particularly urgent where access to public services and public funding is at stake. State assistance in obtaining money for Islamic religious facilities (prayer halls, religious education, the formation of future imams, fees for imams or religious instructors, cemeteries, etc.) is requested where such assistance is already given for analogous Protestant, Catholic, and Jewish religious facilities. There is a general Muslim demand for the teaching of Islamic religion, with a recognised curriculum, to Muslim children in state schools and in schools receiving public funding. There also is an increasing demand for recognition of the eligibility of Islamic schools for government subsidies.

There have been several test cases as to the nature of the border-lines between the European nation-oriented societies on the one hand, and the Muslim communities living in these societies, on the other. Attempts to convert Muslims in Europe to Christianity meet with resistance from all Muslim organisations. However, there have been some conversions of asylum seekers from Muslim countries.

Three major problems facing Muslims in Europe can be identi-fied that are less frequently discussed in Muslim publications, their importance notwithstanding. The first concerns the need to con-stitute a common national representation of Muslims to national governments. The latter are prepared to discuss problems related to Islam in their countries only with a Muslim body that represents the great majority of Muslims living there. Only in a few cases (Austria and Belgium, for example) has such a body been legally constituted in the framework of existing legislation. The onus is on Muslims to take initiatives themselves to establish such bodies. The second problem concerns the need to promote intellectual development and social emancipation for all persons within the Muslim commu-nities, including women. Here too, Muslims have to take initiatives themselves. In all European countries adequate Muslim leadership (social, organisational, intellectual and cultural) is at present lacking. There is also the question of where and how future imams should receive their education. The third problem is how to avoid Muslim immigrant communities in Europe (in the near or distant future) constituting a kind of under-class or under-developed proletariat, on the fringe of established society and bearing its burdens. Since the majority of the immigrants coming from outside Europe are Mus-lims, they have to give thought to this problem and take their own initiatives toward further integration before it is too late.

Some Observations by way of Conclusion

The study of Muslim perceptions of the West, Muslim encounters with people from the West, and Muslim thinking about the West dur-ing the twentieth century is a field of research in itself.[53] A number of studies have dealt with historical, social, and political relations between Western and Muslim countries. Attention has then been paid mostly to Western perceptions of these relations, and actions following them. There is urgent need to bring to light how these relations were seen from the Muslim side, what kind of action Muslims took when they invoked Islam, and how they related to non-Muslims. Such a study of Muslim positions by implication will also reveal a lot about Western ones, about Western actors, and about the interaction between the two sides.[54] Three arguments for this kind of research can be advanced:

(1) In both Western and Muslim parts of the world, there is a lack of solid knowledge about their mutual relationships, current and historical. Most studies used by policy-makers and entrepreneurs are produced from a perspective of political and economic interests. These studies remain ethnocentric, and often view Islam as a potential threat. There is an urgent need to disentangle scholarly research from ethnocentrism, and to study the various aspects of these relationships, including their ideological expressions, in an impartial way.

(2) Political, economic and ideological pursuits on both sides need to be better known and illuminated. On both sides political, ideological and religious interests have been greatly mixed. Religious and moral aims have been pursued by socio-political means; likewise, political and economic strategies have been implemented with ideological as well as religious legitimations.

(3) If Jews and Christians have their memories of suffering and persecution, Muslims also have theirs. Impartial study in search of historical truth is needed to overcome existing traumatisations. Scholarship can bring enlightenment, and perhaps some relief.

This exploration of Muslim perceptions of the West during the twentieth century exposes four major questions requiring further exploration:

(1) During the twentieth century, Muslim societies had to respond

to ever-new situations. A major challenge was the intrusion of the 'foreign' into the Muslims' 'own' society, culture and religion. How did Muslims articulate Islam, in their search for an adequate response to what was foreign to them?

(2) New situations gave rise to new ways of thinking about Islam. What kinds of new interpretations have been developed during the twentieth century?

(3) If it is true that the West imposed itself on the Muslim part of the world during the twentieth century (if not earlier), what positive expectations did Muslims have of the West for their own future? When they went out to learn from the West, what exactly were they striving for?

(4) With whom in the West did specific Muslim persons and groups communicate? Can one distinguish particular networks? What did they ask of Westerners, and what could they offer them in return? How did they look at the Western counterparts with whom they were ready to co-operate? What kind of structures of communication, transient or enduring, have existed between Muslims and Westerners in the course of the twentieth century?

It may well be that during the twentieth century the West has had at least as many stereotypes about Islam, as Muslims have had about the West. Perhaps it is the case that Muslim images and interpretations of the West show no particular Islamic aggressiveness towards it, but constitute a response to its aggression.[55]

Notes

1. There is an immense Muslim literature about the West from the beginning of the nineteenth century, both in 'Islamic' and Western languages. Much of it concerns attitudes or actions that Muslims are encouraged to adopt, giving moral and religious directives. The more reflective literature is historical, sociological or political, concerned respectively with historical relations between Muslim countries and the West, contemporary relations (including Western influences on contemporary Muslim societies), and attitudes that should be adopted toward the West as power. (There are other genres, such as travelogues, personal memoirs and literary texts, but these do not fall under the heading of what are here termed 'reflections'.)

The texts explored here have their origin in very different groups, varying from typically 'Islamic' circles that refer directly to Islam as a norm (in accordance with their own particular interpretation of it), 'Muslim' circles that combine co-operation with non-Muslims with Islam as their religion (as they formulate it), and 'modernist' circles of what may be termed 'social' Muslims, who consider religion a private matter. An attempt is made to distinguish four kinds of discourse on the West: political, socio-economic, cultural, and spiritual. Muslim discourses on Muslim minorities living in Europe are also considered.

2. Hichem Djaït, *Europe and Islam* (Berkeley, CA, 1985). See also Albert Hourani, *Europe and the Middle East* (Berkeley, CA, 1980). Compare Bernard Lewis, *Islam and the West* (New York, 1993).

3. Ibrahim Abu-Lughod, *Arab Rediscovery of Europe* (Princeton, NJ, 1963). Compare Bernard Lewis, *The Muslim Discovery of Europe* (New York and London, 1982). There was also a discovery of America. See Ami Ayalon, 'The Arab Discovery of America in the Nineteenth Century', *MES*, 20, 4 (1984), pp. 5–17.

4. Anouar Louca, *Voyageurs et écrivains égyptiens en France au XIXe siècle* (Paris, 1970). See also Nazik Saba Yared, *Arab Travellers and Western Civilization* (London, 1996).

5. Emad Eldin Shahin, *Through Muslim Eyes: M. Rashid Rida and the West* (Herndon, VI, 1993). An in-depth study of *al-Manar*'s views of the world at large at the time of its writing is needed.

6. For a succinct history of successive images of the West including Europe, see Gerhard Höpp, 'Feindbild "Westen"; Zur Rolle historischer Zäsuren im 20. Jarhundert', in Henner Fürtig and Gerhard Höpp, ed., *Wessen Geschichte? Muslimische Erfahrungen historischer Zäsuren im 20. Jahrhundert* (Berlin, 1998), pp. 11–26.

7. The role of the factor and use of power in relations between Western and Muslim countries cannot be overestimated. Subjugation has been (and remains) a determinant factor in Muslim perceptions of the West. The experience of various forms of Western domination has given rise to negative attitudes among Muslims. This experience, which has become part of Muslim collective memory, comprises expropriations of Muslims' land; alienation from their culture; imposition of a Western economic system; destruction of potential bases of Muslim power; creation of 'bridgeheads' for the West in the Muslim world; humiliation of Muslim populations; and the frustration of expectations awakened through Euro-Arab and other dialogues between Westerners and Muslims.

8. The mutuality of perceptions is important. See Gerhard Höpp and Thomas Scheffler, ed., *Gegenseitige Wahrnehmungen – Orient und Okzident*

seit dem 18. Jahrhundert. Special issue of *Asien, Afrika, Lateinamerika,* 25, 1–3 (1997). In this volume see especially Henner Fürtig, 'Ayatollah Chomeinis Bild vom Westen' (pp. 355–375). See also A. Bendaoud and M. Berriane, ed., *Marocains et Allemands; la perception de l'autre* (Rabat, 1995). Compare Moustafa Maher, *Das Bild des Deutschen in der arabischen und das Bild des Arabers in der deutschen Literatur* (Hamburg, 1978). The ways in which Europeans perceived Islam and Muslims is beyond the scope of this discussion.

9. The expression 'Islam and the West' is conceptually problematic, since it suggests the existence of two definable entities. However, it has caught much public attention. On 27 October, 1993 Prince Charles delivered a much-referred to speech 'Islam and the West', in Oxford (Text in *Islam and Christian-Muslim Relations,* 5, 1 (1994), pp. 67–74). See also the statement paper by Khurshid Ahmad (Pakistan), 'Islam and the West: Confrontation or Cooperation?' (for text see *MW,* 85, 1–2 (1995), pp. 63–81.) See also Annemarie Schimmel's speech on receiving the 1995 Peace Prize of the German Book Trade Association (text in *CSIC Papers* (Birmingham), 6 (1996), pp. 7–13). Compare also with Seyyed Hossein Nasr, 'Islam and the West: Yesterday and Today', *The American Journal of Islamic Social Sciences,* 13, 4 (1996), pp. 551–562; Ali A. Mazrui, 'Islamic and Western Values', *Foreign Affairs,* 76, 5 (1997), pp. 118–132. The expression 'Islam and the West' seems to have become especially current since the Gulf War of 1991.

10. The Cold War prevented relations between the West and Islam from becoming dualistic; there was always the third factor of the Eastern Bloc countries. For the impact of the Cold War on Western and Eastern Block attitudes toward and views of Islam, see Jacques Waardenburg, 'The Study of Religion during the Cold War: Views of Islam', in Iva Oležalová, Luther H. Martin, and Dalibor Papoušek, ed., *The Academic Study of Religion during the Cold War* (New York, 2001), pp. 291–311. The end of the Cold War implied re-orientations on the part of Muslim countries, too. See Ellinor Schöne, 'Die islamische Staatengruppe und das Ende des Ost-West-Konflikts – die Sicht der Organisation der Islamischen Konferenz', in Fürtig and Höpp, ed., *Wessen Geschichte?,* pp. 97–115. See also Henner Fürtig, 'Die Islamische Republik Iran und das Ende des Ost-West-Konflikts', in Fürtig and Höpp, ed., *Wessen Geschichte?,* pp. 73–95.

11. Jacob M. Landau, *The Politics of Pan-Islam. Ideology and Organization* (Oxford, 1994).

12. Perceptions of Europe among well-known Egyptian authors are particularly interesting. See Werner Ende, *Europabild und kulturelles Selbstbewusstsein bei den Muslimen am Ende des 19. Jahrhunderts. Dargestellt an den Schriften der beiden ägyptischen Schriftsteller Ibrahim und Muhammad al-Muwailihi* (Hamburg, 1965). Also Baber Johansen, *Muhammad Husain Haikal. Europa*

und der Orient im Weltbild eines ägyptischen Liberalen (Beirut and Wiesbaden, 1967). A fundamental study is Rotraud Wielandt, *Das Bild der Europäer in der modernen arabischen Erzähl und Theaterliteratur* (Beirut and Wiesbaden, 1980). On contemporary perceptions of Europe, see Mohammed Arkoun, 'The Arab Perception of Europe', *Awrâq*, 10 (1989), pp. 25–39 (Ar.). Although European perceptions of Islam are beyond the scope of this discussion the illuminating article by Talal Asad, 'Europe against Islam: Islam in Europe', *MW*, 87, 2 (1997), pp. 183–195 might be mentioned.

13. Taha Hussein, *The Future of Culture in Egypt*, tr. Sidney Glazer [Or. 1936] (Washington, DC, 1954).

14. Fazlur Rahman, *Islam and Modernity; Transformation of an Intellectual Tradition* (Chicago and London, 1982).

15. Ali Shariati, *On the Sociology of Islam: Lectures by Ali Shariati*, tr. Hamid Algar (Berkeley, CA, 1979). Shariati, *Marxism and Other Western Fallacies; An Islamic Critique*, tr. R. Campbell (Berkeley, CA, 1980).

16. Mohammed Arkoun, *Pour une critique de la raison islamique* (Paris, 1984).

17. Abdallah Laroui, *Islam et modernité* (Paris, 1987); Laroui, *Islamisme, modernisme, libéralisme* (Casablanca, 1997).

18. Mohamed Talbi, 'Possibilities and Conditions for a Better Understanding between Islam and the West', *Journal of Ecumenical Studies*, 25 (1988), pp. 161–193.

19. Tariq Ramadan, *Islam. Le face à face des civilisations: Quel projet pour quelle modernité?* (Lyon, 1995).

20. Farid Esack, *On Being a Muslim: Finding a Religious Path in the World Today* (Oxford, 1999).

21. Nasr Abou Zeid, *Critique du discours religieux*, tr. Mohamed Chairet (Paris, 1999).

22. Hubert Dobers and Ulrich Haarmann, ed., *The Euro-Arab Dialogue – Le dialogue euro-arabe* (Symposium Bonn, June 1982) (St. Augustin, 1983). See also *Euro-Arab Dialogue: The Relations between the two Cultures*. Acts of the Hamburg Symposium, April 11–15, 1983. English version ed. Derek Hopwood (London, 1985).

23. Jalal Al-Ahmad, *Occidentosis: A Plague from the West*, tr. R. Campbell (Berkeley, CA, 1984). See also Sayid Mujtaba Rukni Musawi Lari, *Western Civilisation through Muslim Eyes*, tr. F.J. Goulding (Guildford, UK, 1977).

24. On Sayyid Qutb (1906–66), see Ahmad S. Moussalli, *Radical Islamic Fundamentalism: The Ideological and Political Discourse of Sayyid Qutb* (Beirut, 1992).

25. On Abu al-A'la Mawdudi (1903–1979) see Seyyed Vali Reza Nasr, 'Mawdudi and the Jama'at-i Islami: The Origins, Theory and Practice of Is-

lamic Revivalism', in Ali Rahnema, ed., *Pioneers of Islamic Revival* (London, 1994), pp 98–124.

26. The phenomenon of Islamism itself (and what are at times ideologically oriented interpretations of it) is left aside here.

27. The author is indebted here to Paul Khoury, *L'Islam critique de l'Occident dans la pensée arabe actuelle; Islam et sécularité* (Religionswissenschaftliche Studien 35), 2 vols. (Würzburg and Altenberge, 1994/5).

28. Leif Stenberg, *The Islamization of Science; Four Muslim Positions Developing an Islamic Modernity* (Stockholm, 1996).

29. Isma'il Raji al-Faruqi, *Islamization of Knowledge* (Islamabad, 1982) and 'Islamizing the Social Sciences', *Studies in Islam*, 16, 2 (1979), pp. 108–121.

30. Samuel P. Huntington, 'The Clash of Civilizations?', *Foreign Affairs*, 72, 3 (1993), pp. 22–49; Huntington, *The Clash of Civilizations and the Remaking of World Order* (New York, 1996). Compare Roy P. Mottahedeh, 'The Clash of Civilizations: An Islamicist's Critique', *Harvard Middle Eastern and Islamic Review*, 2, 2 (1995), pp. 1–26.

31. Regular meetings have been organised by the CERES in Tunisia and the Ahl al-Bayt Foundation and the Institute for Interfaith Relations in Jordan. Dialogue conferences have been organised in Indonesia, Iran, Malaysia, Pakistan and Turkey. Many meetings have been held in Europe. For example, at one such meeting in the Netherlands in October 1994, genuine dialogue appears to have been achieved. See Ruud Hoff and Hanneke Mulder, ed. *Islamic Revival and the West. Common Values, Common Goals*. Final report of a conference held in Oegstgeest, The Netherlands, 22–24 October 1994 (The Hague, 1995).

32. As a consequence, this discourse touches issues that are sensitive to traditional societies as well as to political regimes: it spreads critical thought. See, for example, Abdullahi Ahmed an-Na'im, *Toward an Islamic Reformation: Civil Liberties, Human Rights, and International Law* (Syracuse, NY, 1990).

33. As such, its position is oriented more broadly toward the West, especially in current debates on North-South relations and globalisation.

34. In the last quarter of the nineteenth century, the Egyptian periodical *al-Muqtataf* regularly published pieces concerning relations between East and West. See L. M. Kenny, 'East versus West in Al-Muqtataf, 1875–1900', in D. P. Little, ed., *Essays on Islamic Civilization* (Leiden, 1976), pp. 140–154. Just after World War II, a prominent Egyptian intellectual wondered why there was so much misunderstanding between Europe and Muslims, and what could be done about it. See M. H. Haekal (sic.), 'Les causes de l'incompréhension entre l'Europe et les musulmans et les moyens d'y remédier', in *L'Islam et l'Occident* (Paris, 1947), pp. 52–58.

35.   The debate on Western culture is then part of the broader debate on Islam and modernity.

36.   This position is forcefully presented by Seyyed Hossein Nasr. See, for example, *Islam and the Plight of Modern Man* (London, 1975; 2nd ed., 1981), *Knowledge and the Sacred* (Edinburgh, 1981), *Traditional Islam in the Modern World* (London, 1981; 2nd ed., 1987).

37.   There is an urgent need for a comparative study of these, as well as various Muslim educational models.

38.   Some observations made at the time remain valuable. See Jacques Waardenburg, *Les Universités dans le monde arabe actuel. Documentation et essai d'interprétation.* Vol. 1: Texte (Recherches méditerranéennes, Études 8) (Paris and The Hague, 1966).

39.   See, for example, Hasan Hanafi, *Muqaddima fi 'ilm al-istighrab* (Cairo, 1991). 'Occidentalism' as a critical study of the West would be the counterpart of 'Orientalism' as the critical study of the East.

40.   The desirability (and even the possibility) of inter-cultural studies and dialogue has sometimes been denied.

41.   One thinks here of the academic status of the international Islamic universities in Islamabad, Kuala Lumpur and Khartoum.

42.   Examples arise in the calls of the Sudanese scholar Abdullahi Ahmed an-Na'im concerning human rights, and the work of the Egyptian scholar Sa'ad ad-Din Ibrahim on civil society, to mention two well-known names. Throughout the Muslim world, independent activists are working for human rights (including women's rights), without paying lip-service to Western interests.

43.   For the development of ideas on the Islamic state, see, for example, Hamid Enayat, *Modern Islamic Political Thought* (London and Austin, TX, 1982).

44.   See Mehrzad Boroujerdi, *Iranian Intellectuals and the West; The Tormented Triumph of Nativism* (Syracuse, NY, 1996). This provides ample details about the life and work of intellectuals like Al-e Ahmad, Makarem-Shirazi, Ali Shari'ati, Abolhasan Jalili, Ehsan Naraqi, Hamid Enayat, Daryush Shayegan, Seyyed Hossein Nasr, Abdolkarim Sorush, and others.

45.   It is noteworthy that interesting studies of Christianity have emerged in Iran. See Isabel Stümpel-Hatami, *Das Christentum aus der Sicht zeitgenössischer iranischer Autoren. Eine Untersuchung religionskundlicher Publikationen in persischer Sprache* (Berlin, 1996).

46.   This is evident in the work of Seyyed Hossein Nasr. See n. 36.

47.   The idea prevails that in the West religion has made place for a secular order. See Paul Khoury, *L'Islam critique de l'Occident* (1994-5) mentioned above, n. 27.

48. An exemplary historical study is Avril Ann Powell, *Muslims and Missionaries in pre-Mutiny India* (Richmond, UK, 1993). Another is Karel A. Steenbrink, *Dutch Colonialism and Islam: Contacts and Conflicts 1596–1950* (Amsterdam and Atlanta, 1993). More such historical studies are needed.

49. Smail Balic, *Der Islam – Europakonform?* (Religionswissenschaftliche Studien 32) (Würzburg and Altenberge, 1994), pp. 281–282.

50. Compare Jacques Waardenburg, 'Politics and Religion in the Balkans', in *Islam in the Balkans*, special issue of *Islamic Studies*, 36, 2–3 (1997), pp. 383–402.

51. 'Das islamische religiöse Leben muss sich neue Prioritäten zu eigen machen. Nur als ständige Aufgabe verstanden, die aus der alltäglichen Wirklichkeit erwächst, vermag sich der Islam im europäischen Westen dauernd anzusiedeln' (Smail Balic, *Der Islam – Europakonform?* p. 286). Cf. note 49.

52. See, for example, Syed Abul Hasan Ali Nadwi, *Muslims in the West: The Message and Mission*, ed., Khurram Murad (Markfield, Leicester, 1983). See also *Vivre et défendre l'Islam à l'étranger*. Causeries et études recueillies par le Bureau de Paris, Ligue Islamique Mondiale (Madrid, 1981). Compare *Reciprocity and Beyond: A Muslim Response to the European Churches' Document on Islam* (Markfield, Leicester, 1997).

53. Bernard Lewis was among the first to identify this as a task. See, for example, 'Muslim Perceptions of the West', in Lewis, Edmund Leites and Margaret Case, ed., *As Others See Us: Mutual Perceptions, East and West*. Special issue *Comparative Civilizations Review*, 13–14 (1985/6).

54. The plea here is for a 'communicative perception' in such studies. See Jacques Waardenburg, 'L'Europe dans le miroir de l'Islam', *Asiatische Studien/Études Asiatiques*, 53, 1 (1999), pp. 103–128.

55. There remains, of course, the problem of how to interpret the images that one party gives of the other. See Ibid., pp. 113–117.

Perceptions of Christians and Christianity

Hugh Goddard

Introduction

In the contemporary world, Christians and Muslims together make up something between one-third and one-half of the world's population. Precise statistics are, of course, virtually impossible to obtain, but the best estimates fall somewhere in this range, with Christians probably outnumbering Muslims in a rough proportion of three to two. Both communities have their origins in the Middle East, with Jerusalem and Mecca separated by a distance of only around 800 miles. Both traditions therefore grew up enjoying considerable interaction with different aspects of Middle-Eastern culture. Christianity, however, spread first in the Mediterranean world, moving towards Rome, the capital city of the empire within which it was first established, while Islam's centre of gravity shifted to the east, with its new capital of Baghdad, founded in 762 CE, serving as its intellectual as well as political centre during its classical period. Correspondingly Christian thought was heavily influenced by Hellenistic thought, not least as a result of the fact that its scriptures, the various books of the New Testament, were written in Greek, while Islamic thought was considerably influenced by Persian patterns and ideas, though Arabic was always the language of the Muslim scripture, the Qur'an.

The geographical spread of the two faiths in later centuries has also been different, with Islam gradually becoming the dominant faith in the northern half of Africa and south-western and Central Asia, and Christianity coming to dominate Europe and the Americas. Each has a significant presence outside these areas, however, with Christianity being the main faith in southern Africa, Australasia, and the Philippines, and Islam being the majority faith of much of South-East Asia, with Indonesia being the largest Muslim nation in the world today in terms of population. Moreover, as a result of the ease of modern travel and increasing economic migration, each community has now established a not inconsiderable presence in parts of the world traditionally dominated by the other, so that Western Europe, for example, now has a Muslim population of around twelve million, and the Gulf region, in Arabia itself, now has a significant Christian presence, consisting of Westerners, Christians from the Middle East (especially Lebanon, Palestine and Egypt), and Christians from the Philippines and South Asia, resident there.

In those parts of the world where the Christian and Muslim worlds meet, relationships between the two communities have often been conflictual. Recent decades have seen civil conflicts in which religious differences appear to have been one of the causes in such places as the Lebanon, Nigeria, the Sudan, the Philippines and, within Europe, Bosnia and Kosovo. International conflicts such as the Gulf War of 1991 or the more recent war in Afghanistan following the events of 11 September 2001 may appear to pitch certain parts of the Islamic world against the West, whose ancestral religion is Christianity, though there is an important difference between referring to Christianity and Islam, as systems of religious thought and practice, on the one hand, and the Islamic world and the West, as geographical and political labels, on the other. And within other societies, where one or the other faith has traditionally been seen as the dominant or majority one, there are also many recent instances of tension. The Christians of the Middle East, whose history goes back to before the coming of Islam, the three centuries when Byzantine Christianity was the dominant political and religious force in the region, often feel that their presence in the Middle East is increasingly resented, and in Western Europe Muslims sometimes feel that their presence is increasingly just tolerated rather than appreciated.

This is the context for this discussion of twentieth-century Islamic thought about Christians and about Christianity. To some Muslim writers and thinkers Christianity is basically a synonym for the West: all Westerners are Christian, and therefore the failings of the West are due to Christianity. For others there is an awareness that the modern West may in practice be secular or post-Christian, and this may be true both of those writing in the Muslim world, that is in a Muslim majority context, and those working from a base in the West, that is in a Muslim minority context. Others are fully alert to the fact that there is a substantial Christian minority presence in such places as Egypt or Palestine, and are sensitive to the concerns of these Arab Christians, who wish to affirm their difference from Western Christians very vigorously, especially if Western Christians turn out, as many do, to be Zionist in their sympathies. Many of the different Muslim perceptions of Christianity which we will examine will be shown to be caused, quite simply, by the different contexts within which they are written.[1]

In this chapter, we will look first at the historical background to modern Muslim perceptions of Christians and of Christianity, and then in the main body of the chapter we will investigate the topic under four main headings: Jesus, Christianity, Christians and Interfaith Dialogue.

Historical Background

Taken as a whole, the Islamic tradition offers a wide range of opinions and attitudes concerning both Christianity as a religious system and Christians as people. In the Qur'an itself, as regards Christians, we can thus discern some contrast or tension between a statement such as 'you will find the nearest in affection to those who believe to be those who say: We are Christians' (Q.5: 82), and statements which come only a few verses earlier in the same Sura to the effect that 'they disbelieve (*kafara*) who say: God is the Messiah, son of Mary' (Q.5:72), and 'they disbelieve who say: God is the third of three' (Q.5:73). Given the general Qur'anic strictures about *kufr* (disbelief), these latter judgements are clearly fairly negative.[2]

Equally, concerning Jesus, the Qur'an combines a number of very positive affirmations about the person of Jesus with some very radical criticisms of some of the statements which Christians make about him, most notably in Q.4:171:

> People of the Book [i.e. in this instance Christians], do not go too far in your religion: Jesus the son of Mary was the messenger of God, and His word (*kalimatuhu*) which He cast into Mary, and a spirit from Him (*ruhun minhu*), so believe in God and His messengers, and do not say "Three". Stop! It is better for you. God is one god. Far removed is it from His transcendent majesty that He should have a son. His is all that is in the heavens and all that is in the earth, and He is sufficient as defender.

The Qur'an's positive statements here are made about no other figure in the whole scripture, thus hinting at some kind of particular significance being given to Jesus in the Qur'anic view of history, yet they are combined with sharp condemnation of any idea that Jesus is one of three gods or a son of God, which have usually been taken by later Muslim interpreters to mean condemnation of the Christian doctrines of the Trinity (though the Qur'an does not use that word explicitly) and the Incarnation.[3]

On this foundation, the formative and classical periods of Islamic thought evolved a view of Christians (and Jews) which was based primarily on the concept of *dhimma* (protection), whereby in return for accepting Islamic rule Christians were offered security concerning their lives and property, and were permitted to continue to practise Christian worship (albeit with some restrictions on public manifestations of that worship), in return for paying a special tax or tribute, the *jizya* (sometimes called the 'poll-tax'), and for accepting that certain careers, especially in government and the army, would not be open to them. On this basis the position of Christians (and Jews) in medieval Islamic society has sometimes been described as being that of second-class citizens, but the *dhimmis* were certainly far better off under this arrangement than were religious minorities in some other parts of the world at the time, particularly Western Europe, so the arrangement should probably be seen as being relatively liberal for its day.[4]

Religious communities do not always live up to their ideals, however, and even if the theory of *dhimma* was relatively tolerant, there are a number of instances in medieval Islamic societies of outbreaks of antagonism towards non-Muslims, and attitudes were therefore not always as positive in practice as Islamic theologians and legal scholars would have liked.[5]

Further elaboration also took place in this period in Muslim thinking about Jesus and about Christianity, and again quite a broad spectrum of thought developed. On the one hand a tradition of warm appreciation of Jesus as a figure of special spiritual significance developed, particularly among Sufi and Shi'i Muslim thinkers who sometimes, as in the works of the great Spanish Sufi, Ibn 'Arabi (d. 1240), presented Jesus as the 'seal of the saints', corresponding in some way in spiritual terms to the status of Muhammad, the 'seal of the prophets', in prophecy.[6] On the other hand a much more polemical tradition also developed, and while it was never disrespectful of the person of Jesus, given the respect shown to him in the Qur'an, it was sometimes extremely hostile to Christianity, the religious system which in Christian eyes had developed on the basis of the teaching and life of Jesus but which Muslim polemicists came to see as having been corrupted by his followers. Jesus himself, in other words, was always highly respected, but over the course of the centuries the faith which he established came to be regarded as having become the victim of a serious process of historical corruption, resulting, according to some Muslim writers such as Ibn Taymiyya, in the virtually complete loss of its original authenticity.[7]

The early modern period, in the sense of the period in which the majority of the Muslim world came to be occupied by one or another European power, beginning in the eighteenth century and perhaps most powerfully symbolised by Napoleon's invasion of Egypt in 1798, saw some further elaboration of Muslim thinking about Christians and about Christianity, often based on a more or less complete identification of Christianity with the West. Generally speaking this consisted of the further elaboration, or accentuation, of existing trends of thought, though there were one or two significant exceptions to this such as Sayyid Ahmad Khan in India, whose Commentary on the Bible was a demonstration of a significantly new Muslim approach to both the Old and the New Testaments.[8] The twentieth century, however, has seen this change, with the appearance of a significant amount of fresh thinking about both the religious ideas of Christianity and the position of Christians in Islamic societies.

The Twentieth Century

(a) Jesus

In terms of fresh twentieth-century Muslim thought on our theme, a number of biographical studies of Jesus should first be mentioned. Two in particular, both of which first appeared in Egypt in the 1950s, should be mentioned. 'Abqariyat al-Masih, by 'Abbas Mahmud al-'Aqqad, was first published in 1953 as part of a series of works on geniuses which included studies of the Prophet Muhammad, of a number of significant figures from early Islamic history including both caliphs and military commanders, and of the early modern re-formist thinker Muhammad 'Abduh.[9] In the series as a whole, how-ever, it is noteworthy that among the figures discussed Christ is the only non-Muslim person to be included. (Al-'Aqqad did produce a very positive study of one other such figure, Mahatma Gandhi, but this was under the title Ruh 'azim.)

What was new about al-'Aqqad's study of Jesus was essentially his reliance upon Christian sources, in other words the New Testament, as his main source of information, so that although the introduction consists of five quotations from the Qur'an, which are all more rel-evant to the significance of genius in general than to Jesus in particu-lar, the main body of the text relies primarily on Christian accounts of the life of Jesus. One significant influence on al-'Aqqad's view of Jesus was the Life of Jesus by the German scholar Emil Ludwig, which again was part of a series of books on great men, but this too is used positively, and even when al-'Aqqad comes to the controversial area of the end of Jesus' life, namely whether or not Jesus was crucified, he comes up with a careful choice of words to outline the different traditional views of Christians and Muslims on this topic, 'Here we leave the realm of history and enter the realm of faith' (p. 212), and although this could be seen as being a re-assertion of the mainstream Muslim view that Jesus was not crucified, it could also be seen as an open and candid recognition that Christians and Muslims differ on this topic, and it is not for Muslims to insist on the correctness of their view over and against the Christian view.

Further evidence of al-'Aqqad's readiness to reconsider traditional Muslim thinking about Jesus is provided by the fact that the whole

study of Christian origins was revolutionised in the years immediately after the publication of his book by the discovery of the Dead
Sea Scrolls, and in the light of these discoveries al-'Aqqad produced
a second edition of his book, with the new title of *Hayat al-Masih* in
1958.[10] This included a new introduction, without the Qur'anic quotations, and a new Part I on the significance of the discoveries of Wadi
Qumran, and once again provides clear evidence of the author's
readiness to take account of new discoveries and perspectives.

The other significant new study of Jesus emanating from Egypt of
the 1950s was *Qarya zalima* by Muhammad Kamil Husain, professor
of surgery in Cairo University and first rector of what later became
'Ain Shams University in the same city.[11] This work received the State
Prize for Literature in Egypt in 1957, and arguably remains the most
original study of any aspect of Christianity by a Muslim author, with
its Preface in particular probably being the only piece of Muslim literature which could profitably be read in the context of a Christian
Good Friday service of meditation on the death of Christ.

As the sub-title of the English translation of the work by Kenneth
Cragg, *A Friday in Jerusalem*, suggests, Husain's work concentrates
on the events leading up to death of Christ, which are investigated
primarily with reference to the motivations and intentions of all
who participated in those events. It is a work of fiction, therefore,
rather than a work of history, but in the process there are profound
insights on the operation, and stifling, of the human conscience, by
the Jewish participants in the events, Jesus' own disciples, and Roman figures such as Pilate.

> The day was a Friday. But it was quite unlike any other day. It was a day
> when men went very grievously astray ... On that day the Jewish peo-
> ple conspired together to require from the Romans the crucifixion of
> Christ, so that they might destroy his message ... On that day men willed
> to murder their conscience and that decision constitutes the supreme
> tragedy of humanity ... The events of that day do not simply belong
> to the annals of the early centuries. They are disasters renewed daily
> in the life of every individual. Men to the end of time will be contem-
> poraries of that memorable day, perpetually in danger of the same sin
> and wrongdoing into which the inhabitants of Jerusalem then fell. The
> same darkness will be theirs until they are resolute not to transgress the
> bounds of conscience.[12]

A similar interest in the crucifixion as a symbol of innocent suffering and as a powerful indicator of the depth of human oppression and evil can also be found in the writings of a number of poetic writers from different parts of the Muslim world. Just to quote two, the Iranian Ahmad Shamlu's poem *The Death of the Nazarene* charts the pain which Jesus had to endure on his way to death, culminating towards the end in the memorable words 'The low sky sank heavily/Over the dying voice of mercy.'[13] And in Urdu poetry, a poem entitled *Crucifixion of the Word*, by Ahmad Faraz, begins 'Come, let us mourn the bloodied corpse of that Jesus whom we crucified, and weep.'[14]

Alongside all this rather new Muslim thinking about Jesus, however, there is also much material of a more traditional, even polemical, kind which has been produced in the twentieth century, and although it is never negative about Jesus himself, it insists that the image of him which has been passed down among Christians is fatally flawed.[15]

(b) Christianity

Something of the same spectrum of Islamic thought is also evident in writings about Christianity as a religious system (in contrast to studies of Jesus in particular). In general, however, although a much greater knowledge about Christianity is evident in many of these writings, not least because many of their authors have studied in the West and have learned many of the languages in which much modern Christian discussion takes place, there has not been as much significantly new and creative Muslim thinking as we have seen with reference to the person of Jesus.

Thus the study *Islam and Christianity* by Ulfat Aziz us-Samad of the English Department of the University of Peshawar in Pakistan, is a fairly traditional study in that it draws a clear contrast between the unreliability of the New Testament Gospels and the authenticity of the Qur'an, and it focuses on the Christian doctrines of the Trinity, the Divinity and Sonship of Jesus, and the Atonement, all of which are described as irrational dogmas, in contrast with the rationality of Islam. It is also suggested that while there is much in common between the moral teachings of the two faiths, with respect to such things as the treatment of women in society, attitudes towards slavery, the development of scientific knowledge and the ideal of the brotherhood of humanity, Islam has a better historical record than Christianity.[16]

Other studies demonstrate a deeper understanding. Isma'il R. al-Faruqi's *Christian Ethics: A Historical and Systematic Analysis of its Dominant Ideas* demonstrates a serious intention to get to grips with Christian ethical thinking on the basis of a detailed knowledge of both the Christian scriptures and the later thought of some of the key figures in the development of the Christian tradition. In particular, al-Faruqi suggests that Jesus' great breakthrough in understanding was his interiorisation of ethics, with special reference to the ethic of intent:

> With his usual contempt for utility, Jesus saw that the higher place belongs not to the effect of the act, but to the intent of the moral agent. The intent of the doer is the fulcrum of ethics; the effects he actually produces may be good or bad according to the law of utility. But intention is that which gives to the act its moral character.[17]

But later Christian history, according to al-Faruqi, undermined this achievement by coming to lay an unhealthy emphasis on what he calls 'peccatism', the claim that sin is universal and rooted in the nature of humanity, and 'saviourism', the view that humanity must therefore necessarily rely on an outside party in order to bring about salvation.

> In the foregoing, we sought to present the dominant ideas of Christian ethics, to analyse them systematically and historically. These ideas were found to be peccatism and saviourism; or the principles governing the Christian understanding of sin and salvation. As held by the minds which formed and cystallized the Christian faith, peccatism and saviourism deviated widely from the faith and teaching of Jesus ... (but) ... this pristine Christian faith has never disappeared from history; but has survived, alongside the other traditions, within Scripture as well as within thought and history, as the cornerstone of the Christian faith as a whole.[18]

The task for modern Christianity, he therefore suggests, is to push through a kind of second Reformation, which will produce a new Christian theology which will set aside these deviations and return to the pristine understanding of Jesus himself.

In addition to this major study, a number of articles by al-Faruqi, helpfully collected into one volume recently by Ataullah Siddiqui, address many of the broader issues connected with the relationship between Islam and other faiths, including not only Christianity but also Judaism and other traditions also, and here too he indicates his readiness to break new ground, perhaps most notably in an article originally published in the *Journal of Ecumenical Studies*, entitled 'Islam and Christianity: Diatribe or Dialogue'.[19]

In the context of the Middle East, some of the work of Hasan Hanafi, professor of philosophy in Cairo University, also displays great erudition in its knowledge of Christian history and thought, partly on the basis of Hanafi's doctoral studies at the Sorbonne on the subject of the exegesis of the New Testament. But a work such as *Religious Dialogue and Revolution: Essays on Judaism, Christianity and Islam*, despite the range of topics covered and the passion with which the discussion is invested, somehow fails to demonstrate much sympathy for Christianity, so that while there is plenty of information about Christianity, there is perhaps rather less understanding of Christianity.[20]

A deeper understanding of at least some aspects of Christianity is provided by two Turkish writers who have recently undertaken doctoral research in the UK. Adnan Aslan's thesis at the University of Lancaster compared the approaches of the Iranian Shi'i thinker, Seyyed Hossein Nasr, and the British philosopher of religion, John Hick, to religious pluralism and manifests a good understanding of both the biographies and thought of the two thinkers.[21] Mahmud Aydin, whose research at the University of Birmingham traced the process whereby Christians have re-thought their views of Islam over the past forty years, suggests in his conclusion that this is a process which Muslims, too, need to undergo in their thinking about Christianity, which might even include a re-reading of the Qur'an.[22]

A readiness to go this far in reappraising traditional attitudes is rare, however, as may be seen in the views of Christianity expressed by five modern Muslim writers which have been helpfully collected by Paul Griffiths in Part II of his *Christianity through non-Christian Eyes*. The five are Sayyid Qutb (Egypt), Mohamed Talbi (Tunisia), Fazlur Rahman (Pakistan and the United States), Syed Muhammad Naquib al-Attas (Malaysia) and Seyyed Hossein Nasr (Iran), and while Talbi certainly represents fresh thinking of the kind represented by the two Turkish writers just mentioned, some of the others, especially al-Attas and Qutb, see Christianity's history essentially as providing a precedent which Muslims should definitely seek not to follow, rather than being in any sense a model or helpful example. [23]

(c) Christians

Thirdly, in personalising the discussion, and focusing in other words on Christians as people rather than on Christianity as a religious system, we again find a broad range of Muslim opinion and considerable debate. A good example of debate can be found in the series of articles that were published in the *Journal of Muslim Minority Affairs* from 1985 onwards in response to an article by Tom Michel.[24] The article was entitled 'The Rights of non-Muslims in Islam: An Opening Statement', and it summarised the discussion and conclusions of a conference which had been held in Colombo, Sri Lanka, in 1982, with primary sponsorship from the World Council of Churches and the World Muslim Congress, before going on to outline the author's own statement of the implications of the recommendations made by the conference at its conclusion. If the intention of the editor of the journal, Syed Z. Abedin, in publishing the article, was to initiate a debate, he certainly succeeded as subsequent issues of the journal contained a series of responses by such distinguished Muslim thinkers as Muhammad Hamidullah, Fazlur Rahman and Hasan Askari, as well as comment by Christian scholars such as William Shepard and Achilles D'Souza, among others.[25]

One key point in this debate, and in discussion elsewhere, is the validity or otherwise of the traditional model of *dhimma* (protection), as it evolved in medieval Islamic thought. Generally speaking, scholars trained in the traditional disciplines of fiqh tend to argue for the continued relevance, and justice, of this model. This is true, for example, of Abdur Rahman I. Doi, the Director of the Centre for Islamic Legal Studies at Ahmadu Bello University in Zaria, Nigeria, and Yusuf al-Qaradawi, the Dean of the Faculty of Shari'a (Islamic Law) in the University of Qatar.[26] Both Doi and al-Qaradawi sometimes feel free to re-define the traditional models of *dhimma* to some extent, with Doi, for example, suggesting at one point that the payment of the *jizya*, while obligatory in an Islamic state, is *symbolic*, and al-Qaradawi insisting that the traditional framework does not mean severing relations with non-Muslims, or kindling hatred and contempt towards them, but for each of these scholars it is the classical framework which undoubtedly provides the fundamental basis for the position of Christians (and Jews) in modern Islamic societies, even if the detail is amenable to some re-definition.

For other Muslim thinkers, however, the *dhimma* model is essentially part of history, and is no longer to be taken as prescriptive in modern society. Thus for Muhammad Salim al-'Awa, professor of comparative law in the University of Cairo, the nature of the modern state, particularly with reference to the ideas of sovereignty within local borders which underpin its existence, is so different from that of the classical caliphate, with its universal claims, that the *dhimma* model is simply no longer applicable, since it is essentially a contract (*'aqd*), rather than a fixed rule (*wad'*).[27] For the Egyptian journalist Fahmi al-Huwaydi things are even clearer. For him the Copts in Egypt are not *dhimmiyyun* (protected people), but *muwatinun* (fellow-countrymen), and in their relationships with other people Muslims have three circles of people to whom they should relate positively: firstly, naturally enough, are fellow-Muslims; secondly Christians and Jews, the followers of other divinely-inspired religions; and thirdly there is the rest of humanity, whether or not the religions involved are of divine or of human origin.[28] And at the other end of the Islamic world, in Indonesia, scholars such as Nurcholish Majid and Abdurrahman Wahid, have subjected the concept of *dhimma* to a very radical critique, the former to the extent of suggesting that at the very least it should be extended to include not only Jews and Christians but also Hindus, Buddhists, Confucians and Taoists, and the latter going so far as to suggest that it should be rejected. Asked about the *jizya*, he once replied:

> It is very problematic for me until now, because it concerns the concept of *dhimmi*. To be frank I do know what to do with it. It is there. But my belief and the very core of my own existence, you see, reject *dhimmism* because, as an Indonesian and because of our national priorities, my main thinking is that I have to reject it. All citizens are equal, you see. That is the problem. That is why I do not know what to do with it. It is there, but I reject it.[29]

A useful selection of further Muslim thinking on the whole question of the rights of non-Muslims can be found in *Liberal Islam*, edited by Charles Kurzman, in which Part 5 includes texts illustrating the views of Humayun Kabir (India), Chandra Muzaffar (Malaysia), Mohamed Talbi (Tunisia), Ali Bulaç (Turkey) and Rusmir Mahmutcehajic (Bosnia), the last of which is perhaps particularly interesting, reflecting as it does something of the thinking of Muslims in Europe.[30]

(d) Inter-Faith Dialogue

Finally, one area in which the latter half of the twentieth century has seen substantial new development is in the whole area of dialogue between members of different religious traditions, especially between Muslims and Christians. In the context of the religious history of the world as a whole it has to be said that the idea of dialogue is a rather new one, but some Christians have taken to it enthusiastically and so too have some Muslims.

A landmark in the development of dialogue between the two communities came in 1965 with an important pronouncement from the Second Vatican Council:

> The Church also regards with esteem the Muslims who worship the one, subsistent, merciful and almighty God, the Creator of heaven and earth, who has spoken to man. Islam willingly traces its descent back to Abraham, and just as he submitted himself to God, the Muslims endeavour to submit themselves to his mysterious decrees. They venerate Jesus as a prophet, without, however, recognising him as God, and they pay honour to his virgin mother Mary and sometimes also invoke her with devotion. Further, they expect a day of judgement when God will raise all men from the dead and reward them. For this reason they attach importance to the moral life and worship God, mainly by prayer, alms-giving and fasting.
>
> If in the course of the centuries there has arisen not infrequent discussion and hostility between Christian and Muslim, this sacred Council now urges everyone to forget the past, to make sincere efforts at mutual understanding and to work together in protecting and promoting for the good and benefit of all men, social justice, good morals as well as peace and freedom.[31]

The word 'dialogue' does not actually occur in this ground-breaking statement, but on the strength of it the Roman Catholic church undertook a number of initiatives to promote dialogue with Muslims, and other Christian churches, both Protestant and Orthodox, soon followed suit, particularly under the auspices of the World Council of Churches.

Muslim scholars and organisations were keen participants in such dialogues, as can be seen in the detailed study of the subject by Ataullah Siddiqui, the Director of the Inter-Faith Unit of the Islamic Foundation in Leicester. His book investigates the factors which proved favourable to the development of the dialogue, as well as the personalities and institutions which moved the process along in both the Christian and Muslim communities, focusing particularly on Mahmoud Ayoub, Hasan Askari, Khurshid Ahmad, Mohamed Talbi and Seyyed Hossein Nasr as individuals, and the Mu'tamar al-'Alam al-Islami (World Muslim Congress), Rabitat al-'Alam al-Islami (Muslim World League), and Jam'iyyat al-Da'wa al-Islamiyya al-'Alamiyya (World Islamic Call Society) as organisations.[32]

A large number of dialogues have thus been arranged, under the sponsorship of different Christian and Muslim organisations, over the course of the last three or four decades, and the results of their deliberations can be seen in such publications as those edited by Rousseau and Swidler, as well as the journals and newsletters produced by the different participants, such as *Islamochristiana*, produced annually since 1975 by the Pontifical Institute for Arabic and Islamic Studies in Rome, and *Encounters: Journal of Inter-Cultural Perspectives*, produced biannually by the Islamic Foundation in Leicester since 1995.[33] Given the high quality of the discussion and interaction reported in these various publications, it seems somewhat invidious to select particular examples for discussion here, but special mention must be made of the work of the Muslim-Christian Research Group, a group of French-speaking Christians and Muslims, mainly from France, Belgium and North Africa, who have met regularly over the course of a number of years and have produced reports which demonstrate clearly the high quality of their discussion.

Perhaps the best example of the group's work is *The Challenge of the Scriptures: The Bible and the Qur'an*, which is noteworthy as almost certainly the first attempt in religious history by Christians and Muslims to look seriously together at their two scriptures. Given the centrality of scripture to each tradition, and the long history of bitter polemical attacks by members of each community on the scripture of the other community, this is no mean achievement. The published report of the group's deliberations did not gloss over the difficulties which the group had encountered, referring to 'some tense exchanges, often passionate but always friendly', 'the discussion was ardent, even strained, with occasional moments of suspense', and 'some major difficulties and even some serious tension developed', but given the importance of the topic the group persevered, inspired by the realisation that 'the mutual recognition of our respective scriptures raises serious questions which are at the heart of the friction between our religious traditions, and which have not as yet received an adequate reply'.[34]

The genesis of the group and the principles according to which it operates were described by one of its founders, Robert Caspar, in an article in *Islamochristiana*.[35] And since the production of its report on the scriptures, the group has gone on to investigate more socio-political questions such as the relationship between religion and the state, pluralism, and secularisation.[36] These are questions which several other dialogue groups have also investigated, and just to mention two, *Religion, Law and Society: A Christian-Muslim Discussion* brings together papers presented by an equal number of Christian and Muslim scholars at two conferences in Switzerland in 1992 and 1993 on such issues as the implementation of the sharia in plural societies and the relationship between concepts of human rights and religious revivalism.[37] And, more recently, dialogue between Christians and Muslims in the context of the British Commonwealth has been discussed in a conference held in Windsor in 2000, which surveyed the very different situations pertaining in Australasia, Britain, Africa, India and South-east Asia.[38]

In the Middle East too, not least in the aftermath of the fifteen-year civil war in the Lebanon between 1975 and 1990, considerable interest has developed in some quarters in dialogue between Christians and Muslims. Thus in the Lebanon interesting books have been produced on the subject by both the Sunni writer Muhammad al-Sammak and the Shi'i author Sa'ud al-Mawla, both of whom have been intimately involved in the activities of the Islamic-Christian National Dialogue Committee in the country.[39] Leading Lebanese journals have also devoted special issues to the subject, for example, the journal of the Islamic Supreme Shi'i Council, *al-Ghadir*, which devoted two issues (nos. 27–28, and 29–30) to the subject in 1995, and the Sunni journal *al-Ijtihad*, which devoted four consecutive issues (nos. 28, 29, 30, and 31–32) of the journal to Christian-Muslim relations and Christian-Muslim dialogue between the summers of 1995 and 1996, and the Center for Strategic Studies, Research and Documentation also produced a book of readings on Muslim-Christian relations at around the same time.[40]

Perhaps most remarkable of all has been a series of conferences involving large numbers of Middle-Eastern Christians and Muslims which have met in Beirut, Cairo and a number of other venues in order to discuss issues of shared concern such as the status of Jerusalem and wider issues connected with the relationship between the two communities in the region. At its meeting in Cairo in December 2001 this Arab Working Group on Muslim-Christian Dialogue formulated an Arab Muslim-Christian Covenant, under the title 'Dialogue and Coexistence', of which it is worth quoting substantial elements:

> 1. In the firm belief in coexistence between Muslims and Christians in a society where freedom, justice, equality, and the rights of citizenship prevail; cogniscent of the need to work together in facing the internal concerns and external dangers that threaten the people, Muslims and Christians, of the one Arab homeland; and aware of the obligation of people of faith to reflect the duty to their Arab nation and homeland which their religious belief dictates, to share in the strengthening of national unity and of belonging to one homeland, which encompasses all of its people with their different religious adherences and which through them rises above confessional and ethnic bigotry so that all their efforts may be for the whole nation; a number of prominent Arab Muslims and Christians – intellectuals, religious scholars, and people engaged in public life – met together in Beirut in May 1995. The Middle East Council of Churches facilitated this meeting, and it resulted in founding 'The Arab Working Group on Muslim-Christian Dialogue', including members from Lebanon, Syria, Egypt, Jordan, Palestine, the Sudan, and the United Arab Emirates.
>
> 2. Every member of the working group is moved to participate in it because of personal conviction and does not pretend to officially represent

anything else. The activity of each member springs solely from his or her religious commitment, aims only to realize the general well-being, and in so doing has regard to the whole nation, not to any one section, community, confession, party or the like. The consensus of the group's members is that the dialogue they are engaged in is a 'dialogue of life' which will be achieved through intellectual research, and programs of work conducted jointly by the adherents of both faiths so as to facilitate a common stance against the dangers faced by the nation in the social, educational, moral and cultural spheres.

Muslim-Christian dialogue is, in the view of the Working Group, not merely a dialogue between those who, as fellow citizens, belong to the national group as such. It is also a dialogue among believers. They perceive this endeavor as a practical expression of their religious values, values which give substance to the meaning of pluralism, mutual awareness, and the unqualified dignity of the human being, and of the values of justice, fairness, truth, decency, fellow feeling, affection, mercy and the stewardship of creation.

3. Taking as its key these defining ideas, the Arab Working Group on Muslim-Christian Dialogue has launched several related initiatives. It has convened several seminars which dealt with topics as various as citizenship, equality, pluralism, political participation, coexistence, and the Abrahamic heritage. It also called together an Arab conference, the first of its kind, on the cause of Jerusalem. Its participants were the cream of the Christian and Muslim intellectual and religions leadership in the Arab world. The group also initiated several other events among the most important of which have been meetings of Muslim and Christian in Egypt and Lebanon.

4. Drawing upon its growing experience and upon the products of conferences and activities over the past years, the Working Group thought it good to prepare this document on dialogue and coexistence so as to articulate principles and broad guidelines which might help give wider currency to the culture of dialogue, mutual understanding, coexistence and common action. It might encourage the development of a society of shared citizenship, justice and freedom, and enable people to confront those dangers which threaten to unravel the national fabric.

5. The Arab Working Group on Dialogue observes that securing coexistence is a necessity informed by a single set of national and social concerns and objectives, one historical and cultural context, and a common destiny. These are core issues that bring everyone together; obligations

and rights and their consequences do not involve just one party. Religious differences do not cancel out the fact of belonging all together to the Arab Islamic culture, in whose making Christians and Muslims participated side by side.[41]

This statement is clear evidence of the importance which, in the context of the Middle East, at least some Muslim thinkers attach to the promotion of better understanding between Christians and Muslims in order to achieve a good level of co-existence. And what is true in the context of the region in which both Christianity and Islam have their historical origins is also true on a global level, with members of each community sharing profound concerns about such ethical issues as poverty, population growth, social conflict, community relations especially in an urban context, influencing public policy especially with respect to science and technology, and influencing the ideas which are propagated on the Internet.[42]

Conclusion

On each of these aspects of Islamic thought in the twentieth century, then, we have seen lively debate and discussion. Of the four areas which have been focused on particularly, new creative thinking has perhaps been less evident with respect to Muslim thinking about Christianity in general, but it is certainly true that with reference to Christians as people, with reference to Muslim views of Jesus, and even more so in the arena of inter-religious dialogue, there has been much original Islamic thought evolving in the course of the twentieth century.

In some cases this has been stimulated by the opportunities presented by studying abroad and spending a considerable length of time in parts of the world which have been influenced over many centuries by Christianity rather than Islam, as in the case of a thinker like Mohamed Talbi, for example. In others it has been influenced by personal friendships with Christians, as may be seen in the case of Muhammad Kamil Husain in Egypt. Other writers have re-examined traditional assumptions simply on the basis of their own reading and reflection, as was the case with 'Abbas Mahmud al-'Aqqad. And in others fresh thinking has been caused by prolonged and regular meeting and discussion with Christians on the highest and most demanding intellectual level, most obviously in the case of those who have participated in the deliberations of the Muslim-Christian Research Group. In the light of the increased potential for all of these things to happen in the modern world, it will be interesting in the twenty-first century to see whether this fresh thinking continues to develop, and, if so, whether it leads to a wider re-examination of Christianity as a whole.

Notes

1. See Hugh Goddard, *Muslim Perceptions of Christianity* (London, 1996), and Hugh Goddard, *A History of Christian-Muslim Relations* (Edinburgh, 2000).

2. See Jane Dammen McAuliffe, *Qur'anic Christians* (Cambridge, 1991), and Ahmad von Denffer, *Christians in the Qur'an and the Sunna* (Leicester, 1979). Translations from the Qur'an are by the author.

3. See Geoffrey Parrinder, *Jesus in the Qur'an* (London, 1965; repr. Oxford, 1995), and Neal Robinson, *Christ in Islam and Christianity* (London, 1991).

4. See A. S. Tritton, *The Caliphs and their Non-Muslim Subjects* (London, 1970).

5. See the controversial study of Bat Ye'or, *The Dhimmi: Jews and Christians under Islam* (New York, 1985), and the more nuanced study by Youssef Courbage and Philippe Fargues, *Christians and Jews under Islam* (London, 1997).

6. See Andreas D'Souza, 'Jesus in Ibn 'Arabi's *Fusus al-Hikam*', *Islamochristiana*, 8 (1982), pp. 185–200. On Shi'i views, see Mahmoud Ayoub, 'Towards an Islamic Christology: An Image of Jesus in Early Shi'i Muslim Literature', *Muslim World*, 66 (1976), pp. 163–188.

7. See Tom Michel, *A Muslim Theologian's Response to Christianity: Ibn Taimiyya's 'Al-jawab al-sahih'* (Delmar, NY, 1984).

8. See Christian Troll, *Sayyid Ahmad Khan: A Reinterpretation of Muslim Theology* (Delhi, 1978).

9. See 'Abbas Mahmud al-'Aqqad, *'Abqariyat al-Masih* (Cairo, 1953), tr. F. Peter Ford, *The Genius of Christ* (New York, 2001).

10. See 'Abbas Mahmud al-'Aqqad, *Hayat al-Masih* (Cairo, 1958).

11. See Muhammad Kamil Husain, *Qarya zalima* (Cairo, 1954), tr. Kenneth Cragg, *City of Wrong* (Amsterdam, 1959; repr. Oxford, 1994), and Harold Vogelaar, *The Religious and Philosophical Thought of Dr. M. Kamel Hussein, an Egyptian Humanist* (unpublished Ph.D. thesis, University of Columbia,

1978).

12. Cragg, *City of Wrong*, pp. 3–4.

13. See Sorour S. Souroudi, 'On Jesus' Image in Modern Persian Poetry', *Muslim World*, 69 (1979), pp. 221–228, esp. pp. 224–227.

14. See Jonathan S. Addleton, 'Images of Jesus in the Literatures of Pakistan', *Muslim World*, 80 (1990), pp. 96–106, esp. p. 104.

15. See, for example, Muhammad 'Ata ur-Rahim, *Jesus Prophet of Islam*, (Norwich, 1977, repr. many times under the title *Jesus – A Prophet of Islam*), and discussion in Hugh Goddard, 'Modern Pakistani and Indian Muslim Perceptions of Christianity', *Islam and Christian-Muslim Relations*, 5 (1994), pp. 165–166.

16. See Ulfat Aziz us-Samad, *Islam and Christianity* (Karachi, 1970), and discussion in Goddard, 'Modern Pakistani and Indian Muslim Perceptions of Christianity', pp. 166–168.

17. Isma'il al-Faruqi, *Christian Ethics: A Historical and Systematic Analysis of its Dominant Ideas* (Montreal, 1967), p. 78.

18. Ibid., p. 311.

19. See Isma'il al-Faruqi, *Islam and Other Faiths*, ed., Ataullah Siddiqui (Leicester, 1998), pp. 241–280.

20. See Hasan Hanafi, *Religious Dialogue and Revolution: Essays on Judaism, Christianity and Islam* (Cairo, 1977), and discussion in Hugh Goddard, *Muslim Perceptions*, pp. 141–149.

21. See Adnan Aslan, *Religious Pluralism in Christian and Islamic Philosophy: The Thought of John Hick and Seyyed Hossein Nasr* (London, 1998).

22. See Mahmud Aydin, *Modern Western Christian Theological Understanding of Muslims since the Second Vatican Council* (Ph.D. dissertation, University of Birmingham, 1998).

23. Paul J. Griffiths, ed., *Christianity through non-Christian Eyes* (Maryknoll, NY, 1990).

24. See Tom Michel, 'The Rights of non-Muslims in Islam: An Opening Statement', *Journal of Muslim Minority Affairs*, 6 (1985), pp. 7–20.

25. See Muhammad Hamidullah, 'Relations of Muslims with non-Muslims', *Journal of Muslim Minority Affairs*, 7 (1986), pp. 7–12, Fazlur Rahman, 'Non-Muslim Minorities in an Islamic State', *Journal of Muslim Minority Affairs*, 7 (1986), pp. 13–24, Hasan Askari, 'Christian Mission to Islam: A Muslim Response', *Journal of Muslim Minority Affairs*, 7 (1986), pp. 314–330, William Shepard, 'Rights of non-Muslims in Islam', *Journal of Muslim Minority Affairs*, 7 (1986), pp. 303–307, and Achilles D'Souza, 'Non-Muslims in Pakistan: Leaven in the Dough', *Journal of Muslim Minority Affairs*, 7 (1986), pp. 308–313.

26. See Abdur Rahman Doi, *Non-Muslims under Shari'ah* (London, 1983),

and Yusuf al-Qaradawi, *Non-Muslims in the Islamic Society* (Indianapolis, IN, 1985).

27. See Yvonne Yazbeck Haddad, 'Christians in a Muslim State: The Recent Egyptian Debate', in Y. Y. Haddad and W. Z. Haddad, ed., *Christian-Muslim Encounters* (Gainseville, 1995), pp. 381–398, esp. pp. 389–391, and Muhammad Salim al-'Awa, *Fi'l-nizam al-siyasi li'l-dawla al-Islamiyya* (Cairo, 7th printing 1989), esp. pp. 255–260.

28. See Haddad, 'Christians in a Muslim State', esp. pp. 391–394, and Fahmi al-Huwaydi, *Muwatinun la dhimmiyyun: ghayr al-Muslimin fi mujtama' al-Muslimin* (Beirut, 1985).

29. See Abdullah Saeed, '*Ijtihad* and Innovation in neo-Modernist Thought in Indonesia', *Islam and Christian-Muslim Relations*, 8 (1997), pp. 279–95, esp. pp. 291–292.

30. Charles Kurzman, ed., *Liberal Islam: A Sourcebook* (New York, 1998).

31. See John Hick and Brian Hebblethwaite, ed., *Christianity and Other Religions* (2nd ed., Oxford, 2001), p. 41.

32. See Ataullah Siddiqui, *Christian-Muslim Dialogue in the Twentieth Century* (London, 1997).

33. See Richard W. Rousseau, ed., *Christianity and Islam: The Struggling Dialogue* (Scranton, PA, 1985), and Leonard Swidler, ed., *Muslims in Dialogue; the Evolution of a Dialogue* (Lewiston, NY, 1992).

34. See Muslim-Christian Research Group, *The Challenge of the Scriptures: The Bible and the Qur'an* (Maryknoll, NY, 1989), pp. 4–5.

35. See Robert Caspar, 'Le Groupe de Recherches Islamo-Chrétien (GRIC)', *Islamochristiana*, 4 (1978), pp. 175–186.

36. See Groupe de Recherches Islamo-Chrétien, 'État et Religion', *Islamochristiana*, 12 (1986), pp. 49–72 (Eng. trans. in *Encounter* [Documents for Christian-Muslim Understanding, Rome], nos. 149–150, 1988, 32 pp.), and *Pluralisme et laïcité: Chrétiens et Musulmans proposent* (Paris, 1996).

37. See Tarek Mitri, ed., *Religion, Law and Society: A Christian-Muslim Discussion* (Geneva, 1995).

38. See Anthony O'Mahony and Ataullah Siddiqui, ed., *Christians and Muslims in the Commonwealth: A Dynamic Role in the Future* (London, 2001).

39. See Muhammad al-Sammak, *Muqaddima ila'l-hiwar al-Islami al-Masihi* (Beirut, 1998), and Sa'ud al-Mawla, *al-Hiwar al-Islami al-Masihi: darurat al-mughadira* (Beirut, 1996).

40. See Samir Sulaiman, ed., *al-'Alaqat al-Islamiyya al-Masihiyya: qira'at marja'iyya fi'l-ta'rikh wa'l-hadir wa'l-mustaqbal* (Beirut, 1994).

41. See Arab Working Group on Muslim-Christian Dialogue, *Dialogue and Coexistence (An Arab Muslim-Christian Covenant adopted in Cairo, Shawwal 1402/December 2001)* (Beirut and Cairo, 2001).

42. See Suha Taji-Farouki, 'Muslim-Christian Cooperation in the Twenty-First Century: Some Global Challenges and Strategic Responses', *Islam and Christian-Muslim Relations,* 11 (2000), pp. 167–193.

Thinking on the Jews

Suha Taji-Farouki

Introduction

The defining context for any discussion of Muslim thinking on the Jews in the twentieth century, and on Muslim perceptions of the Muslim-Jewish relationship, is the Zionist project and the creation of the Jewish state in Palestine. This chapter explores the impact of this development and the resultant shifts in formulations characteristic of the pre-modern Islamic tradition. The focus is mainly (but not exclusively) on expressions emanating from the Arab world.[1] By way of background, the chapter begins with a sketch of Muslim-Jewish relations from the earliest encounter through the centuries of Jewish life under Muslim rule, into the modern period. Thereafter it surveys Arab-Muslim responses to the Zionist project prior to 1948 in the central arenas of Palestine and Egypt. During the closing decades of the nineteenth century and the early part of the twentieth century, the issue of the Jews and their heritage was raised in the context of Islamic reformist projects conceived under the shadow of European domination. Out of such discussions emerged the foundations of what developed after 1948 into an influential Islamic meta-narrative.[2] This made sense out of the contemporary Muslim experience of the Jews' project of Zionism and set out a prescription for dealing with them, based on a particular reading of the foundational texts of Islam. While perhaps best developed in its Islamist articulations, this meta-narrative is not confined to these articulations, and is found equally in the formulations of ulama and non-Islamist intellectuals, for example. It is explored here through two central themes. First is the notion of the 'essential Jew', with which is linked the rise of anti-Jewishness as a new tradition in contemporary Muslim thinking, and which represents a shift in traditional Islamic formulations. Second is the notion of a jihad to dismantle the Jewish state which, as an embodiment of Jewish ascendancy, is ultimately regarded as an aberration. Finally, approaches to the issue of the Jews which proceed outside of the meta-narrative framework, and which are somewhat less influential in Muslim thinking and popular opinion, are explored.

Muslim-Jewish Relations: from Qur'anic Portrayals to a Modern Islamic Meta-narrative

The Islamic revelation reflected the encounter of Islam, in its formative period, with Judaism. It evinced ideas and stories, enjoined practices and established institutions with clear Jewish resonances or forms. At the same time, the Qur'anic profile of the Jews (Banu Isra'il; the Israelites) indicates the process of Islamic self-definition in regard to the Jewish 'other'. According to this profile, the Jews are in covenant with God, but they repeatedly violate both this and the Torah, and oppose the prophets. Consequently they incur divine wrath and God rejects them. There is no mention of Jewish redemption. The Qur'an presents Islam as the final, complete and divinely chosen faith, superseding Judaism (and Christianity). At the same time, however, it demonstrates a clear respect for Judaism and the Jews, who are often mentioned as the main example of *ahl al-kitab* (People of the Book), who have received a divine scripture. This is in spite of the Qur'anic doctrine of *tahrif*, which holds that the scriptures of the Jews (and Christians) have been knowingly corrupted.

The Qur'anic portrayal of the Jews also reflects the situation in contemporary Medina, with references to machinations by specific Jewish tribes in the city against the Prophet and the Muslims, and their forging alliances with the Prophet's opponents. This tense situation added a concrete dimension to its more abstract depictions of the historical Banu Isra'il's rebellion against prophecy, and informed this somewhat negative portrayal of the Jews. The subjugation of the Jews of Khaybar in 628CE marked the end of a series of Muslim campaigns against the treacherous Jewish tribes. At this point, a practical arrangement for relations between Jews living under the Muslim order was established. According to this, the Jews would live as a protected minority, in return for payment of a special tax.

In its final form, this institution (the *dhimma* or covenant of protection) was to govern the relationship between the two communities from then onwards, throughout the classical and post-classical eras, and up until its dissolution in the modern period.[3] As the Islamic conquests expanded, diverse Jewish communities were gradually brought within the realm of Islam, and assumed the administrative status of 'protected peoples'. While subject to certain legal and social restrictions reflecting the reality of Islamic political ascendancy, their lives, property and right to worship were guaranteed. They enjoyed a considerable measure of economic opportunity, and autonomy in their internal communal life. Interaction with the majority culture was widespread, and there were periods of profound cultural and intellectual exchange in fields of theology, exegesis, philosophy, law, mysticism, the sciences and poetry, exemplified in the lives of such men as the great Jewish philosopher Moses Maimonides (d. 1204).[4]

The *dhimma* system was not uniform in its application over time and space. In general, during times of political, economic and social stability, it tended towards a more liberal application. During periods of stress, its harsher or more restrictive elements might come to the fore. The relative political and economic decline that afflicted parts of the Islamic world in the post-classical and pre-modern periods gradually impacted on the situation of the *dhimmi*s there, during the seventeenth, eighteenth, and early nineteenth centuries, for example. With the extension by the Western powers of far-reaching influence and ultimately domination over the lands of the Middle East, the *dhimma* institution came under direct challenge. By the end of the nineteenth century, political developments and legal changes implemented under European pressure had effectively done away with it.[5] The demise of the Ottoman state, the implantation of territorial nation-states in its former territories and the rise of Arab nationalism and political Zionism each contributed to the comprehensive disruption of Muslim-Jewish relations from their traditional forms, sealing their fate in the context of an altogether new configuration.[6]

Following steady deterioration of the situation in Palestine with the launch of the Zionist project and Jewish immigration, the creation of the state of Israel in 1948 signalled a new era of confrontation, shaping Muslim attitudes towards the Jews for the remainder of the century. The gradual departure of most of Middle-Eastern Jewry from the Arab countries and their concentration in Israel meant that they became physically and intellectually isolated from the Muslim majority. From the Muslim perspective, concrete relations with the Jews had thus become confined to the theatre of conflict.

The foundation of the first truly popular Zionist movement in Russia in 1881 and the accelerated arrival of Jews in Palestine shortly thereafter gradually heralded new beginnings in Muslim thinking on the Jews: these early foundations would develop further after 1948. During the closing years of the nineteenth century, Palestinians grasped at first hand the far-reaching significance of Zionism for their own situation. Steps were taken to lobby the Ottoman Parliament and later the Committee of Union and Progress (CUP), which came to power following the Young Turks' Revolution in 1908, concerning the threat posed by Zionism. The Ottoman state was regarded as deficient in opposing Zionism; Palestinians accused the CUP, which was preoccupied with internal affairs, of being dominated by Jews and freemasons.[7] An anonymous 'General Summons to Palestinians' distributed in Jerusalem in June 1914 foreshadowed later declarations in its use of a range of Islamic symbols. For example, it invoked the names of 'Umar ibn al-Khattab and Salah al-Din, the conquerors of Jerusalem, and claimed that those who did not fight for their Islamic heritage were not true Muslims, and would be punished by God.[8]

From 1918 onwards, the leadership of the Palestinian nationalist movement drew on Islamic arguments and sentiment in mobilising popular support around specific threats, in the struggle against the Jewish National Home and the British Mandate.[9] The Grand Mufti Hajj Amin al-Husayni and the Supreme Muslim Council consistently highlighted the Islamic importance of Jerusalem, and the threat posed by Zionism to the Muslim holy sites there, particularly after the Wailing Wall disturbances of 1929.[10] In 1934, against the background of a dramatic surge in Jewish immigration and land purchases, al-Husayni issued a fatwa linking the sale of land to Jews with *kufr*, and treachery towards God and His Messenger. It also portrayed the Jews as seeking 'the extinction of the light of Islam and of the Arabs from this holy land', which had been granted to the Palestinians as a divine trust (*amana*).[11] From the early 1930s, various factors combined to create a climate ripe for the emergence of a number of clandestine groups committed to the notion of an armed struggle against the Zionist enterprise, and British rule. The first to take action was al-Kaff al-Aswad, a peasant-based resistance movement led by 'Izz al-Din al-Qassam, a Syrian student of Muhammad 'Abduh. After he carried out a series of attacks on Jewish settlements in northern Palestine, al-Qassam was himself killed by the British in November 1935. His martyrdom was an important immediate trigger for popular support for the General Strike, and the Arab revolt that followed it (1936–1939). Beyond this, the Islamic discourse and symbolism of his enterprise (centring on such notions as umma, jihad and *shahada*, for example) became widely accepted within the Palestinian nationalist movement, providing a basis around which the Arab-Muslim population as a whole could coalesce. Al-Qassam's views thus perhaps held more appeal for Palestinians in general than the Islamic rhetoric of the ruling notables in Jerusalem, who were regarded as a somewhat detached elite.[12] Indeed, al-Qassam became an enduring symbol of commitment to jihad through self-sacrifice, in an effort to repel those who threatened to wrest Palestine (or had indeed wrested it) from the Arab-Muslim fold.[13] In the years following the revolt, it became firmly established in the discourse of ulama (in Palestine as elsewhere)[14] that no Jewish authority must be allowed to rise on this holy land, which belonged not only to the Palestinians, but to all Muslims.

The reaction in Egypt to the advent of Zionism differed in pace and in character from that in Palestine. Before 1914, Egyptian opinion was not monolithically anti-Zionist. After 1918, and throughout the 1920s, there was virtually no official support for the Palestinian Arab political cause: the friendly approach of the palace and the government towards the British Mandate in Palestine carried no opposition to the idea of a Jewish National Homeland.[15] The Wailing Wall disturbances of 1929 constituted a turning point, however, as various Muslim organisations (especially the Young Men's Muslim Association [YMMA] and the Muslim Brotherhood [MB]) began to foster popular interest in the situation in Palestine, by pointing to the threat to the Muslim holy sites. From its beginning in 1936, the General Strike sparked much activity on the part of these and other Egyptian organisations. (The strike and the following revolt gave the Palestine conflict a new centrality in Arab politics in general.) The attitude of the Egyptian elite towards the British gradually became less conciliatory, especially in the approach to the Second World War, and greater sympathy was expressed for the Palestinian cause. The MB sent volunteers to Palestine during the General Strike: following the Partition Plan of 1947, both the MB and the YMMA participated in efforts to raise money and arms for further volunteers.

Throughout the 1930s and 1940s, a rising tide of popular anti-Zionist sentiment swept Egyptian society. This was substantially led and consolidated by the efforts of the YMMA and the MB while, in contrast, the government always lagged behind. In issues from the late 1930s of the salafi-oriented *Majallat al-Fath*, a number of major themes were reiterated.[16] The fear of a gradual Judaisation (*tahwid*) of Palestine was intertwined with a concern for the safety of the Islamic sacred sites. Writers consistently portrayed the struggle to defend Palestine (part of *dar al-Islam*) against the British and the Jews as a jihad, holding up for emulation the great heroes of the early Islamic conquests, and Muslim resistance to the Crusades. They recalled the sacrifices of the Companions in the course of their own jihad, alongside the Prophet. The fear of a displacement of Palestinians was another prominent theme in *al-Fath* at this time, as was an appeal to the Jews of Arab and Muslim lands not to abjure the centuries-old symbiosis of Muslims and Jews in favour of Zionism, which was described as 'un-Jewish'. In this context, the mercy with which the Arabs of Palestine had treated the Jews while 'they were being slaughtered in civilised Europe' was emphasised. Zionist aspirations were construed as ingratitude to Islam, which had long embraced and sheltered the Jews, 'in the blackest hours of their history'.

It is in the Egyptian arena specifically, and in reformist or salafi circles there during the late nineteenth and early twentieth centuries

in particular, that one can trace the foundations of what was to become an influential approach to understanding the issue of the Jews,
and their relation to the fate of Islam and Muslims, in Muslim thinking of the twentieth century. Confronted by a dominant Europe,
reformist ulama, statesmen and intellectuals in Arab urban centres
of the Ottoman state advanced a synthesis of Islamic and European
values as a foundation for the rehabilitation of their societies in the
modern world. The reformists construed their formulation of Islam
as a retrieval of the pristine or 'original' Islam. Properly understood,
the latter was held to be a religion of reason, above all else. It had
become distorted during its historical development, however, largely
as a result of the incorporation of sources at odds with its rational
essence. Prominent among these, according to reformist formulations, were the *Isra'iliyyat*, a traditional category which denotes in
Islamic thought early literatures of various types attributed to Jewish sources, and deemed to be borrowed Jewish content within Islam. Stories and legends within it thus often contained irrational,
fantastical elements.[17]

The great Egyptian reformist Muhammad 'Abduh (d. 1905),
for example, questioned the acceptability of the *Isra'iliyyat* within
hadith, *tafsir* and fiqh, in the context of a broad critique of *taqlid*
(the uncritical emulation of tradition). As Ronald L. Nettler points
out,[18] however, it was 'Abduh's disciple Rashid Rida (d. 1935) who
laid the foundations for what would soon develop into a pointed
modern critique both of the *Isra'iliyyat*, and of those reported Jewish
converts to Islam who had transmitted this material, and brought it
into Islam.[19] Rida made reference to traditional Islamic narratives
of alleged political machinations against the early Muslims and Islam by these transmitters and their colleagues. He suspected, for
example, that Ka'b al-Ahbar (d. 652) and Wahb b. Munabbih (d.
728/32), the two main transmitters of irrational *Isra'iliyyat*, who were
of Persian descent and who were generally believed to have been
Jews before their conversion to Islam,[20] retained covert sympathies
with the Persians, who harboured anti-Islamic sentiments as a result
of the defeat of their empire at the hands of Arab Muslims. Again
reflecting some traditional arguments, Rida was of the opinion that
all political strife within the early Muslim community, and all false
narrative traditions from this time, emanated from 'the society of

[the Jew] Abdallah b. Saba's followers, and the Persian groups'.[21]

Not all modern Muslim writers on the subject abjure the *Isra'iliyyat* wholesale, insisting instead on upholding the early Islamic permission to accept material transmitted from the Jews, as there was no harm in it.[22] In so doing, such writers call into question a widespread tendency in modern Muslim thinking to emphasise the prominent presence of the *Isra'iliyyat* and the Jews in the Islamic literatures of hadith and *tafsir* as a case of contamination of the pure by the impure. Some are indeed at pains to exonerate Ka'b and other Jewish convert transmitters from the traditional charges against them, which Rida had foregrounded.[23] By developing Rida's critical position further, however, his controversial and less circumspect disciple Mahmud Abu Rayya (d. 1970), widely known for his critical analysis of hadith,[24] elaborated a formula that was destined to assume a more central and persistent presence in Islamic discourses on the Jews for the remainder of the twentieth century. As Nettler has suggested, Abu Rayya conflated early Jewish convert transmitters with Zionist Jews in pre-1948 Palestine. He had interwoven perceptions concerning the *Isra'iliyyat* and their 'Jewish' transmitters as a critical problem in early Islam with the contemporary challenge posed by Zionist Jews in Palestine.

In an article in the April 1946 issue of the Egyptian weekly *al-Risala* (which was among the country's foremost intellectual fora of the time), Abu Rayya denounced those Jewish converts and their followers who had been responsible for incorporating the *Isra'iliyyat* into Islam as 'cunning deceivers'. Although they had declared their Islam, they actually worked to undermine the faith. The foremost of them was Ka'b.[25] Abu Rayya argues that Ka'b had allied himself with the group that had conspired to assassinate the second caliph, 'Umar ibn al-Khattab. He argues that Ka'b wished to see 'Umar eliminated because the latter had recognised him as 'the first Zionist', who had issued 'the first Zionist cry in Jerusalem', a cry which the caliph had proscribed. Abu Rayya attributes to Ka'b many irrational and dangerous *Isra'iliyyat* stories, which became part of Islamic tradition and *tafsir*. He points out that, 'Umar's suspicions notwithstanding, the Companions and their Followers (especially the prolific Abu Hurayra) continued to transmit from this former Jew.[26] For Abu Rayya, Ka'b was in fact 'the first Zionist'.

Presentism of the type that underpinned Abu Rayya's reading
of alleged Jewish designs linked to the *Isra'iliyyat* and intra-Islamic
strife in the early Islamic period was to become a characteristic approach in Islamic discourses on the Jews in the Zionist era, setting
it apart from its pre-modern counterparts. As they sought illumina-
tion of contemporary difficulties with the Jews in the sacred texts,
other writers applied present-minded hermeneutics beyond the issue of the *Isra'iliyyat* to other representations of the early Muslim-
Jewish encounter as recorded in the Qur'an, hadith, *Sira* and early
historiographical literature. References to the Jews which reflected
the Prophet's dispute in Medina with the Jewish clans there, or the
gradual consolidation of Islamic self-identity, were now read by Muslim writers through the lens of their own present, and particularly
the new realities created by twentieth-century Jews in Palestine. Seen
thus, these references were upheld as transcendent and universally
relevant exegetical archetypes, which could be applied to make sense
of the twentieth-century Muslim encounter with Jews.[27]

Abu Rayya's discussion reflects the impact by the mid 1940s of
increasingly pressing Muslim concerns over the intentions of Zionist Jews in Palestine and the future of the land and its people. The
Arab-Islamic reformist discourse had been frustrated by the Arab defeat of the First World War, and the ensuing policies of the colonial
powers. As a culture of jihad construed as defensive armed struggle
against colonial oppression and occupation emerged, certain reformist elements indeed diverted their attention to the defence of
Muslim freedom by force, including within the Palestinian arena,
where the Zionist project was gathering momentum.[28] The emphasis on jihad was to assume further importance among the heirs of
the reformist legacy following the *nakba* in 1948. It appeared in the
context of an emerging meta-narrative, which served to make sense
of the new realities. This provided an explanation, derived from the
sacred texts and the experience of the early Islamic community, for
Arab-Muslim losses and Zionist-Jewish successes, and offered an understanding of the new enemy.[29] Reflecting the central themes and
concerns of the emerging genre of the *Adab al-Nakba*, it also pointed
a way towards reversing the situation. In the course of its elaboration, hermeneutic approaches, assumptions and constructs of the
Jewish/Zionist other (and the Muslim self) which were to shape a

broad sector of Muslim thinking on the Jews for the remainder of the century crystallised. The 'Jewish question', experienced within the broader context of the impact of modernity and colonialism on Muslim societies, had gradually assumed a profound existential significance. Western modernity had effectively brought the Jews, as part of its new order for the region, into the heart of Arab-Muslim existence. An intertwining of two prominent landscapes is hence discernible in many writings from after 1948. These are Jewish political ascendancy in Palestine, and Western subjugation of the Arab-Muslim region in its entirety.

The influential meta-narrative concerning the Jews and Palestine recruits the Islamic texts and tradition to define the nature of the conflict, the enemy, and the solution, building upon the repertoire of motifs, texts and historical precedents that had been mobilised by earlier Arab-Muslim responses to the Zionist project. It is undergirded by the notion that Palestine is an Islamic territory (a part of the historical *dar al-Islam*), and that a particular importance attaches to it, as home to Islam's third holiest city.[30] The Pan-Islamic framing of the challenge to be confronted is thus emphasised, issuing in a position that has at times jostled for support with that of the secular (Pan-) Arab nationalists, and at others found tactical common ground with it.[31] The meta-narrative (and its constituent themes) has been asserted with growing emphasis and clarity during the last half-century. It has gained widespread prominence in the writings of conservative ulama (including those attached to state-establishments), Islamists, and scholars and intellectuals of diverse Islamic orientations. It also informs a broad band of popular Muslim opinion. Arab defeats of the past decades have contributed to its entrenchment, while Islamist formulations have added both to its conceptual elaboration, and to the endeavour to materialise its conclusion, especially since the loss of Jerusalem in 1967.

The 'plot', protagonists, motifs and methods of this meta-narrative are explored here in relation to two salient themes. First is the construction in this narrative of the 'essential' Jew, and the concomitant foundation of a new tradition of anti-Jewishness in Muslim thinking. The relationship of this new tradition to anti-Zionism is considered in this context, as well as the role of 'anti-Semitism' within it. The second theme is encapsulated in the notion of Jewish ascendancy in

Israel as an aberration, and the crystallisation of the idea of a jihad
to dismantle the Jewish state as the obligatory means to bring about
the divinely-ordained conclusion of the narrative.

The Essential Jew and the New Tradition of anti-Jewishness

The presentist approach to portrayals of the Jews in the sacred texts
issued inevitably in an essentialising perspective. In the eternal present forged out of the collapsing of past-time with present-time, the
Jew came to be seen to possess qualities of character and tendencies
of conduct that persist across the ages, finding expression in all times
and places.[32] A line of continuity was posited between Qur'anic and
other early Islamic depictions of the Jews (both in their ancient Is-
raelite and seventh-century Arabian representatives), and the mod-
ern-day adversary in Palestine. The Jews who had resisted Islam in
seventh-century Arabia, and their ancient ancestors who had rebelled against the prophets, were now perceived as representative
of all Jews in all times and places and, par excellence, in the Zionist
project and the Jewish state. This was the essential Jew, whose reprehensible character and conduct were detailed with unequivocal
clarity in the early Islamic sources. The meta-narrative thus describes
the establishment of Israel on the Islamic land of Palestine and the
policies of the Jewish state as an explicit re-enactment of the Jews'
historical rebellious conduct. Accordingly, accounts of the Prophet's
trials with the Jews of Medina are recruited to explain the character and actions of the state of Israel. And after the manner of their
ancestors in Medina, contemporary Jews are also held to be plotting
to weaken and corrupt Muslim societies (particularly through the
agency of their state).

The essential Jewish nature and its characteristic qualities are elucidated on the basis of historically conditioned Qur'anic texts target-
ing specific groups of Jews, and in relation to concrete situations.
In the meta-narrative, however, this material is developed into a
systematic and detailed exposition of what is construed in an abstract
sense as the Jews' *innate* evil and vices. Among these are ingratitude, selfishness, disbelief in the truth, hatred of good for others,
love of life and cowardice, for example. Their in-built hostility to
the interests of non-Jews is underlined, and their sufferings across

the ages are held to be the inevitable fruit of their own character and conduct.[33]

Sayyid Qutb's seminal essays from the turn of the 1950s, known collectively as *Ma'rakatuna ma'a al-Yahud*, showcase the construction of the essential Jew. Qutb developed the Prophet's encounter with the Jews in Medina into a notion of an ongoing, cosmic struggle between the Jews and Islam, claiming that the former would be satisfied only with the destruction of the latter:

> The Jews have confronted Islam with enmity from the moment the Islamic state was established in Medina ... the Muslim community continues to suffer the same Jewish machinations and double-dealing which discomfited the early Muslims.... This is a war which has not been extinguished ... for close on fourteen centuries its blaze has raged in all the corners of the earth and continues to this moment.[34]

He attacked the ruling elites in Egypt as agents of this anti-Islamic Jewish conspiracy, arguing that the Jews had infiltrated Muslim societies and states in the form of religious, professional and political elites and an intelligentsia who betrayed their own people, on behalf of their Jewish/Zionist masters. The collapsing of past and present is clear from the following passage:

> Just as, in the past, it was the Jews who had disrupted the early Islamic community ... it was the Jews who had more recently undermined Islam by installing a generation of fifth-columnists in its midst, posing as true Muslims but in reality betraying the Muslim cause.... The Jews have installed ... a massive army of agents in the form of professors, philosophers, doctors, researchers ... some even from the ranks of the Muslim religious authorities ... intending to break the creed of the Muslims by weakening the Shari'a in many ways ... with this and that they fulfil the ancient role of the Jews.[35]

A natural consequence of the construction of the essential, evil Jew has been the crystallisation of anti-Jewishness in Muslim thinking. Few areas are as polemically or politically charged as the discussion of what we term here the new, twentieth-century, Muslim tradition of anti-Jewishness, its relationship to anti-Zionism and anti-Semitism, and the relationship of these three twentieth-century trends and attitudes to the pre-modern Islamic tradition. We will consider the relationship between anti-Jewishness and anti-Zionism first, and then proceed to examine what has been termed 'anti-Semitism' in twentieth-century Muslim thinking.

The starting-point for any consideration of the two trends of anti-Jewishness and anti-Zionism in modern Islamic discourses, both in theoretical and chronological terms, must be the Arab-Muslim response to the Zionist project. Anti-Jewishness in twentieth-century Islamic discourses (and broader Muslim perspectives) has developed within, and is ultimately predicated upon, this response, which takes the form of an uncompromising anti-Zionism. As such, current Muslim anti-Jewishness represents an entirely new tradition, established within *modern* Islam.

In contrast, some scholars reduce Muslim anti-Zionism to a contemporary expression of an essential Islamic anti-Jewishness (at times citing in relation to the latter the Qur'anic content concerning the Jews). For example, in her discussion of Egyptian writings from the 1980s, Rivka Yadlin argues that Zionism is perceived as 'the essence of Judaism'. On this basis, she concludes that anti-Zionism is 'inherently an expression of an anti-Jewish attitude'.[36] In a similar vein, Amal Saad-Ghorayeb emphasises the identification of Zionism with Judaism in the outlook of the Lebanese Islamist movement Hizb Allah. She suggests that Zionism merely brought to the fore the party's 'latent anti-Judaism', which is 'rooted in a vehemently anti-Judaic Islamic tradition'.[37] Such scholars assume that there has persisted an unchanging Muslim anti-Jewishness/anti-Judaism, across the centuries of Islamic history since the Prophet's time. Zionism has merely inflamed this pre-existent (if perhaps latent), essential, Muslim anti-Jewish tendency.[38]

To understand expressions of anti-Jewishness in contemporary Islamic thinking, however, it is necessary to underline the elements of its *qualitative difference* from traditional Islamic prejudice against Judaism. To illuminate the latter, a few observations can be made concerning traditional Muslim treatment of and attitudes towards the Jews, and Muslim-Jewish relations in general, in pre-modern Islamic history.

In a recent critical historiographical overview of modern scholarly reconstructions of the Judeo-Muslim historical encounter, Norman Stillman traces the origins of what he terms the *idée reçue* of an idealised vision of the Judeo-Muslim symbiosis in the medieval world.[39] This leads him particularly to the work of a scholar of the nineteenth-century Wissenschaft des Judentums movement in Germany, Heinrich Graetz. The 'mythic vision' here reflected a disappointment with Graetz's own day, given the spread of a new, virulent form of racial anti-Semitism in Europe. It pointed to a selectively reconstructed past (that of Islamic tolerance) as 'proof' of what could be possible in the way of Jewish creativity, in an enlightened environment.[40] Stillman notes that the idealised picture of Jewish history under Islam has been adopted in the twentieth century in polemical writings by Arab and Muslim authors, and by others sympathetic to the Arab cause in the Middle East conflict. Its antithesis has appeared in a counter-myth in polemical works of the opposite political sympathy, which emphasises the darker side of Jewish history under Islam. Stillman thus describes a polemical 'golden age' myth or school, and an opposing 'persecution and pogrom' myth or school. Between these two tendentious extremes, he recognises the existence of a considerable body of literature produced during the second half of the twentieth century with 'a more balanced, nuanced and deeply textured vision' of the history of the Jews of the Islamic world. 'Indubitably', Stillman notes, 'the single greatest contributor to this corpus is the late S. D. Goitein'.[41] In his assessment, Goitein constructs a vision of the Judeo-Muslim historical experience that is not monochromatic, but balanced (this assessment is extended to the work of Bernard Lewis and Stillman himself).

Goitein, whose work has provided a framework for later discussions of the nature of Muslim-Jewish relations, characterised the central relationship between Jews and Muslims in the first centuries of Islam as one of 'creative symbiosis'. This characterisation has become institutionalised in the study of the Jews of Islam, and has been adopted by almost all of the leading scholars in the field.[42] In spite of a few recent calls for caution concerning Goitein's paradigm, and fresh assessments resulting from new research, as S. M. Wasserstrom recently noted, the overarching consensus has not been seriously shaken: 'creative symbiosis' remains the central concept in the study of early Muslim-Jewish relations.[43] (That is, the period from the dawn of Islam to approximately 1300 CE, encompassing the formative and classical centuries of Islam, the most important part for the field being the last four centuries of this period.)

Stillman criticises Mark R. Cohen for in fact 'offering a subtle form of the original myth' in his endeavour to counter the counter-myth of persecution and pogrom, by striking a balance between the two.[44] While this criticism must perhaps be held in mind, Cohen's later work nevertheless offers important insights regarding Muslim treatment of the Jews during this period of Islamic history. Cohen describes the existence of an intolerance and discrimination that was considered 'normal' in the medieval societies in which Jews lived. He points out that the Jews' experience of persecution under Islam at this time was on a scale that did not remotely approach Jewish suffering in Western Christendom. Furthermore, those persecutions that did take place in the Islamic world (he lists six major ones) differed significantly from those in Christendom. They were 'not directed at the Jews *per se*, but at non-Muslim *dhimmi*s as a group, or at the Jews as members of the *dhimmi* class'. Persecutions did not accompany 'irrational' accusations against the Jews, such as the ritual murder, or blood libel, and Jewish expulsions during this period of Islamic history have not been recorded.[45] Accounting for the dearth of Jewish literary sources devoted to the suffering and persecution of Jews in the Islamic world during this time (the first such sources appeared only in the sixteenth century), Cohen advances his most significant arguments. He suggests that the Jews of Islam lacked a collective historical memory of persecution at the hands of Muslims. Their adaptation of certain Biblical motifs to the recording of intra-Jewish persecution reveals 'a Jewish perception of persecution as a general phenomenon, and not the monopoly of the Muslims'.[46] During the post-classical period of Islamic history (after 1300 CE), the situation of Jews began to deteriorate as a result of general economic, social and political decline in the Islamic world. Concomitantly, the level of intolerance and persecution intensified, but even when the *dhimmi*s as a group experienced growing oppression, by and large, according to Cohen, 'the grim conditions of Europe were not matched'.[47]

Turning to Islamic textual traditions from the formative and classical periods, it is clear that Qur'anic depictions of the Jews and those developed in the earliest Islamic sources were elaborated further by later scholars. While their treatment might reflect the more critical in addition to the positive portrayal of the Jews, straightforward

vilification was not the norm. Scholars might hold up the Jews to
fellow Muslims as a 'warning model' of a people who had strayed
from the right path, and been chastised by God for this. Such discussions were abstract in nature, however, and were not related to
Jewish communities living within the Islamic fold.[48] At the same
time, as pointed out above, sources of *Isra'iliyyat* (and the related
genre of *Qisas al-Anbiya'* or 'tales of the prophets') achieved a widespread and comfortable presence in Islamic textual traditions from
tafsir to Sufism.

Ancient Islamic archetypes of the Jews persisted across the centuries, appearing in diverse textual traditions as a routine part of
doctrine and historiography. The Jews were portrayed as rejectors
of God's truth and persecutors of His prophets, mortal enemies of
Islam who had conspired with his enemies against the Prophet, had
had a hand in his death (through his poisoning by a Jewess), and
afterwards had fomented sectarian civil strife among Muslims. According to Nettler, throughout the long history of Islamic rule these
archetypes 'were prosaically recounted as part of Islam's portrayal of
the "proper" world order where the malevolent, conspiratorial Jews
were finally humbled under Muslim rule'. Crucially, he notes, the
treatment was 'devoid of hatred'.[49] By way of illustration, reference
can be made to a recent survey by Camilla Adang (who participates
in the same tradition of balanced and detailed textual scholarship as
Nettler), of a selection of classical Muslim discussions of Judaism, its
scriptures and the Jews, located within the genres of *kalam* and *tafsir*
as well as historical and polemical literatures. She concludes that, in
these writings, Judaism was indeed not treated any differently from,
say, Christianity or Zoroastrianism. Some of the authors were also
concerned to discuss *contemporary* Judaism, thereby according the
religion 'a place among the great cultures of their own period'.[50]
For the most part, according to Adang, the discussions of Judaism,
its scriptures and its beliefs were 'courteous and fair'.[51]

From the establishment of the *dhimma* system to the late pre-modern period of Islamic history it can be argued that, for the most part,
Islamic textual traditions assimilated the Qur'anic and early Islamic
treatments of the Jews, with their negative archetypes, in a detached
manner. Such discussions evinced a matter-of-fact tone and, as a
rule, showed no interest in systematic vilification. When negative

archetypes were transferred out of the realm of the abstract and applied to specific contemporary social realities, it served to confirm implementation in the world of the Qur'anic paradigm for relations with the Jews. The latter was manifest in their subordinate position in the context of the *dhimma* system, within which they posed no existential threat to Islam and Muslims.[52] The negative Qur'anic content (the timeless Word of God) thus typically did not form the basis of a focused anti-Jewishness directed at specific communities of Jews, or a general anti-Jewishness aimed at all Jews.

The collapse of traditional political and social structures in the Islamic world (including the *dhimma* institution) and the concomitant rise of political Zionism provided the backdrop to an appropriation of the Qur'anic and early Islamic treatment of the Jews that is both new, and unique to the specific circumstances of the twentieth century. The rupture of the old framework of relations was rapidly followed by an emerging situation where the Jews (for the first time since the Medinan period of Islam), through their liberation and political entrenchment in the heart of the Muslim world, represented a potentially existential danger to Islam. Muslim thinkers and writers (who were not always familiar with the classical Islamic legacy) now connected the Qur'anic content concerning the Jews, and the negative archetypes elaborated in early Islamic sources, with contemporary realities in Palestine.

It is in this context that virulent Islamic anti-Jewishness, applied to specific communities but extended beyond them also to Jews in general, has become established as a new tradition within modern Muslim thinking, where it has found widespread expression. The nature of current Muslim anti-Jewishness as a new construct, qualitatively distinct from any prejudiced treatment of the Jews and Judaism in the textual traditions and socio-political practice of earlier Islam, cannot be over-emphasised. This new tradition can be understood only within the complex matrix of the Arab-Muslim religious, intellectual and political response to Zionism, in the broader context of modernity and its political, cultural and ideological impacts.[53]

Undoubtedly, since its establishment (and against the background of the enduring enmity between Israel and the Arab world) the new tradition of Muslim anti-Jewishness has acquired an existence that is partially, and perhaps increasingly, independent of its origins in anti-Zionism. Moreover, vilification of the Jew as enemy has played an important part in anti-Israeli propaganda in the Arab world, during its long confrontation with the Jewish state.[54] Such observations point to the complexity of the relationship between the two trends: it cannot be precisely captured in reductionist formulae and essentialising assumptions, which are all too readily recruited to serve ideological and political ends.[55]

It has been argued thus far that virulent, targeted anti-Jewishness of the kind that has been expressed during the last century was not to be found, as a rule, in traditional Islam. In a similar vein, Bernard Lewis points out that *anti-Semitism* did not exist in the traditional Islamic world, in that prejudice against Jews and cases of persecution 'were not accompanied by the demonological beliefs and conspiratorial fantasies characteristic of Christian anti-Semitism in both medieval and modern Europe'.[56] Lewis cites the collapse of traditional political structures in the Islamic World, the importation from Europe of anti-Semitic ideologies and literature, and the establishment of the Zionist project in Palestine as major factors in the development of aspects of European-style anti-Semitism there during the nineteenth and twentieth centuries. This provides a useful broad framework for any discussion of 'anti-Semitism' in the twentieth-century Muslim context. A few comments can be made in relation to Lewis' second and third points, by way of emphasis and illustration.

In considering the impact of imported European anti-Semitic ideologies and literatures, it is important to underline the fact that Nazi Germany's efforts to promote its own brand of anti-Semitism in the Arab world from 1933–1945 met with limited success. With reference to Egypt during the 1930s, for example, Israel Gershoni deconstructs the dominant scholarly narrative, which is founded on the assumption that the Egyptian public's sympathy for fascism and Nazism was 'built into the social and cultural fabric of Egypt as a Muslim-Arab community', and that the intellectual elite 'venerated fascism and Nazism', in the context of the impact upon them of 'reactionary, Islamic mass culture'. Arguing that Egyptian responses to fascism and Nazism were neither monolithic nor homogeneous, he exposes the 'clear-cut anti-fascist' positions of such prominent Egyptian Muslim intellectuals as Taha Husayn and 'Abbas Mahmoud al-'Aqqad. Gershoni demonstrates that a key element of the Egyptian critique of fascist totalitarianism was a 'systematic condemnation of the racism inherent in its ideology and practices'. Intellectuals described Nazi racism as a 'cosmic enemy' of all humankind, which was anti-Arab and anti-Muslim to the same extent that it was anti-Jewish. The Jew was upheld as a metaphor for all Semites, and it was argued that if the racist persecution in Germany was not stopped, all Arab Semites might suffer a similar fate. The Egyptian press thus rejected the anti-Semitic repertoire ascribed to the Jews.[57]

The promotion of anti-Semitic ideologies among Arabs by Europeans of course significantly pre-dated the rise of European fascism. Anti-Semitism thus flowed through the same channels through which the transfer of notions such as liberalism and constitutionalism proceeded. Among the earliest and most influential imported works of European anti-Semitism in the Arab-Muslim world is the late nineteenth-century forgery *The Protocols of the Elders of Zion*. This was first translated into Arabic in the early twentieth century, and circulates in several translations in Arab countries, where many discussions of its implications have been published.[58] It is commonly referred to as a 'support-text' for the new Muslim constructions of Jewish nature, intentions and conduct. Its stamp is evident, for example, in Qutb's *Ma'rakatuna ma'a al-Yahud* (see above).[59] At about the same time, Qutb wrote in *al-'Adala al-ijtima'iyya fi'l-Islam* of Jews weakening all modern societies by smashing barriers of creed through the dissemination of secular philosophy. Their aim in this was to penetrate them with their 'satanic usurious activity', in order to 'deliver the proceeds of all human toil' to Jewish financial institutions.[60]

Such examples notwithstanding, the characteristic motifs and constructs of modern European anti-Semitism have been more prominent in secular Arab nationalist works,[61] than in those articulated through a specifically Islamic discourse, which have generally made greater use of internal Islamic sources rich in material relevant to the construction of an anti-Jewish stance. Furthermore, a question must be posed concerning the extent to which, strictly speaking, a contemporary Islamic discourse can accommodate the racial substratum of modern European anti-Semitism, given that such a discourse can lay legitimate claim to an Islamic tradition of explicit *anti*-racism.[62] In the Islamic discourse, the focus is not on the Jews as a race or racial group, but as the adherents of a religion, a religious-cultural community. This is an important theoretical distinction, which perhaps parallels that between modern, racial, anti-Semitism, and the anti-Jewish ideas and theories which pre-dated the rise of racial theory. Hence while for the anti-Semite Jewish characteristics are congenital (and hence the Jew's innate evil is incontrovertible), in Islamic discourses these characteristics (which arise out of adherence to the corrupted Jewish faith) are capable of rejection by individual Jews.[63]

This distinction should be held in mind when considering Lewis' third point, which concerns the impact of the Zionist project on the development of anti-Semitism in the Arab world. Lewis concedes that the specifically anti-Semitic element in the Arab response to unfolding events in Palestine remained consistently minor, until after the war of 1956. After the 1967 war, the change was much accelerated, and eventually 'a torrent' of anti-Semitic outpourings appeared, saturating the media in the Arab countries of the Middle East. The dominant sources in this were Rohling's *Talmud Jew*, and the (by now) ubiquitous *Protocols*.[64] Lewis attributes this development to the swiftness and completeness of the Israeli victories of 1956 and 1967, which he maintains presented a 'terrible problem of explanation' for the Arabs, especially in light of the general description of the Jews in the Arab media as a cowardly people. He argues that this propelled them towards irrational explanations, which they found in the (imported, European) literature of anti-Semitism and specifically, perhaps, its notion of a universal Jewish plot against God and mankind, aiming at world domination. He points here to the impact of this notion on the reconstruction of the Qur'anic account of the Prophet's encounter with the Jews in Medina, portraying this as an 'anti-Semitic innovation' that is 'explicitly Islamic, or at least presented in Islamic terms':

> Jews are now presented in a role which obviously reflects the narrative of the Christian gospels. They are depicted as a dark and evil force, conspiring to destroy the Prophet, and continuing as the main danger to Islam from that time to this.[65]

It is difficult to assess the relative extent to which the new, twentieth-century reading of portrayals of the Jews and the Prophet's

encounter with them in the early Islamic sources reflects the influence of European anti-Semitic motifs, or embodies a development
internal to the Islamic discourse.[66] What is noteworthy, however, is
the way in which Muslim authors use European anti-Semitic sources
in elaborating their views. In examples surveyed, as suggested earlier, the tendency is to adduce the anti-Semitic literature as external
'proof' of the nature of the Jews, and the allegations against them,
which is put forward based on the *Islamic* sources. For example, in
his discussion of the Jews in the Qur'an (1966), 'Abd al-Fattah Tabbara refers liberally to *Mein Kampf*. He clarifies his intentions in this
in the following terms:

> I include frequent quotations from Hitler to demonstrate the nature
> of Zionist Jews in a way that corresponds to the Qur'anic description of
> them, not out of admiration for their persecution ....[67]

In like fashion, the editor of a Saudi edition of Qutb's *Ma'rakatuna
ma'a al-Yahud* (1970) provides additional annotation, which consistently emphasises the *Protocols* as a 'proof-text' for Qutb's ideas.[68]

This manner of relating to European anti-Semitic literature might
suggest that, rather than becoming synthesised with the Islamic
sources, its motifs and themes have been kept somewhat distinct,
and hence have not effectively penetrated the Islamic discourse. A
parallel point might be advanced, which both reflects and flows from
this, in assessing the overall place of modern European anti-Semitism
in the Arab-Muslim context: it is functional, rather than organic.[69]
This interpretation illuminates further the growth of European-style
anti-Semitism in the Muslim context over the past few decades. The
magnitude and entrenchment of the Zionist-Israeli challenge and its
denial of Palestinian-Arab-Muslim rights have become ever clearer
in Arab-Muslim perception. Concomitant with this, Lewis' 'terrible
problem of explanation' has grown more pressing.

The failures of Arab nationalism, the strengthening of consciously
Islamic self-expression and the growth of Islamism in past decades
have brought Islamic discourses on the Jews to the foreground of
the public-political arena. These have been dissected in contemporary scholarship, and especially segments of Israeli scholarship.
Some Israeli scholars (among others) adopt the position that 'anti-
Semitism' (which typically remains undefined, leaving the reader to

assume that what is signified is full-blown, modern European-style racial anti-Semitism, with all that this implies) is intrinsic to modern Islamic discourses.[70] Some find in Arab-Muslim anti-Zionism and its accompanying anti-Israeli and anti-Jewish stances the expression of an underlying and defining 'anti-Semitic' attitude. Such unhelpful assumptions can reflect a reductionist approach that fails to take into account the multi-stranded, complex and nuanced reality of the Arab-Muslim position, and the extent of the antipathy caused by the Zionist project and the state of Israel. To achieve a balance, it is important to elucidate the historical origins and contextual realities of Muslim expressions of modern European anti-Semitism, as one element within the new tradition of anti-Jewishness in modern Islamic discourses.[71]

The Jihad to Dismantle the Jewish State

The second major theme in our discussion of the modern Islamic meta-narrative regarding the Jews is its construction of Jewish ascendancy as an aberration, and its prescription of a jihad to dismantle the Jewish state as the Islamic solution. The notion of the Jews' current ascendancy as a transient aberration is based on the Qur'anic characterisation of their ultimate, enduring destiny as one of abasement, poverty and bearing the burden of God's anger (a fitting punishment for their rebellious behaviour). The relevant verses here are Q.3:110–112. These juxtapose praise for the Muslim umma with censure of the People of the Book (a reference here to the Jews), affirming that the Jews will cause only *minor* harm to the Muslims, except if they are in 'a bond of God', and 'a bond of the people'.[72] Based on a reading of these verses through the prism of contemporary political realities, expressions of the meta-narrative typically construe the Western states that protect and empower Israel (especially the USA) as a 'bond of the people'.[73] This yields a reassuring explanation of current Jewish ascendancy. It provides scriptural confirmation for Muslim characterisations of Israel as the West's 'colonialist springboard' or 'spearhead' in the region, established to dominate it and to thwart Muslim interests. This explains the widespread tendency to denounce Israel and the West in the same breath,[74] collaborating in a common effort to subjugate Muslims and ultimately to destroy Islam. Some Islamists articulate this conviction in terms of a perennial conspiracy against Islam hatched by the forces of unbelief, in this context the Christians and Jews.[75] However the struggle against it is conceived, Israel is thus regarded as a 'cancer' or 'poisoned dagger' plunged into the heart of the Muslim world. It is an inherently expansionist state, and constitutes an existential danger to the Muslim world.[76] Occasionally, the Western powers are themselves construed as victims of the international Zionist conspiracy, used to serve Zionist goals,[77] and Israel is described as an enemy of humanity as a whole.[78] The militaristic character of Israeli society, which is geared towards protecting the illegitimate state, is construed as further evidence of its aberrant nature as an encapsulation of Jewish ascendancy.

While underlining the contingency of current Jewish ascendancy upon Western support, the meta-narrative also sees in this ascendancy an indictment of Muslim shortcomings. In Q.3:110–112, God promised the believers (in this context the Muslims) victory over the Jews. Having neglected their faith, however, they have failed to meet the fundamental condition for fulfilment of the divine promise. Building on these premises, the conclusion is that a turnaround in the fortune of the Arab-Muslim claim to Palestine requires a sincere commitment from the umma (with the Arabs at its vanguard) to re-embrace Islam, and on this foundation to strive to restore Palestine to the Islamic fold through the duty of jihad. Some expressions of the meta-narrative indeed construe the Palestinian tragedy as an *opportunity* granted Muslims by God, so that they might wake from their heedless state and retrieve their dignity.[79] There are frequent recommendations concerning economic, political and military preparations for the inevitable battle, in which Muslims will fulfil their divinely-ordained destiny to defeat the Jews. The inevitability of a Muslim victory and a comprehensive Jewish defeat is a central motif of the meta-narrative.[80]

The struggle to retrieve Palestine from its occupiers is construed as a defensive jihad: its theoretical legitimacy derives from its intended purpose of rebutting Zionist aggression. In 1968, for example, the conference of ulama convened by al-Azhar issued a series of resolutions, first of which was a call for such a jihad against Israel. The following rationale was advanced:

[T]he causes for which combat and Jihad must be taken up as defined in the Holy Qur'an are all manifest in the Israeli aggression, since the Israelis had launched attacks against the Arab and Muslim territories, violated what is regarded as most sacred in Islam ... Equally did they expel Muslims and Arabs from their homes, and ... killed old men, women and children ... For all these reasons, striving with one's life and wealth against the aggressors has become a binding duty every Muslim has to fulfil ....[81]

The jihad is typically held to be incumbent upon the umma as a whole, and appeals to launch it are often addressed to all Muslims.[82] While a collective duty (*fard al-kifaya*) for Muslims in general, for Muslims whose land is actually occupied the jihad constitutes an individual duty (*fard 'ayn*).[83] While the status of Palestine in its entirety as usurped Islamic land is universally underlined, many Islamists further emphasise this by describing it as a waqf (Islamic patrimonium) specifically.[84] As such, it 'belongs' to all generations of Muslims, past, present and future, and it is hence the duty and the right of the umma as a whole to participate in determining its destiny. This has clear implications for perceptions of the legitimacy of attempts by various leaderships (Arab and Palestinian) to achieve a negotiated settlement with Israel, based on a recognition of its right to exist in exchange for partial territorial concessions. Many Islamists insist that no one can negotiate on behalf of Palestine, or relinquish any part of it, and denounce such attempts as treacherous, and a heinous crime.[85] While a finite truce with the usurper-occupier based on non-recognition of its right to the land might be entertained for tactical purposes, they generally deny the permissibility of a permanent reconciliation.[86] Some uphold the historical Crusades as a paradigm in this respect, pointing out that, although temporary truces were concluded, the war was prosecuted relentlessly for two centuries, until the Crusaders were finally expelled.[87] Muslims today are hence obliged to fight to the expulsion of the last man, 'even if', according to one Islamist movement, 'this costs them millions of martyrs, and takes centuries'.[88]

Islamist attitudes towards the peace process since the late 1970s echo broader Muslim opinion, demonstrating the extent of the influence of various aspects of the meta-narrative on a substantial popular mode of perception and thinking. The Egyptian MB organ *al-Da'wa* led the way in condemning the Egyptian-Israeli peace process, insisting that the Islamic position could only be one of rejection. Both *al-Da'wa* and *al-I'itsam* (a second MB publication) argued that, if a peace agreement ensued from Sadat's visit to Jerusalem, the Israelis would use it to try to subvert the foundation of Islamic faith in Egypt:[89] Qutb's portrayal of Jewish intentions towards Islam had thus acquired a new relevancy. This line of argument persisted after the peace treaty had been signed. For example, *al-I'tisam* insisted that Israel be prevented from participating in the Cairo Book Fair, warning of the threat of an Israeli 'cultural assault' that would 'attempt to undermine the Muslim Egyptian personality' by falsifying Islam, spreading secular ideas, and corrupting morals.[90] Since Camp David, Islamists have consistently rejected the various peace proposals that have been mooted across the decades, from the Fahd Plan of 1981,[91] to the Saudi Crown Prince Abdullah's initiative of early 2002.[92] They have condemned the Oslo (Palestinian-Israeli) Agreement as a sell-out,[93] during which the PLO had clearly waved the 'flag of surrender'.[94]

The 'coldness' of Egypt's bi-lateral relations with Israel at the popular level provides specific evidence of the persistence of motifs and attitudes characteristic of the meta-narrative, and the continuing failure of any culture of peace to take root. Following the March 1979 agreement, Sadat introduced official measures to enhance the image of Israel in Egypt, to improve the atmosphere in the media, and to promote good relations. In spite of this, however, Egyptian public discourse (including the media) remains coloured by hostility towards Israel and the Jews, as highlighted by recent Israeli studies.[95] Writing in 2000, for example, Ephraim Dowek maintained that

> Twenty years of peace did not bring about the slightest change in the attitude of the Egyptian media towards Israel, the Israelis and the Jewish people.... To this day, the intensity and virulence of the attacks against Israel and the Jews in the Egyptian media are the equal of the warmongering and anti-Semitic incitement of the Nasser regime in its darkest period.[96]

In Egypt as in Jordan (which signed its own peace agreement with Israel in late 1994), there has been widespread opposition in intellectual and popular opinion to normalisation of relations with Israel, constituting a de facto repudiation of the peace agreements that call for this.[97] While influenced by concerns relating to the 'cultural assault' referred to above, popular aversion to normalisation is especially rooted in fears of regional Israeli economic domination.[98] It is equally fuelled by the cumulative impact of continued Israeli intransigence concerning Palestinian rights.

Popular perceptions across the Muslim world attribute Israel's virtual immunity from international censure to its *raison-d'être* as a proxy through which the West secures its strategic regional interests (interests that are inherently inimical to those of Arabs and Muslims). It is also construed as evidence of the success of Jews world-wide in using Western political elites to serve Zionist goals. The 'peace' process is widely seen as a means through which the Arab-Muslim peoples can be finally subjugated by Israel-America, and efficiently exploited. The inaction of Arab states in the face of Palestinian suffering is construed as evidence that the Arab regimes secretly collude with the West in its interests, and in the interest of its proxy Israel, at the expense of their own populations. In recent years, the chasm between popular Arab-Muslim opinion and the official stances of Arab regimes has reached unprecedented depths. In the context of the al-Aqsa intifada and Israeli reoccupation of Palestinian towns during 2002, for example, the Arab-Muslim 'street' has called repeatedly for borders with Israel to be opened, so that volunteers might join their personal efforts, construed as a jihad, with the Palestinians. The stark contrast with official positions, signalled at the Beirut Arab Summit in March 2002, hardly need be pointed out.

Through the implementation of a jihad, however this is achieved, the meta-narrative points to a conclusion in which Palestine, in its entirety, is restored to the Islamic fold. Many Islamists envisage the establishment there of an Islamic state, typically defined in terms of the implementation, in some form, of the sharia. Some call for a reversion at this point to the *dhimma* arrangement. For example, Isma'il R. al-Faruqi argued that, once the *bouleversement* engendered by implementation of the Islamic solution of a jihad to liberate Palestine has settled down, 'there is no reason why the Jews, as *dhimmi* citizens of the Islamic state, may not keep all the public institutions they have so far developed in Palestine'. Indeed he envisaged the future pan-Islamic sate (stretching from the Atlantic to the Malay

Basin) opening its gates to Jewish immigration, and becoming 'a haven for world Jewry'.[99] Other Islamists and intellectuals of various Islamic orientations deny this institution any contemporary role in relation to Jews or other minorities. For example, Fahmi Huwaydi argues within the framework of modern notions of citizenship, in his discussion of the place of non-Muslims in a Muslim society and state.[100]

Alternative Approaches?

Some Islamic formulations appear to break with the characteristic themes, motifs and prescriptions of the widely-spread meta-narrative. Examples arise in pronouncements since the late 1970s by certain ulama, in particular those associated with state establishments, addressing the related issues of jihad and peace with the Jews. When it decided to embark upon 'peace' with Israel, the Egyptian regime looked to its official religious institutions to confer on this a stamp of Islamic legitimacy. Only two years prior to Sadat's visit to Jerusalem in 1977, the al-Azhar ulama had issued a fatwa judging any ruler who might conclude peace with Israel a *kafir*.[101] After the event, however, the then Shaykh al-Azhar, 'Abd al-Halim Mahmud, declared his support for Sadat's initiative, and the Camp David Accords that followed. Once the peace treaty had been signed, the al-Azhar ulama issued a detailed statement outlining the Islamic position on peace treaties and war, citing texts from the Qur'an and hadith and the opinions of early Islamic jurists. In defence of Egypt's treaty with Israel, they pointed out that it neither gave up Muslim rights, nor approved the occupation. Rather it encapsulated a peace concluded from a position of strength (following Egypt's 1973 'victory'), and provided a means to restore Muslim rights. Indeed, the ulama argued, it represented a starting point in the march towards liberation of Jerusalem. Explaining their *volte-face*, they pointed out that while their earlier opposition to peace had been based on a belief in the possibility of defeating Israel, it had since become clear that Egypt could not bear the material cost of war with a superior military power. Based on the historical precedent of Muslim rulers concluding peace due to their enemies' overwhelming power, they insisted that Sadat himself had made peace for no lesser goal than, ultimately, to save the umma and its interests.[102] The Mufti of the time (Gad al-Haqq 'Ali Gad al-Haqq) adopted the same line in his own pronouncement emphasising that, in Islamic law, a peace treaty is permissible when it averts greater harm from Muslims. He also stressed that, thanks to Sadat's treaty, Jerusalem might eventually be returned to Muslim rule.[103] From the late 1970s up until late 1995 (towards the end of his life), Gad al-Haqq's position (both as Mufti and later as Shaykh al-Azhar) remained rooted in a pragmatic recognition of the fact of Israel's existence, and the futility of the attempt to achieve Arab-Islamic goals on the battlefield.[104]

In a publication that first appeared in the late 1960s, Muhammad Sayyid Tantawi (Shaykh al-Azhar at the time of writing) had called on Muslims to prepare for the obligatory, inevitable war 'to purify the Holy Land from the Jews', while launching an all-out campaign to stem international support for Zionism.[105] His response to a question about normalisation during an interview in 1995 (when he was serving as Mufti) revealed a profound evolution in this position:

> I believe in President Sadat's approach (may God have mercy on his soul): he went to his enemy in his own home from a position of strength ... I think I should go to my enemy in his own home and demonstrate his error to him. I should use all possible means to secure my rights. What does boycotting the enemy actually achieve – when I boycott my enemy while he occupies my land what is the result?[106]

Such politically conditioned arguments may appear to break with the assumption of the jihad to dismantle the Jewish state as the solution to the contemporary problem of the Jews, as prescribed by the meta-narrative. Understood within the tradition of Islamic fiqh, however, they clearly reflect a pragmatic, tactical response that remains theoretically committed to this solution. In contrast with this are the contributions of intellectuals, including both Islamists and others, who work outside of the meta-narrative framework, or consciously break with or critique it, and offer alternative ways of approaching the issue of the Jews. In the current climate, such voices represent a marginal trend. A significant example arises in the repudiation of the essentialist approach that underpins the meta-narrative, with its construct of Jewish nature and its notion of a 'cosmic' Muslim-Jewish struggle. Instead, concrete historical Muslim perceptions of

Jews are highlighted, accompanied by an attempt to account for the shift in these generated by the impact of Zionism. It is conceded that Arab-Muslim hostility to the Zionist project has resulted in a blurring of the traditional Islamic distinction between the Qur'anic condemnation of specific Jews (a response to their reprehensible conduct), and the injunction to grant Jews in general (as People of Book) inviolable rights under the *dhimma* covenant. Accordingly, Muslims are urged to distinguish between Zionist and non-Zionist Jews, and there is a call for resuming a *contextual* reading of the Qur'anic texts concerning the Jews, distinguishing between those who do wrong and those who are righteous.[107] The great modernist thinker Fazlur Rahman highlights the relatively positive character of the Muslim-Jewish encounter across history, with the exception of political tensions created by the political role of the Jews of Medina and Khaybar, and the political situation generated by Israel as a Western colonial creation. In what might be construed as an implicit critique of the conflation of categories characteristic of the metanarrative, he points out that the analogy between these seventh-century Jews and contemporary ones is not wholly accurate. The former were thus a segment of the indigenous population, who as such felt entitled to take sides in the unfolding political conflict; in contrast, Israel constitutes an entirely foreign element.[108]

For certain liberal Muslim intellectuals, the study of comparative religion, motivated by a concern to refashion conceptions of Islam for contemporary times, has brought greater familiarity with the central themes and motifs of Judaism. This has led some to attribute profound distortions in Muslim understandings of Islam (contributing to the declined state of Muslim societies) to the direct influence of Jewish notions. Here the emphasis is on Muslim culpability, through ignorance or neglect, rather than some active Jewish conspiracy. Examples arise in the writings of the Egyptian judge Muhammad Sa'id al-'Ashmawi and the late Libyan intellectual Sadiq Nayhum. In the context of his polemic against 'political Islam', 'Ashmawi argues that, through the vehicle of the *Isra'iliyyat*, the Jewish notion of religion has entered Islam and led to a distorted understanding of it. Muslim notions of Islam thus have effectively been 'Judaised'. While the characteristic of a legal system predominates in Judaism, where it is wholly appropriate (Moses was thus 'the giver of the Law'),

'Ashmawi characterises the essence of Muhammad's prophetic mission as one of 'mercy and ethics'. Here, legislation is a peripheral characteristic. In spite of this essential difference, Islamic thought has followed in the footsteps of Judaism, attaching importance to the small legislative content of the Qur'an and construing the term sharia as law (in contrast with the Qur'an's own notion of it as 'a spiritual and ethical way'). 'Ashmawi sees this process of 'Judaisation' behind Islam's long historical decline. It culminates today in the appearance of political Islam, with its misplaced religious formulation and expression of law and politics.[109]

Like 'Ashmawi, Nayhum is also concerned to expose political Islam as a distortion of 'original' Islam. His own preoccupation is with a historical conspiracy 'between Islamic fiqh and the forces of feudalism', aimed at wrenching the authority to rule themselves away from the people. His critique of the *fuqaha'* encompasses the accusation that they serve the Old Testament by incorporating its rules within what is erroneously termed the 'prophetic' Sunna. Examples of such rules, which he insists have no basis in the Qur'an, include the requirement of circumcision and the death penalty for apostasy. Nayhum suggests that, although its intentions were revolutionary, Islam has barely changed the condition of Muslims, since they remain 'surrounded by Jews from every side'. By 'erasing the boundaries between Judaism and Islam to the extent that they became wholly similar, even in the smallest details', he argues that the fiqh has caused unimaginable destruction. The *fuqaha'* have transformed Islam into 'magical rites' and 'archaic Jewish laws', brainwashing generations of Muslims with these under the pretext of preserving the prophetic Sunna. They have subverted Islam's original mission to liberate people from the authoritarian structures of feudalism, which uses religion as a tool of their oppression, by instituting a system of collective self-rule.[110]

The Tunisian historian Mohamed Talbi also rejects the assumptions of 'political Islam', emphasising in his own conception of 'pristine' Islam universal values, ethical principles and a fundamental tolerance. The latter informs a theory of religious pluralism, rooted in the early Islamic sources and having as its ultimate aim dialogue between all religions and peoples, and particularly between Muslims and the People of the Book.[111] Indeed Talbi argues that Islam

obliges Muslims (as the community which received God's final Word
in a series of revelations) to engage Jews and Christians in dialogue.
From the Qur'anic notion of its own finality and completeness in
relation to the earlier revelations, he constructs a message of con-
ciliation and unity of outlook and purpose among the three mono-
theistic faiths, which are accepted as equal in value. Talbi points out
that the Muslim-Jewish encounter in Medina both occasioned the
Constitution of Medina, and exemplified the pluralistic dimension
of Islam manifested in it (the Jews were thus integrated within the
umma and included in the political life and defence of Medina). As
such, the early Muslim-Jewish encounter is paradigmatic for Talbi:
through it, early Islam had perfected its vision for the inclusive,
pluralist society.[112]

While there are various individual contributions echoing that
of Talbi, the establishment of a broad-based Muslim-Jewish dialogue has been precluded by the conflict over Palestine. This has
remained the case in spite of the (politically driven) intensification
and international expansion of the field of inter-religious dialogue
per se in recent years. Fundamental disagreements concerning the
meaning of the state of Israel and the legitimacy of Palestinian griev-
ances pose a serious obstacle to successful conversation, while some
would-be participants fear stigmatisation by members of their own
community, for associating with the other. Most dialogue events involving Muslims and Jews in recent years have taken place in Europe
and the USA, where a handful of prominent religious leaders have
met in the context of international inter-faith colloquia. These are
typically organised under an 'Abrahamic' rubric bringing together
Muslims, Christians and Jews. They tend to focus on general issues
(ethics, youth or education, for example) and invite elite groups
of religious and community leaders, academics and intellectuals to
participate. In the UK, the Interfaith Foundation exemplifies such
elite associations: it was set up under the patronage of Prince Hassan of Jordan, Sir Evelyn de Rothschild, and HRH Prince Philip the
Duke of Edinburgh. The London-based Maimonides Foundation
describes itself as 'the only Jewish-Muslim interfaith foundation in
Britain' and seeks to promote harmonious Muslim-Jewish relations
there, built though dialogue, as a role model for other contexts.
It claims the Ambassadors of many Arab and Muslim countries as

members of its International Consultative Council. The Foundation has endeavoured to break the mould of closed academic seminars and occasional public lectures by organising meetings between Muslim and Jewish students on university campuses,[113] and joint activities for children. Within the Muslim world and especially the Middle East, inter-faith initiatives involving Jewish participation have been few and far between. These events are also confined to elite circles, and have no impact on popular opinion. During the past decade, Morocco has hosted such events in collaboration with UNESCO, while in Jordan closed meetings were held for a number of years under the patronage of Prince Hassan, following Wadi 'Araba. Within Israel, there has been a very marginal local Palestinian Muslim response to Jewish initiatives for dialogue or education/scholarship-in-dialogue, such as those launched in Jerusalem by the Shalom Hartman Institute, and the Elijah School for the Study of Wisdom in World Religions.[114] An interesting example of the transcendence of political conflict through the expression of a common spirituality arises in the recently established *Tariqa* Ibrahimiyya, a Jewish-Muslim mystical group whose Jewish founding members include a conservative Rabbi and academics knowledgeable in Islamic mystical traditions.[115] Among the founding Muslim members is a Palestinian Qadiri shaykh. Members meet to read Sufi texts and peform the *dhikr* together.

Concluding Remarks

Muslim thinking in the twentieth century concerning the Jews has been overwhelmingly shaped by the impact of Zionism on Muslim perceptions of the Jews and the Muslim-Jewish relationship, in the broader context of the ruptures occasioned by modernity and the colonial enterprise. The extent of that impact is reflected in the characteristic preoccupations and aspirations of the integrating meta-narrative that has crystallised in Muslim thought and popular opinion, and has come to stamp a broad range of Muslim discourses. While the new tradition of anti-Jewishness that has emerged within it encapsulates a shift in the traditional Muslim discourse, there is little indication at present of any change that might ultimately cause this tradition to recede. Indeed, the current international climate would appear set to add to its entrenchment and intensification. Few images are thus as potent in contemporary Islam as that of the al-Aqsa Mosque, captive to Zionist Jews and their Western backers.[116] The intensity of Muslim sentiment concerning Palestine is unmatched,[117] while as a symbol of injustice and oppression its appeal cuts across national and ethnic boundaries.[118] Arab leaders recognise its potency as a legitimising motif or rallying cry[119] (and fear popular sentiments concerning it for the same reason). In contrast, leading Western circles tend to underestimate its centrality in Muslim perceptions. Furthermore, they show relatively little interest in understanding what lies behind contemporary Muslim formulations and attitudes.[120] An informed and balanced understanding of these must acknowledge the magnitude of the impact of Zionism, and of its broader context of Western modernity, on the Muslim experience. Western modernity occasioned unprecedented and fundamental upheavals in all aspects of Muslim life, bringing (and often imposing by force) alien institutions and concepts, and creating a sense of crisis and a concomitant mood of self-defence. For twentieth-century Islam, the issue of the Jews and their new Jewish state epitomised this broader experience, and the threat to traditional Islamic assumptions and Muslim social and cultural modes inherent within it. The new intellectual traditions and constructs that have emerged out of Muslim efforts to make sense of this novel situation reflect the disjunctures and complexities characteristic of Muslim responses to this century, and the changes it has wrought.

Notes

1. While necessarily touching on aspects of Muslim attitudes and perceptions concerning Judaism (both as a religion in its own right and in its relation to Jews, Zionism and Israel, and both according to Islam and as presented in the Jewish scriptures), this area is not addressed directly in this chapter. For an example of a widely-circulated discussion of Judaism by a well-known Arab-Muslim author, see Ahmad Shalabi, *Muqarana al-adyan, al-juz' al-awwal: al-Yahudiyya* (5th ed., Cairo, 1978). See also M. Y. S. Haddad, *Arab Perspectives of Judaism: A Study of Image Formation in the Writings of Muslim Arab Authors, 1948–1978* (PhD dissertation, University of Utrecht, 1984), ch. 4–8.

2. As used here, the term describes a particular way of integrating reality

through an overarching, story-like plot.

3. For a historical survey of the *dhimma* institution see Youssef Courbage and Philippe Fargues, *Christians and Jews under Islam*, tr. Judy Mabro (London and New York, 1998). For a survey of Jewish life in the Arab world up to approximately 1875, see Norman A. Stillman, *The Jews of Arab Lands: A History and Source Book* (Philadelphia, PA, 1979).

4. See, for example, G. F. Hourani, 'Maimonides and Islam', in W. M. Brinner and S. Ricks, ed., *Studies in Islamic and Judaic Traditions* (Atlanta, GA, 1986), pp. 153–166.

5. For an overview, see Bernard Lewis, *The Jews of Islam* (London, 1984) ch. 3–4.

6. For a discussion of the impact of European penetration and colonialism, Zionism and Arab nationalism on the undermining of traditional inter-group relations between Jews and Muslims (and the evolving '*crise d'identité* engendered by these forces among Arabic-speaking Jewry), see Norman A. Stillman, 'Frenchmen, Jews, or Arabs? The Jews of the Arab World between European Colonialism, Zionism and Arab Nationalism', in Benjamin H. Hary, John L. Hayes and Fred Astren, ed., *Judaism and Islam: Boundaries, Communication and Interaction* (Essays in Honour of William M. Brinner) (Leiden, 2000), pp. 123–138. For an overview of the period from the late nineteenth century to the 1960s, see Norman A. Stillman, *The Jews of Arab Lands in Modern Times* (Philadelphia, PA, 1991). See further, Aron Rodrigue, *Jews among Muslims: Images of Sephardi and Eastern Jewries in Modern Times* (Seattle, WA, 2003).

7. For a discussion of Arab concerns regarding Zionism during the late Ottoman period, see Neville Mandel, *The Arabs and Zionism before World War I* (Berkeley, CA, 1976).

8. For excerpts, see Ibid., pp. 220–222.

9. See, for example, Uri M. Kupferschmidt, 'Islam on the Defensive: The Supreme Muslim Council's Role in Mandatory Palestine', in G. R. Warburg and G. G. Gilbar, ed., *Studies in Islamic Society* (Haifa, 1984), pp. 175–206.

10. For an analysis of statements of the 'Committee for the Defence of the Noble al-Buraq and the Muslim Holy Places', established in 1928, see Ilan Pappé, 'Understanding the Enemy: A Comparative Analysis of Palestinian Islamist and Nationalist Leaflets, 1920s–1980s', in Ronald L. Nettler and Suha Taji-Farouki, ed., *Muslim-Jewish Encounters: Intellectual Traditions and Modern Politics* (Amsterdam, 1998), pp. 92–97

11. For the collection of fatwas issued by religious authorities across the Muslim world and published together with al-Husayni's see *al-Fatwa al-khatira bi-sha'n bay' al-ard li'l-sahyuniyyin* (Jerusalem, 1935).

12. This argument is developed in Nels Johnson, *Islam and the Politics of*

Meaning in Palestinian Nationalism (London, 1982), pp. 38 ff, especially pp. 53 ff.

13. On al-Qassam see further Shai Lachman, 'Arab Rebellion and Terrorism in Palestine 1929–39: The Case of Sheikh Izz al-Din al-Qassam and his Movement', in Elie Kedourie and Sylvia G. Haim, ed., *Zionism and Arabism in Palestine and Israel* (London, 1982), pp. 59–78; Basheer M. Nafi, 'Shaykh 'Izz al-Din al-Qassam: A Reformist and a Rebel Leader', *JIS*, 8, 2 (1997), pp. 185–215.

14. For examples from Syria, Saudi Arabia and Iraq, see Basheer M. Nafi, *Arabism, Islamism and the Palestine Question, 1908–1941: A Political History* (Reading, 1998), p. 324, n. 248.

15. Israel Gershoni and James P. Jankowski, *Egypt, Islam and the Arabs: The Search for Egyptian Nationhood, 1900–1930* (New York, 1986), p. 40.

16. The journal was established in 1926–7 and edited by Muhib al-Din al-Khatib. For a translation and analysis of a selection of articles from 1938–9, from which the examples given here are drawn, see Nigel Meir, *Some Islamic Writings of the 1930s on the Palestine Problem: Translations and Commentary* (M.Phil dissertation, Oxford, 1993), p. 35 ff. Similar concerns occupied the Muslim Brotherhood at this time. See for example 'Abd al-Fattah El-Awaisi, *The Muslim Brothers and the Palestine Question, 1928–1949* (London and New York, 1998).

17. In its main Sunni traditions, classical Islam typically accepted whatever was held not to be contrary to Islam within this 'alien' material, and thereby allowed a substantial element of it to become assimilated within the textual traditions of hadith and *tafsir*, and the literatures of historiography and Sufism. While there is ongoing debate about its status and role in classical and medieval Islam, Muslim scholars from this time appear themselves to have proceeded largely from a presumed integration and continuity of sources within the Jewish, Christian and Islamic religions. Muslim debates regarding the issue of the *Isra'iliyyat* have been ongoing since ancient times, but the significance attributed to this issue has been subject to a qualitative shift in the modern period. For an introduction to the reception of Biblical materials in early Islam see Camilla Adang, *Muslim Writers on Judaism and the Hebrew Bible: From Ibn Rabban to Ibn Hazm* (Leiden, 1996), pp. 1–22. For further discussion of the *Isra'iliyyat* see G. Vajda, 'Isra'iliyat', *EI2*, pp. 211–212; M. J. Kister, '"Haddithu 'an Bani Isra'ila wa la haraja": A Study of an Early Tradition', *Israel Oriental Studies*, 2 (1972), pp. 215–239.

18. See Nettler, 'Early Islam, Modern Islam and Judaism: The *Isra'iliyyat* in Modern Islamic Thought', in Ronald L. Nettler and Suha Taji-Farouki, ed., *Muslim-Jewish Encounters: Intellectual Traditions and Modern Politics* (Amsterdam, 1998), pp. 1–14.

19. Rida was to become an active party to the Palestinian struggle. As early as 1902, he had warned that the aim of Zionism was national sovereignty. For him, Zionism was in essence a Western imperialist phenomenon, having little to do with Judaism as a religion.

20. A Yemeni of Persian descent, Wahb himself may have been born a Muslim, although his ancestors appeared to have been Jewish. See Adang, *Muslim Writers*, p. 11.

21. Muhammad Rashid Rida, *Tafsir al-Qur'an al-karim al-shahir bi-tafsir al-Manar* (Cairo, n.d.), pp. 44–45. For further discussion of Rida's views in this regard, see G. H. A. Juynboll, *The Authenticity of the Tradition Literature; Discussions in Modern Egypt* (Leiden, 1969), ch. 10. On 'Abdallah b. Saba', who is often regarded as the originator of the Shi'a, and whose alleged mission in converting to Islam was to lead the Muslims astray by trying to persuade them to profess Ali's divinity, see Adang, *Muslim Writers*, p. 105, n. 165. The author here also relays Ibn Hazm's views to this effect. The linking of Jews and Shi'ites was a standard feature of Sunni polemics.

22. This permission was encapsulated in a hadith, '*haddithu 'an Bani Isra'ila wa la haraja ...*', that became widely current among the Muslims in the first half of the second century of Islam.

23. A prominent example arises in the work of the late Azharite shaykh Muhammad al-Dhahabi: *al-Isra'iliyyat fi'l-tafsir wa'l-hadith* (Cairo, 1986): see Nettler, 'Early Islam, Modern Islam and Judaism', p. 12. Compare with 'A'isha Bint 'Abd al-Rahman, *al-Isra'iliyyat fi'l-ghazw al-fikri* (Cairo, 1975).

24. For example, *Awda' 'ala al-sunna al-Muhammadiyya* (Cairo, n. d.).

25. Mahmud Abu Rayya, '*Ka'b al-Ahbar huwa al-sahyuni al-awwal*', *al-Risala*, 665 (April 1946), pp. 360–363. For a discussion of the role of converted Jews in general, and Ka'b in particular, in the transmission of Biblical material, see D. J. Halperin and G. D. Newby, 'Two Castrated Bulls: A Study of the Haggadah of Ka'b al-Ahbar', *JAOS*, 102 (1982), pp. 631–638.

26. It must be pointed out that Abu Rayya's critical writings on the transmitters and substance of hadith (indeed his outright denial of their authenticity or authority), and particularly his book on Abu Hurayra (*Abu Hurayra, Shaykh al-Madina,* Cairo, 1969), were rejected by more traditional scholars. Nettler, 'Early Islam, Modern Islam and Judaism', p. 8; see further Daniel Brown, *Rethinking Tradition in Modern Islamic Thought* (Cambridge, 1999), p. 158 n. 27, for example.

27. This application of present-minded hermeneutics reflected an emerging trend in twentieth-century Muslim thought, which has become particularly pronounced in Islamist formulations. It represents an attempt to relate the sacred text and tradition to Muslim experience in the profoundly reordered context of the modern era. The characteristic approach proceeds

from a perception of the literal transcendence of this text (and of the defining moments of sacred history) which renders its surface meanings relevant to all contexts, and involves the reader in 'an interaction among past, present and future having a bearing on both understanding and action'. (See Dominick LaCapra, 'Rethinking Intellectual History and Reading Texts', in Dominick LaCapra and Steven Kaplan, ed., *Modern European Intellectual History: Reappraisals and New Perspectives* [Ithaca, NY, 1982], p. 81.) In the course of this anti-historicist approach, timeless elements of universal relevancy are abstracted from their own context, construed in light of the reader's perceptions of their own reality, and applied on the basis of this present and contextually-driven reading. For a discussion of approaches to the understanding and interpretation of historical texts which can illuminate the relationship between reader and sacred text in the present discussion see Quentin Skinner, 'Meaning and Understanding in the History of Ideas', *History and Theory*, 8 (1969), pp. 3–53, and 'Motives, Intentions and the Interpretation of Texts', *New Literary History*, 3 (1972), pp. 393–408.

28. While the positive reformist view of the West was necessarily revised in light of the 'ugly face of imperialism', doubts surrounding this view of the West were most acute in relation to the Palestinian arena, where Western plans looked set to pose a lethal challenge to Arab-Islamic assumptions. See Basheer M. Nafi, *The Rise and Decline of the Arab-Islamic Reform Movement* (London, 2000), pp. 60–61.

29. The impulse to derive understanding of the new enemy from the ancient Qur'anic text is reflected in the titles of the many works that appeared in the Arab world after 1948. For a sample from the mid-1960s through to the mid-1990s, see S. Taji-Farouki, 'A Contemporary Construction of the Jews in the Qur'an: A Review of Muhammad Sayyid Tantawi's *Banu Isra'il fi'l-Qur'an wa'l-Sunna* and 'Afif 'Abd al-Fattah Tabbara's *al-Yahud fi'l-Qur'an*', in Nettler and Taji-Farouki, *Muslim-Jewish Encounters*, p. 34 n. 1. Further examples include Sabir 'Abd al-Rahman Tu'ayma, *Banu Isra'il fi mizan al-Qur'an al-karim* (n. p., 1975) and 'Abd al-Karim Khatib, *al-Yahud fi'l-Qur'an* (Cairo, 1974).

30. Islamic doctrine identifies Jerusalem, which was Islam's first *qibla*, as the starting point for the Prophet's ascension into the heavens (Q.17: 1). It is home to al-Haram al-Sharif, encompassing the area of the former Jewish Temple Mount and the rock upon which Ibrahim, according to Islamic tradition, resolved to sacrifice Isma'il. During the late seventh/early eighth century, the Dome was constructed over this (together with the al-Aqsa mosque). It is the oldest surviving Islamic monument, and contains the earliest extant extensive portions of the Qur'anic text.

31. For a typical Islamist critique of the Arab nationalist approach to the

issue of Palestine see Mohamed Yehia, 'A Criticism of the Idea of Arab Nationalism', in M. Ghayasuddin, ed., *The Impact of Nationalism on the Muslim World* (London, 1986), pp. 48–49. The author sees both Israel and Arab nationalism as tools created by the West to engender the disintegration of Islam.

32. Essentialist constructs of self and other have become a characteristic motif in much Islamist thinking. This is illustrated in Islamist readings of world history, which is frequently framed in terms of an ongoing struggle between 'Muslims' (or 'Islam'), and 'unbelievers' (or 'unbelief'), the latter often being broken down into Jewish and Christian elements. Each category is held to enjoy a coherent collective existence that transcends time and space, characterised by a single psychology, and united behind a single pre-determined aim. In this scheme, perceptions and purposes float unanchored across the ages, rather than being part of immediate realities and circumstances. Timeless civilisations are pitted against each other, and in different times and places 'grand themes' and essences are manifest, ever unchanging. Hence, medieval and modern history is construed as an endurance of seventh-century episodes and paradigms, or indeed ancient episodes and paradigms as depicted in the seventh-century text.

33. The treatment is harsh and uncompromising, and the essentialism far-reaching. According to one discussion, for example, the Qur'anic depiction of the Jews' vices (whether in ancient times or during the seventh century) applies 'in all times and places', and the passage of time 'increases the deep-rootedness of these qualities in them'. Muhammad Sayyid Tantawi, *Banu Isra'il fi'l-Qur'an wa'l-Sunna* (Cairo, 1986), p. 11. For further examples from this publication and others, see S. Taji-Farouki, 'A Contemporary Construction of the Jews in the Qur'an', pp. 15–38. A brief overview of the 'odium of the Jews' as elaborated in Egyptian writings from the 1980s is provided in Rivka Yadlin, *An Arrogant Oppressive Spirit: Anti-Zionism as Anti-Judaism in Egypt* (Oxford, 1989), pp. 107–109; for Hasan Hanafi's treatment, see pp. 50–60. Hizb Allah's discussion of Jewish nature is summarised in Amal Saad-Ghorayeb, *Hizbu'llah: Politics and Religion* (London, 2002), pp. 174–86.

34. Translated in Ronald L. Nettler, *Past Trials and Present Tribulations: A Muslim Fundamentalist's View of the Jews* (Oxford, 1987), p. 9.

35. Ibid. Echoes of Qutb's suspicions concerning the academic study of Islam specifically arise in Muslim perceptions of recent Western scholarship on the Qur'an, especially that which portrays Islam as a heretical offshoot of Judaism, and its sacred text as owing much to the Talmud. Examples include John Wansbrough, *The Sectarian Milieu: Content and Composition of Islamic Salvation History* (Oxford, 1978); Michael Cook and Patricia Crone, *Hagarism: The Making of the Islamic World* (Cambridge, 1977). Some Muslims

thus construe the 'Orientalist' enterprise of Qur'anic studies as a conspiracy to sow doubt among Muslims in the Qur'an's historical authenticity and doctrinal autonomy. See for example comments by S. Parvez Manzoor cited in Toby Lester, 'What is the Koran?', *The Atlantic Monthly* (January 1999).

36. Yadlin, *An Arrogant Oppressive Spirit*, p. 106. The author argues that the state of Israel is rejected in these writings 'not only because of its invasion of Arab territory but also because, as an expression of Judaism, it represents an existential danger for Egyptians-Arabs-Muslims'. The main aspect of the danger embodied in the Jews lies 'in their reprehensibility, their cultural nature and the consequent aberrations in the right order of things'. She emphasises the fact that, in the Muslim view, Judaism can coexist with Arab-Islamic culture only in a status that is inferior to it. It is against this background that the establishment of Israel represents an aberration. For further discussion of this notion see below.

37. Saad-Ghorayeb, *Hizbu'llah*, p. 174.

38. This essentialising assumption can lead to some absurd conclusions. Referring to the Qur'anic discussion of the Jews and the Prophet's dealings with them in Medina, for example, Saad-Ghorayeb comments: 'It is against this historical and scriptural backdrop that Hizbu'llah's struggle against Israel can be viewed as a continuation of Muhammad's conflict with the Jews of his day.' *Hizbu'llah*, p. 177. Hizb Allah itself might indeed construe its struggle against Israel in these terms. However, a critical distinction must be drawn between expressions of anti-Judaism in early, medieval and premodern Islam, and in the modern situation, reflecting the fundamental and comprehensive disruption in political, social, intellectual and religious contexts that sets the latter apart from its predecessors. See below.

39. Norman A. Stillman, 'The Judeo-Islamic Historical Encounter: Visions and Revisions', in Tudor Parfitt, ed., *Israel and Ishmael: Studies in Muslim-Jewish Relations* (Richmond, 2000), pp. 1–12.

40. The 'golden age' mythic vision among scholars such as Graetz was allegedly reinforced by the concomitant work of pioneering European scholars of Islam who were either Jewish or of Jewish extraction (the so-called 'pro-Islamic Jews'), such as Ignaz Goldziher. See ibid.

41. Ibid., p. 8. His major works are *Jews and Arabs: Their Contacts through the Ages* (New York, 1955; 3rd ed., 1974); *A Mediterranean Society: The Jews of the Arab World as Portrayed in the Documents of the Cairo Geniza* (Berkeley and Los Angeles, CA, 1967–1988).

42. Bernard Lewis himself speaks of '… in earlier though not later Islamic times, a kind of symbiosis between Jews and their [Muslim] neighbours that has no parallel in the Western world between the Hellenistic and modern ages.' Bernard Lewis, *The Jews of Islam* (London, 1984), p. 88.

43. Steven M. Wasserstrom, *Between Muslim and Jew: The Problem of Symbiosis under Early Islam* (Princeton, NJ, 1995), pp. 3–5.

44. Stillman, 'The Judeo-Islamic Historical Encounter', p. 8. The author refers specifically to two controversial earlier articles by Cohen. References below are to slightly later works in which, Stillman concedes, Cohen has slightly 'moderated' his views.

45. Mark R. Cohen, 'Persecution, Response, and Collective Memory: The Jews of Islam in the Classical Period', in Daniel Frank, ed., *The Jews of Medieval Islam: Community, Society and Identity* (Leiden, 1995), pp. 147–148. His *Under Crescent and Cross: The Jews in the Middle Ages* (Princeton, NJ, 1994) addresses the same issue, but also offers a broad comparative study of medieval Jewish life in Muslim and Christian lands.

46. Ibid., p. 162.

47. Ibid., p. 148.

48. It was commonplace in classical *tafsir*, for example, to identify 'those against whom God is wrathful' (Q.1:7) with the Jews in a matter-of-fact way, at times without further comment. By way of illustration, see the fifteenth-century *Tafsir al-Jalalayn* (Beirut, n. d.), p. 1.

49. Ronald L. Nettler, 'Islamic Archetypes of the Jews: Then and Now', in Robert S. Wistrich, ed., *Anti-Zionism and Anti-Semitism in the Contemporary World* (London, 1990), p. 67. From this perspective, the general use of the term 'Jew-hatred' in the context of pre-modern Islam is questionable. For an example, see Haggai Ben-Shammai, 'Jew-Hatred in the Islamic Tradition and the Koranic Exegesis', in Shmuel Almog, ed., *Antisemitism Through the Ages*, tr. Nathan Reisner (Oxford, 1988), pp. 161–169.

50. Adang, *Muslim Writers*, p. 252. The authors discussed are Ibn Rabban al-Tabari, Ibn Qutayba, al-Ya'qubi, al-Tabari, al-Baqillani, al-Mas'udi, al-Maqdisi, al-Biruni and Ibn Hazm.

51. Ibid., p. 253. Ibn Hazm's avowedly polemical writings form an exception here, although the author points out that his legal decisions concerning *dhimmi*s in *al-Muhalla* present a milder view, and indeed leave open all kinds of possibilities for Muslims to interact socially with *dhimmi*s. On his approach to the Bible see further Hava Lazarus-Yafeh, *Intertwined Worlds: Medieval Islam and Bible Criticism* (Princeton, NJ, 1992), ch. 2; 6.

52. An interesting example is the case of the legality of the Karaite Synagogue in Mamluk Cairo of the mid-fifteenth century, and the renewal of the Covenant of 'Umar in relation to this. The background was one of gathering pressure on *dhimmi* communities in Egypt in general from the end of the thirteenth century, involving periods of mob violence. See Donald S. Richards, '*Dhimmi* Problems in Fifteenth-Century Cairo: Reconsideration of a Court Document', *Studies in Muslim-Jewish Relations*, 1 (1993), pp. 127–164.

53. Saad-Ghorayeb, *Hizbu'llah*, p. 174 hence fails to situate in its proper context Hizb Allah's alleged insistence 'that its strong aversion to Judaism is unrelated to its abomination of Zionism, and hence exists irrespective of the existence of Zionism'. The party's anti-Jewishness is an Islamic construct of the modern, Zionist, era, and would be unthinkable, in its vehemence and its application to specific Jewish communities, in any other context. See below.

54. For a discussion of such propaganda, see Yehoshua Harkabi, 'On Arab Anti-Semitism Once More', in Almog, ed., *Antisemitism Through the Ages*, p. 228.

55. The equation of Muslim anti-Zionism with Muslim anti-Jewishness can be constructed on the basis of the careless conflation of the categories 'Jews' and 'Zionists' in many Muslim writings, reflected in the use of these terms interchangeably, in spite of a commonly and explicitly claimed acknowledgement of the distinction between the two communities. In respect of the latter, see, for example, Isma'il R. al-Faruqi, 'Islam and Zionism', in John L. Esposito, ed., *Voices of Resurgent Islam* (New York and Oxford, 1983), pp. 261–267. The author underlines the fact that Islam regards Judaism as the religion of God, but is opposed 'to Zionism, to Zionist politics and conduct'. For a detailed explication of his views, see Isma'il Raji al-Faruqi, *Islam and the Problem of Israel* (London, 1980). According to Ayat Allah Ruh Allah Khumayni, 'Jews are different from Zionists; if the Muslims overcome the Zionists, they will leave the Jews alone'. *The Imam versus Zionism* (Tehran, 1983), p. 42. Hizb al-Tahrir distinguishes between Jews who were resident in Palestine prior to the demise of the Ottoman Empire, and those who arrived thereafter. In theory, it permits individuals from the former category who have not acted violently against Muslims to remain, after the proposed destruction of Israel. (Interview with official spokesman, Amman, 1994.) It should be pointed out that confusion concerning Muslim anti-Zionism and anti-Jewishness is further compounded by the fact that Muslims who are at pains to explicitly repudiate anti-Jewishness are commonly plagued by such charges (and indeed charges of anti-Semitism) when they are openly critical of Israel or its policies.

56. Bernard Lewis, in Sander L. Gilman and Steven T. Katz, ed., *Anti-Semitism in Times of Crisis* (New York, 1991), p. 346. Lewis here describes anti-Semitism in the 'specialised sense' as 'that … peculiar hatred of Jews, which has its origins in the role assigned to Jews in certain Christian writings and beliefs concerning the genesis of their faith, and which has found expression in … portrayals of a universal Jewish plot against both God and mankind'. Unlike other forms of ethnic and racial prejudice, he explains, 'anti-Semitism goes beyond mere denigration or even persecution, and attributes

to its adversary a quality of cosmic and eternal evil'. This notion of 'European-style' anti-Semitism is adopted throughout the following discussion. Its peculiarly Christian origins are here less important than certain of the motifs and constructs that came to characterise its modern elaborations in particular, following the rise of racial theory in the mid-nineteenth century. The presence of these characteristic motifs and constructs is what marks anti-Semitism, and sets it apart from what has been termed anti-Jewishness, in our discussion of the Muslim context. It is important to emphasise that European-style anti-Semitism thus forms only one of several strands within expressions of anti-Jewishness in the contemporary Muslim arena.

57. Israel Gershoni, *Beyond Anti-Semitism: Egyptian Responses to German Nazism and Italian Fascism in the 1930s*, EU Working Papers, RSC No. 2001/32. Compare, for example, with the following: 'Arab admiration of German National Socialism and Italian fascism in the 1930s and 1940s and a concomitant receptivity to their anti-Semitic rhetoric ... ensured that the Jews would find no place for themselves in the Arab nationalist camp and the society it would create.' Stillman, 'Frenchmen, Jews, or Arabs?', p. 135.

58. See, for example, *Brutukulat hukama' Sahyun* [Kutub Siyasiyya, no. 5] (Cairo, 1960); Muhammad Khalifa al-Tunisi, *al-Khatar al-Yahudi: brutukulat hukama' Sahyun* (Beirut, 1952). The latter has appeared in many editions and circulates widely. Extracts of the *Protocols* have reportedly been published in Persian newspapers: see David Menashri, 'The Jews of Iran: Between the Shah and Khomeini', in Gilman and Katz, *Anti-Semitism in Times of Crisis*, p. 366. On the *Protocols* in general see Norman Cohen, *Warrant for Genocide: The Myth of Jewish World-Conspiracy and the Protocols of the Elders of Zion* (Chicago, IL, 1981); Stephen Eric Bronner, *A Rumor about the Jews: Reflections on Antisemitism and the Protocols of the Learned Elders of Zion* (New York, 2000).

59. For a translation and analysis, see Nettler, *Past Trials and Present Tribulations*.

60. William E. Shepard, *Sayyid Qutb and Islamic Activism: A Translation and Critical Analysis of 'Social Justice in Islam'* (Leiden, 1996), p. 303.

61. For an overview of writings by Arab intellectuals from the 1950s and 1960s framed in the then dominant nationalist discourses see Yehoshua Harkabi, *Arab Attitudes to Israel* (Jerusalem, 1968; 2nd ed., 1976).

62. See also the example of Egyptian intellectuals from the 1930s, above.

63. Compare with Saad-Ghorayeb, *Hizbu'llah*, pp. 172–173.

64. For further details, see Harkabi, 'On Arab Anti-Semitism', pp. 231; 234–235. The author reviews internal criticisms of Arab use of anti-Semitic sources.

65. Lewis, 'The Arab World Discovers Anti-Semitism', pp. 351–352

66. For example, Harkabi, 'On Arab Anti-Semitism', p. 229 notes that the Western anti-Semitic notion of the Jewish plot ascribes to the Jews a malevolent power, while the 'dominant image of the Jews in Islam is one of degradation and weakness'. It might be argued, however, that twentieth-century Jewish military and political successes brought to the fore those Islamic archetypes of the Jews that emphasised their potential danger to Islam and Muslims.

67. Tabbara, *al-Yahud fi'l-Qur'an*, p. 48, n. 1. The author provides several examples of the Qur'an having established points made in *Mein Kampf* concerning the Jewish nature fourteen hundred years earlier. The latter is cited, followed by a Qur'anic verse that 'corresponds' to the citation. See Ibid., pp. 46; 49.

68. Nettler, *Past Trials and Present Tribulations*, p. 71.

69. Compare with Harkabi's thesis ('On Arab Anti-Semitism', p. 233) that 'Arab antisemitism' is primarily ideological and political (and orchestrated from above), and is not necessarily 'social' (emerging from below).

70. This assumption is at times extended to encompass in addition traditional Islam. Mapping the rising objections to Jewish settlement in pre-World War I Palestine, Porath, for example (in an otherwise balanced treatment), notes that charges levelled against the Jews began to be heard 'based upon the anti-Semitic infrastructure extant in Islam'. Yehoshua Porath, 'Anti-Zionist and Anti-Jewish Ideology in the Arab Nationalist Movement in Palestine', in Almog, ed., *Antisemitism Through the Ages*, p. 220.

71. This is not to say, however, that modern European anti-Semitic motifs have had no impact on perceptions in Muslim societies in the course of the last century.

72. Hizb al-Tahrir leaflet, 30 November 1981; Tantawi, *Banu Isra'il*, pp. 625–630; Tabbara, *al-Yahud fi'l-Qur'an*, p. 43, for example.

73. For example, in its comment on these verses, Hizb al-Tahrir maintains that the Jews' 'attainment of statehood, their elevated standing and their arrogance today are due to the bond afforded them by America and the unbelieving Western states'. Hizb al-Tahrir leaflet, 30 November 1984. For further examples, see Taji-Farouki, 'A Contemporary Construction of the Jews', pp. 22–23; cf. p. 25.

74. Khumayni, for example, argued that Israel 'has always been an American base'. *The Imam versus Zionism*, p. 42. In May 1981, he asked the Muslims, 'How long should your Quds be trampled on by the scum of America, the usurper, Israel?' Ibid., p. 43. The views of Khumayni and Hizb Allah must be situated within the bi-polar model of the world, divided among oppressed and oppressors, that is typical of contemporary politicised Shi'ism. See, for example Saad-Ghorayeb, *Hizbu'llah*. This framework for understanding the

problem of Israel was recently reiterated by Muhammad Husayn Fadlallah: interview, al-Jazeera TV, 30 March, 2002.

75. For example, Hizb al-Tahrir argues that the 'Jewish unbelievers' seek revenge for their ancestors who suffered at the Prophet's hands in Medina, while the 'Christian unbelievers' seek revenge for their ultimate defeat during the Crusades. Hizb al-Tahrir leaflet 15 May 1991, for example.

76. See, for example, *The Imam versus Zionism*, p. 60.

77. See, for example, 'Conversation with Terror', interview with Usama Bin Laden, *Time Magazine* (11 January 1999).

78. This view clearly reflects the influence of European anti-Semitic ideas. See, for example, Saad-Ghorayeb, *Hizbu'llah*, p. 141. On the Muslim Brotherhood's view (in Egypt), see Walid M. Abdelnasser, *The Islamic Movement in Egypt: Perceptions of International Relations 1967–1981* (London and New York, 1994), p. 122.

79. For example, in 1968 the Secretary General of the Academy of Islamic Research at al-Azhar referred to the events of 1967 in the following terms: 'Indeed, this has been decreed by God, the Almighty, as a trial to present-day Muslim societies. Because of the latter's prolonged neglect and heedlessness, God has empowered against them a queer medley of people … In our view, there is no alternative for contemporary Muslims but to realise the significance of this exalted lesson that present circumstances have set before their eyes'. *The Fourth Conference of the Academy of Islamic Research at al-Azhar*, September 1968 (Cairo, 1970), pp. ix–x.

80. This is commonly supported by reference to a hadith recorded in the Sahih collections of Bukhari and Muslim. In the recension recorded by Muslim: 'The Day of Resurrection will not arrive until the Muslims fight and kill the Jews [with such success that] they will hide behind stones and trees, which will then speak up: "O Muslim, servant of God! There is a Jew behind me – come and kill him", except for the *gharqad* tree, which is a Jewish tree'.

81. *The Fourth Conference of the Academy of Islamic Research at al-Azhar*, p. 921.

82. For example, Yusuf al-Qaradawi, *al-Shari'a wa'l-hayat*, al-Jazeera TV, April 2002. Khaled Mish'al, the Head of the Political Office of HAMAS, recently reminded the umma that God would call it to account if it failed in its responsibility: interview, al-Jazeera TV, 30 March, 2002. Muhammad Husyan Fadlallah recently called on Muslims everywhere to assist Palestinian resistance to Israeli assaults with volunteers and material aid: interview, al-Jazeera TV, 30 March, 2002. Hizb Allah speaks of a Pan-Islamic 'Jerusalem Army' that will liberate the city. See Saad-Ghorayeb, *Hizbu'llah*, p. 73; also 163. In general, emphasis is placed on the potential resources and strength

of Muslims, if they join their forces. Shortly after the Iranian revolution, for example, Khumayni argued that 'If the Muslims united, and if each of them poured a bucket of water over Israel, it would be washed away'. *The Imam versus Zionism*, p. 40. See also Abdelnasser, *The Islamic Movement in Egypt*, p. 125 on the views of the Muslim Brotherhood in this regard.

83. See, for example, Taji-Farouki, 'A Case-Study', p. 49; Saad-Ghorayeb, *Hizbu'llah*, pp. 124–125. The concrete implementation of the individual duty of jihad in the Palestinian context as a strategy to confront the occupation has been discussed at length in several studies. See Taji-Farouki, 'A Case-Study', p. 49; 'Islamists and the Threat of *Jihad*: Hizb al-Tahrir and al-Muhajiroun on Israel and the Jews', *MES*, 36, 4 (2000), pp. 21–46; Ziad Abu-Amr, *Islamic Fundamentalism in the West Bank and Gaza: Muslim Brotherhood and Islamic Jihad* (Bloomington and Indianapolis, IN, 1994); Shaul Mishal and Avraham Sela, *The Palestinian Hamas: Vision, Violence and Coexistence* (New York, 2000); Andrea Nusse, *Muslim Palestine: The Ideology of HAMAS* (Amsterdam, 1998); Beverley Milton Edwards, *Islamic Politics in Palestine* (London, 1996) and Meir Hatina, *Islam and Salvation in Palestine: The Islamic Jihad Movement* (Syracuse, NY, 2001). Of particular interest are the differences between Palestinian Islamists concerning the *timing* of the jihad as legitimate defensive struggle (whether immediate or deferred). Among certain Egyptian Islamists, the debate has been whether the jihad against the nearest enemy (the regime) takes precedence over the enemy who is further away (Israel): see, for example, Johannes J. G. Jansen, *The Neglected Duty: The Creed of Sadat's Assassins and Islamic Resurgence in the Middle East* (New York and London, 1986).

84. HAMAS communique, 30 October 1991; HAMAS Charter, in Mishal and Sela, *The Palestinian Hamas*, Appendix 2; Hizb al-Tahrir leaflet, 25 October 1991; Saad-Ghorayeb, *Hizbu'llah*, p. 73; 152.

85. Such views are commonly expressed by Islamists. Hizb Allah denounces any states and organisations that enter negotiations with Israel as deviant. Saad-Ghorayeb, *Hizbu'llah*, pp. 151–161. Hizb al-Tahrir insists that any agreement struck by the Palestinian and other Arab leaders with the Jews to cede 'as much as a grain of Palestine's soil' are null and void. It holds that 'the only legally permissible encounter between the Jews and ourselves is on the *jihad* battlefield': the state of war with unbelievers occupying Islamic land can be terminated only through their expulsion from it, or their conversion to Islam. (Hizb al-Tahrir leaflets, 14 September 1993; 29 March 2001).

86. Citing the precedent of the Prophet's treaty at al-Hudaybiyya, some argue that a truce must have a maximum limit of ten years.

87. See, for example, Hizb al-Tahrir leaflets 27 July 1982; 10 November

1982; 19 November 1984; 21 October 1991; Taji-Farouki, 'A Case-Study', pp. 47–48.

88. Hizb al-Tahrir leaflets 21 October 1991; 30 November 1984.

89. See Abdelnasser, *The Islamic Movement in Egypt*, pp. 128–133. For the response of the Egyptian Jihad to Sadat's initiative, see ibid., pp. 137–138. For an example from the Islamic left, see the essay by Hasan Hanafi reviewed in Yadlin, *An Arrogant Oppressive Spirit*, pp. 44–61.

90. *al-I'tisam*, January-February 1985, quoted in Yadlin, *An Arrogant Oppressive Spirit*, p. 23. The author also provides examples of the 'cultural assault' argument drawn from the non-Islamic Egyptian press. These include allegations that Israel distributes pornographic movies and smuggles drugs into Egypt, aiming to lure the youth away from Islam, the greatest threat to Zionism. Ibid., p. 25.

91. Khumayni called on the Muslim peoples to oppose the 'corrupt, one hundred percent anti-Islamic' Fahd Plan (which was the basis of the Fez resolutions adopted the following year), arguing that anyone who failed to do so was a traitor. Message to hajj pilgrims, 7 August 1981: *The Imam versus Zionism*, p. 52.

92. One of the most consistent responses across the years is that of Hizb al-Tahrir. The party construes the peace process as the tool of a grand conspiracy, enlisting the co-operation of the United Nations, Arab heads of state, and the PLO leadership. Behind it are the 'unbelievers', a reference here to Christians, who are assisted in its implementation by the Jews. Thus: 'The Crusaders' malice remained concealed in their hearts, until they disclosed it when they succeeded in doing away with the Ottoman Caliphal state and then establishing a Jewish state in Palestine. They deemed this a twofold revenge for their defeat at the hands of the heroic Muslim leader Salah al-Din.' (leaflet, 15 May 1991). For Hizb al-Tahrir's view of the peace process and the dangers implicit in negotiations, see Taji-Farouki, 'A Case-Study', pp. 39–46; Taji-Farouki, 'Islamists and the Threat of *Jihad*', pp. 24–27.

93. Far from liberating Palestine, Hizb al-Tahrir has consistently construed the *raison d'être* of the PLO as surrendering it to Israel. See, for example, Taji-Farouki, 'A Case-Study', p. 42. For the response of HAMAS, see Nusse, *Muslim Palestine*, ch. 14. Hizb Allah has consistently denounced Palestinian-Israeli negotiations, accusing Arafat and the PLO of betraying the cause by legitimising the Israeli state. Saad-Ghorayeb, *Hizbu'llah*, pp. 151–160.

94. Islamist arguments have not been couched exclusively in Islamic doctrinal or legal terms. For example, in recent years much has been made of the failure of bi-lateral agreements to provide the promised economic boost to the Arab states concerned. See below.

95. For examples from the first half of the 1980s, which the author

describes as a period that was 'at the height of the peace', see Yadlin, *An Arrogant Oppressive Spirit*. The author claims to illustrate 'those streams that are central and common to the bulk of the thinking public' [pp. 6; 103]. For further discussion of anti-Israeli and anti-Jewish sentiment in the media, extending to the 1990s, see Ephraim Dowek, *Israeli-Egyptian Relations, 1980–2000* (London, 2001), pp. 85–98. Referring to the process of controlled political liberalisation implemented in Egypt from the mid-1970s and accelerated following the assassination of Sadat, Yadlin (*An Arrogant Oppressive Spirit*, pp. 6–7) maintains that expressions of hostility in Egyptian writings (including the print media) are spontaneous and autonomous. She sees neither inspiration nor instigation in this regard on the part of the regime. Dowek's opinion (*Israeli-Egyptian Relations*, p. 86), in contrast, is that there is no freedom of press in Egypt, and that everything that is published or broadcast by the media is 'orchestrated from above in a very minute manner'. In his view (p. 90), the media is used as a tool by the Egyptian authorities in all that pertains to Israel and the peace process.

96. Dowek, *Israeli-Egyptian Relations*, p. 85. The author spent time in Egypt as an Israeli diplomat.

97. In Lebanon, Hizb Allah has pledged to confront normalisation of relations with Israel should the Lebanese state sign a peace agreement with it, even if it withdraws from Lebanese land. A major thrust of its anti-normalisation campaign will be to counter Israel's efforts to dominate the region politically, and to infiltrate it culturally and economically. Saad-Ghorayeb, *Hizbu'llah*, pp. 159–161.

98. In the case of Egypt, Dowek (*Israeli-Egyptian Relations*, pp. 123–124) maintains that, being convinced of the assumptions underlying *The Protocols of the Elders of Zion*, the leadership (and the people) genuinely fear that 'Israel, with the help of world Jewry, will take control of its economy, and gradually come to pervade all walks of life within Egypt itself'. In his opinion, this accounts for the Egyptian regime's systematic hampering of the 'normal flow of relations' between the two countries, which hence functions as 'a legitimate means of self-defence'. In Jordan the economic argument played an important part in forestalling political opposition to the peace process. A few years after Wadi 'Araba, however, it became clear that the expected economic benefits of peace would prove meagre. For an analysis, see Waleed Hazbun, 'Mapping the Landscape of the 'New Middle East': The Politics of Tourism Development in the Peace Process in Jordan', in George Joffe, ed., *Jordan in Transition* (London, 2002), pp. 330–345.

99. al-Faruqi, 'Islam and Zionism', pp. 264; 267. For a polemical discussion of the 'survival' of the '*dhimmi* archetype', in modern Arab nationalism (including the PLO Charter), see Bat Ye'or, *The Dhimmi: Jews and Christians*

under Islam, rev. English ed., tr. David Maisel, Paul Fenton and David Littman (Rutherford, NJ, 1985), ch. 5–6.

100. Fahmi Huwaydi, *Muwatinun la dhimmiyyun; mawqi' ghayr al-Muslimin fi mujtama' al-Muslimin* (Cairo and London, 1985). Mohamed Talbi (see below) repudiates the *dhimma* institution as the Islamic model for the good society, and calls for its abolition. See Ronald L. Nettler, 'Mohamed Talbi: "For Dialogue between all Religions"', in Nettler and Taji-Farouki, ed., *Muslim-Jewish Encounters*, pp. 191–193; Kate Zebiri, 'Relations between Muslims and Non-Muslims in the Thought of Western-Educated Muslim Intellectuals', *Islam and Christian-Muslim Relations*, 6, 2 (1995), pp. 262–267.

101. See Abdelnasser, *The Islamic Movement in Egypt*, p. 140. The author summarises the institution's responses to the Palestinian situation from 1957.

102. For a detailed survey of their arguments, based on *Bayan ulama al-Azhar hawl ahkam al-mu'ahadat fi'l-Islam* (Cairo, 1979), see ibid., pp. 140–143.

103. Gad al-Haqq, al-Dasuqi, Hamza and Mahmoud, ed., *al-Fatawa al-Islamiyya min Dar al-Ifta' al-Misriyya* (Cairo, 1980–1993) vol. 10, pp. 3621–3636. For further discussion of fatwas relating to the 1979 peace treaty, see D. F. R. Pohl, *Nationhood and Peace: Challenges to Official Islam in Egypt* (D.Phil. dissertation, Oxford University, 1987).

104. *al-Ra'i*, Amman, 13 October, 1995, for example.

105. Tantawi, *Banu Isra'il*, p. 689.

106. The text of the interview appears in *Majallat al-Musawwar* (Cairo) no. 3668 (27 January, 1995), pp. 30–33; 76–77.

107. Such views were expressed recently by the moderate Islamist Azzam Tamimi. See 'Jews and Muslims in Post-Israel Middle East', MSANEWS (30 June, 1999). http://msanews.mynet/Scholars/Tamimi/kitabi.html. In a similar vein, the conservative Muslim scholar M. Abdul Ra'uf underscores the fact that 'Islam never condemned the Jewish people *in toto*, since the critical verses stand side by side with those others which justify [sic.] the Jews, both enjoying the same divine authority. And in order to dispel any such confusion, the Qur'an explicitly distinguished the righteous from the unrighteous.' M. Abdul Ra'uf, 'Judaism and Christianity in the Perspective of Islam', in Isma'il Raji al-Faruqi, ed., *Trialogue of the Abrahamic Faiths* (Herndon, VA, 1986), p. 28.

108. Fazlur Rahman, 'Islam's Attitude Toward Judaism', *MW*, 72, 1 (1982), pp. 8–9.

109. For a translation and discussion of the relevant section in *al-Islam al-siyasi* see Ronald L. Nettler, 'A Post-Colonial Encounter of Traditions: Muhammad Sa'id al-'Ashmawi on Islam and Judaism', in Ronald L. Nettler, ed., *Medieval and Modern Perspectives on Muslim-Jewish Relations* [*Studies*

in Muslim-Jewish Relations, vol. 2] (Luxembourg, 1995), pp. 179–182.

110. Sadiq Nayhum, *Islam didda al-Islam; shari'a min waraq* (Beirut and London, 1994), pp. 137–146; for further examples see p. 201ff.

111. For a personal statement see Mohamed Talbi, 'Unavoidable Dialogue in a Pluralist World: A Personal Account', *Encounters: Journal of Inter-Cultural Perspectives*, 1, 1 (1995), pp. 56–69. See further Nettler, 'Mohamed Talbi: "For Dialogue between all Religions"'. For a further example of Muslim attitudes towards dialogue see what the author himself describes as a 'liberal, modern, humanist, Muslim proposal', in Mohammed Arkoun, 'New Perspectives for a Jewish-Christian-Muslim Dialogue', in Leonard Swidler, ed., *Muslims in Dialogue: The Evolution of a Dialogue* (Lewiston, 1992), pp. 345–352. See also Isma'il Raji al-Faruqi, *Trialogue of the Abrahamic Faiths*; Muhammad Shafiq, 'Trialogue of the Abrahamic Faiths: Guidelines for Jewish, Christian and Muslim Dialogue; Analysis of the Views of Isma'il Raji al-Faruqi', *Hamdard Islamicus*, 15 (1992), pp. 59–74.

112. The Constitution of Medina (along with specific Qur'anic verses) is thus upheld as a formula for the organisation of inter-religious relations in the modern world, based on religious freedom and co-operation. See further Zebiri, 'Relations between Muslims and Non-Muslims', pp. 267–270; Ronald L. Nettler, 'Mohamed Talbi's Theory of Religious Pluralism: A Modernist Islamic Outlook', *The Maghreb Review*, 24, 3–4 (1999), pp. 98–107.

113. The aim is to defuse tension caused by anti-Jewish rhetoric, in statements against Israeli policies circulated by certain Islamist groups.

114. The Shalom Hartman Institute has a Muslim Director of the desk for 'Dialogue and Teaching for Peace' (see http://www.hartmaninstitute.com). The Elijah School has two Muslim academics from the USA on its Advisory Panel (see http://www.elijah.org.il/), but there has been very limited participation by local Muslims in its activities. For an interesting Israeli Jewish perspective on the absence of Muslim-Jewish dialogue in Israel and its implications see Haim Gordon, 'The Lack of Jewish-Arab Dialogue in Israel and the Spirit of Judaism: A Testimony', in Swidler, ed., *Muslims in Dialogue*, pp. 389–401.

115. The Jewish founding members relate themselves to the Jewish Sufi tradition inaugurated by Rabbi Abraham, son of Maimonides, in the thirteenth century. See Itzchak Weismann, 'Sufi Brotherhoods in the Syrian Area: Religious Strategies and Political Implications', paper read at Conference on 'The Role of Sufism and Sufi Brotherhoods in Contemporary Islam: An Alternative to Political Islam?', Turin, 20–22 November 2002. For a discussion of the historical interaction between Islam and Judaism in the domain of mysticism and the mutual influences of Islamic and Jewish mysticism see Paul B. Fenton, 'Sufism and Judaism', in Seyyed Hossein Nasr and

Oliver Leaman, ed., *The History of Islamic Philosophy*, Part 1 (London, 1996), pp. 755–768.

116. Popular poetry and song renew pledges to retrieve it for Islam, as did Salah al-Din, while images of the Dome of the Rock adorn Muslim homes across the world.

117. This is evidenced by religious occasions (Ramadan and the Islamic festivals), when Palestine is remembered in emotional supplications.

118. For example, the arson attack on the al-Aqsa Mosque was the immediate cause behind the establishment of the Organisation of the Islamic Conference (Rabat, 1969); since its inception, it has consistently addressed the issue of Palestine. In 1980, Khumayni instituted the last Friday of Ramadan as 'al-Quds Day', on which 'the Iranian nation' would display its enmity towards Israel through mass demonstrations: *The Imam versus Zionism*, p. 64, n. 14. In popular art, Palestine appears as a bleeding limb of the Muslim umma, which rallies to its rescue.

119. During the 1990s, for example, King Hussein of Jordan personally funded the renewal of the gold leaf covering of the Dome of the Rock, Saddam Hussein 'linked' resolution of his 'occupation' of Kuwait with that of Palestine, and Usama Bin Laden justified his anti-Americanism with references to Palestinian suffering.

120. These are not infrequently put down to some irrational Islamic hatred, not only of the Jews, but of the democratic and progressive values they have come to represent (in Israel, that is) in many Western perceptions of the region.

Further Readings

Chapter 2: The Rise of Islamic Reformist Thought and its Challenge to Traditional Islam

Adams, Charles. *Islam and Modernism in Egypt: A Study of the Reform Movements Inaugurated by Muhammad Abduh.* New York, 1968.

Ahmad, Aziz. *Islamic Modernism in India and Pakistan, 1857 – 1964.* London, 1967.

Ahmad, Jamal M. *The Intellectual Origins of Egyptian Nationalism.* London, 1960.

Brown, Daniel. *Rethinking Tradition in Modern Islamic Thought.* Cambridge, 1996.

Commins, David Dean. *Islamic Reform: Politics and Social Change in Late Ottoman Syria.* New York, 1990.

Gibb, Hamilton A. R. *Modern Trends in Islam.* Chicago, 1947.

Hourani, Albert. *Arabic Thought in the Liberal Age, 1798 – 1939.* London, 1962.

Kerr, Malcolm. *Islamic Reform, The Political and Legal Theory of Muhammad Abduh and Rashid Rida.* Berkeley, CA, 1966.

Khaled, Adeep. *The Politics of Muslim Cultural Reform: Jadidism in Central Asia.* Berkeley, CA, 1998.

Metcalf, Barbara Daly. *Islamic Revival in British India: Deodband, 1860–1900.* Princeton, NJ, 1982.

Noer, Deliar. *The Modernist Muslim Movement in Indonesia, 1900–1942.* Kuala Lampur, 1978.

Qureshi, Ishtiaq Husain. *The Muslim Community of the Indo-Pakistani Subcontinent, 610–1947.* The Hague, 1962.

Rahman, Fazlur. *Islam and Modernity: Transformation of an Intellectual Tradition.* Chicago, 1982.

Sharabi, Hisham. *Arab Intellectuals and the West: The Formative Years, 1875–1914.* Baltimore, 1970.

Voll, John. *Islam: Continuity and Change in the Modern World.* Boulder, CO, 1982.

Chapter 3: The Diversity of Islamic Thought: Towards a Typology

Ahmad, A. and G. E. von Grunebaum, ed. *Muslim Self-Statement in India and Pakistan, 1857–1968.* Weisbaden, 1970.

Barton, Greg and Greg Fealy, ed. *Nahdatul Ulama: Traditional Islam and Modernity in Indonesia.* Clayton, Victoria, Australia, 1996.

Boland, B. J. *The Struggle of Islam in Modern Indonesia.* The Hague, 1971.

Dabashi, Hamid. *Theology of Discontent.* New York and London, 1993.

Esposito, John L. *Islam and Politics,* 3rd ed. Syracuse, NY, 1991

——ed. *Islam and Development.* Syracuse, NY, 1980.

Esposito, John L. and John O. Voll. *Islam and Democracy.* Oxford, 1996.

Hourani, A. *Arabic Thought in the Liberal Age, 1798–1939.* Cambridge, 1983.

Mottahedeh, Roy. *The Mantle of the Prophet: Politics and Religion in Iran.* London, 1986.

Nasr, Sayyed Vali Reza. *The Vanguard of the Islamic Revolution: The Jama'at-i-Islami of Pakistan.* Berkeley, CA, 1994.

Rahnema, Ali, ed. *Pioneers of Islamic Revival.* London, 1994.

Sivan, Emmanuel. *Radical Islam: Medieval Theology and Modern Politics.* New Haven, CT and London, 1985.

Smith, Wilfred Cantwell. *Islam in Modern History.* Princeton, NJ, 1957.

Toprak, B. *Islam and Political Development in Turkey.* Leiden, 1981.

Voll, John Obert. *Islam: Continuity and Change in the Modern World.* 2nd ed., Syracuse, NY, 1994.

Chapter 4: Sufi Thought and its Reconstruction

Clarke, Peter B., ed. *New Trends and Developments in the World of Islam.* London, 1997.

De Jong, Frederick and Bernd Radtke, ed. *Islamic Mysticism Contested: Thirteen Centuries of Controversies and Polemics.* Leiden, 1999.

Ernst, Carl. *The Shambhala Guide to Sufism.* Boston, 1997.

Hermansen, Marcia. 'Hybrid Identity Formations in Muslim America. The Case of American Sufi Movements', *MW*, 90 (2000), pp. 158–197.

Hoffman, Valerie J. *Sufism, Mystics and Saints in Modern Egypt.* Columbia, SC, 1995.

Iqbal, Muhammad. *The Reconstruction of Religious Thought in Islam.* Lahore, 1930; 2nd ed., 1977.

Johansen, Julian. *Sufism and Islamic Reform in Egypt: The Battle for Islamic Tradition.* Oxford, 1996.

Lings, Martin. *A Sufi Saint of the Twentieth Century: Shaikh Ahmad al-'Alawi, his Spiritual Heritage and Legacy.* Cambridge, 1961; 2nd ed., 1993.

Sanyal, Usha. *Devotional Islam and Politics in British India. Ahmad Riza Khan Barelwi and his Movement, 1870–1920.* Oxford and Delhi, 1996.

Schimmel, Annemarie. *Gabriel's Wing: A Study into the Religious Ideas of Sir Muhammad Iqbal.* 2nd ed., Lahore, 1989.

Sirriyeh, Elizabeth. *Sufis and Anti-Sufis: The Defence, Rethinking and Rejection of Sufism in the Modern World.* London, 1999.

Triaud, Jean-Louis and David Robinson, ed. *La Tijaniyya. Une confrerie musulmane a la conquête de l'Afrique.* Paris, 2000.

Werbner, Pnina and Helene Basu, ed. *Embodying Charisma: Modernity, Locality and the Performance of Emotion in Sufi Cults.* London, 1998.

Westerlund, David and Eva Evers Rosander, ed. *African Islam and Islam in Africa: Encounters between Sufis and Islamists.* London, 1997.

Westerlund, David and Ingvar Svanberg, ed. *Islam Outside the Arab World.* London, 1999.

Chapter 5: Nationalism and Culture in the Arab and Islamic Worlds: A Critique of Modern Scholarship

Ahmad, Aijaz. *In Theory: Classes, Nations and Literatures.* London, 1992.

Ayubi, Nazih N. *Political Islam: Religion and Politics in the Arab World.* London, 1991.

—*Over-stating the Arab State: Politics and Society in the Middle East.* London, 1997.

Al-Azmeh, Aziz. *al-'Ilmaniyya fi manzur mukhtalif.* Beirut, 1992.

—*Islams and Modernities.* London, 1993.

Balakrishnan, Gopal, ed. *Mapping the Nation.* London, 1996.

Boggs, Carl. *The End of Politics: Corporate Power and the Decline of the Public Sphere.* New York, 2000.

Choueiri, Youssef. *Arab Nationalism: A History.* Oxford, 2000.

Coury, Ralph M. *The Making of an Egyptian Arab Nationalist: The Early Years of Azzam Pasha, 1893–1936.* Reading, 1998.

Eagleton, Terry. *The Idea of Culture*. Oxford, 2000.

Gilsenan, Michael. *Recognizing Islam*. London, 1982.

Hudson, Michael, ed. *Middle East Dilemmas: The Politics and Economics of Arab Integration*. New York, 1999.

Khalidi, Rashid, et al., ed. *The Origins of Arab Nationalism*. New York, 1991.

Salvatore, Armando. *Islam and the Political Discourse of Modernity*. Reading, 1997.

Schulze, Reinhard. *A Modern History of the Islamic World*. New York, 2000.

Zubaida, Sami. *Islam, the People and the State*. London, 1989.

Chapter 6: On the State, Democracy and Pluralism

Abrahamian, Ervand. *Iran Between Two Revolutions*. Princeton, NJ, 1982.

Algar, Hamid. *Islam and Revolution I: Writings and Declarations of Imam Khomeyni: 1941–1980*. Berkeley, CA, 1981.

Binder, Leonard. *Islamic Liberalism: A Critique of Development Ideologies*. Chicago, IL, 1988.

Cotran, Eugene and Adel Omar Sherif, ed. *Democracy, the Rule of Law and Islam*. London, 1999.

Eickelman, Dale F. and James Piscatori. *Muslim Politics*. Princeton, NJ, 1996.

El-Affendi, Abdelwahab. *Who Needs an Islamic State?* London, 1991.

Enayat, Hamid. *Modern Islamic Political Thought*. London, 1982.

Esposito, John, ed. *Voices of Resurgent Islam*. Oxford, 1983.

Esposito, John and John Voll. *Islam and Democracy*. Oxford, 1996.

Hourani, Albert. *Arabic Thought in the Liberal Age: 1789–1939*. Cambridge, 1989.

Lewis, Bernard. *The Emergence of Modern Turkey*. London, 1961.

Ozdalga, Elizabeth and Sune Persson, ed. *Civil Society, Democracy and the Muslim World*. Istanbul, 1997.

Rahnema, Ali, ed. *Pioneers of Islamic Revival*. London, 1994.

Soroush, Abdolkarim. *Reason, Freedom and Democracy: Essential Writings of Abdolkarim Soroush*, tr. and ed., Mahmoud Sadri and Ahmad Sadri. Oxford, 2000.

Sachedina, Abdulaziz. *The Islamic Roots of Democratic Pluralism*. Oxford, 2001.

Chapter 7: The Development of Islamic Economics: Theory and Practice

Aghnides, Nicolas P. *Mohammedan Theories of Finance*. Lahore, 1961.

Ahmad, Khurshid. *Studies in Islamic Economics*. Leicester, 1980.

Chapra, M. Umer. *Towards a Just Monetary System*. Leicester, 1985.

——*Islam and the Economic Challenge*. Leicester, 1992.

Ghazali, Aidit. *Development: An Islamic Perspective*. Selangor, 1990.

Kuran, Timur. 'Islamic Economics and the Islamic Sub-economy', *Journal of Economic Perspectives*, 9, 1 (1995), pp. 155–173. Reprinted in Tim Niblock and Rodney Wilson, ed., *The Political Economy of the Middle East*. Cheltenham, 1999, vol. 3 'Islamic Economics', pp. 57–75.

Mannan, Muhammad Abdul. *Islamic Economics: Theory and Practice*. Lahore, 1970; Sevenoaks, Kent, 1986.

Naqvi, Syed Nawab. *Islam, Economics and Society*. London, 1994.

Nomani, Farhad and Ali Rahnema. *Islamic Economic Systems*. London, 1994.

Rodinson, Maxime. *Islam and Capitalism*. Harmondsworth, 1977.

al-Sadr, Muhammad Baqir. *Iqtisaduna*. Beirut, 1961, repr. 1968. English tr., Tehran World Services, 1981; further English tr., Kadom Jawad Shubber, London, 2000. German tr., Andreas Rieck, Berlin, 1984.

Siddiqi, Muhammad Nejatullah. *Muslim Economic Thinking: A Survey of Contemporary Literature*. Leicester, 1981.

Siddiqi, S. A. *Public Finance in Islam*. Lahore, 1948.

Vogel, Frank E. and Samuel L. Hayes. *Islamic Law and Finance: Religion, Risk and Return*. The Hague, 1998.

Wilson, Rodney. 'The Contribution of Muhammed Baqir al-Sadr to Contemporary Islamic Economic Thought', *JIS*, 9,1 (1998), pp. 46–59.

Chapter 8: On Gender and the Family

Abou El Fadl, Khaled. *Speaking in God's Name: Islamic Law, Authority and Women*. Oxford, 2001.

Abugideiri, Hibba. 'Allegorical Gender: The Figure of Eve Revisited', *The American Journal of Islamic Social Sciences*, 13, 4 (1996), pp. 518–35.

Abu-Lughod, Lila. 'Feminist Longings and Postcolonial Conditions', in Lila Abu-Lughod, ed., *Remaking Women: Feminism and Modernity in the Middle East*. Princeton, NJ, 1998, pp. 3–31.

Abu Shuqqah, Abd al-Halim. *Tahrir al-mar'a fi 'asr al-risala*. Kuwait, 1991.

Ahmed, Leila. *Women and Gender in Islam: Historical Roots of a Modern Debate*. New Haven, CT, 1992.

Barlas, Asma. *'Believing Women' in Islam: Unreading Patriarchal Interpretations of the Qur'an*. Austin, TX, 2002.

Esposito, John L. and John O. Voll. *Makers of Contemporary Islam*. New York, 2001.

Mawdudi, Syed Abu al-A'la. *Purdah and the Status of Woman in Islam.* Lahore, 1972.

Mernissi, Fatima. *The Veil and the Male Elite: A Feminist Interpretation of Women's Rights in Islam,* tr. Mary Jo Lakeland. Reading, 1991.

Mir-Hosseini, Ziba. *Islam and Gender: The Religious Debate in Contemporary Iran.* Princeton, NJ, 1999.

Mohanty, Chandra Talpade, 'Under Western Eyes: Feminist Scholarship and Colonial Discourses', in Chandra Talpade Mohanty et al., ed., *Third World Women and the Politics of Feminism.* Bloomington, IN, 1991.

Narayan, Uma. *Dislocating Cultures.* New York, 1997.

al-Qaradawi, Yusuf. *The Lawful and the Prohibited in Islam,* tr. Ahmad Zaki Hammad. Indianapolis, IN, n.d.

Sonbol, Amira el-Azhary, ed., *Women, the Family and Divorce Laws in Islamic History.* NY, 1996.

Stowasser, Barbara Freyer. *Women in the Qur'an, Traditions and Interpretation.* New York, 1994.

Wadud, Amina. *Qur'an and Woman.* New York, 1999.

Chapter 9: Muslim Reflections on the West

Abul-Fadl, Mona. *Where East meets West: The West on the Agenda of Islamic Revival.* Herndon, VI, 1992.

Ansari, Zafar Ishaq and John L. Esposito, ed. *Muslims and the West: Encounter and Dialogue.* Islamabad and Washington, DC, 2001.

Boroujerdi, Mehrzad. *Iranian Intellectuals and the West: The Tormented Triumph of Nativism.* Syracuse and New York, 1996.

Djaït, Hichem. *Europe and Islam.* Berkeley, CA, 1985.

Hourani, Albert. *Europe and the Middle East.* Berkeley, CA, 1980.

Khoury, Paul. *L'Islam critique de l'Occident dans la pensée arabe actuelle. Islam et sécularité* (Religionswissenschaftliche Studien 35), 2 vols. Würzburg and Altenberge, 1994–1995.

Lamchichi, Abderrahim. *Islam-Occident, Islam-Europe. Choc des civilisations ou coexistence des cultures?* Paris, 1999.

Lewis, Bernard. *Islam and the West.* New York, 1993.

Martin Muñoz, Gema, ed. *Islam, Modernism and the West: Cultural and Political Relations at the End of the Millennium.* London and New York, 1999.

Nielsen, Jörgen S. and Sami A. Khasawnih, ed. *Arabs and the West: Mutual Images.* Proceedings of a three-day seminar organised by the University of Jordan (April 3–5, 1998). Amman, 1998.

Rahimieh, Nasrin. *Oriental Responses to the West.* Leiden, 1990.

Shayegan, Daryush. *Cultural Schizophrenia: Islamic Societies Confronting the*

West. Syracuse, NY, 1997.

Steenbrink, K. A. *Dutch Colonialism and Islam: Contacts and Conflicts 1596–1950*. Amsterdam and Atlanta, 1993.

Waardenburg, Jacques. *Islam et Occident face à face: Regards de l'histoire des religions*. Geneva, 1998.

Yared, Nazik Saba. *Arab Travellers and Western Civilization*. London, 1996.

Chapter 10: Perceptions of Christians and Christianity

Cragg, Kenneth. *City of Wrong*. Amsterdam, 1959; repr. Oxford, 1994.

Doi, Abdur Rahman I. *Non-Muslims under Shari'ah*. London, 1983.

al-Faruqi, Isma'il. *Christian Ethics: A Historical and Systematic Analysis of its Dominant Ideas*. Montreal, 1967.

——*Islam and Other Faiths*, ed., Ataullah Siddiqui. Leicester, 1998.

Ford, F. Peter. *The Genius of Christ*. New York, 2001.

Goddard, Hugh. *Muslim Perceptions of Christianity*. London, 1996.

——*A History of Christian-Muslim Relations*. Edinburgh, 2000.

Griffiths, Paul J., ed. *Christianity through non-Christian Eyes*. Maryknoll, NY, 1990.

Leirvik, Oddbjorn. *Images of Jesus Christ in Islam: Introduction, Survey of Research, Issues of Dialogue*. Uppsala, 1999.

Muslim-Christian Research Group. *The Challenge of the Scriptures: The Bible and the Qur'an*. Maryknoll, NY, 1989.

Al-Qaradawi, Yusuf. *Non-Muslims in the Islamic Society*. Indianapolis, IN, 1985.

Siddiqui, Ataullah. *Christian-Muslim Dialogue in the Twentieth Century*, London, 1997.

Waardenburg, Jacques, ed., *Islam and Christianity: Mutual Perceptions since the Mid-20th century*. Louvain, 1998.

——*Muslim Perceptions of Other Religions*. New York, 1999.

——*Muslim-Christian Perceptions of Dialogue Today: Experiences and Expectations*. Louvain, 2000

Chapter 11: Thinking on the Jews

Abu-Amr, Ziad. *Islamic Fundamentalism in the West Bank and Gaza: Muslim Brotherhood and Islamic Jihad*. Bloomington, IN, 1994.

Adang, Camilla. *Muslim Writers on Judaism and the Hebrew Bible: From Ibn Rabban to Ibn Hazm*. Leiden, 1996.

Cohen, Mark R. *Under Crescent and Cross: The Jews in the Middle Ages*. Princeton, NJ, 1994.

al-Faruqi, Isma'il Raji. *Islam and the Problem of Israel*. London, 1980.

Goitein, S. D. *Jews and Arabs: Their Contacts through the Ages*. New York, 1974.

Haddad, M. Y. S. 'Arab Perspectives of Judaism: A Study of Image Formation in the Writings of Muslim Arab Authors, 1948–1978', Ph.D. dissertation, University of Utrecht, 1984.

Landau, Jacob M. 'Muslim Turkish Attitudes towards Jews, Zionism and Israel', *WI*, 28 (1988), pp. 291–300.

Lewis, Bernard. *The Jews of Islam*. London, 1984.

Nettler, Ronald L. and Suha Taji-Farouki, ed. *Muslim-Jewish Encounters: Intellectual Traditions and Modern Politics*. Amsterdam, 1998.

Qutb, Sayyid. *Ma'rakatuna ma'a al-Yahud*. Beirut, 1979; tr. Ronald L. Nettler, *Past Trials and Present Tribulations: A Muslim Fundamentalist's View of the Jews*. Oxford, 1987.

Rahman, Fazlur. 'Islam's Attitude Toward Judaism', *MW*, 72, (1982), pp. 1–13.

Stillman, Norman A. *The Jews of Arab Lands: A History and Source Book*. Philadelphia, PA, 1979.

——*The Jews of Arab Lands in Modern Times*. Philadelphia, PA, 1991.

Tabbara, 'Afif 'Abd al-Fattah. *al-Yahud fi'l-Qur'an: tahlil 'ilmi li-nusus al-Qur'an fi'l-Yahud 'ala dau' al-ahdath al-hadira, ma'a dirasa wa tafsir qisas anbiya' Allah Ibrahim wa Yusuf wa Musa*. 13th ed., Beirut, 1986.

Taji-Farouki, Suha. 'Islamists and the Threat of *Jihad*: Hizb al-Tahrir and al-Muhajiroun on Israel and the Jews', *MES*, 36, 4 (2000), pp. 21–46.

The Fourth Conference of the Academy of Islamic Research at al-Azhar, September 1968. Cairo, 1970.

Index